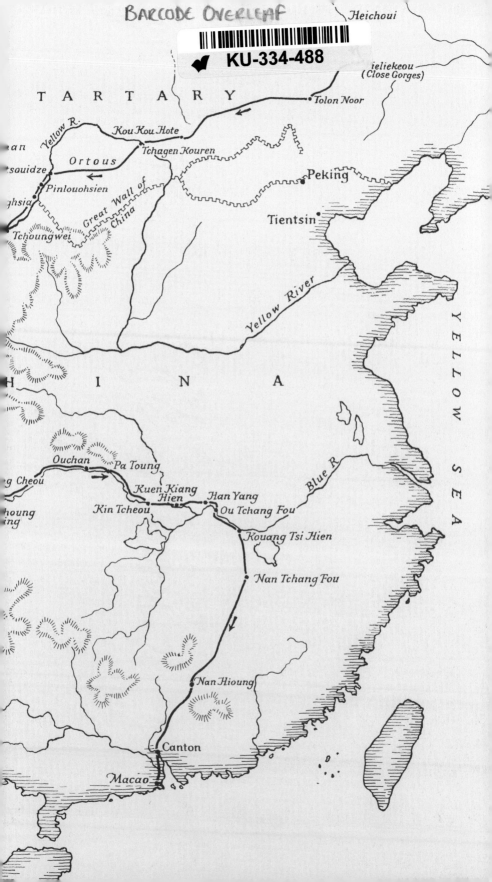

Heichoui

ieliekeou
(Close Gorges)

T A R T A R Y

Tolon Noor

Yellow R.

Kou Kou Hote

an

Ortous

Tchagen Kouren

tsouidze

Peking

Pinlouohsien

ghsia

Great Wall of China

Tientsin

Tchoungwei

Yellow River

H   I   N   A

Y
E
L
L
O
W

S
E
A

Ouchan

Pa Toung

g Cheou

Kuen Kiang
Hien

Blue R.

Kin Tcheou

Han Yang

houng
ing

Ou Tchang Fou

Kouang Tsi Hien

Nan Tchang Fou

Nan Hioung

Canton

Macao

LAMAS OF THE WESTERN HEAVENS

Lamas of the Western Heavens

Régis-Evariste Huc

*Translated by Charles de Salis
with an introduction by John Keay*

*Engravings taken from the first English
edition*

The Folio Society 1982

Souvenirs d'un voyage dans la Tartarie et le Thibet by Régis-Evariste Huc was first published in two volumes in 1851. A third volume, *L'Empire Chinois*, was published in 1854. This edition includes the whole of the second volume with summaries of the first and third.

Set in eleven point 'Monophoto' Apollo type, spaced one point
by BAS Printers Limited, Over Wallop.
Printed by Jolly & Barber Ltd, Rugby
on white Antique Laid paper.
Bound by The Pitman Press Ltd, Bath
using BBN Canvas cloth
blocked with a design based on a
19th-century Tibetan maskers apron from the
mystery play Tag-mar-ch'am.

Printed in Great Britain

CONTENTS

ILLUSTRATIONS

INTRODUCTION

If Tibet did not exist, some visionary would surely have invented it. The notion of a forbidden sanctuary at the heart of the world's greatest landmass, of a citadel fenced about with mighty mountains and so elevated as to seem half way to heaven, is more appropriate to a fairy tale. Indeed, to George Bogle, the first Briton to enter Tibet, it seemed truly 'a fairy dream . . . a perfect illusion'. Yet, as Bogle would willingly have conceded, the real Tibet boasted wonders and contradictions that the most fertile imagination could never have conjured.

For a start, this land, so devastatingly harsh and inhospitable, is nonetheless beautiful—unbelievably so. Nothing can be grander than the trans-Himalayan panorama of jagged peaks and plunging glaciers, nothing weirder than its contorted rock formations, nothing more startling than their bright shades of crimson, purple and ochre. In this geological wilderness, evidence of fertility is wholly unexpected. Yet, marooned in a sea of pebbles or cradled by crumbling precipices, lie islets of dazzling verdure, oases of a serene and gentle charm. The leaves of the tapering poplars rustle in the wind, a vivid green against the bare slopes. Willows shade the grassy banks of a timid stream, and in the terraced fields villagers in long skirts and turquoise blouses work their way through a harvest of golden barley.

The scene—and the fairy tale image—would be incomplete without, high above, some towering palace, its walls sheer and white-washed, its roof gilded, and its many storeys stacked up the mountainside or teetering on an inaccessible bluff. The great lamaseries of Tibet only look like palaces; they are, in fact—or they were—centres of scholarship and worship, Buddhist universities rather than feudal strongholds. In a terrain which could barely produce the essentials of human subsistence, and in a climate which for much of the year rivalled that of the Arctic, it was remarkable that the population, far from being reduced to a state of brutish savagery, seemed more unworldly, more aloof from mundane anxieties and more dedicated to learning and mysticism than any other. At the remote lamasery of Kumbum [Kounboum in Huc's text],

where the Lamas of the Western Heavens, Fathers Huc and
Gabet, spent much of 1845, there were 4,000 monks, and in
Lhasa the three principal monasteries each had a complement
of 15,000. Close on half the Tibetan population was in religious
orders. The monasteries were the seats of political, as well as of
religious authority just as, ultimately, all sovereignty, both
temporal and spiritual, was vested in the person of a god-
king, the Dalai Lama. It was the most theocratic polity ever
devised.

Religion, then, was all-powerful and all-pervasive. The
Buddhist doctrine of reincarnation enjoined respect for life in
all its forms, and so strictly was this interpreted that Father
Huc would hesitate before subjecting a louse to the perils of
examination under his microscope. Yet by way of contrast,
these same ultra-humane Tibetans were considered by their
Mongol and Chinese neighbours as the most warlike of peoples—
and with good reason. Huc found the mountain wastes infested
with blood-thirsty brigands; even the lamas of rival monasteries would settle their disputes in pitched battles.

In this topsy-turvy land, the women used make-up, not to
enhance their appearance, but to render it repulsive. Sticking
out one's tongue, accompanied by a nonchalant scratching of
the ear, was reckoned the politest form of salutation. And the
bones, over which packs of mangy dogs fought in the streets of
Lhasa, might be those of their deceased masters. This city,
which looked so romantic from a distance, invariably disappointed the visitor. Beggars were as plentiful and impor-
tunate as the dogs. Inside, the houses were bare, cheerless and
filthy; even the wealthy lived largely on a diet of barley meal
and buttered tea. Yet Tibet was far from poor. Silver, weighed
by the ounce, was the common currency. The gilded roofs of
the monasteries were real; and the gold, panned from every
stream, was legendary.

Eighty years before Huc's visit it was the fabulous wealth of
Tibet which had spurred the first initiative to penetrate its
political isolation. Following the phenomenal success of British
arms in India during the 1750s and 60s the East India
Company found itself master of Bengal and Bihar, including the
city of Patna. It was from Patna, on the Ganges, that the
existing trade between India and Tibet by way of Nepal was
conducted. Here for the first time factors of the Honourable

Company came face to face with trans-Himalayan traders. They knew them as the men from 'Botton' (literally Bhutan, but the word was used to designate Tibet as well) and, as one factor delightfully put it, 'they had but few hares [sic] in their beards'. The trade was small but highly advantageous since 'a considerable quantity of gold and many other valuable commodities were imported'.

And gold, or specie of some sort, happened to be precisely what the East India Company most needed. To meet the ever-growing demand for tea on the home market a three-way trade had developed between Britain, India and China. Manufactured goods were exported to India and tea was brought back from China (it would be fifty years before the first attempts were made to grow tea in India). But until the Chinese developed a taste for Indian-grown opium, it was British bullion which filled the ships' holds between Calcutta and Canton and financed the tea trade. Clearly Tibet's gold would be the ideal substitute. And given that country's cruel climate and backward condition, English broadcloth and manufactures should command a ready sale there. The Tibetan trade was scheduled for rapid expansion.

Unfortunately, though, the East India Company did not quite have a common frontier with Tibet. Interposed between the two was the main Himalayan chain, a formidable obstacle in itself, but even more so since it was the home of several small but troublesome peoples. One of these, the Gurkhas of Nepal, was in the process of overwhelming its mountain neighbours just as the British were expanding in the plains. In the process the Gurkhas antagonised the Tibetans and mercilessly taxed all traders. Thus, no sooner had Patna fallen into British hands, than the trickle of Tibetan trade from which so much was expected promptly dried up. A British expedition was sent to Nepal in 1767 and a trade mission was planned for 1769. But neither reached its destination and all commerce across the mountains remained frozen.

Such was the situation when in 1772 Warren Hastings, the first and greatest of India's Governors-General, took over as Governor of Bengal and gave the matter his personal attention. Conveniently, events suddenly took a more favourable turn. The Bhutanese, only slightly less belligerent than the Gurkhas, started raiding into the plains. Hastings sent a force to repel them and appeared poised to invade the country. Bhutan had traditional links with Tibet and in early 1774 a Tibetan mission turned up in Calcutta to plead for clemency on behalf of the wayward Bhutanese. The opportunity was too good to miss. Hastings welcomed the unexpected overture, agreed to spare Bhutan and, as a quid pro quo, despatched a small mission to explain and exploit the situation. In October 1774 two Scots, George Bogle and Alexander Hamilton, became the first Britons ever to enter Tibet.

The Tibetan initiative had come, not from the Dalai Lama at Lhasa, but from the Panchen Lama at Tashilunpo. As yet Hastings was unaware of the friction between these two centres and fondly imagined that Bogle and his companion would proceed to Lhasa as a matter of course. They soon discovered otherwise. The Panchen Lama had acted quite independently and the Lhasa authorities bitterly resented his entertaining a British mission. Bogle and Hamilton got no further than Tashilunpo and Namling, places only a hundred miles inside Tibet and situated in the, by Tibetan standards, comparatively fertile and populous Tsangpo valley. They were categorically refused access to Lhasa and they were spared a taste of the barren wastes which comprise the core of the country.

But Bogle, at least, formed a highly favourable opinion of the people. Their gaiety and unaffected kindness were revelations, the personal friendship of the Panchen Lama moved him deeply, and the six months spent in Tibet he reckoned amongst the happiest and most relaxed of his life. His sentiments on leaving the country would do much to foster the nineteenth century's romantic image of Tibet.

Farewell ye honest and simple people [he wrote]. May ye long enjoy that happiness which is denied to more polished nations; and while they are engaged in the endless pursuit of avarice and ambition, defended by your barren mountains, may ye continue to live in peace and contentment, and know no wants but those of nature.

These were odd sentiments from a man who was supposed to be engineering the commercial and political penetration of the country. But it was through no fault of his that the mission failed to achieve anything. The good offices of the Panchen

Lama were simply not enough in themselves to open Tibet. For one thing, while Nepal remained closed to trade, the only known route between India and Tibet was through Bhutan; and the Bhutanese had yet to be convinced that an open frontier was in their best interests. Then there were the Lhasa authorities. The Dalai Lama was, as so often, a minor. His regent opposed the aspirations of the rival Panchen Lama and could therefore be expected to continue to resist all approaches from India. And finally there were the Chinese *ambans*, or residents, in Lhasa. If the regent ever changed his mind about contacts with India, the Chinese could be guaranteed to resist to the last all outside interference.

Bogle confirmed that Tibet was under Chinese protection and that its foreign relations were the responsibility of Peking. Given the appalling restrictions placed on British trade in Canton, this news might have been expected to kill off all hopes of access to the Tibetan market. But Hastings and Bogle saw it very differently. The existence of regular contacts between Lhasa and Peking held out the prospect of a new line of communications with the emperor. Thus the wall of Chinese officialdom in Canton might be circumvented and the markets, not just of Tibet but of all inland China, opened to British commerce.

With such high stakes to play for, Hastings determined to stay in the game. In 1776 he sent Hamilton to renew contacts with the Panchen Lama. But then, and in 1777, Hamilton was refused entry into Tibet. Two years later Bogle himself was appointed to a new Tibetan mission. This time the Panchen Lama was about to leave for Peking. There were plans for Bogle to accompany him there and suddenly the prize seemed within reach. But the lama died in Peking and Bogle himself died a few weeks later. The only positive link between India and Tibet—the personal friendship between Bogle and the lama—was broken.

To the Tibetans, of course, the Panchen Lama's death was nothing of the sort; he was still alive and, by 1783, kicking, in the shape of an eighteen-month-old baby. Hastings, who would have spotted a silver lining even in a smog, suddenly realised that in Tibetan eyes it might be proper and acceptable for him to pay his respects to his old friend, now embarking on his seventh term of office. The Governor-General stopped short of despatching an eighteen-month-old reincarnation of Bogle, and, instead, sent Lieutenant Samuel Turner, his own first cousin. Turner duly entered Tibet, reached Tashilunpo, and had a touching interview with the infant lama. His dealings were largely with the child's ineffectual regent and he was thus still further than Bogle from any contact with the high authorities in Lhasa. But Turner does seem to have seized upon an important point—that wooing the lamas with British-led missions was not essential to the initiation of a modest degree of Indo-Tibetan commerce. This trade, after all, was what had prompted the first British moves and, although the Tibetans had refused to condone any regular arrangement, they had never actually banned the trade as such. Clearly what they objected to most was the involvement of British officers. Turner therefore proposed that Indian merchants be encouraged to try their luck and, to this end, at last persuaded the Bhutanese to cooperate.

In 1785 the first Indo-Tibetan commercial 'adventure' proved a modest success and, in spite of Hastings' departure from India, further exchanges continued encouraging. But again it was the Gurkhas who frustrated matters. In 1788 they invaded Tibet. During four years of intermittent war, British intervention, and non-intervention, was sought by both sides. Hastings' successor failed to take advantage of either. Instead it was the Chinese who came to Tibet's aid. By 1793 Gurkhas, Tibetans and Chinese all believed that the British had helped the other side; in Tibet the influence of Peking was stronger than ever, and the possibility of either commercial or political links with India was dead. It would be over a century before they were revived.

Thus ended the first Anglo-Tibetan flirtation. Only two British missions had actually entered Tibet and neither had reached Lhasa. There was, though, a curious postscript. For in 1810 an Englishman did at last reach Lhasa. His name was Thomas Manning and, in the century preceding Huc and Gabet's visit, he was the only European to see the Tibetan capital.

Strangely, this achievement attracted little attention. At the outset the East India Company refused Manning any diplomatic status—probably no bad thing from his point of view—and, on his return, failed to take note of his recommendations.

Moreover he himself regarded the journey as a failure. Lhasa had not been his goal and Tibet interested him little. For Manning, an eccentric genius and traveller extraordinary, was first and foremost a sinologist. After a brilliant career as a mathematician he had conceived a passion for all things Chinese and determined to pursue his interests to their fountainhead. In the early 1800s he tried to enter China from Canton, from Macao and from Vietnam. Failing in each case he came to Calcutta, adopted a disguise which he claimed to be that of 'a Tartar gentleman', and set off for Peking by way of Tibet. His disguise probably fooled few, but his very un-English behaviour and, above all, his cold-shouldering of the 'barbarian' Tibetans in favour of the more cultured Chinese, worked much to his advantage. The Chinese in Tibet were now far more in evidence than in Bogle's day and it was in the entourage of a Chinese general that he finally entered Lhasa. There he stayed for four months, considerably longer than Huc and Gabet, although his observations were neither as full nor as intriguing as theirs. Manning, like the fathers, was perpetually on the defensive; the question of proceeding to Peking was scarcely broached and, once his money had run out, his only hope was that he might be expelled via China. But, just as the fathers hoped to be sent to Calcutta and were in fact sent to Canton, so Manning, desperate to be sent to Canton, was simply packed off back to India. Bitterly disappointed, he went back to Canton by sea, and in 1815 at last entered Peking as part of an official British mission. But then, as now, this proved an unsatisfactory way of seeing the country. To the distrust of the Chinese was added that of his own colleagues. The party was closely escorted and carefully quarantined. They saw nothing of the real China and Manning returned to England in disgust. In retrospect the Tibetan journey must have seemed infinitely preferable.

Whether Huc and Gabet had ever heard of Manning seems doubtful. For one thing, no account of his travels had been published by 1846, and for another, it was thirty-six years since his visit to Lhasa. More intriguingly, Huc's perspective on the subject of previous Europeans in Tibet was foreshortened by the discovery of a much more recent visitor to Lhasa. This again was an Englishman, none other in fact than William Moorcroft, the father of exploration in both the

Western Himalayas and Central Asia. Furthermore, according to Huc's information, Moorcroft had lived in Lhasa for an incredible twelve years.

For English readers this must have been one of the most fascinating snippets from Huc's entire narrative. It was known that William Moorcroft had indeed visited Tibet. In 1812 he had crossed the Himalayas just west of Nepal and spent the summer exploring Western Tibet including the sacred lake of Manasarowar and the commercial centre of Gartok. As superintendent of the East India Company's stud farm he claimed that he was reconnoitring a possible route to the horse breeding areas of Central Asia. In fact he was travelling without authorisation and spent most of his time investigating the trade in goat's wool between Tibet, where the goats flourished, and Kashmir, where the wool was turned into the valuable shawls. But there was no question of his reaching Lhasa during this foray; indeed, he was back in India, meeting a stiff reprimand from the Company with a broadside of political and commercial recommendations, by September 1812.

Seven years later Moorcroft again headed north into the Himalayas on what would prove to be one of the greatest marathons in the history of exploration. His early plans included Lhasa, but by the time his considerable caravan reached the Tibetan passes they were already closed for the winter. He was forced to take a much more westerly route, via Ladakh instead of Tibet, and was thus never within a thousand miles of Lhasa. On the other hand, he did spend two years in and around Leh, the capital of Ladakh. It is just possible that Huc misunderstood his informants, and that when they talked of Moorcroft living amongst them they meant in Leh not Lhasa. These informants seem to have been mainly from Lhasa's Kashmiri community and such people might well have been in Leh in the early 1820s.

It is clear, however, that Huc checked this strange story very carefully. It was substantiated by the Dalai Lama's regent (a Tibetan), by the head of Lhasa's Mohammedan community and by a man who claimed to have been Moorcroft's servant, as well as by 'other inhabitants of Lhasa'. 'We had never heard of Moorcroft before we arrived there,' wrote Huc, 'but with all these independent sources it would seem beyond doubt that he really did arrive there in 1826, lived there twelve years and was murdered on the road from Lhasa to Ladakh.' The date, 1826, of his arrival in Tibet was particularly significant. For one thing, this meant that he had left only eight years before Huc arrived on the scene; the scandal of his having avoided detection for so long was still fresh in the minds of the authorities and their chronology might be taken as fairly accurate. More significant still, 1826 happened to be the year after that in which, according to the East India Company, Moorcroft had died in Afghanistan.

As recorded in his voluminous papers, Moorcroft had left Ladakh in 1822 heading west for Kashmir and Afghanistan. After being detained for six months at Kunduz near the Oxus river, he crossed into Western Turkestan and, in 1825, reached Bukhara; he was the first Englishman to visit this famous city since Tudor times. Still searching for bloodstock to improve the East India Company's cavalry, he then headed south for the oasis town of Andkhui. For some reason he went alone, leaving his companions—a young Englishman called Trebeck and an Anglo-Indian doctor called Guthrie—to proceed to Balkh. They never saw their leader again. A servant returned to report that he had died of fever; and his body was eventually brought to Balkh. But by then Guthrie was also dead. Trebeck was too ill to inspect the body and, anyway, it was probably unrecognisable. It was buried at Balkh and almost the last message from Trebeck, before he too died, was that 'Mr M. died of fever on 27th August 1825.'

At the time there was no reason to doubt this and, since the same fate befell all the principal members of the expedition, no enquiry could be held. There were suspicions that Moorcroft— and perhaps his companions—had not died of natural causes; it seemed too much of a coincidence that after six years of travel they should all succumb within six weeks. But there was no reason to suppose Moorcroft had simply absconded. The last entry in his journal, three weeks before his death, gave no hint of anything untoward; and Moorcroft was not one to leave his colleagues in the lurch.

On the other hand 'it is clearly impossible', as Huc rightly noted, 'to reconcile these two accounts. But if Moorcroft never went to Lhasa, how is it that the Tibetans knew so much about him? Why should they want to invent such a tale?' If still alive, he could well have reached Lhasa in 1826. He had always planned to retire to the mountains and breed sheep; he had always wanted to go to Lhasa, and where better to hide from the wrath of his employers who had long since washed their hands of his activities? But another problem arises. Not the least of Moorcroft's achievements was to undertake his greatest journey when he was already in his fifties. By 1826 he was in his sixtieth year and, after twelve years in Lhasa, he would have been seventy-two.

Those who know their Moorcroft will not be hasty in discrediting the wildest of rumours about this extraordinary man. If any septuagenarian Englishman should have elected to see out his days wandering the Tibetan plateau with a herd of sheep and yaks, it would have been Moorcroft. But, to put it mildly, it seems improbable. Some scholars have suggested that Huc's informants must have mistaken one of his erstwhile servants for the man himself. Yet the two obvious candidates, one of whom was indeed a Kashmiri, are both accounted for. And who but Moorcroft himself, who had already purchased flocks of sheep in Ladakh, would have thought of combining map-making with husbandry? But there can be no proof in a case like this. The story is in itself a measure of the legend that surrounded—and still surrounds—the name of William Moorcroft.

And so to Fathers Huc and Gabet, the only Europeans apart from Manning who certainly saw Lhasa in the whole of the nineteenth century. In contrast to their immediate European antecedents in Tibet, Huc and Gabet were not interested in trade or politics. They came in search of converts and, to this extent, belong to a much earlier tradition of pioneers. For the first Europeans ever to enter Tibet had also been missionaries. In 1624 two Portuguese Jesuit fathers, lured on by the similarities between Tibetan Buddhism and Roman Catholicism which would so intrigue Huc, had established a mission at Tsaparang in Western Tibet. Forty years later two more Jesuits reached Lhasa and in 1707 two Capuchin fathers actually set up a mission there. It lasted for nearly forty years but with little success. An unseemly quarrel with the Jesuits as to who had the exclusive conversion rights for Tibet is very reminiscent of Huc's fury when his Lazarist order was eventually relieved of the same concession. Such bickering did Christianity little credit in the eyes of the Tibetans and, by the time of their expulsion in 1745, the Capuchins had left a legacy of intolerance which still rankled a hundred years later.

Though charged with the same zeal for conversions, Huc and Gabet showed none of the bigotry of their clerical predecessors. They were willing to conform to Tibetan ways, to seek out common ground in matters of doctrine and ritual, and to acknowledge piety in whatever guise. Bogle, who was much attracted towards Tibetan Buddhism, would have approved. Indeed, as a traveller and observer, Huc belongs far more to the tradition of Bogle, Turner, Manning and Moorcroft than to that of the earlier Jesuits and Capuchins. Moorcroft would have been delighted with his long and careful analysis of the burning qualities of different types of animal dung. Manning, himself an appalling judge of character, would have relished the picture of Huc being endlessly terrorised by his servants. And all would have appreciated the truly Gallic fervour with which the fathers set about their cuisine.

But what sets Huc's visit in a class apart, even from these, is the extent of his Tibetan travels. While the others all entered Tibet from the south, Huc and Gabet came from Mongolia in the north. To reach Lhasa they had thus to cross the core of the country, the bleakness and difficulty of which no previous European traveller had so much as suspected. Similarly, when they left, they headed east for Szechwan, across the axis of those most formidable mountain barriers along the upper reaches of the Mekong and Yangtse rivers. Throughout it was winter, the cold so intense on their first journey that men were freezing to death in their saddles, the snow so deep on the second that the yaks had to be sent ahead as steam-rollers. Were it simply a story of physical endurance it could stand with the best of polar endeavours.

And then there is the very considerable power and pace of Huc's narrative. The novelty of his surroundings never palls on him, and the danger of his situation never interferes with a lively curiosity. Yet somehow he manages to contain the large chunks of information which result—on Tibetan religion for instance—within the rhythm of his narrative. It was no mean achievement. Bogle and Manning had never attempted to prepare their notes for publication, although an edited narrative of both did eventually appear in 1867. Only Turner produced his own published account—and one that is none the more readable for that. Huc thus had a clear field. Until the present century his was the only popular account of Tibet. It is also—which is perhaps of more lasting appeal—a most enthralling and dramatic travelogue.

JOHN KEAY

TRANSLATOR'S NOTE

In August 1844, two young French Catholic missionaries, Joseph Gabet and Régis-Evariste Huc, set out on what proved to be a remarkable journey. Dressed as lamas, they started from a point some 400 miles north of Peking, and travelled south-west, traversing the whole of what is now Inner Mongolia, until they reached the foot of the Tibetan mountains. There, they joined the caravan of a Tibetan ambassador returning to Lhasa from Peking. In Lhasa they managed to win the confidence and friendship of the regent of the child Dalai Lama, were allowed to set up a chapel and to expound the Christian doctrine. But the Chinese authorities soon realised the dangers of this European penetration, and they were expelled after only forty-six days in Lhasa. They were sent under honourable escort through Eastern Tibet and South China to Macao, where they arrived in October 1846 and where Huc wrote his account of the journey. It was published in 1851 in two volumes under the title *Souvenirs d'un voyage dans la Tartarie et le Thibet*. This told the story only up to the point where the two missionaries re-entered China from Tibet. In 1854 Huc wrote a final volume, which he called *L'Empire Chinois*, describing the last stage of the journey across South China.

Meanwhile the *Souvenirs d'un voyage* seems to have had an immediate success. It was enjoyed rather as an adventure story than as a book of instruction and, according to one nineteenth-century orientalist, was given to French children to read, as a later generation was given the novels of Jules Verne. It was translated into many languages, including English, but then seems to have been forgotten. It was re-published in France by Huc's missionary society in 1923, and in 1962 the Livre de Poche Chrétien brought out a two volume paperback edition, Volume I, *Tartarie* and Volume II, *Thibet*. The first English translation was made by W. Hazlitt (1811–1893), son of the essayist, and was published in 1851. A second translation, by Mrs P. Sinnett, *Recollections of a Journey through Tartary, Tibet and China*, appeared in 1851. Hazlitt's version was reprinted a number of times, its last appearance being in an abridged edition in 1937, published by Herbert Joseph in the Great Explorations series. It was a poor translation, as Hazlitt's knowledge of French was inadequate, and there are gross mistranslations on nearly every page. The style is also uphill work for the modern reader.

Of the three volumes written by Huc, the second is by far the most interesting. This new translation of it has been made in the belief that it has a wide potential readership in the English-speaking world. Readability has therefore been a main consideration.

The Foreword is based on Volume I and explains how and why the journey was undertaken. The Postscript is based on Volume III and summarises the rest of the story.

FOREWORD

How the Journey Began

Father Huc set sail for China in February 1839, a few days after his ordination. He was twenty-six, a member of the Lazarist Order, full of zeal but with a lump in his throat at leaving his beloved France, as he thought, for ever.

Five and a half months later he arrived at the Portuguese colony of Macao, the jumping off place for Catholic missions into the forbidden territory of the Chinese Empire. While there he learned of the execution of a fellow Lazarist missionary, Father Perboyre. The bloodstained clothes of this martyr eventually reached Macao, and Huc was granted the right to wear them, as a symbol of his determination to follow if need be the same path. Using the missionaries' clandestine route, he set off for Peking in February 1841, across a China in the throes of a British attack, and arrived there three months later. From there he made his way across the Great Wall into Mongolia, where Lazarist missions had been set up for the benefit of Chinese Christians who had fled there to avoid persecution. Here he spent three years in the study of Chinese, Manchu and Mongolian.

Here also he met Father Gabet, five years his senior, who had been in Mongolia since 1837, and was now head of a mission at the town of Heichoui. Out of their friendship came an idea. The vast area known as Mongolia or Tartary was inhabited by nomad peoples who all embraced the Buddhist religion in the form practised in Lhasa, capital of Tibet: from Lhasa came the spiritual direction of the numerous lamaseries which were almost the only permanent settlements in a land of herdsmen and brigands. The two young missionaries resolved to go, as they said, 'to the source of the superstitions which dominate the peoples of Upper Asia,' that is, to Lhasa itself, a journey which involved crossing the whole of Tartary from the extreme north-east to the extreme south-west, before entering Tibet from the north.

The likelihood of their being able to accomplish this feat and return alive must have seemed small indeed; nevertheless permission was granted by Monseigneur Mouly who held the title of Apostolic Vicar of Mongolia, and they received official

instructions and financial resources. There was no mention of
Lhasa in the instructions; they were to study the character and
customs of the Mongols and to determine, if possible, the
extent and limits of Mongolian territory. 'You are to go from
tent to tent, from tribe to tribe, until God shows you the place
where he wishes you to stop, and there begin your mission.'
The story of how they set off in August 1844 is told below in
the words of Father Huc, taken from the first volume of the
account that he wrote over two years later, back in Macao
when the journey had ended.

The Narrative of Father Huc

This journey, which we had contemplated for so long, could
now begin, and we dispatched a young lama, a recent convert
named Samdadchiemba who was to accompany us on our
pilgrimage, to fetch some camels which we had put out to grass
in the kingdom of Naiman. Whilst waiting for his return, we
finished off the Mongolian texts on which we had been working for some time.

These small books of prayer and doctrine were ready but our
young lama had not returned. However, we thought that he
could not be long in coming, and so left the Valley of Black
Waters to wait for him at the Close Gorges, which was in any
case a more suitable base for mounting an expedition. But days
passed in fruitless waiting; the cool of autumn became sharper,
and we dreaded the thought of beginning our crossing of the
wilds of Tartary in the cold of winter. We therefore decided to
send someone to look for our camels and our lama. One of the
native teachers of the mission, a man of goodwill and an
excellent walker, set off. He returned on the day appointed,
but his search had been more or less fruitless. He had only
learned from a Tartar that our lama had started back some days
before with our camels. Our courier was therefore most surprised at their non-arrival.

'What?' he said, 'do I walk faster than a camel? Reverend
Fathers, be patient for another day; I am sure that the camels
and the lama will all be here tomorrow.' Several days passed
and nothing happened. We sent our courier off scouting again,
with the suggestion that he should go right to the spot

where the camels had been grazing, in order to see things with his own eyes without putting his trust in hearsay . . . The day fixed for his return arrived; still no camels, still no lama and—even more astonishing—no courier either. We were at our wits' end: we could not afford to waste more time in this way. We made new plans, since our old ones had come to nought. We fixed a day for our departure, and arranged for one of the Christians to take us in his cart as far as Tolon Noor, about 150 miles. There we would dismiss our driver, and go off alone into the wilderness, and so start our pilgrimage. This plan alarmed the Chinese Christians; they could not conceive how two Europeans could undertake a long journey alone in an unknown and hostile country; but we had reasons for maintaining our decision. We did not want a Chinese companion. It seemed to us absolutely necessary to break out from the cocoon which had been spun round us as missionaries in China. The services of one of the native teachers, full of prudence and timidity, would have done us no good in Tartary; a Chinaman would have been a burden.

On the Sunday, eve of our departure, all was ready; our two small trunks were padlocked and the Christians had come to say goodbye. However, to everyone's surprise, at sunset the courier returned. We could see at once from his gloomy expression what sort of news he brought.

'Reverend Fathers,' he said, 'the news is bad; all is lost, there is no hope; in the whole kingdom of Naiman there are no camels belonging to the Holy Church. The lama must have been killed; in my opinion the devil has been at work.'

Doubts and fears are often harder to bear than certainty of misfortune. This news, although distressing, removed our perplexity, without affecting our plan. After listening to the wordy condolences of our Christians, we went to bed, certain that the morrow would be the first day of our nomadic life.

The night was already far advanced when we were woken suddenly by a babble of voices; our door shook with loud and repeated knocks. Everyone jumped out of bed, to discover that our young lama had arrived complete with the camels! It was like a minor revolution. Plans were changed on the spot. We would leave not on Monday but on Tuesday, not on the cart but with our camels in Tartar fashion as originally planned. We went to bed again, in great excitement, but not to sleep: we both spent the remaining few hours thinking out the quickest way of equipping the caravan.

Next day, as we made our preparations, Samdadchiemba explained the reasons for his mysterious delay. First, he had been sick for a long time; next he had gone off in pursuit of a camel that had escaped in the wilderness; finally he had been obliged to attend the law-courts to get back a stolen mule. A law-suit, an illness and animals gone astray were more than sufficient reasons to explain his long absence. Our courier alone did not share in the general rejoicing; for it was clear to everyone that he had bungled his mission.

Monday was entirely devoted to fitting up the caravan. Everyone lent a hand. Some worked at repairing our mobile home, that is, they patched up a coarse blue canvas tent, whilst others fashioned a good store of tent-pegs. In one corner a brass cauldron was being scoured out, in another a broken trivet was being repaired; elsewhere ropes were being made, and the hundred and one pieces of the camels' pack-saddles were being fitted together. The small courtyard of our house was crowded with tailors, carpenters, coppersmiths, rope-makers, harness-makers, men of all crafts and of all trades. For, man and boy, all our Christians had made up their minds that their reverend fathers should be provided with every possible comfort when they set out.

By Tuesday morning, all that remained to be done was to pierce the camels' noses, and insert in the hole a wooden peg which would function as a kind of bit. This task was left to

Samdadchiemba. The wild shrill cries uttered by the poor beasts during this painful operation brought all the Christians of the village together as spectators. Our young lama then became the hero of the expedition. The crowd stood round him watching how, by little tugs on the rope tied to the peg in the camels' noses, he could control them and make them kneel down when he wished. It was a fascinating novelty for the Chinese to see how our lama tied our luggage on to the camels. When all was ready, we drank a cup of tea and went to the chapel. The Christians sang the prayers for travellers; then came tearful goodbyes and we set off. Samdadchiemba, solemnly riding on a stocky black mule, went first, leading two camels loaded with our baggage; we then followed, Father Gabet riding on a large she-camel, and I on a white horse.

We set off, determined to give up our old way of life and adopt the Tartar way. However, we could not shake off the Chinese system immediately. Apart from the fact that we had a temporary escort of Chinese Christians who, some on foot and some on horseback, were providing a guard of honour, the first night of our journey was to be spent at an inn owned by the chief native teacher of the Close Gorges mission.

The advance of our small caravan was not at first entirely successful. We were still novices in the art of saddling and leading camels; again and again we had to halt, sometimes to rearrange a bit of rope or wood which was chafing one of the animals, sometimes to attach our baggage more securely to stop it toppling off. Despite these setbacks we made progress, but only at a snail's pace. After about a dozen miles we left the cultivated fields behind us and came out on to the grasslands. We now made better progress, the camels were more at home in these wilds and seemed to put on speed.

We climbed a high mountain; but the camels knew how to get their own back for the trouble we caused them by browsing on the tender elder shoots and wild rose bushes by the wayside. The shouts we had to make to get the lazy brutes to get a move on alarmed some foxes, which came out of their earths and fled at our approach. As soon as we reached the top of this steep hill we saw in the hollow below the Christian-owned inn of Yan Pa Eul. Our path from then on followed a number of brooks of clear water which sprang from the mountainside and met at its foot in a fine wide stream which encircled the inn. We were welcomed by the chief innkeeper, or, as he is called by the Chinese, the 'steward of the cash-box'.

This inn was typical of a number that we came across in Tartary, isolated in the wilderness but not far from the Chinese frontier. They usually consisted of a vast square enclosure, fenced by tall stakes interwoven with brushwood. In the middle there would be an adobe building, not more than ten feet high. Apart from a few poor small rooms on either side, this building consisted of one big apartment which served as kitchen, dining room and dormitory. When travellers arrived, they all congregated in this room, which was extremely dirty, smelly and smoky. Their place was on the large *kang* which occupied more than three-quarters of the room. This *kang* was both bed and stove: it was a platform some four foot high, with a flat smooth top, spread with a rush mat; the rich put felt carpets or skins on top of this. In front, three large cauldrons set in earthenware contained the broth for the guests. These great cauldrons were heated from below by fires which connected by flues with the interior of the *kang*, so that even in the bitterest cold of winter it remained very well heated. When travellers arrived the 'steward of the cash-box' invited them to climb on the *kang*; there one sat, cross-legged like a tailor, at a

big table whose feet were no more than five or six inches high. The rest of the room was for the folk of the inn, who came and went tending the fires under the cauldrons, making tea or kneading oatmeal and buckwheat flour for the guests' supper. The *kang* in these half-Chinese, half-Tartar inns was a stage on which the most lively and picturesque scenes were enacted: there the guests ate, drank, smoked, gambled, shouted or fought. When the day was over, from dining-room and gambling den it changed to dormitory. The guests unrolled their blankets, if they had any, or covered themselves with their overcoats and lay down side by side. When there were many guests, they lay in two rows, feet always to the middle. Everyone lay down, but it did not follow that everyone slept; whilst some were snoring away, others smoked, drank tea or conversed in loud voices. This strange scene, dimly lit by the pale gleam of the lamp, would often conjure up sensations of fear and foreboding in us. The lamp itself was a crude affair, usually a chipped cup, containing a long wick coiled up in a thick nauseating oil; it stood in a niche in the wall or was wedged between two wooden pegs doing duty as a lampstand.

On this occasion the innkeeper had given up his little room for us. We ate supper there, but decided not to sleep there; since we were Tartar nomads and owners of a fine tent, we wanted to practise putting it up. No one was upset at our decision; it was realised that we behaved in this way, not out of contempt for the inn, but out of love for pastoral life. When the tent was up and we had spread our goatskins on the ground, we lit a blaze of brushwood to warm ourselves up, for the nights were already beginning to be cold. No sooner were we in bed than the night-watchman, or 'inspector of darkness', began to sound a drum-roll on the gong, whose ringing tones echoed across the valleys and startled the tigers and wolves which frequent these wildernesses.

We were up before dawn. Before setting off we had a most important operation to perform: we had to change our clothes, and in a sense transform ourselves. The missionaries who live in China all wear, without exception, Chinese clothes; nothing distinguishes them from merchants, there is no visible indication of religion. This is a great disadvantage, for these laymen's clothes are most unsuitable for a man who preaches the Gospel. A Tartar would react with amusement or contempt if he heard a 'black' man, that is, a layman, speaking of religion. A black man is expected to deal with the things of this world; religion is not his business, but that of the lamas exclusively. Since the conditions which caused missionaries in China to adopt worldly clothes no longer applied to us, we felt that we could abandon them. The instructions we had received from our Apostolic Vicar gave us sanction, so we had no doubts about going ahead. We had decided to wear the secular costume of Tibetan lamas: we say secular, because they also have a specifically religious costume, which they put on when they pray in the temples or take part in their idolatrous ceremonies. We had fixed on this particular dress because it was that worn by our young convert Samdadchiemba.

We told the Christians at the inn that we had decided not to resemble Chinese merchants any more, and that we wished to cut off our pig-tails and shave our heads completely. This announcement was greeted with a gush of sentiment; some appeared to shed tears; others even tried to make us change our minds; but their eloquence was completely wasted on us; a razor, which we took out of a small packet, was the only answer we made to their arguments. We handed it to Samdadchiemba, and in an instant off came the long locks we had grown since we left France. We each put on a long yellow robe, which fastened on the right-hand side with five gilt buttons; it was drawn in at the waist by a long red sash; at the neck there was a small purple velvet collar; a yellow cap with a red pom-pom completed our new costume.

Lunch followed this critical operation; but it was a sad and silent meal. When the innkeeper brought us the little glasses and the bowl steaming with hot rice wine, we told him that having changed our clothes we must now change our way of life. 'Take away,' we said, 'that wine and that chafing dish; from today we must give up our wine and our pipe of tobacco. You know,' we added with a laugh, 'that good lamas neither drink nor smoke.' The Chinese Christians who had gathered round us did not find it in their hearts to laugh, for they were all secretly convinced that we should die of hardship and hunger in the wilds of Tartary.

When lunch was over, whilst the people of the inn packed up our tent, saddled the camels and got all ready for our departure, we took with us some steamed bread rolls and went

and picked our own dessert from the wild gooseberry bushes
which grew along the nearby stream. Soon a message came that
everything was ready. We mounted and set off towards Tolon
Noor, accompanied only by Samdadchiemba.

We were now launched, alone and without a guide, into the
midst of a new world. From now on we should not be treading
paths beaten before us by earlier missionaries; for we were to
enter a land where the Gospel had never been preached. The
die was cast: there would no longer be a band of Christians at
our side anxious to serve and always trying to make us feel at
home. We were on our own, in enemy territory, having to

handle everything ourselves, without any prospect of hearing
a friendly or brotherly voice on our way. But what matter? We
were in good heart and health; we went forward in the
strength of Him who said: 'Go ye therefore, and teach all
nations; . . . and lo, I am with you alway, even unto the end of
the world.'

As already said, Samdadchiemba was our only travelling
companion. This young man was neither a Chinaman, a Tartar
nor a Tibetan, yet from his features it was immediately clear
that he belonged to the Mongolian race. His broad, cheekily
turned-up nose, his wide straight mouth, his thick protruding
lips, his dark complexion all helped to make him look like a
savage, but a proud one. When his little eyes looked at you
under his long lids without lashes you felt an odd mixture of
trust and fear. There was nothing clear-cut about this strange
face: there was neither the cunning of the Chinaman, the open
good-nature of the Tartar nor the bravery of the Tibetan; but

there was a little of each. Samdadchiemba was a Dchiahour. Later on we shall have an opportunity of saying more about the native land of our young camel driver.

At eleven years of age, Samdadchiemba had escaped from his lamasery to avoid the blows of a master whose punishments he considered to be too severe. He had then passed most of his youth wandering like a tramp, sometimes in Chinese cities, sometimes in Tartar wildernesses. It was clear that this life of freedom had added little polish to the natural roughness of his character; his mind was completely untutored: but on the other hand his muscular strength was prodigious, and he was very proud of this and liked to show it off. After being instructed and baptised by Father Gabet, he wanted to become a servant of missionaries. The journey we had embarked on was exactly what suited his wandering temperament. This young man was no use as a guide across the wilds of Tartary; he knew no more about the country than we did. Our only guides were a compass and the Andriveau-Goujon map of the Chinese Empire.

Two months later, the small caravan had made its way across the greater part of Mongolia. It had passed through the Tchakar, crossed the Yellow River in flood and entered the kingdom of Ortou. Receiving warning that owing to extreme drought conditions the Alachan desert was impassable, the missionaries decided to alter their route. This would involve re-entering China.

Before setting off that morning we opened our map in order to work out a route avoiding the terrible Alachan, without however deviating too far from our true direction. We came to the conclusion that the only way was to cross the Yellow River once more, pass through the Great Wall and travel through the Chinese province of Kansou until we reached the Tartar lands of the Koukou Noor.

There was a time when such an idea would have filled us with alarm; used as we were to living clandestinely amongst our Chinese Christians, it would have seemed impossible to launch ourselves into Chinese territory alone without a native Christian as a guide; obviously the only possible outcome would have been death by strangulation for ourselves and the persecution of all missions in China. But by now we had thrown off such fears. Armed by two months' experience on the road we had reached the conclusion that we could travel within the Chinese Empire as securely as in Tartary. Staying in various market towns where we had had to handle our own affairs had given us practice and accustomed us to Chinese ways. The language was by now no problem: apart from the fact that we could speak the Tartar tongue, we had by now mastered the everyday language of the Chinese; when we had lived in missions this had been most difficult to do, because the Christians had, out of flattery, always been careful to use in our

presence the simple vocabulary we had learned in the text-books. But our long journey had not only endowed us with these purely moral and intellectual advantages, it had greatly toughened us up physically. For two whole months rain, wind and sun had done battle against our European complexions, and our faces were now so tanned that we bore a fair resemblance to men of the wilds. We no longer felt the slightest fear of being recognised as Westerners by the Chinese.

So when we started out we changed from the westerly direction that we had been consistently following during our journey, and turned slightly southward. After two days' march we came to the foot of a chain of mountains whose summits were hidden in clouds. We began the climb in good heart, hoping that on the other side we would reach the Yellow River. This day's march was very hard, especially for the camels, which had to tread continually on sharp rocks. As a result their soft feet began to bleed almost immediately. We however hardly noticed any discomfort, because we were so

fascinated by the bizarre appearance of the mountains themselves.

In the gorges and at the foot of the precipices formed by
these high mountains there were large heaps of mica and
foliated rock, broken up, crushed and even pulverised. All
these accumulations of slate and shale seemed to have been
washed into the hollows by the action of water, for they did not
belong to these mountains, which were granitic. The higher we
climbed the more bizarre grew the shapes of the rocks. There
were great lumps of stone tumbled and heaped on each other
and seemingly cemented tightly together. These rocks were
nearly all covered with incrustations of sea-shells and plants
resembling seaweed; but the most remarkable thing of all was
the way they were hollowed out and burrowed into in every
direction. Wherever we looked there were cavities, and long
winding tunnels; it looked as though the whole of the upper
part of the range had been eaten into by a race of gigantic
worms. Here and there we saw deep imprints in the granite, as
if it had been used to make moulds for monsters, whose shape
was perfectly well preserved.

We could not help feeling that we were walking on a dried-
up seabed. Everything testified to the belief that these mountains had in fact undergone the slow action of the sea. It was
impossible to imagine that what we saw had been brought
about by rainfall, and even less likely that it was caused by the
flooding of the Yellow River, which, however great, could not
be imagined as reaching such a height. Those geologists who
claim that the Flood took place by subsidence, rather than by
the melting of the Polar ice, might find in these mountains
enough evidence to support their theory.

When we reached the crest we could see the Yellow River
below us, flowing majestically from south to north; it was
about midday, and we hoped that we should be able to cross it
that evening and spend the night in an inn at the little town of
Chetsouidze, which we could see from where we stood on the
slope of a hill on the far side of the river.

The steep descent took the whole afternoon, as we had to
pick our way over the rough ground. It was still light however
when at last we reached the river bank. The crossing was
unexpectedly successful. First, the Mongols who ran the ferry
asked for less than we had previously been charged by Chinese

boatmen. Secondly, the animals embarked without any trouble.
On the other side we were in China. So we said goodbye for a
while to Tartary, to the wilderness and to our nomadic life.

*The rest of the present volume continues the narrative of Father
Huc from this point. It is an unabridged translation of the second
part of his trilogy, dealing with the most dramatic part of the
story: the journey through Kansou; the stay at the lamaseries of
Kounboum and Tchogortan; the journey to Lhasa by the northern
route; the adventures of the two missionaries in Lhasa and finally
their forced return by the eastern route.*

A TIBETAN JOURNEY

[1]
ACROSS KANSOU

It was now two months since we had left the Valley of Black Waters, and during all this time we had suffered hardships and privations of every sort. Our health, it is true, had not yet been seriously affected; but we felt weak and in need of a few days' holiday from our life of hardship. For this purpose, a country where the inhabitants were Chinese would suit us perfectly; compared with Tartary, it would have all the comforts one could ask for.

As soon as we had crossed the Yellow River we entered the little frontier town of Chetsouidze, which was separated from the river only by a sandy beach. We put up at the Inn of Justice and Mercy. The house was vast and of recent construction. Apart from solid foundations of grey brick, it was built entirely of wood. The innkeeper greeted us with the courtesy and eagerness invariably shown by those trying to build up a clientèle for a new establishment, and with ingratiating manners he tried to make up for his unprepossessing appearance. He had such a violent squint that his eyes were always turned askance from the person addressed; but if his sight was defective his tongue made amends by being marvellously supple. As a former member of a great man's retinue he had seen much, heard much and above all remembered much; he knew every country and had met everybody. His talk was, however, by no means always a nuisance; he provided all sorts of facts about towns and villages through which we would pass on our way to the Koukou Noor. He even had a good knowledge of the Koukou Noor itself, for when a serving soldier he had fought against the Si Fan. The day after our arrival he appeared at early dawn with a large sheet of paper on which were written, in the right order, the names of every single town, village, hamlet and straggling settlement that we would pass through in the province of Kansou; he then launched into a spate of topographical detail, with such a wealth of gesture and so much shouting that it left us stunned.

The time not occupied, willingly or unwillingly, in conversations with our host was spent in exploring the town. Chetsouidze was tucked into an angle formed on one side by the Alachan Hills and on the other by the Yellow River. At the eastern end blackish hills rose from the river's edge, rich in coal-mines which the inhabitants actively exploited and which were the main source of their wealth. In the suburbs, great pottery works made enormous urns destined to contain the family water supply, impressive and well-constructed stoves and a large number of pots of every shape and size. The province of Kansou imported a great quantity of these goods.

Food in Chetsouidze was abundant, varied and extraordin-arily cheap; there is probably nowhere else in the world where life is so easy. At all hours of the day and night travelling restaurants brought all sorts of cooked dishes to the home: soups, mutton and beef stews, vermicelli and so forth. There were dinners for all appetites and every pocket, from the rich man's elaborate feast down to the thin and simple beggar's broth. These caterers came and went constantly. They usually belonged to the Mohammedan caste, and were distinguishable from the Chinese only by a blue skull-cap.

When, after two days at the Inn of Justice and Mercy, we felt sufficiently rested and restored, we resumed our journey. The country round Chetsouidze was barren; there was nothing to be seen but sand and gravel deposited each year by the floods of the Yellow River. However, as we advanced the ground rose slightly and the soil improved. At some three miles from the town we crossed the Great Wall, or rather we passed through some pathetic ruins which still marked the place where the ancient bastion of China had stood. Soon the country became magnificent and we were filled with admiration for the Chinese genius for agriculture. The part of Kansou that we were cross-ing was especially remarkable for its large-scale and ingenious irrigation works. By means of cuts made in the banks of the Yellow River the waters flowed into great artificial canals from which they passed into narrower channels and finally into the ditches which surrounded every field. A system of large and small locks, of an admirably simple design, was used to raise the level of the water and to distribute it where the terrain was uneven. It was shared out amongst the landowners in perfect order. Each one watered his land in turn; no one would ever open his sluices before the appointed day.

We came across few villages, but everywhere there were scattered farms of varying sizes only a few fields apart. There were no groves of trees nor pleasure gardens. Apart from a few tall trees round the houses, the entire land was devoted to the culture of grain; there was not even a little space left to put the sheaves when harvested: they were all piled on top of the houses, which were always flat-roofed. When the river overflowed its banks, as was now the case, the countryside was an exact replica of the floods in the Nile valley which have so often been described; to move about in their fields the inhabitants used little skiffs or light carts on very high wheels, usually drawn by buffaloes.

Such floods, however valuable for soil fertility, are most unpleasant for travellers; we were forced to use the embankments which divided the fields as causeways. Leading camels along such paths is an agonising experience. At every step we feared that our luggage would go down into the mud; and indeed this happened on more than one occasion, causing a considerable nuisance; it would have done so more frequently had it not been for the ability of our camels to cope with mud, a skill which they had learned on their long journey through the Ortou marshes.

In the evening of our first day's march, we arrived at a small village named Wang Ho Po. We expected to find the same easy living as at Chetsouidze, but we were disappointed. Customs were different; there were none of those splendid travelling restaurants laden with ready-cooked meals. Only the forage-dealers appeared. So we first fed the animals, then went into the village to find provisions for our supper. On returning to the inn, we found that we had to do our own cooking, since the innkeeper provided only the water, the coal and the pot. Whilst we were peaceably engaged in enjoying the results of our culinary efforts, a great hubbub arose in the courtyard of the inn: it was a caravan of camels led by some Chinese merchants on their way to the city of Ninghsia. Since we were going in the same direction, we soon got into conversation; they told us that the roads to Ninghsia were impassable, and that our camels, however expert, would be unlikely to get through. However, they knew a less dangerous short-cut, and invited us to accompany them. As they intended to set off during the night, we called the innkeeper so as to settle our account. According to the Chinese custom, whenever money is involved one side asks a high sum and the other offers a low one; there follows a long argument and after concessions on each side a price is agreed. As we were taken for Tartars, it was quite normal procedure to ask for about three times the proper price; as a result the ensuing argument was twice as long as it normally would be. We had to bargain very hard, first for ourselves, then for the animals; for the room, for the stable, for the water-trough, for the cooking-pot, for the coal, for the lamp, for each item in turn, until the innkeeper had come down to the prices charged for 'civilised' clients. This unfortunate Tartar appearance of ours led to our acquiring a certain skill in this type of debate, for not one day passed during our journey through the province of Kansou without a wrangle with an innkeeper. Such quarrels, however, were not to be taken at all seriously: when they were over, we were always better friends than ever.

Shortly after midnight the Chinese camel drivers were already up and noisily preparing to depart. We rose hurriedly, but although we saddled our beasts as fast as we could, our travelling companions were ready first. They set off before us, promising to go slowly until we caught up with them. As soon as our camels were laden we set off, but the night was dark, and we could see nothing of our guides: with the help of a little lantern we tried to follow their tracks, but in this too we were unsuccessful. So we had to follow our noses, surrounded by watery plains completely unknown to us. We soon found ourselves so deep into flooded country that we dared advance no further. We stopped by the edge of a field, and there waited for day.

As soon as dawn began to break we led our beasts by the bridles and made our way, by a circuitous route, towards a large walled town which we could see in the distance. It was Pinlouohsien, a town of the third class. Our arrival within the walls caused the most frightful havoc. The district was noted for the number and quality of its mules: at that hour of the day there was a mule tethered in front of nearly every house in the long street which traversed the town from north to south. As we advanced, all these beasts, struck with terror at the sight of our camels, began to rear and kick violently at the nearest merchant's stall; some broke their halters and galloped off, upsetting the stalls as they went. The crowd became angry, shouting and swearing at the 'stinking Tartars', cursing the camels and increasing the disorder instead of quelling it. We were deeply grieved that our arrival should have provoked such dire consequences, but what could we do? We had no control over the shyness of the mules nor the fearsome appearance of the camels. One of our party decided to run ahead, to warn the people of the caravan's approach: this had some effect, but the trouble continued until we were again outside the walls.

We had intended to breakfast at Pinlouohsien; but having failed to win the goodwill of the inhabitants, we dared not stop. However we plucked up enough courage to buy some provisions, horribly expensive because it was an unfavourable moment for bargaining. At a little distance from the town, we came across a guardhouse. We stopped there to rest and eat our morning meal. These guardhouses are very numerous in China, the rule being that there should be one every mile and a half along the main roads. Very quaintly built in a typical Chinese style, they are constructed either of wood or earth and always whitewashed; the central part is a bare barn-like shelter with a wide opening on to the front intended for travellers benighted in bad weather and unable to reach an inn. On each side of this shelter there is a room with door and window, sometimes only furnished with a red-painted bench. The exterior of the guard-house is decorated with crude paintings of all the weapons in use in China: matchlocks, bows, arrows, lances, shields and sabres of many different shapes. A little way from the guard-house there is always a square tower on the right-hand side, and on the left five small milestones in a line: they indicate the five *li* or Chinese miles to the next guardhouse. There is often a large notice-board on two poles giving the traveller the names of the next towns on the road. The board we saw here read as follows:

From Pinlouohsien to Ninghsia, fifty *li*.
Northwards, to Pinlouohsien, five *li*.
Southward to Ninghsia, forty-five *li*.

In times of war the square tower is used at night for signalling, by means of fires arranged according to a certain code. The Chinese relate that an emperor, yielding to the foolish whim of his wife, one night gave the order for the alarm signals to be lit. The empress wanted to make merry at the soldiers' expense, also to test whether the beacons would really bring the soldiers to the defence of the capital. As the signals spread through the provinces, the governors ordered the military mandarins to set off for Peking; but learning on arrival that the alarm was merely a joke, a woman's whim, they made their way home full of indignation. Soon afterwards, the Tartars invaded the empire, advancing rapidly right to the walls of the capital. This time the emperor gave the order for the beacons to be lit in earnest for the summoning of aid; but in the provinces no one moved, for it was assumed that it was another of the empress's little jokes. The Tartars, so ends the story, entered the capital without meeting resistance and the imperial family was massacred.

The long peace which China has enjoyed has much lessened the importance of these guardhouses; when they fall into ruin they are seldom repaired. The windows and doors are usually missing and they are unoccupied. On certain very busy roads only the notice-boards and the five milestones are usually kept in repair.

The guardhouse at which we had stopped was deserted. We tied our beasts to a large stake and went into one of the rooms, where we peacefully enjoyed a reviving meal. The travellers looked at us as they went by, apparently surprised to see their watchtower used as a restaurant. The more refined could not suppress a smile, at the sight of three Mongolians so unused to civilised ways.

We did not stay long. The notice-board informed us officially that we were still forty-five *li* from Ninghsia; what with the bad road and the slowness of our camels we had no time to lose. We set off alongside a very fine canal fed by the waters of the Yellow River, a part of the irrigation system. Whilst our little caravan advanced slowly over the wet slippery ground, we saw coming towards us a large troop of horsemen. As they advanced, the numerous workers who were repairing the banks of the canal flung themselves to the ground and called out: 'Peace and happiness to our father and mother!' We realised that an eminent mandarin was approaching. According to Chinese usage, we should have got off our mounts and prostrated ourselves like the rest, but we thought that as Lamas of the Western Heavens we could be excused such a tiresome and unpleasant custom. So we remained stolidly on our mounts, and went calmly on. Seeing our camels, the horsemen kept a respectful distance. But the mandarin himself, the brave man, urged on his horse and forced it to come near to us. He greeted us politely and asked, in Mongolian, after our health and our journey. As his horse became more and more restive at the sight of our camels, he was forced to cut the conversation short and rejoin his suite. He went off full of triumph at having found an opportunity to speak Mongolian, and thus demonstrate to his people the extent of his knowledge. This mandarin was probably a Tartar-Mandchou; he was on an official tour of inspection of the irrigation canals.

We continued to travel for a long while along the banks of this canal, meeting only a few large-wheeled wagons drawn by buffaloes, and travellers who were usually riding large donkeys. At last we saw the high ramparts of Ninghsia and the summits of numerous pagodas, looking from a distance like great cedar trees. The walls of Ninghsia, in brick, were ancient but very well preserved. Owing to their age they were entirely covered with moss and lichen, and the effect was most impressive. They were completely surrounded by marshes full of rushes, reeds and water-lilies. The town itself was wretchedly poor; the streets were dirty, narrow and winding, the houses smoky and tumbledown. The great antiquity of Ninghsia was evident, and although it was not far from the frontiers of Tartary there was very little in the way of commerce.

When we had travelled about half the length of the main street and there seemed to be about three miles more of it, we decided to make a halt. We went into a large inn, and were soon followed by three individuals who had the effrontery to ask for our passports. We realised straightaway that these were three light-fingered gentlemen after our purses.

'Who are you to dare ask for our passports?' we demanded.

'We are employees of the High Court,' they answered. 'Foreigners are forbidden to pass through the city of Ninghsia without passports.' Instead of replying we called the innkeeper and asked him to write his name and that of his inn on a piece of paper. Our request surprised him greatly.

'What for?' he asked. 'What will you do with it?'

'We shall need it by and by. We are going to the High Court to report to the mandarin that at your inn three robbers came and pestered us.' At these words the three passport-seekers took to their heels, followed by the curses of the innkeeper, and the laughter of the already numerous bystanders. Owing to this little episode, we were treated with particular respect.

The next morning, when dawn had hardly broken, we were woken by a frightful din which broke out in the inn yard. Above the uproar of many voices seemingly in violent dispute we made out words such as 'stinking Tartars', 'camel', and 'courthouse'. We dressed quickly and went out to discover the cause of this sudden riot, which seemed to be connected with us. During the night our camels had devoured two cartloads of osiers which had been parked in the yard. The crushed remains could still be seen littered here and there. The owners, who like us were strangers at the inn, were demanding payment for their merchandise, a claim which we thought was entirely justified. But in our opinion the innkeeper alone was responsible, since before going to bed we had warned him of the danger. We had told him the carts should be moved elsewhere, since the camels would certainly break their halters to get them. The owners of the carts had supported us, in order to be able to claim damages, but the innkeeper had laughed at our fears and insisted that camels did not eat osiers. When we had put our case, the bystanders, who in China are a kind of standing jury, decided that the whole loss should be made good by the landlord; however we generously did not claim the price of our camels' halters.

As soon as this unbiased judgment had been passed, we prepared for departure and set off. The southern half of the town looked in an even worse state than the part we had passed through on the previous day. Several whole districts had been destroyed and abandoned. We saw only a few pigs wandering among the ruins or rummaging through the rubbish. The inhabitants of that great city were plunged in a state of utter poverty. They were dressed for the most part in filthy rags and their faces, pale, sick and gaunt, showed that they often lacked the basic necessities of life. Yet Ninghsia had once been a royal city, and no doubt a rich and flourishing one. In the tenth century, a prince of Tartar race from Tou Pa, now occupied by the Si Fan, with a number of hordes under his command, succeeded, in spite of the Chinese, in setting up a small state not far from the banks of the Yellow River. He chose as his capital Hsia Tcheou, later renamed Ninghsia. Hence the kingdom was called Hsia. It flourished for more than two centuries but in 1227 it was enveloped in the general ruin by the victories of Genghis Khan, the founder of the Mongolian dynasty. Today Ninghsia ranks as a city of the first class in the province of Kansou.

On leaving Ninghsia, we found ourselves on a fine road bordered with willows and jujube trees. From time to time we came upon little tea houses, at which the traveller could rest and refresh himself at little cost. They provided tea, hardboiled eggs, broad beans fried in oil, cakes and a great variety of fruits preserved in sugar or salt. This day's march was a day of relaxation for us. Our camels, which knew only the deserts of Tartary, seemed to react to the charms of civilisation; they turned their heads majestically from side to side and observed with interest what was to be seen on the road, both people and things. Yet they were not so absorbed in their study of the crafts and customs of China that they failed to take notice of the marvels of nature. The willows attracted their attention from time to time, and when they were within reach they invariably lopped off the tenderest branches. Sometimes too, craning their long necks, they sniffed at the delicacies displayed in front of the tea-houses, eliciting strong protests from the traders. The Chinese admired our camels as much as our camels admired

China. They came running from everywhere to see the caravan pass by and lined the route, but never dared to come too close, for all over the world men instinctively fear whatever has the appearance of strength and power.

Towards the end of that day's march, which had not been without enjoyment, we arrived at Hsia Ho Po, a large unwalled village. We lodged at the Inn of the Five Felicities. We were busy feeding our beasts when a horseman with a white button on his hat entered the inn yard. Without dismounting or making the usual salutations he began to call loudly to the innkeeper:

'The Great Mandarin is about to arrive,' he said sharply and haughtily. 'See that everything is clean and well-swept. Those Tartars must lodge elsewhere. The Great Mandarin will not want to see camels at the inn.' Coming from a mandarin's courier, these insolent words did not surprise us, but they incensed us considerably. We pretended not to hear them and calmly continued our small task. The innkeeper, seeing that we took no notice of the command that had just been uttered, came up to us and explained the state of affairs with a courtesy mingled with embarrassment.

'Go and tell that White Button,' we told him firmly, 'that you accepted us into your inn and that we shall stay there. Tell him that mandarins have no right to interfere with travellers who have lawfully taken up lodgings.' There was no need for the innkeeper to repeat our words to the White Button: we said them loud enough for him to hear. He immediately dismounted, and addressing us directly said:

'The Great Mandarin is about to arrive; he has a large retinue and the inn is small. In any case, how could horses share this courtyard with your camels?'

'A man in a mandarin's suite, and especially one like you decorated with a white button, should know how to speak both with courtesy and with justice. We have a right to stay here, and will not be evicted. Our camels will stay tethered to the door of our room.'

'The Great Mandarin ordered me to prepare his lodging at the Inn of the Five Felicities.'

'Agreed, prepare his lodging, but without interfering with us. If you can't settle matters satisfactorily here, you will clearly have to go and find another inn.'

'And what about the Great Mandarin?'

'Tell your mandarin that here are three Lamas of the Western Heavens who are quite ready to return to Ninghsia to go to law with him, and that if need be they will go all the way to Peking, for they know the way there.' White Button mounted and departed. The innkeeper immediately came and begged us to remain firm.

'If you stay here,' he said, 'it's a good thing from my point of view: I am sure that with you I shall make a little profit; but if the mandarin takes your place, my inn will be turned upside down, I shall have to work all night and tomorrow morning they will all go off without paying. And then, if I have to send you away, what will happen to the reputation of the Inn of the Five Felicities? Who will ever come to an inn which receives travellers and then sends them away?' Whilst the innkeeper was encouraging us the mandarin's courier reappeared, dismounted and made a deep bow which we returned in the most courteous manner.

'My Lord Lamas,' he said, 'I have been all through Hsia Ho Po and there is no other decent inn. Now, what was all this about your having to leave to make way for us? What an unreasonable idea! For look you, my Lord Lamas, we are all travellers, we are all away from our homes; surely there must be a way of talking this over, of coming to an agreement like brothers?'

'Quite right,' we said, 'men should always agree like brothers, that's the great principle; travellers should learn to live together; a little give and take and everyone is happy.'

'Well said, well said,' replied the courier and we all began to bow deeply once again.

After this short colloquy ending in perfect understanding, we discussed amicably how we could all fit into the Inn of the Five Felicities. It was agreed that we should keep the room in which we had already settled but that we should tether our camels in a corner of the courtyard so that they would not frighten the mandarin's horses. The courier would arrange the rest as he thought best. We quickly untied our camels from outside our room and put them where agreed. Just after sunset we heard the mandarin's party approaching. The two halves of the main gateway opened solemnly and a carriage drawn by three mules stopped in the middle of the inn yard, escorted by a large number of horsemen. In the carriage was a man of some

sixty years of age, with grey moustache and beard and wearing
a kind of red hood. It was the Great Mandarin himself. On
arrival he ran his sharp eyes rapidly round the inn yard; when
he saw us, and in particular the three·camels at the far end, a
scowl passed over his thin face. When all the horsemen had
dismounted, he was invited to descend from his carriage.

'What are those Tartars doing here?' he said in a hard angry
voice, 'and those camels? Send the innkeeper to me.' At this
brusque summons the innkeeper vanished, and White Button
stood petrified. His face turned suddenly pale, then red, then
olive green. However he collected himself, went to the carriage, knelt, rose again, and bent towards his master's ear into
which he whispered for some time. When he had finished the
Great Mandarin deigned to descend, and after greeting us in a
slightly patronising manner, he entered like the mere mortal
that he was the small room that had been prepared for him.

This victory, won in a country forbidden to us under pain of
death, gave us enormous courage. These terrible mandarins,
whom we had so greatly dreaded, scared us no longer now that
we had dared confront them and see them at close hand. We
saw that they were men full of pride and insolence, tyrants
merciless against the weak but utter cowards when faced by
men of some determination. From now on we felt as much at
ease in China as anywhere else; we could travel without fear,
our heads erect in the clear light of day.

After two days' march we arrived at Tchoungwei, on the
banks of the Yellow River. This was a walled city of medium
size. In cleanliness, good condition and air of well-being it
contrasted remarkably with the poverty and ugliness of
Ninghsia. Judging only from its numerous well-stocked shops
and its crowded streets Tchoungwei was a busy trading
centre; yet the Chinese of this region are not navigators: we
saw no shipping on the Yellow River. This fact is quite remarkable; it tends to confirm the view that the inhabitants of this
part of Kansou are really of Tibetan and Tartar origin, for it is
well known that the Chinese are much addicted to the naviga-
tion of rivers great and small.

On leaving Tchoungwei we crossed the Great Wall, which
consisted only of loose stones piled one on another, and for a
few days re-entered Tartary, into the Kingdom of Alachan.
Mongolian lamas had often given us lurid descriptions of the

Alachan Mountains; but we learned from personal experience that the reality of this dreadful country is worse than any words can express. It is a long chain of mountains composed entirely of shifting sands so fine that they run through one's fingers like a liquid. Needless to say that amongst all these mighty heaps of sand there is not the slightest sign of vegetation. The monotony of these vast dunes is broken only by the traces of tiny insects which, as they wander aimlessly about, leave innumerable channels in the sand, so fine that one could follow up the twists and turns of an ant's movements without ever losing track. In crossing these mountains we suffered the greatest hardships and unspeakable difficulties. At each step our camels sank up to their bellies, and they could only advance by plunging. The horses were in an even worse plight, as their hooves had less hold on the sand than the large foot of a camel. We ourselves were forced to go on foot, and had to take great care not to slide down the mountain sides, which seemed to melt under our feet, right into the Yellow River which we could see stretching far below us. Fortunately, the weather was calm. If the wind had been blowing we should certainly have been swallowed up and buried alive under avalanches of sand. The Alachan Mountains seem to have been formed by the sands that the north wind unceasingly sweeps before it in the Chamo or Great Gobi desert. The Yellow River arrests these inundations of sand and thus protects the province of Kansou. The great quantities of sand that the river picks up from the foot of the Alachan Mountains give it the yellowish colour from which it takes its name. Above the Alachan Mountains, its waters are always pure and clear.

However the high mountains became hills and the sand gradually decreased, and towards the end of the day we arrived at the village of Ever Flowing Waters (Tchang Liou Choui). In the midst of these sandy hills, this was a real oasis of exquisite beauty. A multitude of little streams dancing through the streets, many trees, and little houses built on the bare rock and sometimes painted red or white made this a most picturesque place. Exhausted as we were we stopped at Ever Flowing Waters with indescribable pleasure, and savoured its delights. But the poetry only lasted until we came to settle with the innkeeper. As the food and even the forage came from Tchoungwei, and could only be transported with great difficulty, they

were horribly expensive and upset all our economic arrangements. For ourselves and our animals we were obliged to pay
1600 sapeks, about eight francs. Otherwise we should no doubt
have left the charming village of Tchang Liou Choui with
regret. But there is always some circumstance which comes to
help men to detach themselves from the good things of this
world.

On leaving we followed the road used by Chinese deportees
who are being taken to Ili. The country was less awful than the
day before, but it was still very dreary. Sand had given way to
gravel, but apart from occasional tufts of hard grass as prickly
as needles the soil was still arid and barren. We arrived at
Kaotandze, a repulsive and hideous place beyond all powers of
description. It consisted of a few miserable habitations roughly
built of black earth; they were all in use as inns. Provisions
were even rarer than at Ever Flowing Waters, and therefore
even dearer. Here too everything came from Tchoungwei, for
nothing was obtainable locally, not even water. Wells had been
sunk to a very great depth, but nothing was found but dry
stony earth. The inhabitants of Kaotandze were obliged to go
sixty *li* (thirty miles)* to fetch water, and they made passing
travellers pay dearly for it. A bucket of water cost fifty sapeks.
If we had given our camels as much as they wanted we should
have spent many times this amount. We therefore made provision for ourselves and our horses, and the camels had to wait
for better days and a less inhospitable land.

Kaotandze, so poor and so hideous, had not even the advantage of enjoying the peace that its poverty and solitude would
be expected to ensure. It was continually beset by brigands,
and in consequence nearly all the buildings showed signs of
fire or other damage. When we arrived at the inn, we were
asked if we wanted our beasts defended against brigands. This
question filled us with amazement, and we pressed for an
explanation. It was then explained that at Kaotandze there
were two sorts of inn: inns 'where they fight' and inns 'where
they don't fight', and that the price of the former was four
times that of the latter. As we still looked doubtful; 'Don't you

*According to the Larousse Encyclopedia, a Chinese *li* is equivalent to 576
metres. However, it may well be that in such a vast territory it was a rather
flexible measurement; certainly the equivalents given by Father Huc vary
from two to three and a half *li* to one mile. (Trans.)

know that Kaotandze is frequently attacked by brigands?' we were asked.

'Yes, that we know.'

'If you stay at an inn where they fight, there is a good chance that you will keep your beasts, unless the brigands are stronger, which sometimes happens.' All this seemed very strange and very tiresome. However, we had to make up our minds. After very careful consideration we decided to go to an inn where they would fight. It occurred to us that the people of Kaotandze might be in league with the brigands to exploit travellers. In that case it would be better to pay highly rather than lose our animals, since such a loss would soon be followed by the loss of our own skins.

When we entered the inn that we had been recommended we saw that indeed everything was on a war footing. There were lances, arrows, bows and matchlocks everywhere. We did not find the presence of these weapons completely reassuring, and decided to mount guard ourselves during the night.

Kaotandze, with its warlike aspect and its hideous poverty, was a complete mystery to us. We wondered how men could resign themselves to living in a sterile waterless land, far from other habitation and worst of all subject to continual attacks by brigands. What could be their object in life? What advantages could such a position bring them? We sought in vain for an answer, but the mystery remained unsolved. During the first watch of the night we had a long talk with the innkeeper, who seemed to be a trustworthy fellow. He told us many stories of brigands, all full of fights, murders and fires.

'But why then,' we said, 'do you not leave this vile country?'

'Oh,' he replied, 'we are not free. We of Kaotandze are all banished men. We have been exempted from going to Ili, on condition that we stay here on the road, to supply water to the mandarins and soldiers who escort the deportees. We have to supply it free to all government employees who pass through.'

As soon as we realised that we were amongst exiles we were somewhat reassured. We were inclined to think that they would not be in league with the brigands, for there was a kind of junior mandarin in charge to keep an eye on them. For a moment we hoped to find Christians at Kaotandze, but the innkeeper assured us that there were none. He told us that those exiled for belonging to the religion of the Lord of Heaven were all sent to Ili.

After everything that the innkeeper had told us we felt that we could take some rest without much risk. We therefore went to bed and slept fairly soundly until dawn; thank God, the brigands did not appear.

For the greater part of next day we followed the road which led towards Ili. We travelled with a feeling of respect, touched with awe, along this road to exile which the faithful had so often trod. We remembered those brave Christians, those doughty souls who rather than renounce their faith have left their families and their native land to end their days in a strange country. We hoped that Divine Providence would inspire missionaries to bring the consolations of the faith to our exiled brothers.

The road to Ili took us again to the Great Wall, which was still low enough to jump over. That creation of the Chinese people, so often described by those who know too little about it, deserves a few words at this point. Of course the idea of building a wall as a fortification against an invading army is not peculiar to China: the ancient world provides a number of examples. Apart from those constructed by the Syrians, the Egyptians and the Medes, we have in Europe the wall built across the north of England by the Romans. However no nation has made anything on the scale of the Great Wall erected by Tsinchehoanti in the year 244 BC; the Chinese call it Wan Li Tchang Tcheng (The Great Wall of Ten Thousand Li). An enormous number of workers was employed, and the labours of this mighty work lasted for ten years. The Great Wall extends from the westernmost point of Kansou as far as the China sea. The importance of this great enterprise has been rated differently by writers on China: some have praised it beyond measure, and others have tried to turn it to ridicule; no doubt this divergence of opinion comes from the fact that each writer has judged the whole by the parts that he has seen. Mr Barrow, who came to China in 1793 with Lord Macartney as embassy historian, made the following calculation: if we suppose that there are 180,000 houses in England and Scotland and that each one contains 2,000 cubic feet of masonry, taken all together they would not make up the Great Wall of China. According to Mr Barrow, a wall could be built with the material

contained in the Great Wall that would twice encircle the
globe. Clearly Mr Barrow based his calculations on the Great
Wall as he saw it at Koupeko, north of Peking, where it really
is an impressive work; but it would be wrong to think that this
barrier against the Tartar invasions is equally wide, high and
strong throughout all its length. We have had the opportunity
to cross it at more than fifteen different points, and on several
occasions we have travelled along it for a number of days;

often, instead of the double battlemented wall to be seen near
Peking, we have encountered simple masonry and sometimes a
modest earth rampart. We have even found this famous wall
reduced to the bare minimum, a mere heap of pebbles. As for
the foundations of which Mr Barrow speaks, of great cut stones
cemented together, we must admit that we have never found
any trace of them. In any case it is understandable that
Tsinchehoanti, in that great enterprise, should have endeavoured to fortify more strongly the area near the capital of
the empire, as it was the point at which the Tartar hordes
would concentrate first of all. It is also reasonable to suppose
that the mandarins in charge of carrying out Tsinchehoanti's
plan would conscientiously direct those works which were so
to speak under the emperor's nose, but merely put up a token
wall at the furthest points where in any case there was little

danger from the Tartars, as for example on the frontiers of the Ortou and the Alachan Mountains.

The customs post at Sanyentsin, situated a few yards inside the wall, is famed for its severity towards those Tartars who wish to enter the empire. The village possesses only one inn and this is kept by the chief official of the frontier guard. We saw as we came in that there were several groups of camels in the yard; a large Tartar caravan had arrived shortly before. There was still however plenty of room, as the place was very large. We had no sooner been shown to our room than the question of passports arose. The chief guard himself came to ask for them officially.

'We have none,' we told him. At these words his face broke into a happy smile, and he told us that we could not continue our journey without paying a large sum of money.

'What, our passports or our money?' we said. 'We have crossed China from end to end, we have been through the whole of Tartary without ever having had a passport and without spending a single sapek. You are the commander of the guard, and yet you do not know that lamas have the right to travel without passports?'

'What are you saying? Here is a caravan which has just arrived, there are two lamas among them and each of them has shown me his passport like the rest.'

'If what you say is true, the conclusion is that there are lamas who provide themselves with passports and others who do not. We are lamas who do not.' Seeing that the argument was dragging on indefinitely we produced a decisive new point.

'Very well,' we said, 'we will give you any money you like: but you must write and sign a paper in which you say that in order to let us pass you demanded either a passport or a sum of money. We shall apply to the first mandarin we come across and ask him if that is in accordance with the laws of the empire.' The innkeeper-official at once let the matter drop.

'Since you have been to Peking,' he said, 'it may be that the emperor has given you special privileges.' Then he added in a low voice with a smile: 'Don't tell those Tartars that I let you go through without payment.'

It is quite pitiful to see these poor Mongolians travelling in China; everyone thinks he can fleece them, and indeed succeeds in doing so. Everywhere they find customs houses, everywhere there are people to appeal to their generosity for road repairs, bridge building and the erection of pagodas. At first a show is made of doing them a service, they are given advice on how to defend themselves against rascals and thieves, they are flattered and called brother and friend. If this method fails to untie the strings of their purses, intimidation is tried; they are then frightened out of their wits with threats of law-courts, mandarins, prisons and tortures; they are told they will be arrested. In other words they are treated as if they were children. It must be admitted that the Mongolians fall for all these tricks by being totally ignorant of all Chinese ways and customs. When they are at an inn, instead of lodging in the rooms they have been offered and stabling their beasts, they put up their tent in the middle of the courtyard, drive in stakes all round it and tether their animals to them. Sometimes they are not allowed to behave in this unusual way; in that case they will agree to enter the rooms, which they always consider to be prisons; but there they behave in a manner equally comic to the Chinese: they install their tripods and their cooking pots in the middle of the room and light a fire of *argols* (the droppings of animals) of which they have carefully collected a good store. It is no use telling them that there is a large kitchen in the inn where they can cook their meal with greater ease; they will not budge, and it is in their cooking pot, right in the middle of the bedroom that they insist on making tea. When night comes, they unroll felt carpets round the fire and lie down on them. They never sleep on the beds or on the *kangs* provided. The Tartars who were lodging with us at the inn at Sanyentsin did all their housework out of doors. These poor children of the desert were so simple that they came and asked us seriously if the innkeeper would make them pay for letting them stay at his inn.

We continued our journey in a south-westerly direction through the province of Kansou. The country, varied by streams and hills, was generally rich-looking and attractive. There was a remarkable variety of produce, due to the tem-perate climate, the naturally fertile soil, but above all to the skill and hard work of the farmers. The principal crop was wheat, which they made into excellent bread similar to the European. Rice was hardly grown at all; the small quantity consumed came from neighbouring provinces. The goats and sheep were of good quality, and together with bread were the staple diet of the inhabitants. A number of rich coalmines provided enough fuel for all. It seemed to us that in Kansou one could easily and cheaply find an honest livelihood.

At two days' journey from the customs post at Sanyentsin, a hurricane burst upon us, exposing us to very grave danger. It was about ten o'clock in the morning. We had just crossed a small mountain and were about to enter a vast plain, when suddenly there was a great stillness. There was not the slightest movement in the air, and yet the weather was icy cold. Gradually the sky turned white, though without the formation of any clouds. Then a west wind began to blow, which soon rose to such a pitch that our beasts could hardly advance. We had the horrible feeling that nature itself was about to disintegrate. The sky, still cloudless, went a reddish colour. The gale formed whirlwinds which rose like vast columns into the air, laden with dust, sand and pieces of vegetation; then these columns shot off in all directions. The wind blew with such fury, there was such a commotion in the air, that though it was broad daylight we could not see the animals on which we were riding. We dismounted, for it was impossible to advance, and after putting our handkerchiefs over our faces so as not to be blinded by the sand, we crouched down beside our mounts. We had no idea where we were. Again and again we felt that nature was out of joint and that the end of the world had come. It lasted over an hour. When the wind had abated somewhat and we could see clearly around us, we found that we were quite a large distance apart; for at the height of that terrible storm, though we shouted to each other we could hear nothing. As soon as it was possible to move forward a few steps we headed for a farm which was not far off but which previously we had not been able to see. The hurricane had knocked down the main gate into the yard, so it was easy to get in. The housedoor itself soon opened to let us in, for Providence had vouchsafed us, in the midst of our distress, a family truly remarkable for their hospitality.

They immediately heated water so that we could wash. We were in a very bad state; we were shrouded in dust from head to foot; it had even gone through our clothes, and our bodies were covered with it. If we had met such weather in the Alachan Mountains we should have been buried alive in the sand, and never heard of again.

When we saw that the worst of the storm was over and that the wind was now only gusty, we thought of resuming our journey; but the good peasants of the farm simply would not let us go. They said that they would find room for us for the night and that our beasts would lack for neither water nor forage. Their invitation was clearly so genuine and so warm-hearted and we were so much in need of rest, that we willingly accepted their offer. As one gets to know the people of Kansou, one realises that they are not of pure Chinese origin. There is a Tartar-Tibetan strain that predominates. There is none of the affected politeness of the Chinese; but on the other hand they are remarkable for their openness and their hospitality. In their dialect of Chinese there are many expressions taken from the Tartar and Tibetan languages. Their word-order is particularly noticeable, as it is quite different from the Chinese: they use an inversion similar to Mongolian. For example, they do not say as the Chinese do: 'Open the door, shut the window' but 'The door open, the window shut.' Another peculiarity is that milk, butter and curds, none of which the Chinese can stand, are favourite foods of the Kansou people. But above all it is their piety that distinguishes them from the Chinese, who are in general sceptical and indifferent to religion. In Kansou there are many flourishing lamaseries of the reformed Buddhist faith. It is true that the Chinese have a great number of pagodas, and idols of all sorts in their houses; but nothing goes beyond this outward show; whereas in Kansou everyone prays long and often. Now prayer, as we all know, is what distinguishes the religious man from the irreligious.

The inhabitants of Kansou not only differ greatly from the other peoples of China, but are themselves divided into very distinctive groups, of which the Dchiahours are perhaps the most striking. The latter live in the area usually known as San Tchouan, the Three Valleys, homeland of our camel-driver Samdadchiemba. They have all the knavery and guile of the Chinese, but not their courtesy nor their polite forms of address; they are feared and hated by their neighbours. When they think they have been wronged it is always with a dagger that they settle the matter. The most honoured man among them is always the one who has committed most murders. They speak a language of their own, a mixture of Mongolian, Chinese and Eastern Tibetan. They claim to be of Tartar origin. If that

is true, it would seem that they have kept the fierce independence of their ancestors, whereas the present inhabitants
of Mongolia have to a remarkable extent adopted gentler
ways.

Although subject to the Emperor of China the Dchiahours
are governed directly by a kind of hereditary monarch who
belongs to their tribe and who bears the title of Tou Sse. There
are a number of peoples in Kansou and on the frontiers of
Ssetchouan who are self-governing in this way with laws of
their own. Each one is a Tou Sse, to which title is added the
surname of their chief's family. Samdadchiemba belonged to a
Dchiahour tribe called Ki Tou Sse. The Yang Tou Sse are the
best known and the fiercest of the tribes. For many years they
had a great influence in Lhasa, capital of Tibet. But this
influence was broken in 1845 as the result of a famous incident
which we shall describe in its place.

After a good rest, we set off early next day. Everywhere
along the road we encountered traces of yesterday's storm,
trees broken or uprooted, de-roofed houses, fields devastated
and almost stripped of their topsoil. Before sunset we arrived at
an unremarkable town called Tchoang Long, popularly known
as Ping Fang. It was quite prosperous; built on the usual
pattern it had no particular features either beautiful or ugly.
We lodged at the Inn of the Three Social Relationships, whose
innkeeper had the kindest of natures and the sharpest of
tongues that we had ever encountered. To show how clever he
was, he asked us straight out if we were not Englishmen; and to
make himself quite clear he added that by Ing Ki Li he meant
the sea-devils (Yankouidze) who were making war at Canton.

'No, we are not Englishmen,' we said, 'nor are we devils of
any sort, neither of sea nor land.' A bystander very fortunately
made a diversion which got us out of this embarrassing conversation. He said to the innkeeper:

'That's no way to look at men's faces. How can you say that
these men are Yankouidzes? Don't you know that Yankouidzes
have blue eyes and red hair?'

'That's true,' said the innkeeper, 'I hadn't thought.'

'No, you certainly hadn't thought,' we said. 'Do you think
that sea monsters could live on land as we do and ride on
horseback?'

'Yes, you're quite right. They say that the Ing Ki Li never

dare leave the sea; once on land they shiver and die like fish out of water.' There followed much talk of the customs and nature of sea-devils, which all proved conclusively that we were not at all of the same race.

A little before nightfall there was a great commotion at the inn: a Living Buddha had arrived with his large retinue. He was returning from a journey to Tibet, his native land, and was going back to the large lamasery of which he had for many years been the superior. It was in the Khalkas, not far from the Russian frontier. When he had made his entrance into the inn, a great crowd of Buddhist zealots who had been waiting for him in the yard fell prostrate on the ground. The Grand Lama went into the apartment that had been prepared for him; and shortly afterwards at nightfall, the crowd dispersed. As soon as the inn was more or less quiet he began out of curiosity to tour round the whole inn, entering all the rooms, and talking to everybody, without however sitting down or stopping anywhere. We were ready for him when he came into our room. We were sitting solemnly on the *kang*, but deliberately did not get up to receive him, merely greeting him with a humble gesture of the hand. He seemed most surprised at this, but not disconcerted; he stopped in the middle of the room and looked at us for a great while, first at one, then the other. We remained completely silent, and, using the same privilege, examined him at leisure. He was about fifty years old; he wore a long yellow taffeta robe and Tibetan boots in red velvet with remarkably high soles. He was of medium height and somewhat stout; his swarthy face had an extraordinarily good-natured expression; but his eyes, when one looked at them closely, had a haggard look, a weird expression that frightened us. At last he spoke, in fluent Mongolian. At first the conversation was limited to the commonplace questions which travellers ask each other, about the road, their health, the weather and the condition of the animals. When we saw that he wanted to stay we invited him to sit beside us on the *kang*; he hesitated briefly, thinking no doubt that as a Living Buddha it was not fitting that he should put himself on the same level with simple mortals like us. However being very anxious for a chat, he decided to sit down. He could hardly, without compromising his dignity, remain standing any longer whilst we were seated.

A prayer-book which we had beside us on a little table soon

attracted his attention; he asked us if he could examine it. As we agreed, he took it in both his hands, admired the binding and the gilt edge, then opened it and turned over the pages for quite a time; he closed it again and raised it solemnly to his forehead saying:

'It is your prayer-book. Prayers must always be honoured and respected.' He then added: 'Your religion and ours are like that . . .' and saying this he placed the index fingers of his two hands side by side.

'Yes,' we answered, 'you are right, your beliefs and ours are in a state of enmity; the object of our journeys and our efforts, we make no secret of it, is to substitute our prayers for those in use in your lamaseries.'

'I know,' he said smiling, 'I've known it for a long time.' Then he picked up the prayer-book again and asked for explanations of the many illustrations it contained: he showed no astonishment at anything we said. Only when we had explained a picture of the crucifixion, he shook his head in compassion and raised his joined hands to his forehead. After looking at all the pictures he took the book in both hands and raised it again to his brow. He then rose, and with a most friendly bow left the room. We accompanied him to the door.

When he had gone, we felt bewildered for a while after so strange a visit. We tried to guess what this Living Buddha could have been thinking when sitting beside us, and what had been his impression when we gave him an account of our holy religion. At times we felt that very strange stirrings might have been going on in the depths of his heart; at others that he had probably felt nothing, experienced nothing, that he was quite an ordinary man who automatically took advantage of his position without thinking too much about and without attaching any importance to the divinity thrust upon him. We were so fascinated by this extraordinary personage that we determined to see him once again before leaving the inn. As we had to set off very early next morning, we paid him a visit before bedtime. We found him in his room, sitting on great thick cushions magnificently covered in tiger skin. On a little lacquer table in front of him were a silver teapot and a jade cup resting on a richly carved gold saucer. He looked very bored and was delighted at our visit. Just in case he might keep us standing we went without more ado and sat down beside him. His retainers, who were in the next room, were very shocked at this familiarity, and we heard little murmurs of disapproval. The Living Buddha smiled at us mischievously, and rang a little silver bell. When a young lama appeared he ordered tea to be served.

'I have often seen your compatriots,' he said, 'my lamasery is not far from your country; the Oros [Russians] sometimes cross the frontier but they never get as far as this.'

'We are not Russians,' we told him, 'our country is very far from theirs.' This reply seemed to surprise him; he looked at us carefully, then asked:

'Where are you from then?'

'We are from the Western Heavens.'

'Ah, I see, you are Pelings [British from India] from the Dchon Ganga [Eastern Ganges]; the city you live in is called Galgata [Calcutta].' The Living Buddha was thus not so far from the truth, and if he was not quite correct this was no fault of his; he could only place us amongst peoples known to him. In first thinking that we were Russians and then British he showed good powers of discernment. It was in vain that we insisted that we were neither Oros nor Pelings, we could not convince him.

'Well, well,' he said, 'what does it matter which country one comes from, since all men are brothers? Only, whilst you are in China you must be careful and not tell everyone what you are. The Chinese are suspicious and ill-natured, they might do you some harm.' He then talked for a long time about Tibet and the dreadful road that we would have to travel to get there. He doubted, to look at us, whether we would be strong enough to undertake such a journey. The words and the manner of this great lama were throughout extremely affable; but we were still haunted by the strange look in his eyes; there was something diabolical or infernal about it. If it had not been for this— and it may have been due simply to our own worries—we should have found him most likeable.

From Tchoang Long (or Ping Fang) we went to Ho Kiao Y, which appears on maps as Ta Toung, although this ancient name has almost entirely lapsed. The road was everywhere obstructed by oxen, donkeys and little carts, all carrying peat. We decided to stop a few days at Ho Kiao Y to rest our tired beasts. The horse and the mule had large swellings on their flanks caused by the rubbing of the saddles; before going any

further it was important to cut and dress the sores. As we intended to stay a while we had a look at all the inns of the town in order to be sure of the best: our choice was the Inn of the Temperate Climates.

Since we had entered Kansou not a day had passed without Samdadchiemba talking of the Three Valleys of the Dchiahours. Although not sentimental by nature he nevertheless greatly desired to revisit his homeland and any surviving members of his family. We were bound to sympathise with such proper sentiments. As soon as we had settled at the Inn of the Temperate Climates, we gave him a week's leave to revisit his native country, which he had left when he was still a child. He thought that eight days would be enough, two for the journey each way and four to stay with his family and tell them of all the wonders he had seen in the world. We let him take a camel with him, so that he could make something of a triumphal entry into his village; and finally, the five ounces of silver which we put into his purse should, we thought, make him popular amongst his compatriots.

Whilst waiting for the return of our Dchiahour tribesman we did nothing but look after our beasts and ourselves. Every day we went shopping, did our own cooking, and morning and evening watered our animals at some distance from the inn. The innkeeper was one of those good-natured men, always anxious to be of service, who are really such tiresome nuisances that one forgives them only because they mean so well. This man came constantly into our room to give us advice on how we should run our household. After moving everything around according to his whim of the moment, he would go to our small stove, take the lid off the pot, put his finger in the stew and taste it, then add more salt or ginger, to my great vexation, since I was in charge of the cooking. Sometimes he insisted that we had no idea of how to make a fire, and that the coal must be arranged in such a way as to catch the draught on one side; then he would take the tongs and upset the fireplace, to the great irritation of Father Gabet, who was the official stoker. When night came, he considered himself quite indispensable for lengthening or shortening the wick of the lamp to make a good light. Sometimes he seemed to be wondering how we could have survived without him, one of us for thirty-two years and the other for thirty-seven. However, amongst all these attentions which he constantly lavished on us, there was one which we were glad to leave to him, namely the warming of the beds. The method was so strange and so typical of that country that we had never had the opportunity of mastering the craft before.

In Kansou the *kang*, a kind of large stove on which one sleeps, is not made entirely of brick as it is in Northern China. The top is made of loose planks placed side by side so that they fit perfectly. When you want to heat the *kang* you remove these planks, then you spread dried and powdered horse dung over the floor of the stove. You scatter a few hot embers over this, then replace the planks. The dung is gradually kindled, and once alight never goes out. The heat and smoke, there being no chimney, soon warm up the planks which remain hot all night owing to the slow combustion of the dung. The skill consists in knowing exactly how much dung to put in, in spreading it evenly and in scattering the embers so that the combustion commences simultaneously at a number of different points, and all the planks heat up equally. One day, ashamed of being treated like children and having our bed warmed for us, we decided to do it ourselves; but the results were unfortunate, for one of us was nearly roasted alive and the other shivered with cold all night. On one side a plank had caught fire and on the other the dung had not lit at all. The host of the Inn of the Temperate Climates was rightly indignant. To prevent a repetition of this mishap, he locked up the little cupboard in which the dung was kept, and made sure that he alone prepared our bed every evening in future.

The many household chores combined with the recitation of our breviary prevented us from becoming bored during our stay at Ho Kiao Y. The time passed quite quickly, and on the eighth day as agreed Samdadchiemba reappeared, but not alone. He was accompanied by a short young man, who by the likeness of the features could only be his brother and indeed he was introduced as such. The first interview lasted only a moment, for the two Dchiahours left us immediately and went rather conspiratorially into the innkeeper's domain. At first we thought that they wanted to make a polite call on the innkeeper, but this was not the case for they reappeared shortly afterwards with great solemnity. Samdadchiemba came first.

'Babdcho,' he said to his brother, 'bow down before our

masters, and present the offerings of our poor family.' The young Dchiahour made three oriental salutations, and then presented us with two large dishes, one containing fine walnuts and the other three large loaves which in shape reminded us of those of France. In order to show Samdadchiemba how much we appreciated his gifts, we started without more ado to eat one of the loaves and some of the nuts. They made a delicious meal, for since we had left France we had never tasted bread with such a flavour.

We soon noticed that Samdadchiemba's clothing had been reduced to the basic necessities; we were surprised to see him return poorly dressed since he had left us quite well equipped. We asked him to explain the change, and he then told us that he had found his family in utter poverty. His father had been dead many years; his old mother was blind and thus had not had the happiness to see him; he had two brothers, one still a child and the other whom we had met. This young man was the only support of his family; he spent his time tilling a small field that still belonged to them and working as a hired herdsman. We then realised what Samdadchiemba had done with his clothes: he had given everything to his poor mother, including even his travelling rug. We thought it our duty to suggest that he should go and live at home in order to help his unfortunate family, but he said:

'How could I do such a cruel thing? Would it be fair to take the food from their only remaining field out of their mouths? They can hardly live themselves, what would they feed me on? I have no trade, I know nothing of farming, what help could I be to them?' We did not find this decision either noble or generous, but knowing the character of Samdadchiemba, it did not surprise us. We made no attempt to change his mind, for we were even more certain than he was that he was not much good at anything and that his family could get no advantage from his presence; however, we did what we could to relieve the plight of these unfortunate people. We gave Samdadchiemba's brother quite a large charitable gift, and then we made preparations to continue our journey.

During this week of rest the condition of our beasts had sufficiently improved for us to venture on the difficult road that lay before us. The day after we left Ho Kiao Y we began to climb the high mountain of Ping Keou, on tracks which were extremely rough and almost impassable for our camels. As we went along we had to keep uttering loud shouts to warn any muleteers who might be coming in the opposite direction, for the path was so narrow and dangerous that two animals could not pass. Our shouts warned the muleteers to get their mules quickly off the path, since otherwise they would be likely to shy at the sight of our camels and fall over the cliff edge. We began the ascent before daybreak, and did not reach the top until noon. There we found a little hostelry, where instead of tea they sold an infusion of roasted broad beans; we made a short halt and with a ravenous appetite ate a most succulent meal of walnuts and a slice of that excellent Dchiahour bread, which we were using very sparingly. A cup of cold water, we thought, would go well with our repast, but on that mountain all that was obtainable was a liquid with an unbearable stench; so we had to resort to the bean tea, which was nasty and moreover quite expensive.

The cold was not so intense as we had feared, considering the season and the height of the mountain. In the afternoon it even became quite mild; it clouded over and began to snow. As we were obliged to make the descent on foot we soon began to suffer from heat, because we had to work so hard to keep our hold on the slippery pathway. One of our camels fell twice, but was fortunately stopped by rocks which prevented it from rolling right to the bottom of the mountain.

When we had put the fearsome Ping Keou behind us, we spent the night in the village of Old Duck (Lao Ya Pou). There we found a heating system which was different from that of Ho Kiao Y. The *kangs* were fuelled not with horse dung but with powdered coal, made into a paste and then into cakes the shape of bricks; peat was also used. In every street we saw a large number, not of knitting women, but knitting men, for men alone engaged in this occupation. Their products were ugly and crude; they used only coarse wool, which they usually made into shapeless stockings rather like sacks, and sometimes a kind of gauntlet glove. It was most strange to see groups of moustachioed men sitting in the sun in front of their houses, spinning, knitting and chatting like gossips. It was like a parody on the customs of our own country.

From Lao Ya Pou to Sining Fou we had five days' march; on the second day we passed through Nienpaehsien, a town of the third class. Outside the western gate we stopped at a hostelry to eat our morning meal: a number of travellers were gathered in an enormous kitchen; they sat at numerous tables which were ranged along the walls. In the middle of the room stood great stoves at which the innkeeper, his wife, his children and his servants were busily preparing the dishes ordered by the guests. Everyone was occupied either in preparing or in eating food, when suddenly a loud scream was heard. It was the hostess, giving vent to anguish caused by a big blow which her husband had just struck her on the head with a shovel. The guests looked up, the woman ran screaming to a corner of the kitchen, and the host explained to the company why he was justified in punishing his wife, on the grounds that she was disrespectful, wilful and a bad manager who would be the ruin of the inn. Before he had finished, his wife had begun to retort from the corner in which she was cowering; she told all and sundry that her husband was a lazybones, that while she killed herself serving the guests he spent his time smoking and drinking, and that a month's profit went in a few days in tobacco and spirits. During this dramatic interlude, the audience remained calm and unimpressed, showing no signs of approval or disapproval. The woman finally emerged from her corner, and presented her husband with a sort of challenge.

'Since I am a bad wife,' she said, 'then you must kill me. Come on, kill me.' And she stood up proudly in front of the innkeeper. The latter did not kill her straightaway, but he hit her very hard indeed and she went back howling to her corner. At this point the audience roared with laughter; it now found the play amusing, but the play itself soon turned serious. After a further exchange of insults and threats, the innkeeper tightened his belt and rolled his plait of hair round his head: these were his action signals.

'Since you want me to kill you,' he said, 'well, I shall kill you.' At these words he took up some long iron tongs from one of the stoves and furiously attacked his wife. Everyone stood up and shouted, neighbours came running in and attempts were made to part the couple; but by the time these were successful the hostess had a bloody face and her hair was in disorder. Then a middle-aged man, who seemed to enjoy some authority in the house, made a short solemn speech as a kind of epilogue to the affair:

'What!' he said. 'A husband and wife! In their children's presence! In the presence of a company of guests!' These words, repeated three or four times, in a tone which expressed both indignation and authority, had a marvellous effect. A moment later the guests had happily resumed their dinner, the hostess was frying cakes in walnut oil and the head of the family was silently smoking his pipe.

When we were about to leave, the innkeeper in presenting his bill put down fifty sapeks for the animals we had tethered in the courtyard whilst we were dining. Clearly he was charging us the rate for Tartars. Samdadchiemba could not contain his indignation.

'Do you think that we Dchiahours do not know about inn charges? Who ever heard of paying for tying animals to a wooden stake? Tell me, mine host, how many sapeks are you asking for the comedy you have just acted with your wife?' The sarcasm struck home, the laughter of the company decided the matter in Samdadchiemba's favour and we left after paying our own expenses only.

The road to Sining Fou was generally quite good and well maintained. It wound through a fertile countryside, well cultivated and prettily varied with large trees, hills and many streams. Tobacco was the main crop. We came across a number of water-mills of a design that was remarkably simple, like all Chinese inventions. In these mills, the upper millstone was fixed; the lower one turned by means of a single wheel driven by the current. Only a very small quantity of water was needed to keep the mills working, even though some of them were very large, because it was made to fall on the wheel from a height of at least twenty feet, like a waterfall.

The day before we reached Sining Fou we travelled a road which was extremely difficult and dangerous, and which caused us to appeal to Divine Providence for protection. We had to clamber over enormous rocks and along a deep torrent whose rushing waters leapt below us. The chasm yawned before us, one false step would have sent us rolling into it; we were particularly worried about the camels which were always so heavy and clumsy on rough paths. But at last, with God's grace, we arrived safe and sound at Sining Fou. This city occupied an enormous area but was sparsely inhabited and in part falling in ruins. Its commerce had been mostly taken over by Tang Keou Eul, a small town on the frontier between Kansou and the Koukou Noor.

It is usual at Sining Fou, indeed a general rule, that the inns do not accept foreigners such as Tartars, Tibetans and others. These all lodge at establishments called rest houses (*Sie Kia*), from which other travellers are excluded. We therefore went to a rest house and were very well received. The *Sie Kias* differ from the other hostelries in that board, lodging and service are free. As commerce is the normal purpose of foreigners, the owners of these establishments take a percentage on everything bought and sold. In order to open a rest house, the local authorities must give permission and must be paid a certain sum annually, varying according to the amount of trade involved. Foreigners seem to be treated very well, but really they are always dependent on the *Sie Kias*, which being in league with the merchants of the town stand to gain from both sides.

When we left Sining Fou, the *Sie Kia* had of course not made any profit out of us, for we had neither sold nor bought anything. Therefore, as it would have been absurd and unjust to live at the expense of our neighbours, we compensated the head of the rest house by paying him at the normal rate.

After crossing many torrential rivers, climbing a large number of rocky hills and passing twice through the Great Wall, we arrived at Tang Keou Eul. It was January; about four months had passed since we had left the Valley of Black Waters. Tang Keou Eul was a small town, a great centre of trade and very crowded. It was quite a Tower of Babel; there were Eastern Tibetans or Houng Mao Eul (the 'Long Haired Ones'), there were Eleuts, Kolos, Chinese, Tartars from the Blue Sea and Mohammedans descended from peoples who migrated long ago from Turkestan. They all contributed to the violent character of the town. Every man walked through the streets armed with a long sabre, making a show of fierce independence. We could not walk abroad without witnessing a brawl.

[2]
TANG KEOU EUL AND KOUNBOUM

Rest houses are very numerous at Tang Keou Eul, because of the large number of foreigners who come from all parts attracted by the opportunities for trade. It was in one of these establishments, kept by a family of Mohammedans, that we took up our lodging. As we were not engaged in commerce, we frankly informed the headman of the fact, and came to an agreement on terms; it was settled that we should pay the same as at an ordinary hostelry. So far, so good; but what was our next step? This question continually occupied our minds and caused us a certain amount of worry.

As far as Tang Keou Eul we had successfully and fairly rapidly followed the route that we had worked out beforehand; we could even say that this part of our journey had been successful beyond our wildest hopes. It now remained therefore to carry out the rest of our plan and make our way to Lhasa, capital of Tibet. But the project seemed to bristle with almost insurmountable difficulties. For us, Tang Keou Eul was like the columns of Hercules, with their discouraging inscription: *Nec plus ultra*, thou shalt go no further. However, we had already gone too far to be liable to discouragement. We learned that nearly every year caravans left Tang Keou Eul and successfully made their way to the heart of Tibet. That was all we needed to know: what other men had tried and succeeded in doing we were sure we could also do; it did not seem beyond our strength. It was therefore decided that we should continue the journey as planned, and that it should not be said that Catholic missionaries had less courage in the interests of the faith than merchants for a little gain. The decision to go on having thus been made, we now only had to watch out for an opportunity.

Our main occupation then was to collect all possible information about the notorious road to Tibet. What we heard was very frightening indeed: we would have to spend four months crossing a completely uninhabited country and must therefore take all the necessary provisions with us. In the winter season the cold was extreme and travellers were often frozen to death or buried under avalanches of snow. In the summer many were drowned, for great rivers had to be crossed, without bridges, without boats, relying only on the animals, which often could not swim. Then, on top of all that, we might be attacked by hordes of brigands, who at certain times of year scoured the desert, robbed the travellers and left them without clothes and food in the middle of nowhere; in short the stories we heard were enough to make one's hair stand on end. But these stories, apparently fables or at least much exaggerated, were nevertheless always the same whenever we heard them; there was a frightening uniformity about them. Moreover we were able to meet and question, in the streets of Tang Keou Eul, some Tartar-Mongolians who were so to speak documentary evidence of these tragic stories; they were the remains of a caravan which had been attacked the previous year by a troop of Kolos or brigands. They had been able to escape, but their many companions had been left to the mercy of the Kolos. All this information, whilst it left our resolve unshaken, persuaded us not to be overhasty and to await a good opportunity.

We had been six days at Tang Keou Eul when a small caravan

of Tartar-Khalkas arrived at our rest house. They had come from the frontiers of Russia and were on their way to Lhasa to pay homage to a little child, who it was claimed was a new reincarnation of the great Guison Tamba. When these Tartars learned that we were waiting for a good opportunity to travel to Tibet, they were delighted, for they looked forward to an unexpected addition of three pilgrims to their little troop, and in the event of an attack by Kolos, of three fighters. Our beards and moustaches gave them a high notion of our valour, and we were spontaneously honoured with the title of *batourou* or braves. All this was most flattering and attractive. However, before deciding to set off, we had to think the matter over very seriously. The caravan which filled the great courtyard numbered only eight men; all the rest consisted of camels, horses, tents, luggage and cooking utensils. It was true that all these men, in their own opinion, were great warriors. They were certainly armed to the teeth; they displayed for our benefit their matchlocks, their lances, their arrows, and above all their artillery, which consisted of a little cannon about as thick as a man's arm; it was not mounted, but tied securely with rope between the two humps of a camel: it would clearly create a most devastating impression. All this warlike equipment was not particularly reassuring, nor did we feel that we could rely very far on the moral effect of our long beards. However, a decision had to be made; the Tartar-Khalkas were very pressing, and assured us of complete success. Amongst those who gave us advice, some said it was an excellent opportunity and that we should take advantage of it, others that it was most ill-advised, that a small party would infallibly be 'eaten up by the Kolos', and that it would be preferable, since we were in no hurry, to wait for the great Tibetan ambassadorial caravan.

That diplomatic body had only just arrived in Peking and would not be returning until eight months later. This long delay seemed disastrous to us. How with our modest resources could we feed five beasts at an inn for so long? And so, having weighed up all the pros and cons we made up our minds and 'With God's protection,' we said, 'let's be off.' We told the Tartars of our decision, which they received enthusiastically, and commissioned the head of the rest house to buy us enough flour for four months.

'But why four months?' asked the Tartars.

'They say that the journey takes three months at least,' we told them. 'It is good to provide for four in case of accident.'

'True, the Tibetan Embassy takes a long time over the journey. But we Tartars travel differently; we need at most a month and a half; we ride at the gallop and every day we cover about two hundred *li* [sixty miles].' These words changed our minds in a flash. We were absolutely incapable of keeping up with this caravan. Firstly, we ourselves were not accustomed, as the Tartars were, to forced marches, which would have killed us in a few days; secondly, our animals, thin and weakened by four months of continual efforts, would not have been able to keep up the Tartars' pace for long. They had forty camels at their disposal; it would mean nothing to them if they killed off half of them. They agreed that our three camels were inadequate for the journey, and they advised us to buy a dozen more. The advice, in itself, was excellent, but having regard to our purse, it was absurd. Twelve good camels would have cost us three hundred ounces of silver, and we hardly had two hundred.

The eight Tartar-Khalkas were all of princely family. On the eve of their departure they received a visit from the King of Koukou's son, who was then at Tang Keou Eul. As the room that we occupied was the cleanest in the whole rest house, it was there that the interview took place. The young Prince of Koukou Noor surprised us by his good looks and graceful manners; it was easy to see that he spent more time at Tang Keou Eul than under a Mongolian tent. He was dressed in a beautiful robe of sky-blue cloth; over this he wore a kind of waistcoat of purple cloth with wide edging of black velvet. His left ear was adorned, in the Tibetan fashion, with a gold ring from which hung several jewels, his face was almost white with an expression of extreme gentleness; there was nothing Tartar about the perfect cleanliness of his clothes. As a visit from a prince of the Koukou Noor was quite an event in our lives, we really went to town: Samdadchiemba was set to prepare refreshments, namely a large jug full of boiling hot tea with milk. His Royal Highness was kind enough to accept a cupful, and the rest was distributed to his staff, who waited attendance in the snow, in the middle of the courtyard. The conversation turned on the journey to Tibet. The prince promised the Tartar-Khalkas an escort during their passage through his states.

'Beyond that,' he said, 'I can do nothing. Everything will depend on fate, good or bad.' Turning to us he added that we were very wise to await the Tibetan Embassy, with which we could travel in greater safety and less hardship. On leaving, the royal visitor withdrew from an elegantly embroidered purse a little agate box, and offered us a pinch of snuff.

On the following day the Tartar-Khalkas set off. When we saw them go, we felt a twinge of regret, for we would have liked to go with them; but the feeling soon passed. We soon stifled these pointless sentiments and concentrated on how best to spend the waiting time. We decided to try and find a teacher, and to bury ourselves in the study of the Tibetan language and the Buddhist texts.

At some thirty miles from Tang Keou Eul there stands, in the land of the Si Fan or Eastern Tibetans, a lamasery renowned not only in all Tartary but in the furthest corners of Tibet. Pilgrims come from all parts to visit the site celebrated as the birthplace of Tsong Kaba Remboutchi, the famous Buddhist reformer. The lamasery is called Kounboum, and nearly four thousand lamas reside there, Si Fan, Tartars, Tibetans and Dchiahours. We decided to go there on a visit, to try and engage a lama to come and teach us the Tibetan language for a few months. Father Gabet set off with Samdadchiemba, and I remained at Tang Keou Eul to look after the animals and the baggage.

After five days, Father Gabet returned to the rest house. Everything had gone well: he had made a great discovery at the lamasery, and had brought back with him a lama, thirty-two years of age, who had spent ten years in a great lamasery in Lhasa. He was a fluent speaker of pure Tibetan, wrote it with ease and was deeply read in the Buddhist texts; moreover, he had a good knowledge of a number of other languages, such as Mongolian, Si Fan, Chinese and Dchiahour; in a word he was an extremely accomplished language scholar. This young lama was himself a Dchiahour, and first cousin to Samdadchiemba: his name was Sandara; in the lamasery he was called Sandara the Bearded, his beard being remarkably long. When we saw with what enthusiasm Samdadchiemba's cousin immediately entered our service, we felt happy that we had not risked leaving with the caravan of the Tartar-Khalkas. We were now in a position to obtain all the necessary information on

Tibet and to study the language and religion of that country.

We set to work with the greatest enthusiasm. We first of all composed in Mongolian two dialogues containing all the most common words and phrases. Sandara translated them into Tibetan with the greatest care. Every morning we watched as he wrote a page, explaining as he did so the grammatical structure of all the expressions: it was our lesson for the day. We copied it several times, to practise Tibetan writing; then we sang it, as they do in the lamaseries, until it was well fixed in our memories. In the evening our teacher made us recite the passage of dialogue that he had written out that morning, and corrected any mistakes in our pronunciation. Sandara carried out his task with talent and good-nature: sometimes during the day, as a recreation, he talked in a most interesting way about Tibet and the lamaseries he had visited. We listened to this young lama's stories with the greatest admiration: we had never heard anyone speak with such ease and so vividly; the simplest, most ordinary matters became picturesque and full of charm as he described them; he was especially remarkable when he wished to persuade others to see things as he saw them. His eloquence was natural and compelling.

After mastering the first difficulties of the Tibetan language and learning the expressions which are in daily use, we turned our studies in a religious direction. We instructed Sandara to translate in sacred language the most important Catholic prayers, such as the Lord's Prayer, the Hail Mary, the Apostles' Creed and the Ten Commandments; in the process we took the opportunity to explain to him the truths of the Christian religion. He seemed at first extremely impressed by a doctrine which was quite new to him and so different from the vague and incoherent teachings of Buddhism. Soon he attached such great importance to the study of the Christian religion that he completely abandoned the Buddhist books he had brought with him. He began to learn our prayers with an enthusiasm which delighted us. From time to time during the day he would stop what he was doing in order to make the sign of the cross; he made this religious gesture in so grave and respectful a manner that we had no doubt that he was a Christian at heart. His tendencies in this direction gave us the greatest hopes; we liked to think of Sandara as a future apostle who would one day work successfully for the conversion of Buddhists.

Whilst we were entirely absorbed, master and pupils, in these important studies, Samdadchiemba, who had no vocation for intellectual matters, passed his time lounging in the streets of Tang Keou Eul or drinking tea. We did not approve of this kind of life and therefore made a plan aimed at curing his idleness and occupying him in his speciality of camel-drover. It was decided that he would take the three camels to feed in a certain valley of the Koukou Noor which was famous for the abundance and quality of its pastures. A Tartar from that area promised to let him stay in his tent; so the plan would have the double advantage of keeping Samdadchiemba suitably occupied and giving the camels better and cheaper food.

All the marvels that we thought we had discovered in Sandara soon vanished away like a beautiful dream. That young man, who seemed so pure and so devoted, was in reality an artful fellow who was anxious to make money out of us. As soon as he thought he had made himself indispensable, he threw off the mask and revealed all the bad qualities of his character. He was proud and arrogant, and incredibly insolent. During the Tibetan lessons which he gave us he dropped his previous good behaviour and politeness in favour of the most shocking manners, sneering in a way that a schoolmaster would not permit himself in the presence of a pupil: if by chance we asked him for an explanation that he had already given us, we were sure to be treated to sweet words such as these:

'What! Do I have to say everything three times? And you claim to be scholars? I think if I said something three times to a mule, it would remember.' There would no doubt have been quite an easy way to cut short all this impertinence; namely to pack him off home to his lamasery. More than once we felt like doing this; but we preferred to swallow our daily humiliations and keep this lama by us, as he was undoubtedly talented and consequently able to be most valuable to us. His excessive rudeness could even be of use to our progress in the Tibetan language; for we could be sure that he would not allow the slightest mistake of grammar or pronunciation to pass, and that we should always be corrected in a way that we would be unlikely to forget. This system, although unpleasant and sometimes damaging to the self-esteem, was incomparably better than the method used by Chinese Christians when teaching European missionaries. Partly through politeness and partly through piety, they are always enraptured by everything that their spiritual father says; instead of frankly correcting his many mistakes, they sometimes even imitate his accent so that he can understand them more easily. As a result, he gets a shock when he has to converse with non-Christians, who are rarely inclined to compliment him on his pronunciation! For these reasons, we resolved to keep our teacher with all his faults, to suffer his insults and to get all we could from him. As we had discovered that it was money that he was after, it was arranged that he should be properly paid for his lessons; moreover we had to close our eyes to small acts of dishonesty and pretend not to know that he was in league with the dealers who sold us our daily provisions.

Samdadchiemba had only been away a few days when he reappeared unexpectedly. He had been robbed by brigands, who had taken all his store of flour, butter and tea. He had eaten nothing for a day and a half. His voice was hollow, his face pale and sunken. Seeing only one camel in the yard, we thought that the other two had also been stolen; but Samdadchiemba reassured us, saying that he had left them with the Tartar family who had given him hospitality. Hearing this story, Sandara knitted his brows.

'Samdadchiemba,' he said, 'you are my younger cousin; I therefore have the right to ask you a few questions.' He then subjected him to an interrogation with all the cunning and subtlety of a prosecuting counsel with a criminal in the dock. He asked for every detail, and made a point of showing up the contradictions of which the accused was guilty and the improbability of the whole episode. He wanted to know how it was that the brigands had stolen the butter but left the sack it was in, how they had left the little snuff-box but carried off the embroidered purse which contained it. When he had ended his stern interrogation, he said slyly: 'I have just asked my cousin a few questions, but it is purely out of curiosity; it is nothing to me; after all I don't have to buy his provisions.'

Samdadchiemba was famished. We gave him a few sapeks and he went off to a nearby restaurant. As soon as he had gone, Sandara announced:

'I shall never believe that my cousin was robbed. The brigands in these parts do things differently. Samdadchiemba wanted to show off to the Tartars and when he arrived he distributed his provisions to all and sundry in order to make friends. What has he to fear by distributing largesse? Does it cost him anything?' Samdadchiemba's honesty was sufficiently known to us for us to ignore these nasty insinuations. Sandara was jealous of the confidence we had in his cousin. He also wanted to make us believe that he was sincerely attached to our interests, and so allay any suspicions we might have about his own misdemeanours. Samdadchiemba had no inkling of his cousin's treachery. We gave him fresh provisions and he left again for the pastures of Koukou Noor.

On the following day, the town of Tang Keou Eul was the scene of violent disorders. The bandits had irrupted into the area and had carried off two thousand cattle belonging to the Houng Mao Eul or Long Haired Ones. These Eastern Tibetans would set off each year, in great caravans, from their homeland at the foot of the Bayan Khara Mountains, and come to Tang Keou Eul to sell skins, butter and a kind of wild tea which grows in their country. While trading they left their large herds in extensive grazing grounds not far from the town, which were under the jurisdiction of the Chinese authorities. It had never been known, we were told, that the brigands had dared to penetrate so near to the frontiers of the empire. Their audacity in this case and above all the violent character of the Long Haired Ones had provoked a considerable confusion. When these tribesmen discovered that their herds had been carried off they brandished their great sabres and went in a wild mob to the Chinese lawcourts, shouting and demanding justice and vengeance. The mandarin, in alarm, sent two hundred soldiers immediately in pursuit of the robbers. But the Long Haired Ones, aware that foot soldiers would never catch up with the brigands, who were excellent horsemen, themselves set off wildly on horseback following the trail of their cattle. They returned next day, having seen nothing and with rage in their hearts. With complete lack of foresight these half-savages had gone off without provisions of any sort, regardless of the fact that they would find nothing to eat in the wilderness. After one day's forced march, hunger had forced them to return. The Chinese soldiers had not been so simple. They had taken care not to set off on this warlike expedition without a quantity of donkeys and oxen, laden with equipment (but only for cooking!) and ammunition (but only for the pot!). As they had little interest in fighting a battle for two thousand head of cattle which did not belong to them, they executed a short march and stopped by a river, where they spent several days drinking and gambling and having a good time, and dismissing all thought of brigands entirely from their minds. When they had exhausted their stores, they quietly returned to Tang Keou Eul, and told the mandarin they had searched the whole desert but had not been able to catch the bandits. Once, they said, they had been on the point of catching them, but they had cast a magic spell and vanished. At Tang Keou Eul it is believed that brigands are all magicians of a sort; to make themselves invisible, all they have to do is to puff in the air or to throw a few sheep's droppings over their shoulders. The Chinese soldiers may well be responsible for putting these stories into circulation; they certainly make constant use of them during their campaigns. The mandarins are presumably not taken in, but providing the robbers' victims believe these stories, all is well.

For several days the Houng Mao Eul were angry. They paraded the streets waving their sabres and shouting curses on the brigands. No one dared stand in their way; their anger was respected. The sight of these men, even when they are calm and in a good humour, is quite alarming. The Long Haired tribesman wears, in all seasons, a wide sheepskin robe, tucked up at the loins by a thick camel-hair rope. Left to itself the robe would reach the ground, but when it is turned up it reaches only just below the knee, giving the body a bloated and monstrous appearance. He wears big leather boots which reach only as far as the calf, and as he wears no breeches his legs are always half bare. Black greasy hair hangs in long locks over his shoulders, down his forehead and often over part of his face. His right arm is always bare and out of its sleeve, which he throws behind him. A long broad sabre is passed crosswise through his belt, just below the chest; he keeps his right hand always on the hilt. These dwellers in the wilderness move abruptly and jerkily, their speech is short and vigorous. There is something metallic and rasping about their voices. Some of them are extremely rich: their idea of luxury is to adorn their sabre hilts with precious stones and sometimes to edge their robes with tiger skin. The horses that they bring to Tang Keou Eul are remarkably beautiful; they are strong and well-built with a noble bearing. They are far superior to the horses of

Tartary, and prove the truth of the Chinese proverb: *Si ma, Toung niou*: Horses from the West, Oxen from the East.

As the Houng Mao Eul are full of valour and an almost ferocious independence they set the tone of the town of Tang Keou Eul: everyone tries to ape their manner in order to give an impression of toughness and to inspire respect. As a result the whole place looks like a vast den of brigands. Everyone is dishevelled and untidily dressed. The entire population shouts, jostles, fights and often blood flows. In the depths of winter—and in this land the cold is extreme—arms and legs remain bare. To dress properly would be a sign of cowardice. A man of valour, a brave, should fear nothing, neither man nor the elements. The Chinese in this town have lost much of their usual civility and dropped their polite forms of address. They are influenced involuntarily by the Houng Mao Eul, whose conversation resembles that of tigers in the jungle. The day we arrived, just before entering the town, we met a Long-Haired tribesman who had been watering his horse on the banks of the Keou Ho River. Samdadchiemba, who was always attracted towards eccentric-looking people, went up to him courteously and greeted him in the Tartar manner.

'Brother, are you at peace?' The Houng Mao Eul turned quickly round and shouted at the top of his voice:

'You tortoise egg, what is it to you whether I am at war or at peace? What right have you to call brother a man who has never seen you before?' Samdadchiemba was speechless: but this did not prevent him from admiring this proud behaviour of the Long-Haired man.

Tang Keou Eul, owing to filth and over-population, was a most unhealthy town. Everywhere there was a sickening stench of grease and butter. Certain areas where the poor and the vagrants collected were quite unbearable. The homeless lived at the corners of streets and squares and slept hugger-mugger half-naked on piles of rotting straw. There we saw sickly children, the aged and helpless and those suffering from all sorts of diseases. Here and there a corpse would lie, because no one had bothered to bury it: only when it began to putrify would it be dragged into the middle of the street: then the authorities would take it away. This hideous poverty was a breeding ground for petty thieves and crooks, whose daring and skill far outstripped the Artful Dodgers of the West. There were so many of them that the authorities had given up trying to cope with them. It was up to each man therefore to look after his sapeks and guard his belongings. These professionals concentrated on the rest houses and hostelries. They hawked various articles of merchandise such as boots, fur coats and bricks of tea which they offered to strangers. They usually hunted in pairs. Whilst one was acting as salesman the other ferreted around and pocketed anything he could find. They were incredibly skilful at counting sapeks and making some of them mysteriously disappear. One day two of these petty crooks came with a pair of leather boots for sale, first-class boots, they said, impossible to find the like in any shop, rainproof and above all unbelievably cheap; they were a bargain that must not be missed. They had just received an offer of 1200 sapeks. As we were not in need of boots, we said that we did not want them at any price. The vendors then became generous: since we were foreigners, they would let us have them for 1000 sapeks, then 900, then 800, then finally 700.

'It's true,' we thought, 'we don't need boots, but we ought to take advantage of this bargain; they will be useful as spares on the journey.' The bargain was struck; we took a string of coins and, counting out seven hundred, gave them to the fellow. He re-counted them in front of us, found the sum correct, and left them where they were. He then called his companion who was idling in the courtyard.

'Here,' he said, 'I've sold that pair of boots for 700 sapeks.'

'Not on your life,' said the other. '700 sapeks? I won't agree.'

'Very well,' we said, 'take your boots and go.' When they had left we returned the sapeks to their string—but there were 150 missing. That was not all; whilst one was stealing our money under our noses, the other had put into his bag two big iron stakes in the yard which we had driven into the ground for tethering our horses. From then on we decided, a trifle late, never to allow any hawkers into our room.

The rest house, as we have said, was owned by Muslims. One day their mufti, who had just arrived from Lantchow, the capital of Kansou, came to the house to preside over a ceremony the nature of which they would not reveal. Sandara the Bearded suggested that the 'Grand Lama of the Houi Houi' had come to give them a course in cheating. For two days the leading Muslims of the town met in a big room near our own.

They squatted in silence for a long time, their heads bowed. When the mufti appeared they all groaned and sobbed. When they had cried for a while, the mufti recited with incredible speed a number of prayers in Arabic; then there was some more weeping, after which they left. This tearful ceremony was repeated three times daily. On the morning of the third day all the faithful gathered in the courtyard round the mufti, who sat on a stool which was draped with a beautiful red rug. The host led in a fine sheep adorned with flowers and ribbons. It was laid on its side. Whilst the host held its head and two other men its feet, the mufti was offered a knife on a silver dish. He took it gravely and stepping forward he plunged it up to the hilt into the victim's throat. At this, shouts and groans arose on all sides. The sheep was quickly skinned and cut up and taken off to the kitchen to be cooked. A great feast, presided over by the mufti, was the final act of the ceremonies.

The Mohammedans or Houi Houi are very numerous in China. They say that they first arrived in the Tang dynasty (AD 618–907). They were received by the emperor, who at this date resided at Siganfou, today the capital of Chensi, and were benevolently welcomed. The emperor, struck by the beauty of their appearance, heaped them with favours and invited them to settle in the empire. It is said that there were only two hundred of them to begin with, but they have so multiplied that today they are a numerous race feared by the Chinese. Kansou, Yunnan, Ssetchouan, Chansi, Chensi, Chantung, Petchely and Liaoutoung are the provinces where they are most numerous. There are even certain places where they are in a majority over the Chinese. They are so mixed and blended into the empire that it would nowadays be difficult to recognise them if they did not habitually wear little blue skull-caps to distinguish themselves from the Chinese. Their faces have completely lost their original characteristics. Their noses have flattened, their eyes have narrowed and their cheekbones have become prominent. They can no longer understand Arabic; their holy men alone learn to read it. Chinese has become their language. However they have preserved a certain force of character which is rarely found amongst the Chinese. Although they are few in comparison with the enormous population of the empire they nevertheless know how to make themselves feared and respected. The communities, very tightly knit, always support individual members in any affair that interests them. It is owing to this community spirit that they are able everywhere to enjoy religious freedom. No one would dare to criticise their religious beliefs or practices to their faces. They abstain from smoking, from drinking wine, from eating pork and from sitting down to eat with pagans—and no one objects.

At times, when their religious freedom is threatened, they even flout the laws of the empire. In 1840, when we were at our Tartar mission station, the Houi Houi of the town of Hata built a mosque, or *lipaisse* as they are called in China. When it was finished the local mandarins wanted them to pull it down on the grounds that it broke the law by being higher than the courthouse. At this news all the Muslims of the area were astir; they held a meeting and swore that they would go to Peking and jointly bring an action against the mandarins, and that they would not give up the struggle until they had had them disgraced. Since in China in an affair of this type it is always money which counts, they collected subscriptions amongst the faithful and finally defeated the mandarins who had dared interfere with their mosque: these were disgraced and sent into exile.

We have often wondered how it is that the Christians of

China should live in oppression and at the mercy of the lawcourts, whilst the Mohammedans hold their heads high and force the Chinese to respect their beliefs. It is certainly not because the religion of Mahomet is more in harmony with Chinese customs than Christianity; quite the contrary: Christians can, without failing in their religious duties, live with pagans, eat at the same table, send and receive presents, celebrate the feast of the New Year at the same time. These are all things which the Houi Houi are forbidden to do by the authoritarian and exclusive nature of their religion. If Christians are oppressed everywhere in China, the cause is the great isolation in which they live. When one of them is dragged into court all the others hide, instead of coming to his help and forcing the compliance of the mandarins by their numbers. Today especially, now that new imperial decrees have been published favourable to Christianity, if Christians were to rise up simultaneously throughout the empire and firmly take possession of their rights, bringing their religion out into the open without fear, no one would dare to interfere with their liberty. In China as anywhere else, freedom is only for those who are determined to get it, and this determination can derive only from the community spirit.

The first day of the Chinese year was approaching. Preparations were afoot everywhere; the house fronts were being decorated with maxims written on red paper; the shops were full and a greater activity than usual reigned everywhere in the town. The children, who all over the world like to start celebrating before the right day, were letting off occasional fireworks at nightfall. Sandara informed us that he would not be able to spend the New Year festivities at Tang Keou Eul as he was obliged to return to his lamasery where he had duties to perform for his masters and superiors. He added that on the third day of the first moon, when he had carried out all his obligations, he would hurry back in order to resume his duties with us. He said all this with perfect courtesy, as if to obliterate the memory of the rudeness of his daily converse with us. We avoided insisting on his return. Although pleased that he wanted to come back, we did not press him for fear of further raising his already high opinion of his importance. We told him that, since it was proper for him to return to the lamasery for the New Year, he should go. We presented him with three strings of sapeks, saying, according to custom, that it was for drinking a good strong cup of tea with his friends. For some minutes he made a show of not wanting to accept them; we then had to injure his sense of delicacy by forcing them on him and he finally gave up the struggle and put them into his bag. We lent him Samdadchiemba's little mule and he left.

The last days of the year are always, for the Chinese, days of violence and bad temper. It is the time for settling debts, and creditors seek out their debtors and try to get something out of them. But as all Chinamen are both creditors and debtors, everyone is after everyone else in mutual pursuit. The man who has just been round at his neighbour's, raising the roof in an attempt to get paid, returns to find his creditor creating havoc in his own home. There are constant shouts, insults and fights. On the final day the disorder reaches its climax; there is a rush to sell to realise some cash. There are long queues at the government pawnshops, with people carrying clothes, blankets, kitchen utensils and furniture of every description. Those whose homes are already empty have to go looking elsewhere: they rush off to relatives or friends to borrow things which they promise to return quite soon, but which all end up at the *tang pou* (pawnshop). This chaos lasts until midnight. Then calm reigns; debts must no longer be claimed, nor even mentioned. Peace and benevolence are on everybody's lips; all are brothers. Those who, a moment before, were about to cut each other's throats, are now competing in politeness and amiability.

New Year is celebrated in China more or less as it is in Europe. Everyone puts on his best clothes; ceremonial visits, purely matters of etiquette, are paid; presents are exchanged, there is gambling, there are banquets; one goes to the theatre or to see conjurers and jugglers. The whole time is passed in revelling, in which crackers and fireworks always play the leading role. However, after a few days, the shops reopen and business gradually goes back to normal. Then the bankruptcies are declared; this is what the Chinese call 'closing the door'.

The Houi Houi observe their New Year at a different date from the Chinese. They have their own calendar, dating from the Hegira of Mahomet. For this reason we were able to pass those days of disorder and tumult in the greatest tranquillity. The period fixed for the repayment of debts was marked by a few quarrels, but after that perfect peace reigned. The house of rest was not troubled by the sound of fire-crackers. Owing to this calm and the absence of Sandara we were able to revise all our Tibetan lessons. The two dialogues that were our texts were analysed, pulled to pieces, put through the crucible as it were, from beginning to end. Housework took up a certain amount of time of course. However we made up for it at night time, and this did not suit our host. Noticing that we cost him a

lot in lighting expenses, he removed the bottle of oil and told us (like the Turk that he was) to ration our lamp-light. As we did not want to be condemned to darkness before midnight, we bought a packet of candles; we then fashioned a candlestick out of a long nail and half a radish, maybe neither elegant nor beautiful but perfectly practical. When the Turk's oil gave out, we lit our candle and could thus indulge our enthusiasm for the study of Tibetan. But sometimes we would lay down our work, and refresh ourselves by talking of France. After wandering a while, in spirit, in our dear homeland, it was hard to return to reality. It was not easy to believe that we were here, in the silent night, bent over those Tibetan characters, in a strange land almost at the end of the world.

On the third day of the first moon Sandara the Bearded

reappeared. During his absence we had enjoyed such sweet unbroken peace that the sight of him was an unpleasant shock; we were like boys suddenly face to face with their schoolmaster. But Sandara was simply oozing with charm and courtesy. After wishing us a happy New Year and trotting out a number of brotherly, not to say sentimental, phrases, he began to chatter endlessly about the little mule we had lent him. On the outward journey it had thrown him a dozen times, so he had decided to come back on foot; but the mule was such a character, had been so droll, that he had not had time to feel tired. After enough of this nonsense we got down to business. Sandara told us that since we intended to wait for the Tibetan Embassy, he invited us to come and stay at the lamasery of Kounboum. Then with his usual eloquence he expatiated on the advantages that a lamasery had to offer to men of study and prayer like ourselves. This proposal of his was the very thing we most wanted; but we were careful not to show our enthusiasm. We simply said coldly to Sandara: 'We'll try it. Let's go and see.'

Next day we made our preparations. As we no longer had the camels, we hired a cart to carry our luggage. When we gave notice of our departure to the host we asked him for the return of our travelling tent which he had borrowed some twelve days before to go off on a pleasure trip with friends out on the steppes. He said that he would let us have it shortly but that it was stored at a friend's house. We waited, but in vain; night came and the tent did not appear. We were then told that the friend was away and would not be back for a couple of days; the tent would be sent on to us at the lamasery. Sandara had so far kept very quiet in this affair; but when it was dark and we were still not ready he could contain himself no longer.

'Anyone can see,' he said, 'that you are not of this world. Don't you understand that your tent is at the pawnshop?'

'At the pawnshop? Impossible!'

'I personally think that it is more than probable; the Houi Houi must have needed money to pay his debts at the end of the twelfth moon; he was very lucky to have you here to lend him your tent; but instead of going on a pleasure trip be sure that he took it straight to the *tang pou*. Now he has no money to redeem it with. Look, ask him to come here. I'll question him and you'll see.' We sent for him. As soon as he arrived Sandara the

Bearded began to speak with imposing solemnity. 'Listen to me,' he said, 'tonight I have a few words to say to you. Now, you are a Turk and I am a lama, yet the laws of reason are the same for both. You have borrowed our tent, and you have taken it to the pawnshop; if you were in difficulties, you did well: we do not reproach you. But we are leaving tomorrow and our tent is still not here. Which of us is right? We to ask for our property or you not to return it? Don't say that the tent is at a friend's house; I tell you it is at the pawnshop. If before we have finished drinking this jug of tea our tent is not here, I shall go myself to complain to the lawcourts and we shall see if a Dchiahour lama will let himself be robbed by a Turk.' As a peroration to this speech Sandara struck the little table at which we were drinking tea so great a blow with his fist that our three bowls leapt in the air. The Turk had nothing to say, and it was clear that our tent was in fact at the pawnshop. He assured us that we should have it back very soon, and prayed us not to let the story get around as it would damage the reputation of his establishment. He had hardly left us when an uproar arose in the yard; a collection was being made of all the objects which could be taken to the pawnshop: saddles, blankets, old pewter candlesticks and kitchen utensils. That night, before going to bed, we had tied our tent firmly on to the cart which was carrying our baggage to the lamasery.

Next day we set off at dawn. The country we passed through was partly occupied by the Si Fan, leading a nomadic life and grazing their flocks, and partly by the Chinese who, as in Eastern Tartary, were gradually encroaching on the wilderness, building houses and here and there cultivating patches of the steppe-land. This short journey passed without incident, except that as we were crossing a small river on the ice, the cart overturned and came to pieces. In France, in order to get it going again we should have needed a cartwright and blacksmith to repair the damage; but fortunately our charioteer was a Chinaman, that is to say, a man who is never at a loss and who, with stones, pieces of wood and bits of string can get out of any difficulty. All we lost was a little time.

One *li* from the lamasery we met four lamas; they were friends of Sandara who were coming to meet us. Their monastic dress, the red scarves they wore wrapped round them, their tall, mitre-shaped yellow hats, their modesty, their solemnity and the quietness of their voices made a deep impression on us: it was like a breath of air bringing the scent of a life of religious seclusion. It was past nine o'clock when we reached the first building of the lamasery. So as not to break the deep silence that reigned, the lamas made the driver stop a moment, and filled with straw the little bells which hung from the horses' collars. We went slowly forward, in complete silence, through the quiet deserted streets of this great city of lamas. The moon had already set; but the sky was so clear, the stars so bright,

that we could easily distinguish the countless little houses of the lamas scattered over the mountainside and the weird outlines of the great Buddhist temples which loomed above us like gigantic spectres. What struck us most was the profound and solemn silence in which every part of the lamasery was wrapped; it was interrupted only by the occasional barks of a wakeful dog and by the hollow melancholy sound of a marine conch, which was blown from time to time to mark the hours of the night; it sounded like a ghostly osprey. We arrived at last at the little house where Sandara lodged. As it was too late to look for a suitable dwelling for us, our teacher gave up his cell to us and found a lodging for the night in a nearby house. The lamas who had been our guides, before retiring, prepared us milky tea and served us a large dish of mutton, fresh butter and some delicious bread rolls. We supped with an excellent appetite, for we were tired, and moreover we felt within us a happiness that we could not explain.

We tried in vain to sleep that night; it was quite impossible. Our minds were full of thoughts of our situation, which was becoming more and more strange. It was difficult to believe: here we were in the land of Amdo, a country unknown in Europe, lying in a lama's cell in this great lamasery of Kounboum so famous amongst Buddhists far and wide, its monastic life going on all round us. Our heads were in a whirl, and reality seemed like some strange dream. We spent the night making plans.

As soon as day began to dawn we got up. All was still silent around us. We said our morning prayers with a strange new emotion. It was a mixture of joy and pride, that it should be given to us to pray to the true God in this famous lamasery dedicated to a false ungodly religion. We felt as if we had just converted the whole Buddhist world to the faith of Jesus Christ.

Sandara arrived shortly afterwards. He served us tea, raisins and cakes fried in butter. Whilst we were breakfasting, he opened a little cupboard and took out a varnished wooden dish, with gilt patterns and painted flowers on a red background. After giving it a good wipe with a corner of his scarf, he placed on it a large sheet of pink paper, and then on the paper he arranged symmetrically four beautiful pears which he had bought on our behalf at Tang Keou Eul. The whole was then covered with a silk handkerchief, oblong in shape, called a *khata*. It was armed with this offering, he said, that we should go and try to borrow a house.

The *khata* or 'scarf of happiness' plays such an important role in Tibetan life that we must say a few words about it. It is a piece of silk so fine that it resembles gauze. Its colour is a slightly bluish white. Its length is about three times its width; both ends are usually fringed. There are *khatas* of every size and price; no one can be without them, rich or poor. You never go out without carrying a small store of them. When you pay a polite call, when you ask a favour or give thanks for one granted, you start by unfolding a *khata*; you hold it in both hands and offer it to the person you wish to honour. If two friends, who have not seen each other for some time, happen to meet they immediately exchange *khatas*. It is done with as much cordiality and as quickly as a handshake in Europe. It is normal to enclose a small *khata* in a letter. It is difficult to understand the importance attached by the Tibetans, the Si Fan, the Houng Mao Eul and all the peoples who live to the west of the Blue Sea to the ceremonial of the *khata*. For them it is the purest and sincerest symbol of all the most noble sentiments. The most flattering words, the most expensive presents, are nothing without a *khata*. With it, on the other hand, the commonest objects acquire great value. If someone comes with a *khata* in his hand to ask a favour, it is impossible to refuse it without flouting all the conventions. This Tibetan custom has spread widely through Tartary and is especially prevalent in the lamaseries. Trading in *khatas* is an important activity of the Chinese of Tang Keou Eul. The Tibetan embassies never pass through without buying an enormous quantity of them.

When we had finished our modest meal we set off to try and borrow a lodging. Sandara the Bearded walked before us, solemnly carrying the dish with the four pears. We were so unused to such a procedure that we were very embarrassed: we felt that everyone must be watching us. However it was not so; the lamas that we met as we went along passed us silently without turning their heads or paying any attention. Only the little *chabis*, lively and mischievous like all schoolboys, seemed to show any interest. At last we entered the courtyard of a house, where the master was occupied in spreading horse dung to dry in the sun. Seeing us he promptly wrapped himself in his scarf and entered his cell. We followed and Sandara offered him the *khata* and the dish of pears, and made a speech in Eastern Tibetan of which we understood not one word. During this time we stood in modest meditation, like two poor souls who are incapable of asking anything for themselves. The lama invited us to sit on a rug, offered us a cup of tea and told us, speaking in Mongolian, that he was happy to receive strangers who had come from so far, and proud that lamas of the Western Heavens should condescend to visit his humble habitation. If he had understood French, it would have been the moment to reply: *Monsieur, il n'y a pas de quoi*, but as we had to speak Mongolian, we told him that we were indeed from a far land, but that when encountering a hospitality such as his we felt that we had to some extent regained our homeland. After drinking a cup of tea and talking for a while of France, Rome, the Pope and the cardinals, we were shown the rooms that we were to occupy. For poor nomads like us, they were magnificent. We were to have a very spacious apartment with a large *kang*; then there was a separate kitchen with stoves, a cooking pot and some utensils; finally a stable for the horse and the mule: enough to make us weep with joy. We were sorry that we had no spare *khata*, with which to thank this excellent lama.

How strong is the effect of religion on the heart of man, even when that religion is false and knows nothing of its true purpose! What a difference between these lamas, so generous, so hospitable, so brotherly towards strangers, and the Chinese, a nation of shopkeepers, with hard greedy hearts, who will even sell a glass of cold water to the traveller! At the welcome we received in the lamasery of Kounboum, we could not help being reminded of those religious houses, built by our fore-bears, those hospitable monks, as hostelries where travellers and the poor alike could always find relief for the body and comfort for the soul.

We moved straightaway. The lamas who were Sandara's neighbours were keen to help us. They really seemed to enjoy carrying our luggage on their backs. They swept the room, lit the fire under the *kang* and prepared the stable for our animals. When all was ready, the master of the house, in accordance with the rules of hospitality, prepared us a meal. For, when moving, one is not considered to have any time for cooking.

The reader will bear with us if at this point we give a short account of our new dwelling and introduce him to the inhabitants. Through the entrance gate there was an oblong courtyard round which the stables were conveniently arranged. To the left of the gate, a narrow corridor led to a second yard, a square space with the lamas' cells all round it. On the side of this courtyard opposite the corridor was the apartment of the master of the house, whose name was Akayé, that is, Old Brother. He was a man of over sixty, tall, thin, dried up, emaciated. The bones of his long face were covered with dry wrinkled skin. When he was not wrapped in his scarf his sunburnt arms looked like the gnarled roots of old vines.

Although he still stood erect, he tottered as he walked. It looked as though he were mechanically driven, and that each step were a piston-stroke. For thirty-eight years Akayé had been employed in the administration of the lamasery. He had become quite rich, but his fortune had all gone in good works and in loans that had not been repaid. He was now reduced to great poverty, having only this house which he had built during his days of prosperity and which he was now unable to sell. He was not allowed to let it: that was against the rules of the lamasery, which permitted no middle way between selling a house and lending it without any return. To crown all, old Akayé was not allowed to benefit from the occasional distributions of alms made to the lamas who had reached a certain rank in the hierarchy. Having dealt only with temporal matters all his life, he had not been able to study; he was completely unlettered, and could neither read nor write. This did not prevent him from praying from morning till night; he had always his beads in his hand and we could hear him continually muttering some prayer or other. He was a most upright man; but not much respected, for he was old and penniless.

To the right of old Akayé's rooms, on another wall of the courtyard, lived a lama of Chinese origin: he was called the Kitat lama (Chinese lama); although he was seventy he was better preserved than poor Akayé. He was beginning to stoop; but he was still of middle height and very portly; his expressive face was adorned by a fine white beard, a little yellow at the fringe. The Kitat lama was known for his erudition in the sacred books: he spoke and wrote with perfection in Chinese, Mongolian and Tibetan. During many years spent in Tibet and in several Tartar kingdoms he had amassed a large fortune; we were told that he had in his cell a number of boxes full of silver ingots. Yet he was miserly beyond words; he lived meanly and was poorly dressed; he looked continuously from side to side like a man afraid of being robbed. In Tartary he was considered a great lama; but at Kounboum, which abounds in celebrities, he was a little lost in the crowd. With him lived a young *chabi* aged eleven; this child was bright and mischievous but good-natured; every evening we could hear altercations; his master was scolding him for using too much butter, making the tea too strong or turning the wick too high.

Opposite the rooms of the Kitat lama were our own; right

next to ours was a modest little cell in which lived a second year student at the Faculty of Medicine. He was a big strong fellow of twenty-four whose plump form gave witness that a large consumption of butter went on in his tiny room. We could never see him appear at his cabin door without thinking of the rat in La Fontaine's fable which had, out of piety, retired into a Dutch cheese. This young man had a convulsive stammer so bad that he often caught his breath when he tried to speak; this infirmity made him shy and reserved and possibly also helped to make him good-natured and obliging; whenever he could he avoided the young *chabi*, who took a wicked delight in mimicking his way of speaking.

In the wall of the courtyard facing old Akayé's lodging there was a row of separate little kitchens. The master of the house, the Kitat lama, the stammerer and the missionaries each had their own. As was the custom of the lamasery, we lived as four separate families. Despite the presence of several families in one house, there was always order and quiet; people visited each other seldom and each family went about its own business without interfering in the affairs of others. In our house we hardly saw each other except when it was a sunny day. As it was now mid-winter, as soon as the sunlight reached the courtyard the four families left their cells and squatted on a large felt carpet. The Kitat lama, whose eyes were still sharp, patched his torn clothes with pieces of old rag. Akayé muttered prayers whilst noisily scratching the rough skin of his arms. The medical student revised his lessons, singing them aloud without stammering. We found it hard not to watch this strange company; although we had of course our textbooks of Tibetan dialogues on our knees, our eyes were more apt to wander towards the three families warming themselves in the sun.

The lamasery of Kounboum consisted of about four thousand lamas. It stood in an extraordinarily beautiful situation. Imagine a mountain cleft by a wide and deep ravine, in which there are great trees full of crows, magpies and yellow-beaked rooks. On the two flanks of the ravine and up the sides of the mountain the white houses of the lamas are spread as in an amphitheatre. These are of varying sizes, each surrounded by a wall and crowned with a little turret. From amongst these modest dwellings, whose chief charm is their cleanliness and whiteness, rise the gilded roofs of numerous Buddhist temples, sparkling with many colours and surrounded by rows of elegant columns; the houses of the Superiors are distinguished by banners which wave above little hexagonal turrets. Everywhere there are texts from the mystic writings in large Tibetan characters, some red, some black: they are over every door, on the walls, on rocks, on strips of cloth fixed like flags on to numerous little masts on the tops of the houses. Every few yards there are arched niches in the walls where incense,

fragrant woods and cypress leaves are burnt. But the most striking thing of all is to see the throngs of lamas dressed in red robes and wearing yellow mitres walking through the numerous streets of the lamasery. Their bearing is usually solemn; silence is not compulsory, but they speak little and always in a quiet voice. The streets are only crowded at the times fixed for the beginning and end of classes and of the temple services. During the rest of the day the lamas keep pretty well to their cells; at those times only a few can be seen making their way down zig-zag pathways to the bottom of the ravine, or painfully returning, each with a long barrel on his back, with water for household use. One also met a number of strangers on pilgrimage or who had come to visit lamas of their acquaintance.

Kounboum enjoyed so great a reputation that the worshippers of Buddha came as pilgrims from all parts of Tartary and Tibet; parties arrived or departed every day. But for the solemn festivals they came in vast numbers. There were four main festivals in the year; the most famous of all was the Flower Festival, on the fifteenth day of the first moon. It was celebrated with more pomp and circumstance at Kounboum than anywhere else; those in Tartary or Tibet, even at Lhasa, could not compete. We were installed on the sixth day of the first moon, and already caravans of pilgrims could be seen making their way along all the paths leading to the lamasery. The festival was the only subject of conversation: this year the flowers were said to be amazingly beautiful. The Fine Arts Council, which had examined them, had declared them to be better than those of the previous year. As soon as we heard of these marvellous 'flowers', we naturally made enquiries about the festival, of which we knew nothing. These are the details which we were given and which we heard with some surprise.

The Flower Festival of the 15th of the first moon consisted of effigies, both secular and religious, representing all the peoples of Asia with their proper appearance and distinguishing costumes. These figures, their clothing, the backgrounds and decorations were all carved in fresh butter. The preparations for this strange spectacle took three months. Twenty lamas, chosen from the most talented artists of the lamasery, worked daily at the butter, keeping their hands in water all the time for fear that the warmth of their fingers should spoil the sculptures. As this work took place for the most part in the depths of winter the artists had to endure great suffering. They first stirred and kneaded the butter in water so as to make it firm. When the material was ready, each artist worked on the parts of the design to which he had been assigned. They all worked under the direction of a chief who had designed the overall plan for the year and was in charge of its execution. When the works were finished they were handed over to another company of artists, whose task it was to colour them, still under the direction of the same chief. An art exhibition all in butter seemed to us so curious that we rather looked forward to the 15th day of the moon.

The day before the festival, the place was packed with strangers. Kounboum was no longer the peaceful, silent lamasery filled with the gravity and solemnity of religious life; it was a worldly city, full of bustle and turmoil. The air was filled with shrill cries of the camels and the lowing of the long-haired yaks which had brought the pilgrims. On the mountainsides above the lamasery tents were being put up by those who had not been able to find space in the lamas' houses. During the whole of the 14th the number of pilgrims who made their tour of devotions at the lamasery was immense. We found it a strange and pathetic sight: the crowd falling prostrate repeatedly, all muttering their prayers. Amongst these zealous Buddhists there were a large number of Tartar-Mongols, who had all come from a great distance. They looked slow and sullen, but deeply reverent and scrupulously observing all their religious duties. The Long-Haired Ones were there too, and we did not think that they were any better looking than when we saw them at Tang Keou Eul; their primitive piety made a striking contrast to the mysticism of the Mongolians. They walked proudly with their heads high and their right arms free, always carrying their big sabres and slung rifles. The Si Fan of the land of Amdo formed the majority of the pilgrims. Their faces showed neither the roughness of the Long-Haired Ones nor the simple reverence of the Tartars. They performed their pilgrimage in a rather perfunctory manner. They seemed to be saying: 'We're local parishioners; we know all about it.'

The headdress of the Amdo ladies was a pleasant surprise. They wore little hats in black or grey felt, shaped exactly like those little pointed hats which were once so fashionable in France, and which were called, if we recall rightly, *chapeaux à la trois pour cent*. The only difference was that the ribbon round the crown was red or yellow instead of black. The Amdo women let their hair hang over their shoulders, in a number of little plaits adorned with spangles of mother-of-pearl and red coral beads. Otherwise they dressed like the Tartar women; but the heaviness of their long sheepskin dresses was offset by the little 'three per cent' hats, which lent them a certain grace. We were most surprised to find amongst this crowd of pilgrims a few Chinese, beads in hand and going through the same motions as the others. Sandara the Bearded told us that they were *khata* dealers; that they had no faith in Buddha but pretended their piety in order to attract customers and sell more of their merchandise. We cannot say if these words of Sandara were slanderous or not, but they certainly were in accord with the Chinese character.

On the 15th the pilgrims were still touring round the lamasery, but they were less numerous than on the previous days. From curiosity they were congregating in those places where the preparations were being made for the Flower Festival. When it was dark, Sandara came to fetch us to see these wonders in butter of which we had heard so much. We set off, together with the stammering student, the Kitat lama and his *chabi*. Only old Akayé was left to guard the house. The 'flowers' had been set up in the open air, in front of the various temples of the lamasery. The illuminations were brilliant and quite beautiful. Countless brass and copper vessels, calyx-shaped, stood on light frames of fantastic design. All these vessels, of varying sizes, were filled with solid butter in the middle of which was a thick wick wrapped in wadding. These illuminations showed considerable taste; they would not have been out of place in Paris on a day of public festivity.

The 'flowers' themselves were an astonishing sight. It was unbelievable that in this wilderness and amongst these half-savage peoples there could be artists of such talent. The painters and sculptors whose work we had seen in various lamaseries had not led us to suspect the perfection that we now saw in these art-works in butter. These 'flowers' were bas-reliefs of colossal size, representing scenes from Buddhist history. All the figures were astonishingly life-like. The faces were lively and expressive, the postures were natural and they seemed to wear their clothes so well and without the slightest stiffness. The texture of the stuffs was perfectly recognisable: the costumes in fur were particularly well done. The skins of sheep, tiger, fox, wolf and various other animals were so well represented that we were tempted to touch them to make sure they were not real. In all the bas-reliefs, Buddha was easily recognisable. His face, full of nobility and majesty, was Caucasian in type; this followed the Buddhist tradition according to which Buddha, who came from the Western Heavens, had a pale face slightly tinted red, wide eyes, a prominent nose and long wavy hair soft to the touch. The other figures were all of Mongolian type, with Tibetan, Chinese, Tartar and Si Fan variations. The various types were perfectly distinguishable by their faces, even if the costumes were disregarded. There were also some Indian and Negro faces, very well represented. The latter particularly excited the crowd's curiosity. Round these great bas-reliefs were decorations of animals, birds and flowers; these were also in butter and marvellously delicate in their shapes and colouring.

On the route which led from one temple to another, we passed, from time to time, small bas-reliefs picturing miniature battles, hunting scenes, scenes from nomadic life and views of the most famous lamaseries of Tibet and Tartary. And finally, in front of the main temple was a stage on which the actors and the scenery were all made of butter. The actors were only a foot high; the scene represented a community of lamas on their way to a service to recite prayers. To begin with the stage was empty. When the conch sounded, from the side entrances came two lines of little lamas; after them came the superiors in their ceremonial costumes. After standing still for a moment on the stage they went back into the wings and the performance was over. This spectacle was enthusiastically received by all. We who had seen mechanical contrivances of other sorts found these little figures rather dull, arriving and departing as they did without moving their legs. One performance sufficed, and we went back to admiring the bas-reliefs.

Whilst we were examining groups of devils as grotesque, at least, as those of Callot, we suddenly heard the great blast of a number of trumpets and conches. We were told that the Grand Lama was coming out of his sanctuary to visit the 'flowers'. We were delighted; the Grand Lama of Kounboum excited our curiosity. He soon arrived at the spot where we were standing. He was preceded by attendant lamas, who cleared the crowd with long black whips; he was on foot and surrounded by the principal dignitaries of the lamasery. This Living Buddha looked at most about forty years of age; he was of medium height, had a commonplace-looking flat face and a very dark complexion. He glanced glumly at the bas-reliefs as he passed. Seeing the beautiful representations of Buddha, was he per-haps thinking how degenerated he had become after all those reincarnations? If the Grand Lama himself did not impress us, his costume certainly did, for it was exactly like that of a bishop. He wore a yellow mitre; in his right hand he held a long staff shaped like a crozier; his shoulders were draped in a cloak of purple taffeta, fastened on the chest by a clasp and exactly resembling a cope. Later on in this narrative we shall be pointing out a number of similarities between the Catholic and the Buddhist ceremonials.

The spectators showed little apparent interest in their Living Buddha; they preferred the butter Buddhas who were really much better looking. The Tartars alone showed some signs of reverence; they joined their hands and bent their heads as a sign of respect; they seemed upset that the crowd was too dense to allow them to prostrate themselves on the ground.

When the Grand Lama had finished his tour he returned to his sanctuary, and this was a signal for all to indulge in merry-making with the most reckless abandon. They sang at the top of their voices, they danced holding hands, they pushed each other, knocked each other over, shouted and howled like wolves. All these mixed races seemed to have gone mad. As in the midst of this fearful disorder it would have been easy for the illuminations and the butter tableaux to be overturned, lamas armed with big flaming torches stood to keep back the onslaught of the great crowd which surged like a stormy sea. We could not stand this uproar for long. The Kitat lama, noticing our distress, suggested a return home. We accepted readily, for the night was far advanced and we were in need of rest.

Next day at daybreak there was no trace of the great Festival of Flowers. All had gone: the bas-reliefs had been destroyed and that immense quantity of butter had been thrown to the bottom of the ravine as food for the crows. Those mighty creations, which had cost so much labour, so much time and so much talent, had been but the spectacle of a single night. Every year new 'flowers' were made, on a new plan.

With the 'flowers' went the pilgrims. From the morning on we saw them slowly climb the winding mountain paths, returning sadly to their wild countries; they all went with bent heads and in silence: for the heart of man can bear so little joy in this world that the day after a riotous festival is ever filled with bitterness and sorrow.

[3]

KOUNBOUM

The land of Amdo, situated to the south of the Koukou Noor, is inhabited by the Eastern Tibetans who, like the Tartar-Mongols, lead a pastoral and nomadic life. It is a wild and dreary country, a land of red or tawny mountains everywhere divided by a network of deep ravines. However, in the midst of this desolate wilderness, there are a few valleys where pasture is fairly abundant and there the nomadic tribes take their flocks and herds.

According to the Buddhist chronicles, towards the middle of the fourteenth century a shepherd of the land of Amdo, Lombo Moke by name, had put up his black tent at the foot of a mountain, near the brink of a wide ravine, at the bottom of which an ample stream ran over a stony bed. Lombo Moke shared with his wife Chingtsa Tsio the labours of the pastoral life. Their flocks were not large: some twenty goats and a few *sarligues* or yaks were all their wealth. For some years they had lived childless in this wild solitude. Lombo Moke herded his beasts in the surrounding pastures, whilst Chingtsa Tsio, alone in her tent, was occupied with dairy work or with weaving a coarse cloth in the Amdo fashion with the long strands from the coats of the yaks. One day when fetching water from the stream Chingtsa Tsio fainted, falling unconscious on a large rock on which were carved certain characters in honour of the Buddha. When Chingtsa Tsio awoke, she felt a great pain in her side and realised that her fall had made her pregnant. In the year of the fire-hen (1357), nine months after this mysterious event, she gave birth to a child whom Lombo Moke named Tsong Kaba, from the name of the mountain under which his tent stood. This miraculous child had at birth a white beard and an expression of extraordinary majesty. There was nothing child-ish about him. From his very birth he was able to express himself with clarity and precision in the Amdo language. He spoke little, but his words always expressed profound truths about the nature of being and the destiny of man.

When he was three years old, Tsong Kaba decided to give up the world and embrace a religious life. Chingtsa Tsio, out of respect for her son's holy calling, herself shaved his head and dropped his fine long hair at the door of the tent. From this hair grew a tree whose wood gave off a delicious perfume and whose every leaf was engraved with a character of the sacred language of Tibet. From then on, Tsong Kaba withdrew so completely from the world that he even fled the company of his parents. He went to live on the tops of the wildest mountains, or at the bottom of the deepest ravines, and spent his days and nights in prayer and the contemplation of things eternal. He fasted long and often. He respected the life of the tiniest insects and ate no kind of meat.

Whilst Tsong Kaba was thus occupied in purifying his heart through prayer and a life of austerity, a lama from the furthest parts of the West passed by chance through the land of Amdo and received hospitality in the tent of Lombo Moke. Tsong Kaba, amazed at the knowledge and saintliness of the stranger, prostrated himself at his feet and begged him to be his master. Lamaic traditions say that this lama from the West was remarkable not only for his unfathomable wisdom but also for the strangeness of his appearance. He had a prominent nose and his eyes shone with a supernatural light. No less impressed with the wondrous qualities of Tsong Kaba, he accepted him as his disciple without hesitation. He settled in Amdo but lived only a few years. After initiating his disciple into all the teachings of the greatest saints of the West, he fell into a sleep on a rock at the summit of a mountain and his eyes were closed for ever.

Tsong Kaba, deprived of the lessons of the foreign saint, felt an even greater need of religious instruction. He soon decided to leave his tribe and make his way to the farthest West in order to drink the purest doctrines at their source. He set off, staff in hand, alone and without guide but with his heart full of a superhuman courage. He first went due south, and arrived after a long and difficult journey at the frontiers of the province of Yunnan, the furthest outpost of the Chinese empire. There, instead of continuing in the same direction, he turned northwest along the banks of the great Yarou Dsangbo river. He arrived at last at the holy city of the kingdom of Oué. As he was preparing to resume his journey a *Lha* or spirit, bathed in shining light, appeared and forbade him to go any further.

'Tsong Kaba,' he said, 'all these vast lands belong to the great empire which has been bestowed on you. From this place you must proclaim the new rituals and prayers. In this place will come to pass the final unfolding of your immortal life.' Tsong Kaba, obedient to this heavenly voice, entered the 'Land of Spirits', Lha Ssa, Lhasa, and chose a humble dwelling in the remotest part of the city.

The holy man from the tribe of Amdo soon began to gather disciples, and it was not long before the new doctrine and the strange rituals which he introduced into the services began to cause some commotion. Then at last Tsong Kaba boldly came out into the open as a reformer, and declared war on the old religion. His following increased daily, and came to be known as the Yellow Hatted lamas, in contrast to the Red Hatted lamas who supported the old faith. The king of the land of Oué and the Chakdja, a Living Buddha and Chief Lama, were distressed at the rise of this new sect which had brought confusion into the religious ceremonials. The Chakdja sent for Tsong Kaba, in order to discover if his wisdom were as great as his followers claimed. The reformer proudly refused to comply; as the prophet of a new religion which was destined to supplant the old, it was not for him to make an act of submission.

But the sect of the Yellow Hats grew and grew and the multitude paid homage to Tsong Kaba. The Chakdja Buddha, seeing his authority undermined, decided to go himself and seek out the 'little lama from Amdo' as he scornfully called him. He hoped in this interview to hold a discussion with his adversary from which the old doctrine would emerge triumphant. He arrived with great pomp and all the attributes of his religious supremacy. As he entered Tsong Kaba's modest cell his tall red hat struck the top of the door and fell to the ground. This was generally interpreted as an omen of the victory of the Yellow Hatted sect. The reformer was sitting cross-legged on a cushion, and made no sign as the Chakdja entered. He made no attempt to rise and continued solemnly to finger the beads of his chaplet. The Chakdja, ignoring the fall of his hat and the cold reception he had received, launched himself into a discussion. He pompously upheld the ancient rites and explained the basis of his claim to be the final authority. Tsong Kaba, without looking up, interrupted him, saying, 'Cruel man, let go that louse you are pressing in your fingers. I hear its cries of pain, and my heart is torn with anguish.' The Chakdja, whilst singing his own praises, had in fact caught a louse in his clothing and, in contempt of the doctrine of the transmigration of souls, he was crushing it between his fingers. Finding no reply to the harsh words of Tsong Kaba, he prostrated himself at his feet and recognised his authority.

From that moment Tsong Kaba's reforms encountered no opposition; they were adopted throughout Tibet and were subsequently introduced into the various kingdoms of Tartary. In 1409 Tsong Kaba, now fifty years of age, founded the famous lamasery of Kaldan, nine miles from Lhasa; it still exists today and has more than eight thousand lamas. In 1419 the soul of Tsong Kaba, who had become Buddha, left the earth to return to the celestial kingdom where it was admitted into the Heaven of Delight. His body has remained at the lamasery of Kaldan. It is claimed that it has been perfectly preserved and that by a continuous miracle it floats slightly above the ground without any support. Sometimes it has been known to speak to lamas who have progressed far on the road to perfection; but the others cannot hear it.

In addition to his liturgical reforms, Tsong Kaba is famous for his restatement of the sacred texts of the Buddha. The most important of his works is the *Lam Rim Tsien Bo* or *Steps to Perfection.*

It is impossible not to be struck by the similarities between the reforms and innovations introduced by Tsong Kaba and Catholicism. The crozier, the mitre, the dalmatic, the cope or pluvial which the Grand Lamas wear when travelling or when conducting a ceremony outside the temple; the service with two choirs, the singing of psalms, exorcism, the five-chained censer which can be opened and closed at will, the blessing given by raising the right hand over the heads of the faithful; the chaplet, the practice of celibacy, the retreat, the worship of saints, fasting, processions, litanies, holy water: all these are common to both religions. Can it be said that these common factors are Christian in origin? We think so. Although we have found no proof of this either in the traditions or the memorials of the country, it is possible nevertheless to make conjectures that have a high level of probability.

It is well known that in the fourteenth century, at the time of the Mongolian emperors, there were frequent contacts between Europeans and the peoples of Upper Asia. We have already spoken, in the first volume of our travels, of the famous envoys that the Tartar conquerors sent to Rome, to France and to England. These barbarians must have been impressed with the pomp and brilliance of the ceremonial of the Catholic religion, and must have returned to their deserts with indelible memories of them. It is also known that at the same period holy men of various orders set off on far journeys with the intention of bringing Christianity to Tartary; they could also have reached as far as Tibet, the lands of the Si Fan and the Mongolians of the Blue Sea. Jean de Montcorvin, Archbishop of Peking, had already organised a large choir, in which Mongolian monks recited the psalms and the Catholic liturgy. When one realises that Tsong Kaba lived at the very period when the Christian religion was being introduced into Central Asia, it is not surprising that there are striking resemblances to Christian practices in the Buddhist reforms.

But is it not possible to say something more positive than this? Could not this legend of Tsong Kaba, which we have collected at his birthplace from the stories told by a number of lamas, be used to support our theory? When all the miraculous elements added to the story by the lamas' imaginations have been eliminated, it can still be accepted that Tsong Kaba was a man of outstanding qualities, both intellectual and possibly moral; that he was given instruction by a stranger from the West; that after the death of the master, the disciple, making his way westward, stopped in Tibet, where he passed on the teachings he had received. Was not the 'big nosed' stranger a European, one of those Catholic missionaries so many of whom were penetrating into Upper Asia at this period? It is not surprising that the traditions of the lamas have preserved the memory of a European face, so different in type from the Asiatic. During our stay at Kounboum we have several times heard lamas comment on our strange appearance and say, without hesitation, that we must come from the same country as Tsong Kaba's master. It may well be that the Catholic missionary was prevented by an early death from completing his disciple's religious education, and that when the disciple set himself up as a religious leader he either had an inadequate understanding of the Christian dogma or abandoned his beliefs, limiting himself to the introduction of a new liturgy. The weakness of the opposition that he met to his reforms would seem to indicate that an infiltration of Christian ideas had already weakened the Buddhist cult in these areas. We shall later discuss whether frequent contacts between Buddhists and Catholics are an obstacle or an advantage to the propagation of the faith in Tartary and Tibet.

Tsong Kaba's reformation was victorious in all the countries between the Himalayas, the Russian frontiers and the Great Wall of China. It even penetrated into certain regions of the Celestial Empire, such as Kansou, Chansi, Petchely and the whole of Manchuria. The bonzes have preserved the ancient rites, apart from slight innovations that have been adopted in some areas. There are now two kinds of lama, the Yellow and the Red, the reformed and the unreformed. The two sects, which no doubt were once bitter rivals, now live in perfect harmony. The bonzes and the lamas consider that they belong to the same family.

The Amdo tribe, once unknown and of no consequence, has gained great fame since the reformation of Buddhism. The mountain at whose foot Tsong Kaba was born had become a famous place of pilgrimage. Lamas came from all parts to build their cells there, and the flourishing lamasery whose fame spread to the furthest confines of Tartary gradually came into being. It was called Kounboum from two Tibetan words which mean 'Ten Thousand Pictures'. This name refers to the tree which, according to the legend, was born out of the hair of Tsong Kaba, and which bears a Tibetan character on each of its leaves.*

Here the reader will expect us to say something about this tree. Does it still exist? Have we seen it? What is it like? What about those miraculous leaves? All these are justifiable questions. We shall therefore try to reply to them as far as we are able.

Yes, the tree still exists; we had heard so much about it during our journey that we were quite impatient to go and see it. At the foot of the mountain on which the lamasery was built

---

*The miraculous tree of Kounboum (Kumbum). Peter Fleming described it in 1935 as a white sandalwood, and said that the monks sold the leaves which were 'miraculously stamped with the image of Tsong-k'apa'; but he added that there were no leaves on the tree when he visited the lamesery. André Migot, in *Tibetan Marches*, describing a journey made in 1946, said that the leaves were supposed to be marked with the characters of the mani: 'The original tree is now sepulchred in a chorten inside the temple. A new tree has been grown from a cutting, but there was no sign of lettering on the leaves.' (Trans.)

and not far from the main temple was a large enclosure surrounded by a brick wall. We went into this courtyard, and
could examine at leisure the miraculous tree whose branches
we had already glimpsed from outside. We immediately looked
at the leaves with burning curiosity and were dumbfounded to
see that, sure enough, on each leaf there were well-formed
Tibetan characters. They were green, sometimes darker and
sometimes lighter than the leaf itself. Our first reaction was to
suspect a fraud practised by the lamas; but after the most

detailed examination we could find no evidence of this. The
characters gave every appearance of being part of the leaf, like
the veins and nerves; they were not always similarly placed,
but were sometimes on the top and sometimes in the middle of
the leaf, sometimes at its base and sometimes on the sides; the
young leaves had the character in a rudimentary form, only
partly formed; the bark on the trunk and on the branches,
which peeled off rather like the bark of plane-trees, was also
marked with characters. If one removed a piece of the old bark

one could see on the new bark underneath vague shapes of characters which were in the process of formation; the strange thing was that they were often different from the ones on top. We made every effort, until our brows were wet with sweat, to discover some evidence of fraud, but in vain. Others cleverer than we may be able to find a satisfactory explanation of the peculiarities of this tree, but we gave it up. Some will smile at our ignorance, we care little so long as our integrity is not doubted.

The Tree of the Ten Thousand Pictures looked very ancient: its trunk, which three men could hardly encircle, was not more than eight feet high; the branches did not go upwards; they thrust outwards to form a plume and were very bushy; some were dead and decaying with age; the leaves were evergreen; the wood, which was reddish, had a delightful perfume rather like cinnamon. The lamas told us that during the summer, about the eighth moon, it produced large red flowers of great beauty. They also said that no other tree of this kind existed anywhere else; attempts had been made to propagate it by seed and by cuttings in several lamaseries of Tartary and Tibet, but always without success.

The Emperor Kang Hsi, who came to Kounboum on a pilgrimage, paid for a silver dome to be constructed over the Tree of the Ten Thousand Pictures; in addition he presented the Grand Lama with a magnificent black horse which could travel, it is said, a thousand *li* a day, and a saddle adorned with precious stones. The horse is dead, but the saddle can still be seen in one of the temples; it is an object of great veneration. Before leaving the lamasery, Kang Hsi founded an annuity for the upkeep of three hundred and fifty lamas.

The fame of Kounboum, due originally to its connection with Tsong Kaba, is maintained today through the good discipline of the lamasery and the high standard of its teaching. The lamas are regarded as students for life, since the study of religion is considered to be inexhaustible. The students are divided into four schools or faculties, according to the speciality they have chosen:

THE FACULTY OF MYSTICISM, which teaches the rules of the life of contemplation with examples drawn from the lives of the Buddhist saints.

THE FACULTY OF LITURGY, or the study of religious ceremonial and the explanation of all the elements of the cult.

THE FACULTY OF MEDICINE, or the study of the four
hundred and forty diseases of the human body, medical botany
and the pharmacopoeia.

THE FACULTY OF PRAYERS, which is the most highly
esteemed, the best remunerated and therefore the one which
has the greatest number of students.

The great tomes which are used as texts for the teaching of
prayers are divided into thirteen series, which are regarded as
the thirteen degrees in the hierarchy. The place that each
student occupies at the school and in the choir is determined by
the series that he has reached in his study of theological texts.
Amongst these many lamas, there are old men who sit in the
back row thus proclaiming their sloth or their incapacity,
whilst young men can be seen to have reached the top of the
hierarchy.

To qualify in the various grades of the Faculty of Prayers the
student has only to recite the set books without fault. When he
thinks he is ready, he informs the Lama of Prayers, at the same
time presenting him with a magnificent *khata*, a dish of raisins
and some silver ingots, the amount varying according to the
grade; the examining lamas also receive presents. Although it
is generally agreed that the examiners are incorruptible, it is
nevertheless felt, at Kounboum as elsewhere, that an offering to
the senior members of the faculty is not without its effect in
obtaining a good result at the examination. Human nature is
the same everywhere!

In front of the main temple of the lamasery there was a large
paved courtyard surrounded by spiral columns enriched with
coloured sculptures. It was here that the lamas of the Faculty of
Prayers met for their courses when summoned by the conch;
they sat in order of rank on the bare paving stones, enduring
cold wind and snow during the winter and in summer the rain
or the burning sun. Only the teachers were under cover; they
sat on a dais surmounted by a pavilion. It was remarkable to see
all these lamas wrapped in their red scarves and wearing their
yellow mitres and so tightly packed together that the paving-
stones were invisible. After several students had recited the
lessons of the day, the professors in turn gave explanations as

vague and incomprehensible as the text; but nobody objected; everyone was satisfied with an approximation. It was generally considered that the sublimity of a doctrine was in direct proportion to its obscurity and impenetrability.

The lesson normally ends with a thesis defended by a student nominated in advance. All the others had the right to interrogate him on any subject that occurred to them. These theses were thoroughly absurd, and reminded us of the disputations of the medieval schoolmen, who argued passionately *de omni re scibili*. At Kounboum it was the custom that the winner was hoisted on to the shoulders of the loser and carried in triumph round the walls of the school. One day Sandara the Bearded returned from his lessons laughing and looking more radiant than usual. We were soon told that he had been the victor of the thesis; he had beaten his opponent in the important question of why hens and other fowls lacked one of the vital functions common to all other animals. We quote this detail, since it gives an idea of the nobility of the lamaic teaching.

At certain times of the year, the Living Buddha, Grand Lama of the lamasery, comes in person with great pomp to expound the holy books. Although his explanations are neither wiser nor clearer than those of the teachers, they are regarded as sacrosanct. The Tibetan language alone is permitted in the schools.

The discipline of the lamasery is vigilant and strict. During the classes at the faculties and in the choirs during the recitation of prayers, we could always see the proctor-lamas leaning on their iron rods, keeping the student body in silence and in good order. The slightest breach of discipline was immediately checked, first verbally, and then if necessary with the rods. Old men were as liable to these cruel punishments as the young *chabis*.

Constable-lamas were responsible for policing the lamasery; they were dressed like the other lamas, except that their clothes were grey and their mitres black. Day and night they paraded the streets of the city armed with long whips, keeping order when or where necessary. Three courts, presided over by judge-lamas, tried cases which were above the competence of the constables. Those guilty of stealing, however petty, were expelled from the lamasery, after being branded with a hot iron on the forehead and the cheeks with a mark of shame.

Buddhist monasteries are in many ways similar to Christian ones, but in others are essentially different. The lamas are, like Christian monks, subject to a common rule and discipline, but one cannot say that they are a true community. We saw the same degrees of poverty and wealth amongst them as in a worldly city. We saw many lamas dressed in rags, begging a few handfuls of barley flour at the doors of their rich colleagues. Every quarter the administration made a distribution of flour indiscriminately to all the lamas attached to the lamasery, but the quantity was quite insufficient. The donations of pilgrims were a help, but apart from the fact that these were uncertain, they were distributed according to rank, and there were always many who received very little.

There were two types of donation: in tea and in silver. The former was made in the following manner: the pilgrim who wished to offer a treat to the company of lamas would approach the superiors and inform them, at the same time presenting them with a *khata*, that he wished to demonstrate his piety by offering either a tea-for-all or a tea-for-some, the latter being a tea for one of the faculties, at the choice of the pilgrim. On the day fixed for a tea-for-all, the presiding lama after morning prayers would make a sign for all to remain where they were. Then about forty young *chabis*, chosen by lot, would go to the great kitchen and reappear a moment afterwards carrying jugs of milky tea; they went along the rows of lamas with their jugs; each lama produced his wooden bowl from his bosom, and it would be filled to the brim. Each one drank in silence, carefully veiling his bowl with a corner of his scarf, in order to lessen the impropriety of performing this gross act in a holy place. Normally, there was enough tea to go round twice, for two full bowls each. The tea varied in strength according to the generosity of the pilgrim. Some paid for a pat of butter for each lama; those who wanted to be really magnanimous provided cakes made with wheaten flour. When the treat was over, the presiding lama solemnly proclaimed the name of the pious pilgrim who had acquired so much merit by entertaining the holy family of lamas. Straightaway the pilgrim, who was normally present at the ceremony, would prostrate himself: the lamas recited some prayers for him and then walked in procession round their benefactor, who remained prostrate until they had all left.

Donations of this type provided little for each individual lama; but when one thinks that there were more than four thousand tea-drinkers it is easy to see that the expense would be considerable. At Kounboum, a simple tea-for-all, without butter or cakes, cost fifty ounces of silver, that is, more than 500 francs.

Donations in silver were much more costly because they were always accompanied by a tea-for-all. The money was not distributed during the service, but when prayers were over the presiding lama announced that pilgrim so-and-so, from such-and-such a country, had presented so many ounces of silver to the community of lamas, and that the sum had been equally divided to provide a share of so much. The lamas would then go individually to the donations office and draw their exact quota.

There were no fixed times or days for donations: they were always welcome. But at the four great festivals of the year they were more numerous and larger, because of the greater number of pilgrims. After the Flower Festival, and before returning home to Tartary, the King of Souniout presented six hundred ounces of silver and a tea-for-all for eight days, together with butter and cakes: the expense could be reckoned as 15,000 francs. When the donation was made by a distinguished personage it was the custom for the Living Buddha to be present at the ceremony. He then received a personal gift, in a basket adorned with flowers and ribbons, of a silver ingot weighing fifty ounces, a length of red or yellow silk, a pair of boots and a mitre, all covered with a costly *khata*. The pilgrim would prostrate himself on the steps of the altar on which the Living Buddha was seated and place the basket at his feet. A *chabi* would take it and in return give the pilgrim a *khata* from the Living Buddha, who all the while remained motionless as befitted a divine personage.

Apart from such distributions, the lamas of Kounboum had a number of ways of providing income for themselves: some kept cows and sold their comrades the milk and butter to go with their tea and their barley-flour. Some banded together in joint companies for the preparation of the teas which the pilgrims offered to the community; others were tailors, dyers and hatters, making all the articles of a lama's costume in return for payment. And finally there were shopkeepers who sold at

vast profits goods brought from Tang Keou Eul or Sining
Fou.

Amongst the working lamas, however, there were a number
who made their living by occupations more consistent with the
religious life; they printed or copied the holy texts. The Tibetan
script goes horizontally from left to right; it is alphabetical,
rather like a European language; however, movable type
is not used in printing: wooden stereotype plates only are
used. Tibetan books are like large packs of cards; the pages are
loose, and printed on both sides. As they are neither sewn nor
bound together, they are placed between two wooden boards
for protection, and these are fastened with yellow bands. The
Tibetan books printed at Kounboum were very rough; the type
was blotted, coarse and unclear; they were in every way
inferior to those produced by the imperial presses in Peking.
The manuscripts on the other hand were magnificent; they
were highly decorated and the lettering was clear and graceful.
The lamas do not write with a brush like the Chinese; they use
little slips of bamboo which they cut like pens; their inkpot is a
little copper box shaped like a snuffbox with a hinged lid; it
contains cotton-wool soaked in ink. They coat their paper to
prevent it from absorbing the ink: instead of using a solution of
alum like the Chinese, they sprinkle the paper with water
mixed with a tenth part of milk: the method is simple, easy and
gives satisfactory results.

Sandara the Bearded belonged to none of the occupations we
have listed; he formed a class apart. His profession was to
exploit the foreigners who from piety or other reasons visited
the lamascry. The Tartar-Mongols were his most profitable
clients. He offered his services to them as a guide, and owing to
his versatility and his eloquence he ended up as their commercial agent. Sandara enjoyed no great prestige at Kounboum.
The best lamas thought little of him; some of them warned us
benevolently not to put too much faith in his fine words, and to
keep an eye on our purses. We were told that, forced to leave
Lhasa as a swindler, he had toured Ssetchouan and Kansou for
three years as an actor and fortune-teller. We learned this
without surprise. We had noticed that when Sandara really let
himself go he behaved exactly like an actor on the stage.

One evening when he seemed in a particularly good mood,
we tried to draw him on his past experiences.

'Sandara,' we said, 'there are idle gossiping lamas who say that when you left Tibet you spent three years in China.'

'That is true.'

'Some even say that you are a talented dramatic performer.' Sandara smiled, then got up, rhythmically snapped his fingers, assumed a theatrical pose and declaimed a passage of verse in Chinese.

'An actor lama! That's something new!'

'No, no, you are wrong. I was first a lama, then an actor, then I became a lama again. Now, look,' he added, sitting down in his usual place, 'since idle people recount my adventures, I shall tell you them myself.

'After living at Lhasa for ten years, in the lamasery of Sera, I got homesick; I was haunted by the desire to see the Three Valleys again. It became so strong that I had to leave. My travelling companions were four lamas from Amdo who were also returning to their homeland. Instead of taking the eastern route we travelled south, because the desert is not entirely uninhabited on that side. We went on foot, staff in hand with our small packs on our backs; if we came across black tents on our way, we asked for hospitality. If not, we were obliged to spend the nights in ravines or under the shelter of great rocks. You know that Tibet is a land of many great mountains; we continually went up and down them and although it was summer, we often walked through snow. The nights were very cold; but during the day in the valleys it was unbearably hot.

'We were a happy party. All five were in good health and always in good humour, above all when the herdsmen of the black tents had given us in their charity a kid or a big ball of butter. We crossed a land where we found a strange kind of animal. They were no longer than a cat; they were covered in a kind of hair as hard as steel needles. As soon as these animals saw us, they rolled up so that we could no longer see their heads or their tails. They were just big balls, with long quills all round. At first we were afraid of them; we could not think what they were, as the prayerbooks say nothing about them. But we wanted to examine them. As these balls could not be touched by hand, we laid a stick on top of one of them; then we pressed so hard at both ends of the stick that the ball began to open. Out popped a little face like that of a man staring at us. We screamed and ran off terrified. However we eventually got used to them; we even played games with them. We liked to roll them down the mountainsides, bowling them with our staves.

'We also came across some peculiar worms. One day when it was very hot we were walking beside a small stream which wound through a valley where there was high grass. About midday, after preparing and drinking our tea we went to sleep beside the water. You know that by order of Tsong Kaba the Yellow Hatted lamas wear no breeches. Now, when we woke we found that a large number of worms had fixed themselves on to our legs. They were grey, and as big as your finger. We tried to pull them off, but we could not. As we felt no pain, we waited. Soon these creatures swelled up and became round; then they fell off by themselves. Oh, Tibet is a strange country! You see animals there you see nowhere else. The lamas who have not made the journey won't believe what we tell them.'

'They are wrong,' we said, 'what you have just said is entirely true; these strange animals are not only found in Tibet; in our country they are quite common. The ones with the quills are called hedgehogs and the grey worms are leeches.'

'What, you have seen animals like that?'

'Yes, often.'

'Oh, good! Some lamas won't believe in them; you can tell them that it is true.

'Our journey went well until we reached the Bad Mountain. It is very high and is covered with a great forest of pines and holly. We had rested below it for a whole day, in a black tent. When night came, two of us said: "The sky is clear, the moon is bright: we ought to cross over the Bad Mountain in the cool of the night. Tomorrow will be hot, it will be a weary climb." "No," said the others, "night is for wild beasts. Men should only travel by day." So, we were not in agreement. The first two insisted. They took their staves, put their packs on their backs and set off. You can see how bad that was. When pilgrims have said, "Let's travel together," they should stick together.

'At the first light of dawn we also set off. There were only three of us now. When we were just at the top of the Bad Mountain, "Tsong Kaba!" I cried, "Look, I've found a staff!" One of my companions looked at it and said, "It's Lobzan's." We examined it carefully and recognised it. "Well," we said,

"That's what happens when you travel at night. You drop something and can't find it in the dark."

'We went on. After a short steep climb we reached the flat top of the mountain. Then we all gave a shout of horror; there at our feet were another staff, the torn remains of a lama's costume, pieces of human flesh and broken half-gnawed bones. Torn grass and loose earth showed that a great struggle had taken place. We realised immediately that wild beasts, tigers perhaps, or wolves, had eaten our two travelling companions. I stood a moment as if stunned in the midst of this horrible spectacle, then I began to weep like a child. Full of horror, we went down the other side of the Bad Mountain. From then on we travelled in sadness and in silence. But when we came across some black tents, we told the herdsmen of the terrible fate of our companions, and to tell the story was a relief.

'Three moons after leaving Lhasa we arrived at the frontiers of China. There we separated; the two lamas from Amdo went north again, towards their homeland; but I crossed the Wall of Ten Thousand Li and entered the province of Ssetchouan. Some days later, I encountered a troop of players at an inn. All night long we sang, we drank rice wine and we talked nonsense.

'"In this land of Ssetchouan," said the head of the troop, "there are no lamas; what is the use of that red gown and that yellow hat?"

'"You're talking sense," I answered. "In a land of lamas it's fine to be a lama; but in a land of actors, one must be an actor. Will you take me in your troop?"

'"Bravo, bravo," shouted everyone. "Now you're one of us." And at these words they all bowed deeply, to which I responded by putting out my tongue and scratching my ear, which is the Tibetan form of greeting. To begin with it was all meant as a joke, but when I thought how little of my travel allowance I had left, I began to take it seriously. The head of the troop and I came to an agreement, and I was enrolled as an actor.

'Next day I packed up my religious clothes and put on secular ones. As my memory had been thoroughly trained by the study of prayers, I found it easy to learn my parts and in a few days I was a good actor. For over a year we toured the province of Ssetchouan and then the troop decided to move on to Yunnan. I was unwilling to accompany them, because I should be too far from my country, the Three Valleys. So they gave me a goodbye party and I made my way slowly towards my native land. Wherever I passed, I stopped for a few days and gave one-man shows. I was no longer an actor, I was an entertainer.

'I made a fair amount of money, for it is always best to work on one's own. I was able to appear in the streets of my village mounted on a fine donkey I had bought at Lantchow; moreover I had twelve ounces of silver in my purse. I gave a few performances to my fellow villagers, who were amazed at my skill. But I soon had to give up my profession of entertainer.

'One evening when the family had gathered together to hear me tell stories about Tibet, my old mother was silent and her face looked deeply sad; and then I saw that great tears had come into her eyes.

'"Mother," I said, "why are you crying? There is nothing sad about my story."

'"Your story," she answered, "is to me neither sad nor merry; it strikes my ears without reaching my heart. What makes me sad and upset is to think that when you left home fourteen years ago to pay a visit to the land of the saints, you were dressed in the holy dress of a lama, and now you are a 'black' man and an entertainer." These words struck me to the heart. After a moment's silence I stood up and said firmly:

'"It is written in the holy doctrine: 'To honour thy father and thy mother is better than to serve the spirits of heaven and earth.' And so, mother, tell your son what he must do, and he will obey with respect."

'"Take off those secular clothes," said my mother, "cut off those locks of hair and return to the family of saints." I had no words to answer; I bowed three times to the ground as a sign of submission. When a mother speaks, one must obey; filial piety is the basis of all good doctrine. When I translated for you the ten great commandments of Jehovah, I noticed that the fourth said: "Honour thy father and thy mother."

'The following day I again put on my lama's clothing and a few days later I set out for Kounboum, where I am working to achieve perfection.'

Sandara's final words undoubtedly deserved to be received with a great burst of laughter. However we had to contain ourselves and bite our lips; we had had some experience of the fact that, in spite of his great zeal for perfection, he had not yet made much progress in patience and gentleness. When we had heard this account of Sandara's adventures, it was easy to understand why he always showed a great partiality for the Chinese and their way of life. The rules left by Tsong Kaba forbid the use of garlic, of spirits and of smoking tobacco. Garlic is forbidden because it is improper to appear before an image of Buddha with stinking breath which may taint even the perfume of the incense itself; spirits are forbidden because they cloud the reason and incite the passions; tobacco because it encourages laziness and wastes the precious moments which should be devoted to the study of prayers and doctrine. Despite these very sensible prohibitions, the lamas, who in principle were all trying like Sandara to achieve perfection, were quite liable to smoke, get drunk and season their barley flour with garlic. But it all took place secretly and unknown to the police. Sandara was the organiser and go-between of the Chinese pedlars, who dealt in the forbidden goods. He made arrangements for their distribution, in exchange for which he received some slight financial benefits.

A few days after the Flower Festival we returned to our Tibetan studies with determination. Sandara came each morning to work with us. We embarked on a summary of the Bible story, from the creation of the world until the missionary journeys of the Apostles. We cast this in the form of a dialogue. The two speakers were a lama of Jehovah and a lama of Buddha. Sandara carried out his part of the task in a purely mercenary spirit. The inclinations that he had shown at first at Tang Keou Eul, his signs of the cross, his interest in the Christian doctrine, had been mere play-acting. Religious ideas had no longer any hold on his hard greedy heart. He had brought back from his long residence in China a captious cynicism which he often liked to exhibit. In his opinion, all religion was an industry invented by the clever for the exploitation of fools. Virtue was a meaningless word, and the man to be respected was the one who had enough skill to survive better than others.

In spite of these sceptical and irreligious opinions, Sandara could not help admiring Christianity. He was particularly struck by the sequence of historic events which we made him translate for us. It all sounded so much more authentic to him than the fables which filled the Buddhist books; he sometimes admitted it, as if surprised out of the usual role of cynic which he kept up in front of us. When he was with other lamas he was more at his ease: he told everybody that on questions of religious doctrine we could show a trick or two to all the Living Buddhas.

It was not long before we found that we had created something of a sensation in the lamasery; there was much talk of the two lamas of Jehovah and of the new doctrine that they taught; of how we never prostrated ourselves before Buddha; how we recited prayers three times a day which were not in Tibetan; how we spoke a private language that no one understood, but could converse with others in Tartar, Chinese and some Tibetan. This was more than enough to arouse curiosity amongst the lamas. We had visitors daily, and religious matters were always the topic of conversation. Amongst all these lamas we found not one who had the sceptical turn of mind of Sandara the Bearded; they all seemed to be genuinely religious and sincere; there were even many who were real seekers after truth; they came again and again to ask us to teach them about our holy religion.

The teaching method we had adopted was purely historical, omitting all those elements which might give rise to contentious argument. We simply gave them a short account of our religion, leaving them to draw their own conclusions and comparisons with Buddhism. Proper names and precise dates made more impression on them than reasons, however logical; when they knew by heart the names of Jesus, Jerusalem, Pontius Pilate, the date of four thousand years after the creation of the world and the names of the twelve Apostles, they had no more doubts about the mystery of the Redemption and the preaching in the Gospels. The sequence of events in the Old and New Testaments were for them a demonstration of their truth. In any case the mysteries and the miracles themselves never presented any difficulty to them.

All the experience of our long journey and especially of our stay at Kounboum convinced us that it is through teaching and not controversy that one must work for the conversion of the unbeliever. Argument can reduce an adversary to silence, humiliate him even, anger him sometimes, convince him never.

When Jesus Christ instructed his Apostles, he told them: *Ite, docete omnes gentes,* and this does not mean 'Go and argue with all nations'. In our own day, two schools of philosophy, one following the steps of Descartes and the other of Lamennais, have long argued the question as to whether paganism is a crime or an error; in our opinion it is neither one nor the other, but simply the result of ignorance. The mind of the pagan is in darkness; show him a light and the darkness is gone; he needs no Cartesian nor Lamennaisian imputations; he simply needs instruction.

This keenness of the lamas to come and visit us and especially their interest in Christianity finally made Sandara jealous and put his nose out of joint. He became uncivil; after giving us our Tibetan lesson as curtly as he could he retired for the rest of the day into a rude and disgruntled silence. If we happened to ask him politely for the Tibetan word for something or an explanation of some sentences in the dialogues, he would not deign to reply. When this happened we usually turned to our neighbour, the young medical student who was always so friendly and keen to help. Although he was not much of a Tibetan scholar he was very valuable to us. His simplicity and straightforwardness made it possible to ask him many questions about various practices of the lamas, and in return for this we did our very best to satisfy his desire to learn about the Christian religion. Unlike Sandara he was full of respect for the truths we explained to him, but his shy irresolute nature prevented him from breaking with Buddhism. He wanted to be both a good Christian and a devout Buddhist; he prayed in turn to Tsong Kaba and Jehovah; and he was sometimes naive enough to invite us to take part in his religious practices.

One day he suggested that we should all set off next day on a pious expedition in aid of all travellers.

'We have never heard of such a religious practice,' we said. 'Could you give us some explanation?'

'Well, you know how travellers have to take steep and difficult paths. Sometimes these travellers are holy lamas on a pilgrimage: now it often happens that they can no longer go on because they are exhausted; so we are going to help them by sending them horses.'

'Yes, that is a fine thing to do,' we said, 'and full of Christian charity: but remember that we poor travellers are not at the moment in a position to participate in such a generous act; for as you know we have only one horse and one little mule, which are now resting so that they can carry us on our journey to Tibet.'

'Tsong Kaba!' cried our stammering friend, then he clapped his hands in jubilation and burst into a peal of endless laughter.

'Why are you laughing? We are telling the truth, we have only one horse and one little mule.' When his laughter had subsided a little,

'That's not it,' he said. 'You don't understand this religious practice. What we send the travellers are *paper* horses.' And saying these words he ran to his cell. We might well have laughed in our turn on learning that Buddhist charity consisted in giving paper horses to travellers. But we kept straight faces, for we had made it a rule never to laugh at the practices of the lamas. A moment later our friend reappeared, holding some pieces of paper on each of which was printed a picture of a horse, saddled and bridled and galloping at full speed.

'There,' he said, 'those are the horses we send the travellers. Tomorrow we shall climb a high mountain thirty *li* from the lamasery; we'll spend the day saying prayers and sending off the horses.'

'How do you send them?'

'Very easy. After saying certain prayers we take a packet of horses and throw them in the air; the wind takes them; and by the power of Buddha they are changed into real horses and go off to find the travellers.' We told our young friend frankly what we thought of this practice and explained the reasons that prevented us from taking part. He seemed to appreciate everything that we told him; but that did not prevent him from spending most of the night duplicating on a press an enormous quantity of horses.

Next day before dawn he set off with some colleagues who were, like himself, full of pious feelings for the poor travellers. They set off carrying a tent, a cooking pot and some food. For the whole morning it blew a gale, which only abated towards midday; the sky then became overcast and dark, and the snow began to fall in large flakes. We waited impatiently for our friend's return; as night fell the poor fellow came home, shivering with cold and exhaustion. We made him rest awhile in our cell and gave him tea with milk and some rolls fried in butter.

'It was a terrible day,' he said.

'Yes, here the wind blew pretty hard.'

'I think it must have been nothing compared with what we experienced on the top of the mountain; the tent, the pot, everything was blown away in a whirlwind; we had to lie flat so as not to be blown away also.'

'How tiresome that you lost your tent and your cooking-pot.'

'True, that was a misfortune. But on the other hand the weather was excellent for sending horses to travellers. When

we saw that it was going to snow we sent them all off together and the wind carried them to the four parts of the world. If we had waited longer the snow would have wet them and they would have stuck to the sides of the mountain.' So after all this young man was not so discontented with his day.

The twenty-fifth day of each moon is devoted to sending horses to poor travellers. This practice is not general; it is left to the piety of the individual. The twenty-eighth is reserved for another form of religious exercise, in which all lamas are required to take part. On the twenty-seventh our stammering friend warned us about it, saying, 'Tonight we may prevent you from sleeping; we have to attend night-prayers.' We did not take much notice of this warning. We thought that during the night the lamas would recite prayers in their cells, as often happened. We therefore went to bed at our normal time and fell soundly asleep as usual.

As our friend had foretold, our sleep did not remain peaceful for long. First we seemed to be dreaming that we could hear, borne on the air, the sounds of a great multitude singing together. These confused and meaningless voices seemed to become gradually louder and more distinct. We woke, and heard the chant of lamas at prayer. We dressed in a flash and came out into the yard. It was lit by the pale reflection of a light that seemed to come from above. We saw old Akayé squatting in a corner, telling his beads.

'Akayé,' we said, 'what is that strange sound?'

'Those are the night-prayers. If you want to see, climb on the roof.' A ladder had been placed against the wall; we ran up it and a strange sight soon met our eyes. The flat roofs of all the houses were lit by red lanterns hanging from long poles. All the lamas, dressed in their ceremonial robes and wearing their yellow mitres, were sitting on the roofs of their houses chanting prayers in a slow even tone. On the roof of our house we found the stammerer, the Kitat lama and his *chabi* entirely absorbed in their devotions. We were careful not to disturb them and simply looked and listened. The countless lanterns, making a strange reddish glow, the lamasery buildings dimly reflecting the flickering light, the four thousand voices blending together in the air in a mighty concert, punctuated from time to time by conches and trumpets, all this made an impressive scene which filled the soul with a kind of awe.

After watching this strange spectacle for a while we came down into the yard, where Akayé still sat as before.

'Well,' he said, 'did you see the night-prayer ceremony?'

'Yes, but we don't know its significance. Would it be too much trouble to give us a short explanation?'

'Not at all; these prayers were introduced to drive away devils. Previously we were much afflicted by them. They made the animals sick and poisoned the cows' milk; thcy upset the lamas' cells; they even dared to mingle with the choirs as they sang the common prayers, causing confusion, and at night they gathered in great companies in the ravine and caused much terror by uttering cries and groans so strange that no man could imitate them. A lama full of wisdom and holiness invented night-prayers, and since then the devils have almost disappeared from these parts. A few still come from time to time; but they do not do the damage that they used to.'

'Akayé,' we asked him, 'have you by chance ever seen any devils?'

'Oh no, never, and I am sure that you haven't seen any either.'

'Why do you say that?'

'Because devils only appear to bad lamas. Good ones can't see them.' At this moment, the chants of the lamas on the roofs ceased; and suddenly the trumpets, the drums and the conches sounded three times. Then the lamas howled all together like wild beasts—and the ceremony was over. The lanterns went out and silence returned. We wished old Akayé goodnight, and resumed our night's sleep.

We had been in residence at Kounboum for more than three months, enjoying the friendship of the Buddhist monks and the goodwill of the authorities. But for some time we had been in flagrant breach of one of the basic rules of the lamasery. Strangers who were passing through Kounboum, or who were staying only a short time, were allowed to dress as they wished. But anyone who was attached to the lamasery or residing there any length of time was obliged to wear the sacred dress of the lamas, that is, the red robe, the short sleeveless dalmatic which leaves the arms bare, the red scarf and the yellow mitre. They were very strict about this rule of uniformity. The Grand Lama in charge of disciplinary matters sent us one fine day a kind of beadle, to invite us officially to strict observance of the statutes. We made reply to the head disciplinary lama to the effect that, not being of the religion of Buddha, we could not adopt the sacred dress of the lamas without betraying our faith; but that, as we did not wish to be the cause of the slightest trouble in the lamasery, we were perfectly willing to leave if it were not possible to grant us a dispensation in the matter of costume.

Some days passed without any further development in this unfortunate affair. During this time Samdadchiemba arrived with the three camels which he had been grazing in a valley of the Koukou Noor. As we might have to move, he could not have arrived at a better time. Then the envoy of the authorities made a second appearance. He told us that the regulation was inflexible, and that it was much regretted that our 'sublime and holy religion' did not allow us to observe it. He added that we would be most welcome to remain in the neighbourhood of the lamasery and that in consequence we were invited to fix our residence at Tchogortan, where we could wear whatever costume we pleased.

We had often heard about the little lamasery of Tchogortan, which was, as it were, the country house of the Faculty of Medicine. It was at most half an hour's journey from Kounboum. The Grand Lamas and the students of medicine went there every year towards the end of summer and spent about a fortnight collecting medicinal herbs in the surrounding mountains. For the rest of the year most of the houses were empty; there were only a few hermit-lamas, who had hollowed out their cells in the steepest parts of the mountain.

The envoy's proposal suited us perfectly, for spring was at hand. Winter in town, spring in the country, it couldn't be better! During the three months we had spent at Kounboum we had learned a good deal about the rules of courtesy. We therefore bought a *khata* and a little dish of raisins and paid a visit to the administrator of Tchogortan. He received us most affably and promised to give orders immediately for the preparation of a suitable dwelling for us. After inviting old Akayé, the Kitat lama and the stammerer to a sumptuous farewell dinner, we loaded our baggage on the camels and went off merrily towards the little lamasery.

[4]
TCHOGORTAN

It took only half an hour to move our belongings from Kounboum to Tchogortan. For some time we made our way along the barren flanks of a high mountain, then descended into a great valley through which ran a stream whose banks were still edged with ice. The country looked fairly fertile in pasture, but the climate was so cold that everything was extremely backward. Although it was May the grass had only sprouted sufficiently to give the valley a tinge of yellow.

A lama with a red chubby face came to meet us and led us to the quarters which the administrator had had prepared for us. We found ourselves in a large room which until the previous day had housed some small calves which were too tender to follow their mothers on the mountains. A great effort had been made to clean the place up, but without complete success, for here and there numerous traces still remained of the previous tenants; however, we had been allotted the best that the lamasery had to offer.

Tchogortan was, as already mentioned, the country seat of the Faculty of Medicine; the situation was most attractive, especially in summer. The lamas' quarters were tucked under a lofty cliff and were shaded by ancient trees, the haunts of kites and crows. A few steps below the houses ran an ample stream, dammed in places by the lamas for their *tchukor* or prayer-mills. At the bottom of the valley and on the neighbouring hillsides there were the black tents of Si Fan herdsmen and some flocks of goats and herds of yaks. The steep rocky mountain under which the lamasery was built was inhabited by five contemplative hermits who, like eagles, had chosen to build their eyries in the highest and most inaccessible places: some had hewn their refuges out of the sheer rock; the others had constructed wooden cells attached to the mountainside like outsized swallows' nests; wooden stakes in the rock made rungs for climbing up and down. One of these hermits had given up the world completely and had no such means of communication with his fellow men; he had suspended a sack from a long rope, and into this the lamas and the local herdsmen put their charitable gifts.

We were able to meet these contemplative lamas on a number of occasions, but we never discovered exactly what they were contemplating up there in their eyries. They themselves were quite incapable of explaining it clearly; they told us that they had taken up that way of life because they had read in their books that very holy lamas had lived in that way. On the whole they were quite harmless: they had simple, peaceful natures, by no means wild; they spent their time praying, and when they were tired of that they found relaxation in innocent slumber.

Apart from these five who inhabited the rocks above, there were a few lamas who acted as guardians of the empty lamasery buildings below. There was no high-flying mysticism about these; on the contrary their feet were firmly planted on the ground: they were cowmen. In the large building where we lodged there were two hefty lamas who spent their lives in the poetic task of looking after some twenty head of cattle; they tended the calves, milked the cows, churned the butter and pressed the cheeses. As they went about these daily tasks there

seemed little room in their lives for prayer or for contemplation; when they appealed to Tsong Kaba it was always because the bullocks were unruly, the cows wouldn't be milked or the calves had escaped and were frisking across the valley. Our arrival amongst them provided a welcome break in the monotony of their pastoral lives. They sometimes came to see us in our room, and examined our small travelling library with the shy respectful curiosity which simple unlettered folk always show towards any products of the intellect. If by chance we were writing when they arrived, their beasts and their dairy were forgotten: they stood motionless for hours, their eyes fixed on our quill pens which sped over the paper leaving marks which fascinated them by their delicacy and their strangeness.

We enjoyed this little lamasery of Tchogortan much more than we expected. We did not miss Kounboum in the very least, any more than a prisoner misses his cell when he has been set free. We too felt liberated. We were no longer under the iron sway of Sandara the Bearded, that hard pitiless master who, along with his lessons in Tibetan, had apparently taken on the self-imposed task of training us in patience and humility. In our determination to learn we put up with all this bad treatment, but we used our departure from Kounboum as an opportunity to get rid of this fellow, who like a foul leech had clung to our lives for five whole months. In any case we had now reached a stage in our Tibetan studies when we no longer needed a teacher at our elbows: we could go ahead alone, without a pilot.

Our working hours were spent in revising and analysing our dialogues, and in translating a short Tibetan text called *The Forty-two Articles of Buddha's Teachings*. We possessed a magnificent edition of this in four languages, Tibetan, Mongolian, Mandchou and Chinese. With this as an aid we could be independent of instruction from lamas. When the Tibetan baffled us, we only had to consult the other versions, which were in languages with which we were fairly familiar.

This book, attributed to Chakya Mouni, is a collection of precepts and maxims designed to encourage mankind, and especially lamas, to follow the paths of virtue. In order to give the reader an idea of the Buddhist moral code we quote below some extracts from this work, which is regarded as an authority by the lama fraternity.

THE FORTY-TWO ARTICLES OF BUDDHA'S TEACHINGS

I

Buddha, the Supreme Being, revealing his doctrine, spoke these words: 'There are for mankind ten kinds of actions called good, and ten kinds of actions called bad. Of the ten bad actions, three are of the body, four of the word and three of the will. The three of the body are murder, theft and impurity. The four of the word are speech which sows discord, insulting oaths, shameless lies and hypocrisy. The three of the will are envy, anger and depraved thoughts.'

II

Buddha, revealing his doctrine, spoke these words: 'The evil-doer who persecutes the righteous man is like the fool who throws his head back and spits in the sky; his spittle cannot soil the heavens but falls back on himself. He is also like the man who throws dust against the wind; it cannot soil the men at whom he throws it, and it returns against himself. You shall not persecute righteous men, or disaster will destroy you.'

III

Buddha, revealing his doctrine, spoke these words: 'Under Heaven, there are twenty difficult things:
To be poor and in want, and to give: that is difficult.
To be rich and eminent, and to study doctrine: that is difficult.
Having sacrificed one's life, the moment of death: that is difficult.
To be granted to see the prayers of Buddha: that is difficult.
To be blessed enough to be born into the world of Buddha: that is difficult.
To compromise with the pleasures of the flesh and yet to be freed from one's passions: that is difficult.
To see something desirable and not to desire it: that is difficult.
Not to desire what brings riches and honour: that is difficult.
To be insulted and not be angry: that is difficult.
In the whirlwind of affairs, to remain calm: that is difficult.
To study long and deeply: that is difficult.

Not to look down on a man who has not studied: that is difficult.

To remove pride from one's heart: that is difficult.

To find a righteous and clever teacher: that is difficult.

To penetrate the secrets of nature and attain deep knowledge: that is difficult.

Not to envy the prosperity of others: that is difficult.

To leave the paths of righteousness and yet to attain wisdom: that is difficult.

To persuade men to follow their conscience: that is difficult.

To keep one's heartbeat always steady: that is difficult.

To speak no slander: that is difficult.'

IV

'The man who desires riches is like a child who tastes honey on the tip of a sharp knife: he has hardly time to savour it before he feels the pain of the cut on his tongue.'

V

'There is no passion stronger than the desire of the flesh. Happily, there is only one such passion, for if there were two there would not be one man in the whole universe who would be a seeker after truth.'

VI

Buddha spoke these words in the presence of all the Charmanas (holy men): 'Beware of looking on women . . . If you are amongst them, let it be as if none were there. Beware of speaking with women . . . If you speak with them, watch over your heart; your behaviour must be beyond reproach, and you must say to yourselves: "We who are Charmanas, living in this corrupt world, must be like the water-lily, which remains pure in the midst of muddy water."'

VII

'The man who follows the path of virtue must liken the passions to a grass that will burn when a great fire reaches it. A man who wishes to preserve his virtue should flee as the passions approach.'

VIII

A Charmana who spent whole nights singing prayers one day showed by the sadness and weakness of his voice that he was greatly discouraged and unwilling to continue. Buddha called him to him and said:

'When you lived at home, what did you do?'

'I did nothing but play the guitar.'

'If the strings of the guitar became loose, what happened?'

'I got no sound.'

'If the strings became too tight, what happened?'

'The sounds were too sharp.'

'When the strings were perfectly adjusted between tight and loose, what happened?'

'All the sounds were in perfect tune.'

Buddha then spoke as follows: 'So is it with the study of the doctrine. When you have learned to master your heart, and control its movements in rhythm and harmony, you will arrive at the understanding of truth.'

IX

Buddha put this question to the Charmanas:

'How long is the span of a man's life?'

They answered: 'No longer than a few days.'

Buddha told them as follows: 'You have not yet attained the understanding of the doctrine.' Then, turning to one of the Charmanas, he said: 'How long is the span of a man's life?'

The Charmana answered: 'No longer than it takes to eat a meal.'

Buddha then said: 'Away with you: you also have not attained the understanding of the doctrine.' Then turning to another Charmana, he asked the question: 'How long is the span of a man's life?' and the Charmana answered: 'No longer than it takes to utter a breath.'

When he had spoken these words, the Buddha said: 'That is good. You have arrived at the understanding of the doctrine.'

X

'The man who, in the path of virtue, seeks to pluck up his passions by the roots may be likened to one who tells the beads of a chaplet. If he takes them one by one he soon comes to the end; tackling one's faults one by one, one reaches perfection.'

XI

'The Charmana who follows the path of virtue is like the yak which with a full load on its back walks through a deep quagmire; it dares look neither to right nor left, hoping always that the mud will end, and that it will reach a place of rest. The Charmana, though his passions are more fearsome than such a quagmire, will certainly reach the state of beatitude, provided he keeps his eyes fixed on virtue.'

These few extracts will suffice to give an idea of the content and style of this book, which is respected both by the bonzes and by the lamas. It was brought from India to China in the sixty-fifth year of the Christian era, at a time when Buddhism was beginning to reach the Celestial Empire. The Chinese Chronicles describe the event in the following manner:

'In the twenty-fourth year of the reign of Tchao Wang, of the Tchow dynasty [i.e. 1029 BC], on the eighth day of the fourth moon, a light, appearing in the south-west, lit up the royal palace. The king, seeing this splendour, questioned the sooth-sayers. They showed him the books in which it was written that this miracle signified that in the West a great saint had been born, and that, in one thousand years' time, his religion would reach the Celestial Empire.

'In the fifty-third year of the reign of Mou Wang, which was the year of the black monkey [951 BC], on the fifteenth day of the second moon, Buddha became manifest [i.e. died]. One thousand and thirteen years afterwards, in the reign of Ming Ti of the Han Dynasty, in the seventh year of the reign of Young Ping [64 AD], on the fifteenth day of the first moon, the king saw in a dream a man the colour of gold, shining like the sun and over ten feet tall. This man having entered the king's palace said: "My religion will spread through these regions."

'On the following day the king consulted the sages. One of them, named Fou Y, opening the chronicles of the time of the Emperor Tchao Wang of the Tchow dynasty, pointed out the connection between the king's dream and the account in the chronicles. The king studied the ancient books, and finding the relevant passages was filled with joy. He then sent the officials Tsa In and Tsin King and the scholar Wang Tsun and fifteen others to the West to collect information about the doctrine of Buddha.

'In the tenth year [67 AD] Tsa In and the others having arrived in central India, at the house of the great Youei Tchi, met Kas'yamatanga and Tcho Fa Lan, and obtained a statue of Buddha and books in the Fan language [that is, in Sanscrit], and brought them on a white horse as far as the city of Lo Yang. Kas'yamatanga and Tcho Fa Lan paid a visit to the emperor clad in monkish garb and were lodged in the Honh Lon Sse, also known as the Sse Pin Sse or Strangers' Inn.

'In the eleventh year [68 AD] the emperor ordered the construction of the Monastery of the White Horse, outside the Yang Men Gate, to the west of the city of Lo Yang. Matanga there translated the *Holy Book of the Forty-Two Articles*. Six years later, Tsa In and Tcho Fa Lan converted some Tao Sse to Buddhism. Then, rising up into space, they recited the following verses to the king:

'"The fox is not of the race of the lion. The lamp is not as bright as the sun and the moon. The lake cannot be compared to the sea; the hills cannot be compared to the high mountains.

'"The cloud of prayers spreads across the face of the earth, its blessed dew fertilises the seeds of happiness, and as the holy rituals work wondrous changes everywhere, all the nations shall walk according to the laws of renewal." '

We devoted our first days at Tchogortan entirely to the translation of Buddha's book; but we soon had to give up part of our time to grazing our beasts. We began to notice that when they returned each evening they were still hungry, and that instead of putting on weight they were getting thinner each day. The reason was that Samdadchiemba was not bothering to lead them to good grazing. He would drive them a short distance and then let them loose on a barren hillside; after which he would go to sleep happily in the sunshine or go off for tea and a chat in the black tents. Our remonstrances did no good: he went on as before; his easy-going character remained unaffected. We had no alternative but to become herdsmen ourselves.

Indeed it was impossible to remain obstinately and exclusively men of letters whilst everything around us seemed to invite us to share the life of this pastoral people. The Si Fan, or

Eastern Tibetans, are nomads like the Tartars, and devote their lives exclusively to keeping their flocks and herds; however, they do not live, like the Tartar tribes, in yurts covered with felt. Their large black canvas tents are usually hexagonal; the interior is free of any tent pole; the six corners are pegged at the bottom; at the top ropes travel horizontally on to poles, and then dip to ground level where they are fastened to rings. With their odd pattern of poles and ropes these tents are like enormous spiders on long thin legs with fat bellies resting on the ground. They are not a patch on the Tartar yurts; they are neither warmer nor stronger than an ordinary travelling tent. They are icy cold inside, and easily capsize in strong winds.

Yet in certain respects the Si Fan seem to be more advanced than the Tartars: they show some leanings towards the sedentary life. When they have chosen a camp site they build a four to five foot wall around it. Inside their tents they build strong stoves of good workmanship. Yet they put down no roots in the land they occupy; without any good reason they strike camp and on leaving knock down the walls they have made and take the biggest stones with them, as part of their furniture, as it were. Their flocks consist of sheep, goats and yaks; they have fewer horses than the Tartars, but the ones they have are stronger and of a better breed; any camels we saw usually belonged to Tartars.

The long-haired ox is called *tchang mao niou* by the Chinese, *yak* by the Tibetans, *sarligue* by the Tartars and *grunting ox* by the European naturalists. Its grunt is in fact louder and longer than that of a pig. It is shorter and squatter than the ordinary ox; its coat is long, fine and glossy, the coat under the belly reaching to the ground; its hooves are small and crotched like a goat's; it can climb mountains and perch over precipices. When frisky it puts up its tail and waves it: there is a big tuft at the end. Its meat is excellent eating, the cow's milk is delicious and the butter beyond all praise. Malte-Brun says that the milk smells of tallow; in matters of taste one can't argue, but we think that the benefit of the doubt should be ours for surely the learned geographer had fewer opportunities of drinking milk in the black tents and enjoying its flavour.

In the Si Fan herds there are a few 'yellow' oxen, which are of the same breed as we have in France; but they are usually rather poor specimens. The calves cross-bred from a yak cow and a 'yellow' bull are called *karba* and they are seldom much use. The yak cows are so bad-tempered and difficult to milk that they have to be given their calf to lick during the process. Otherwise they would not allow a drop to be taken.

One day one of the cowman-lamas who lived in our building came with a long face to tell us that one of the cows had given birth during the night, and that unfortunately the calf was a *karba*. It died during the course of the day, and the cowman quickly skinned the poor beast and stuffed it with hay. We were at first mystified by this, since our man was hardly the sort to keep specimens in a glass case. When he had finished we noticed that it had neither feet nor head, and we then decided that he had simply made a pillow for himself. However we were quite wrong, and the mystery was only solved next morning when he went off to milk his cow. When we saw him set off with a milk-pail in one hand and the dummy calf under the other arm, we couldn't help following him. He first put the dummy in front of the cow, then set to work to milk her. The cow stared with big eyes at the little one, slowly lowered her head, sniffed it, sneezed several times over it, then began to lick it tenderly. We were really upset to see this; we felt that whoever had invented this parody of nature's most touching sight must have been a monster. However a touch of the absurd cooled our indignation a little: the cow licked her calf to such an extent that one day the belly came unsewn; the hay came out and the cow calmly began to chew her unexpected meal. The Si Fan nomads can easily be distinguished from the Tartars by their more expressive faces and their more energetic natures; the face is less flat, their movements are easy and lively, in contrast to the heaviness of the Tartars. Fun and games, noisy songs and roars of laughter continually fill their camps with cheerfulness; but with all their love of gaiety and pleasure they are of a warlike disposition and dauntless courage. They have thus a profound contempt for Chinese authority; although they are counted as a tributary race they obstinately refuse both obedience and tribute to the emperor. Some of their tribes even harass the frontiers of the empire continually with brigandage, and the mandarins dare not stand up to them. The Si Fan are good horsemen, but not as strong as the Tartars. The care of their flocks leaves them time for crafts, in which the coats of their yaks and the wool of their sheep are put to good use. They can weave coarse cloth, from which they make tents and clothes. When they meet together round a pot of milky tea, they love, like the Tartars, to talk for many hours together, telling stories of lamas and of brigands. Their memories are stored with anecdotes and local traditions; you only have to get them going, and there is an endless repertoire of stories and legends.

One day, whilst our camels were quietly grazing on some prickly bushes at the bottom of the valley, we went for shelter against the north wind to a small tent from which thick smoke was rising. Inside, an old man was on his hands and knees blowing at a heap of *argols* that he had just put on his fire. We sat down on a yak skin. The old man sat cross-legged and held out his hand. We gave him our bowls which he filled with tea and said: '*Temou chi*, drink in peace.' Then he looked at us both in turn with a worried expression.

'*Aka*, brother,' we said, 'it is our first visit to your tent.'

'I am old,' he said, 'my legs will not carry me; otherwise I should have gone to Tchogortan to offer you my *khata*! From what the herdsmen of the black tents tell me, you are from the furthest parts of the Western Heavens.'

'Yes, our country is very far from here.'

'Are you from the kingdom of the Sambas or of the Pobas?'

'Neither; we are from the kingdom of the French.'

'Ah, you are Frambas? I had never heard of them. The West is so big! There are so many kingdoms! But after all, what does it matter? We are all of the same family, are we not?'

'Yes, indeed. All men are brothers, whatever kingdom they come from.'

'Yes, of course what you say is right, all men are brothers. But they say that on earth there are three great families of men: we Westerners are all of the same great Tibetan family: that's all I meant.'

'*Aka*, do you know where the three great families come from?'

'This is what I have learned from the lamas who know about the ancient world: in the beginning there was but one man on the earth; he had neither house nor tent, for in those days the winter was not cold and the summer was not hot; the wind did not blow and there was no rain or snow. Tea grew wild on the mountains and there were no wild beasts for the flocks to fear. This man had three sons, who lived long with him feeding on milk and fruit. When he was very old, the man died. The three sons discussed together what should be done with their father's body; they could not agree, for each one had a different opinion. One wanted to put it into a coffin and bury it, the second wanted to burn it whilst the third wanted to leave it on the top of a mountain. They therefore decided to divide their father's body in three, to take each a part and to separate. The eldest had the head and the arms as his share; he was the ancestor of the great Chinese family. This is why his descendants are famous for their skill in arts and crafts, for their intelligence and for the cunning tricks and stratagems they know how to play. The youngest, who was the founder of the Tibetan family, had the breast as his share. So the Tibetans are full of heart and courage: they are not afraid of death, and amongst them there have always been indomitable tribes. The middle son, from whom the Tartar peoples are descended, was left with the lower part of his father's body. Since you have travelled far in the Eastern wildernesses, you will know that the Tartars are simple and shy, they have neither head nor heart; their only talent is to stay firm on their stirrups and upright in their saddles. That is how the lamas explain the origin of the three great families on the earth, and that is why the Tartars are good horsemen, the Tibetans good soldiers and the Chinese good traders.'

In gratitude to the old man for his interesting chronicle, we in our turn told him the story of the first man, the flood and Noah and his three sons. He was at first very pleased to find that his three families came into our story; but he was most surprised when we said that the Chinese, the Tartars and the Tibetans were all sons of Shem and that moreover there were innumerable races which made up the two other families of Ham and Japheth. He stared at us wide-eyed and open-mouthed, shaking his head from time to time, with an expression which seemed to say: who would have thought that the world was so large?

Time had passed quickly during this archaeological session; we said goodbye to the old man, and drove our camels home to Tchogortan. We tethered them to a stake outside the door and went into our small kitchen to prepare supper.

We were much better off for food here than at Kounboum. First of all, we could help ourselves to all the milk, curd, butter and cheese that we wanted. In addition we had made the marvellous discovery of a hunter in the neighbourhood. A few days after our arrival a man came into our room with a sack on his back, out of which he took a fine hare, and asked us if the *Goucho* (Lamas) of the Western Heavens ate the meat of wild animals.

'Indeed, yes,' we replied. 'A hare is very good eating. Don't you eat it?'

'We "black" men do, sometimes, but the lamas never. It is expressly forbidden in the prayer-books for them to eat black meat.'

'The holy law of Jehovah does not forbid it.'

'Then keep this beast, and if you like I will bring you as many as you want every day; these hillsides are alive with them.'

At this point one of our local lamas happened to come into the room. At the sight of the hare still warm and bleeding on the floor at our feet, he exclaimed: 'Tsong Kaba! Tsong Kaba!' and recoiled in horror covering his eyes with his hands. After cursing the hunter, he asked us if we would dare eat that black meat. 'Why not?' we said, 'since it can hurt neither our body nor our soul.'

Thereupon we expounded a few moral precepts, easily proving that the eating of such meat was no obstacle, in itself, to the attainment of sainthood. The hunter was delighted at our words but the lama was struck dumb. All he could say was that as we were foreigners and followers of Jehovah there was no reason why we should not eat hare; but that he and his fellows must not, because if the Grand Lama heard that they were doing so, they would be expelled from the lamasery without mercy. Having proved our point, we turned to the hunter and asked him if he were serious when he said he could bring us as many hares as we wanted. When he said that he was, we told him that he could bring us one a day, but that we wished to pay him.

'Hares can't be sold in these parts. But if you won't accept them as a gift, you can give me the price of a shot for each one.' So with great generosity we agreed to pay him forty sapeks, or about four sous, every time he brought us a hare.

We made up our minds to eat hare for two reasons. First, for conscience's sake, to prevent the lamas from thinking that we were influenced by Buddhist prejudices. Second, for economy's sake, for a hare was very much cheaper than our insipid barley flour.

One day our tireless hunter brought us, instead of a hare, an enormous roedeer. This also was black meat and forbidden. Away with Buddhist superstition! we thought, and bought it for thirty sous (300 sapeks). For eight whole days our fire burned under it, and Samdadchiemba was a happy man.

For fear of becoming exclusively carnivorous, we did our best to include a vegetable element in our diet. In that wilderness it was not easy. However, by dint of trial and error we finally discovered some wild vegetables which, carefully prepared, were not to be despised. The reader will allow us to treat the matter in some detail. Its intrinsic interest may be small but it may possibly be of use to future travellers in the Tibetan wildernesses.

At the first signs of spring we found about an inch below ground great quantities of creeping roots, long and thin like couch-grass, from which grew a number of small tubercles, full of a starchy substance which was extraordinarily sweet to taste. These were most delicious when carefully washed and fried in butter. An alternative dish, no less remarkable than the first, was supplied by a plant which is very common in France but which has not yet received due appreciation: namely the small shoots of the bracken fern. If they are picked when still tender, before they become downy and whilst the first leaves are still unfurled, all that has to be done is to boil them in clean water and you have a dish of delicious asparagus. If we had any influence with the Minister of Agriculture we would recommend this precious plant strongly to his attention, as a plant which grows abundantly but uselessly on our mountains and in our forests. We would also recommend him the nettle—*urtica urens*—which in our opinion might with advantage replace spinach. We have tried it successfully more than once. Nettles should be picked when very young and the leaves still tender. Pull up the whole plant, with some of the root. To avoid getting stung, wrap the hands in a close-woven cloth. Once steeped in boiling water the nettle is harmless. In spite of its forbidding aspect, it has a most delicate flavour.

We enjoyed this splendid variety of diet for more than a month. Then our little tubercles became hollow and hard-skinned, the bracken was as hard as wood and the nettles, crowned with long white beards, were altogether forbidding. Later, when the season was well advanced, the fragrant wild strawberries on the mountains and the white mushrooms of the valley were honourable substitutes for the early vegetables. But we had to wait a long time for these delicacies; for in that area the cold is prolonged and vegetation very late in developing. During the whole of June snow still fell and the wind was so piercing that it would have been very foolish to leave off one's fur garments. About early July the sun began to be warm, and the rain fell in great downpours. As soon as the sky had cleared a little, warm mists rose from the ground in astonishing quantities. They ran along the hillsides and the valleys; then grew denser, floating a few feet above the ground, and finally became so thick that they shut out the daylight. When these mists had risen sufficiently they formed great clouds, the south wind rose and heavy rain began to fall again. Then the sky cleared once more and the ground-mists started to rise. These atmospheric revolutions lasted about a fortnight. All this time, the earth was as it were in a state of fermentation; the beasts remained lying down and we felt, in every limb, an indescribable sense of discomfort. The Si Fan call this the 'season of ground mists'.

As soon as this crisis was passed the grass in the valley grew fast and the mountains and hillsides were covered, as if by magic, with flowers and verdure. For our camels also it was a moment of rebirth. Their coats fell off completely in large pieces like rags. For some days they remained quite bare, as if shaven from head to tail. They were a hideous sight. When in the shade they shivered all over and at night we had to cover them with big felt carpets to keep out the cold. Four days later their coats began to grow again. At first came an extremely fine down, curly as lamb's wool. The grime and ugliness of their bare state disappeared, to be replaced by this beautiful new coat. After a fortnight the whole process was complete. At this point they attacked the pastures with great enthusiasm, to build up a reserve of fat for the forthcoming journey. To whet their appetites we had bought some sea-salt. Each morning, before sending them off into the valley, we gave them a good dose, and in the evening when they came back another, to help them chew the cud during the night and so dispose of the immense amount of fodder that they had pressed into their stomachs during the day.

The moulting of our camels had provided us with a large amount of hair, half of which we exchanged for some barley flour, and the rest we sought means of using ourselves. One of the lamas, a skilled ropemaker, made an excellent suggestion: he pointed out that during the long journey to Tibet we would need a good store of ropes to tie our baggage, and that camel-hair ropes, being the most supple, were the best for cold countries. We immediately accepted this most excellent advice. He gave us a few free lessons, and we set to work. It was not long before we learnt to twist the flock quite successfully and give it a shape that bore a fair resemblance to rope. Daily, as we went to watch our animals feeding, we tucked a big lump of camel hair under one arm, and as we walked we twisted the yarn which we would later work into rope in our workshop.

Samdadchiemba simply watched us work, with an occasional smile. Partly from laziness, partly from vanity, he abstained from participating. 'My holy fathers,' he said one day, 'how can men of your rank lower themselves to rope-making? Would it not be more proper to buy some ropes or to get a skilled artisan to make them?' We used this remark as a good opportunity to give our cameleer a good scolding. After reminding him that we were not in a position to behave like lords, and that economy was essential, we quoted the example of St Paul, who did not think it beneath his dignity to work with his hands, and so avoid living at the expense of the faithful. As soon as Samdadchiemba learned that St Paul had been at one and the same time tent-maker and apostle he abandoned both his laziness and his pride and set to work on the camel hair. To our amazement, we saw at once that he was a most skilful cord-maker, a fact that he had never revealed. He chose the finest hair and made bridles and halters for our horses with considerable mastery; and so of course we put him in charge and made him director-general of rope production.

The summer season brought a large number of visitors from Kounboum to Tchogortan; they came to take the country air and to rest from their studies. Our room then became a place of pilgrimage, for no one felt he could come to Tchogortan without paying a visit to the Lamas of the Western Heavens. Those who had been our particular friends and who had begun to learn about the Christian religion were drawn by motives other than curiosity; they wanted to hear more about the holy doctrine of Jehovah and consult us about any difficulties they had encountered. What inexpressible joy it was to us, to hear those Buddhist monks pronounce reverently the names of Jesus and Mary, and recite with piety the prayers that we had taught them! We feel confident that God will take into account these first steps of theirs on the road to salvation and will not fail to send shepherds to bring these poor lost sheep home to the fold.

Among the lamas who came on holiday to Tchogortan we noticed a large number of Tartars: they arrived carrying small tents which they put up in the valley, by the banks of the stream or on the most beautiful of the hills. For a few days they would abandon themselves to the joys of freedom and the nomadic life. Forgetting for a while the constraints of the lamasery, they recaptured the happiness of living in a tent in the midst of the wilderness. We saw them running and gambolling in the meadows like children, wrestling and playing games like those they used to play in their homeland. Their urge was so strong that they could not even bear to keep their tents in one place, and would move them three or four times a day; they sometimes even went off and left them; they loaded their cooking utensils and their full water-buckets on to their shoulders, and went off singing to brew up their tea on the top of some mountain, returning only at nightfall.

No less interesting than the Tartars was another type of lama which came to Tchogortan; they would arrive in large parties at dawn. They came with their robes kilted up to the knee and wicker baskets on their backs, and searched the valley and surrounding hillsides, not for strawberries or mushrooms but for the droppings which the Si Fan flocks left everywhere. Because of their trade we had nicknamed them 'dung-lamas' or more politely 'argol-lamas', from the Tartar word argol for the droppings of animals when they are dried and ready to be used as fuel. The lamas engaged in this trade were normally lazy undisciplined fellows who preferred wandering over the mountains to solitude and study; they were divided into several companies, each with a chief responsible for planning and accounts. Before leaving they each brought their contribution to a general collecting point situated under a hill or at the bottom of a ravine. There the raw material was carefully treated, by kneading and pressing into cakes which were then left in the sun to dry out completely; finally these cakes were piled up carefully on top of one another to form large heaps, over which they put a thick layer of dung to keep off the rain. When winter came, this fuel would be transported to Kounboum and there sold.

The quality and variety of fuels available to us favoured Europeans have no doubt made it unnecessary for us to carry out research into the properties of different *argols*. Not so the nomads and the herdsmen: long experience has enabled them to classify *argols* with the accuracy of connoisseurs. They have established the existence of four different categories, and future generations will no doubt have little to add to this classification.

At the top of the list go sheep and goat *argols*; a viscous substance, of which there is a high proportion in their composition, enables this fuel to reach astonishingly high temperatures. The Tibetans and the Tartars use it for smelting; a pig of iron-ore dropped into a fire of these *argols* will quickly reach white heat. The residue which these goat and sheep *argols* leave after burning is a vitreous substance, transparent, greenish and brittle as glass; it forms lumps full of cavities and is extremely light, resembling pumice. There is no ash at all, unless there has been an admixture of other material. The second type consists of camel *argols*; they burn easily, with a good flame; but they give out less heat than those of the first type, because they have a lower proportion of the viscous substance in their make-up. The third type includes all *argols* of the bovine species; when they are very dry they burn easily and are smokeless. They are almost the only form of fuel in use in Tartary and Tibet. At the bottom come the *argols* of horses and other animals of the equine species. These have not undergone, like the others, the process of rumination and consist only of more or less mashed up hay; they throw out thick smoke as they burn and are consumed in a moment. However they are very useful for getting a fire going; they more or less take the place of tinder and are a great help in getting other fuels alight.

We realise that this short and incomplete dissertation on the subject of dung is unlikely to be of interest to the majority of readers. We include it nevertheless as we feel obliged to treat all those subjects which may be of use to anyone who, after us, wishes to adopt the nomadic way of life.

The inhabitants of the valley of Tchogortan, although apparently enjoying perfect peace, were nevertheless living continually in fear of brigands, who from time to time, they said, invaded these mountains and carried off all the cattle they found. We were told that in 1842 they had come in great bands and laid waste the countryside. When least expected they had emerged from all the gorges and mountain passes and spread out over the valley, uttering wild cries and firing their matchlocks in the air. The herdsmen, terrified by this surprise attack, had not even thought of offering any resistance; they had run off in panic haste and in disorder, taking with them only what came to hand. The brigands set fire to their tents and rounded up their cattle into a roped enclosure. They then made their way to the little lamasery of the Faculty of Medicine. But the lamas had disappeared, except for the hermits who had stayed in their eyries up in the rock-face. The brigands ravaged and destroyed everything they came across. They burned the statues of Buddha and broke the dams built to make the prayer-wheels turn. Three years later we could still see traces of their work. The temple which had stood under the mountain had not yet been rebuilt. Ruins blackened by fire and pieces of half-burnt idols were strewn over the grass. The hermit-lamas were however spared. No doubt the brigands felt that it would take too long, or be too difficult, to seek them out in their almost inaccessible dwellings. The excesses they committed against the black tents and the temple of Buddha itself indicate that if they left these poor recluses alone, it was not out of respect or pity.

As soon as the news of the arrival of the brigands reached Kounboum, the whole lamasery was up in arms. The lamas ran to their weapons and shouted. Armed with the first thing they could find they set off pell-mell at the gallop towards Tchogortan. But they arrived too late; the brigands had disappeared with all the Si Fan flocks, and there was nothing in the valley but smoking ruins.

The herdsmen who, since these events, had returned to set up their tents in Tchogortan were always on the look-out in the fear of a new invasion. Occasionally they formed themselves into a patrol armed with lances and rifles and went off to spy out the enemy. Such precautions were inadequate to frighten off the bandits, but they gave the population a sense of security.

Towards the end of August, whilst we were peacefully occupied in our ropemaking, sinister rumours began to circulate. Gradually they hardened into certainty, and everyone became convinced that we were on the brink of a new and terrible brigand invasion. The herdsmen of such-and-such a place had been attacked, their tents burnt and their flocks stolen. Somewhere else, there had been a terrible battle and many people slaughtered. These rumours became so serious that the administration of the lamasery of Kounboum decided to take action. A Grand Lama and twenty students of the Faculty of Prayers were despatched with the mission of preserving the area from any disaster. On arrival they gathered the heads of the Si Fan families together and informed them that there was now nothing to fear. Next day they climbed the highest mountain in the neighbourhood, put up some travelling tents and began reciting prayers with musical accompaniment. They stayed there for two whole days, which they spent in praying, in exorcising and in building a little pyramid of earth which they whitewashed; above, on a flagpole, floated a pennant painted with Tibetan characters. This modest effort was named the Pyramid of Peace. After the ceremony the lamas, great and small, struck camp, came down the mountain and went back to Kounboum, quite convinced that they had erected a barrier that the brigands could not cross.

The Pyramid of Peace did not seem to have completely convinced the herdsmen, for one fine day they departed all together, complete with baggage and flocks, to find a less dangerous place elsewhere. We were urged to do likewise; but we preferred to remain, for in the wilderness one place is as safe as the next. In any case the departure of the herdsmen was a guarantee that our peace would not be disturbed. We thought that when the bandits learned that there were no flocks left in the valley of Tchogortan they would hardly bother to pay us a visit. We also built a pyramid of peace in our hearts, in the form of a firm belief in Divine Protection, and remained calmly where we were.

For some days we enjoyed complete solitude. Since the flocks had gone, the *argol*-lamas stopped coming as there was nothing for them to do. We were alone, apart from the few lamas in charge of the lamasery. Our animals benefited from

the change, for the pastures were all theirs; they could roam anywhere without meeting any competition.

But it was not long before our wilderness became full of life again. In early September the lamas of the Faculty of Medicine came to Tchogortan for herb collection. As many as possible lodged in the buildings and the rest in tents under the shelter of the tall trees of the lamasery. Every morning, after reciting prayers together, drinking buttered tea and eating barley flour, all the medical students kilted up their robes and scattered over the mountains under the guidance of their professors. They each carried a spiked stick and a little pick; a leather purse full of flour hung from each man's belt; some bore great cooking-pots on their backs, for the faculty spent the entire day in the mountains. Before sunset they returned laden with great bundles of branches, roots and all sorts of wild plants. As they laboriously descended leaning on their spiked sticks, they looked more like poachers than doctors of medicine. We often had to provide an escort for those who were specially laden with aromatic plants, for our camels chased them, attracted by the scent, and would unscrupulously have nibbled those precious herbs intended for the relief of human suffering. The rest of the day was spent in cleaning all this herbage and in spreading it on mats. This harvesting lasted eight whole days. Five more were spent in sorting and classifying the different species. On the fourteenth day each student received a small portion, but the major part remained the property of the faculty. The fifteenth day was a holiday. There was a great feast, consisting of tea, barley flour, small cakes fried in butter and some boiled mutton. That was the end of this botanical and medical expedition, and the faculty merrily set off home to the big lamasery.

The medicines collected at Tchogortan were taken to the general pharmacy at Kounboum. When they had dried out in a gentle heat they were ground to a powder, then divided into small doses which were cleanly wrapped in red paper and labelled in Tibetan characters. The pilgrims who came to Kounboum bought these remedies at exorbitant prices. The Tartars never left without taking a good store with them, for they have complete confidence in everything that comes from Kounboum. In their mountains and meadows they would of course find the same plants and the same roots; but how different are these from the ones that grow and ripen in the country of Tsong Kaba!

Tibetan doctors are as empirical as those of other countries; perhaps even more so. They claim that the human body may suffer from four hundred and forty diseases, neither more nor less. The books which the student lamas are obliged to study and learn by heart deal with these four hundred and forty diseases: they explain the nature of each, its diagnosis and cure. These books are a collection of rather obscure statements together with detailed prescriptions. Lamas are not as afraid of blood as the Chinese doctors. They sometimes practise bleeding, and frequently cupping. For the latter operation they first lightly scratch the skin, then they apply to the flesh a cowhorn which has been pierced at the top. They suck at the hole, and when they have a vacuum they stop it up with a little wad of paper, which they have in readiness in their mouths and which they apply with the tongue. To remove the cup, they have only to take off the wad of paper.

They attach great importance to the examination of the patient's urine. They take a number of samples at various times of the day and night. They make a most careful scrutiny and note particularly the changes in colour; they beat it from time to time with a wooden spatula, then they put their ears to the sample and listen to the sound; for they claim that, according to the patient's state of health his urine is either 'dumb' or 'speaking'. A doctor-lama, to be considered competent and master of his profession should be able to treat a patient without seeing him. Examination of the urine should suffice to allow him to prescribe correctly.

As we have said elsewhere in speaking of the Tartars, superstitious practices are used to a considerable extent in the practice of medicine. However, in spite of all the mumbo-jumbo, they undoubtedly possess a large number of valuable prescriptions based on long experience. It would be rash to conclude that medical science has nothing to learn from Tartar, Tibetan and Chinese doctors, on the grounds that they are ignorant of the structure and functioning of the human body. They may in spite of this hold secrets of considerable importance, which no doubt only science can explain but which science is unlikely ever to discover. Without being a scientist, one can often obtain a scientific result. In China, Tartary and

Tibet, everyone knows how to make gunpowder; yet probably there is not one single man in all these countries who can explain the chemical process involved; they have a good recipe, and that is all they need for a satisfactory result.

Towards the end of the month of September, we heard the great news that the Tibetan Embassy had arrived at Tang Keou Eul; it would remain there some days in order to stock up for the journey and form up as a caravan. At last, after this long wearisome wait, we were going to set off for the capital of Tibet. Without loss of time, we got everything ready. We had to pay a short visit to Kounboum in order to buy provisions for four months, as there would be no chance of buying a single thing en route. We had worked out that we should require five tea-bricks, two sheep's stomachs of butter, two sacks of wheaten flour and eight sacks of *tsamba*. The latter is baked barley flour, an insipid food which is the staple diet of the Tibetan peoples. Take a bowlful of hot tea; add several handfuls of *tsamba* and knead it with the fingers; then swallow the resulting paste just as it is, neither raw nor cooked, neither cold nor hot. If you wish to cross the desert and reach Lhasa, you have to make up your mind to eat *tsamba* in this fashion; it's no good being French and accustomed to eat with a fork: it has to be done, and that's that.

Various people of experience and goodwill advised us to take a good stock of garlic, and to eat several cloves a day, if we did not want to be killed on the journey by the deadly plague-bearing vapours which rise from some of the high mountains. Without going into the value or necessity of this health hint we adopted it with uncritical simplicity.

Our stay in the valley of Tchogortan had done our animals a great deal of good; they were fatter than we had ever seen them. The camels were especially fine; their humps had become firm and hard from the quantity of fat they contained, and stood up proudly on their backs in defiance of the fatigues and privations of the desert. However these three beasts were insufficient for carrying our foodstores and baggage, so we added one camel and one horse to our caravan, making our purse lighter by twenty-five ounces of silver; in addition we hired a young lama from the Ratchico Mountains, whom we had known at Kounboum; he joined the party as assistant cameleer. This appointment, whilst raising the social status of

Samdadchiemba, relieved him of much labour. In its new form our little caravan proceeded as follows: the assistant cameleer, Charadchambeul, walked ahead, leading the four camels tied head to tail; Samdadchiemba, head cameleer, travelled along-side astride his little black mule, and we two missionaries brought up the rear, each riding a white horse. After exchang-ing a large number of *khatas* with acquaintances and friends at Kounboum and Tchogortan we set off in the direction of the Blue Sea, where we intended to wait for the Tibetan Embassy.

It took us four days from Tchogortan to the Koukou Noor. On our way we passed a small lamasery called Tansan, of no more than two hundred lamas. Its situation was extraordin-arily beautiful; rocky mountains covered in bushes and great pinetrees encircled it; the lamasery buildings, in the middle, were themselves surrounded by a quiet stream edged with old willows and the high stems of angelica; the stream then tumbled noisily over rocks before making its way into the wilderness. Tansan, they told us, was very rich; the Mongolian princes of the Koukou Noor supported it by generous annual donations.

On leaving Tansan we came out into a wide grassy plain, dotted picturesquely with numerous Mongolian tents and flocks and herds of all kinds. We met two lamas on horseback who were begging butter from the rich herdsmen. They stop-ped at the door of each tent and sounded the conch three times. Immediately someone appeared with a small pat of butter which he put, without a word, into a bag hanging from the horse's saddle. The collectors thus called at all the tents with-out once dismounting; all they did was blow the conch.

As we proceeded, the country became more fertile and less mountainous. At last we came to the vast rich pasturelands of the Koukou Noor. The growth was so strong that the grass reached as high as our camels' bellies. Then we saw far ahead along the horizon a wide band of silver; light white mists floated above it, and melted into the blue of the sky. Our assistant cameleer told us that it was the Blue Sea. These words gave us a thrill of joy: we pushed ahead and before the sun had set we had put up our tent a hundred yards from the shore.

FROM KOUKOU NOOR
TO LHASA

The Blue Lake, in Mongolian Koukou Noor, in Tibetan Tsot Ngon Po, was previously called Si Hai or Western Sea by the Chinese; they now call it Tsing Hai, or Blue Sea. This great stretch of water, with a circumference of more than three hundred miles, certainly deserves to be called a sea rather than a lake. Apart from its vast size, it is salt like the open sea, and tidal. It gives off a sea odour, which can be smelt a long distance off in the desert.

Near its western end there is a barren rocky islet on which live a score of contemplative lamas; they have built themselves a temple and a few houses, where they spend their lives in tranquillity, far from the cares and the pleasures of this world. It is not possible to visit them, for on the whole length and breadth of the lake there is not one single boat; at least we saw none, and the Mongolians assured us that no one in their tribes possessed one. However in the winter season, during the great frosts, the ice is strong enough to allow the local herdsmen to go on pilgrimage to the lamasery. They take their modest offerings of butter, tea and *tsamba* to the lamas and in exchange the lamas bless their pastures, their flocks and their herds.

The Koukou Noor tribes are divided into twenty-nine banners, commanded by three Kiun Wang, two Pele, two Pcize, four Koung and eighteen Taitsi. All these princes are vassals of the Chinese emperor. Each alternate year they visit Peking, taking with them as tribute skins of animals and gold dust from the sands of their rivers. The great plains which surround the Blue Sea are extremely fertile and beautiful—although they are completely treeless; the grass grows to a great height, and the numerous streams which water the land allow the great herds from the wilderness to drink their fill. The Mongolians like to put up their tents in this wonderful grazing land; although the brigand hordes harass them ceaselessly, they never abandon the territory. They simply move frequently from place to place, to avoid pursuit; and when they cannot escape their enemy they accept battle bravely. Their continual need to defend their possessions and their lives against Si Fan attack has made them into good fighting men. They are in readiness all hours of the day and night; they mount guard over their flocks, always on horseback, each with lance in hand, a rifle slung over one shoulder and a large sabre tucked into his belt. How different are these moustachioed braves from the languid shepherds of Virgil, always playing on their pipes or decorating their pretty straw hats with ribbons and spring flowers.

The brigands who keep these Koukou Noor tribes on the constant alert are Si Fan from the Bayen Kharat hills, near the sources of the Yellow River. Locally they are simply given the generic name of Kolo. We were told that their dens were hidden away in mountain gorges where it is impossible to penetrate without a guide, for all approaches are barred by impassable torrents and daunting precipices. They only emerge to scour the wilderness and subject it to pillage and devastation. They are Buddhists, but they also worship a deity of their own, the god of brigandage. He is their main inspiration and is honoured with a special cult. Their lamas pray to him and make sacrifices to him for the success of their expeditions. The story goes that they are in the revolting habit of eating their prisoners' hearts, in order to give themselves greater courage.

Indeed there is no monstrous practice of which they are not accused.

The Kolo are divided into a number of tribes, each with its own name; it is only in this context that we heard of the Kalmucks. We came across no country called Kalmuck, and the Kalmucks themselves hold a less important place in Asia than they do in our geography books. We had to work hard to find anyone who had heard of them, and in territory supposed to be theirs no one had heard of them. At last we were lucky enough to meet a lama who had travelled widely in Eastern Tibet and who told us that a small Kolo tribe existed called the Kolo-Kalmucks. It is possible that the Kalmucks were once of great importance and occupied large areas, but it is also possible that the thirteenth-century travellers, relying on insufficient evidence, made a large nation out of a small one. Neither does the territory of Koukou Noor occupy as much space in reality as it is given on the maps. Although it comprises twenty-nine banners its extent is not large; it is bounded by Khilian Chan to the north, to the south by the Yellow River, to the east by the province of Kansou and to the west by the River Tsaidam, where another Tartar country begins, inhabited by tribes known as the Tsaidam Mongolians.

According to the folklore of the Koukou Noor, the Blue Sea was not always in its present location. All this great mass of water once occupied, says the legend, the place where the city of Lhasa now stands. One fine day it left the great reservoir that held it and travelled by subterranean channels to where it is today. This is the story as we heard it:

In ancient times, the Tibetans of the kingdom of Oué wished to build a temple in the middle of the great valley where they lived; they got together the most precious materials and the building rose rapidly; but just as it was finished it suddenly collapsed, and no one could discover the cause. Next year new preparations were made, with equal enthusiasm, but again the building collapsed; a third attempt was made, followed by the same catastrophe. Everyone was plunged in despair, and there was talk of abandoning the undertaking. The king consulted a famous soothsayer, who told him that he was unable to give the reason why the temple could not be built, but that he knew that a great saint in the East possessed a secret, and that if he could be made to divulge it, the impediment would immediately disappear. He could say nothing more about this great saint or about where he lived. After much discussion, a lama, known for his skill and courage, was sent on the quest. He explored all the lands to the east of the kingdom of Oué, visiting all the Tartar tribes and stopping wherever he heard of any man renowned for his wisdom and holiness. All his enquiries were in vain; no one could answer his questions or understand him when he spoke of the people of Oué and of the temple that they had tried to build. So, sad and disconsolate, he was returning across the great plains which separate China from Tibet when his saddle-girth broke, and he was thrown from his horse. Seeing not far off a poor tattered tent beside a small pond, he went towards it with the idea of repairing his saddle. Tethering his horse to a stake outside the tent door, he went in and found a venerable old man absorbed in prayer.

'Brother,' said the traveller, 'peace on your house!'

'Brother,' answered the old man, without moving, 'sit down by my fireside.' The traveller realised the old man was blind and said: 'I see that, alas, you have not eyes.'

'Yes, it is many years since I lost the joy of seeing the sun and the green fields, but prayer is a great comfort in my misfortunes. Brother, you speak with a strange accent. You are not from these parts?'

'I am a poor lama from the East. I have made a vow to visit the temples which have been built in Mongolia, and to pay homage to the holy men I meet on my journey. I had an accident as I came by here; I broke my saddle-girth and I have come to your tent to repair it.'

'I am blind,' said the old man, 'I cannot help you myself; look down by the side of the tent, and you will find some straps. Take whichever one suits you best for mending your saddle.' Whilst the stranger was choosing the strap, the old man said: 'Oh lama from the East! You are a happy man to spend your days visiting sacred buildings, for the finest temples are in Mongolia. The Poba (Tibetans) will never succeed in making anything so fine: they try in vain to build one in their beautiful valley; the foundations will always be sapped by the waters of a subterranean sea of which they know nothing.' After a moment's silence, the old man added: 'I have spoken these words, because you are a Mongolian lama, but you must keep them in your heart and never tell anyone. If on your pilgrimage you meet a lama of the land of Oué, keep watch over your tongue, for if my secret were revealed it would be the ruin of our country. When a lama of the land of Oué gets to know that there is an underground lake in their valley, the waters will immediately escape and will come and flood our land.'

He had hardly finished speaking when the stranger stood up and said: 'Unhappy man! Run, run fast! The waters will soon come, for I am a lama of the land of Oué!' Saying these words he leapt on his horse and disappeared into the wilderness.

The old man was thunderstruck by his words. After a moment of horrified bewilderment, he fell to crying and groaning. Whilst he was in this desperate state his son arrived with a small herd of yaks that he had been grazing.

'My son,' said the old man, 'saddle your horse quickly, and gird on your sabre. Ride towards the West, and you will meet a foreign lama: you must kill him, for he has stolen my leather strap.'

'What!' cried the young man. 'You command me to commit a murder? You who are regarded by our peoples as a great saint dare order me to kill a poor traveller, just because he stole from your tent a leather strap that he no doubt needed!'

'Go quickly, my son, I beseech you,' repeated the old man, 'and kill this foreigner, otherwise we shall all be drowned.' The young man, thinking that his father was delirious, did not contradict him for fear of exciting him further: he took horse and followed the tracks of the lama from the land of Oué. He caught up with him before nightfall.

'Holy lama,' he said, 'forgive me for interrupting your journey. Today you rested in our tent and on leaving you took a leather strap that my father is calling for; his anger is so great that he ordered me to kill you. But an old man who is delirious need not be obeyed any more than a child. Give me the strap, and I will go back and calm my father.' The lama dismounted, unfastened the strap from the saddle and returned it to the young man, saying 'Your father gave me the strap; since he regrets it, take it back to him; old men are full of whims, but one must always respect them and avoid causing them sorrow.' The lama took off his belt, made it into a saddle-girth and went on his way, whilst the young man returned home in all haste.

It was dark when he arrived, and the tent was surrounded by a crowd of herdsmen, who, not understanding why the local saint was in such distress, awaited his return with anxiety.

'Father, father,' cried the young man, dismounting, 'be comforted, I have brought your strap: here it is.'

'And did you put the stranger to death?' asked the old man.

'I let him go back to his country in peace. Would it not have been a great crime to kill a lama who has done me no harm? Here is the strap that he stole from you.' Saying this, he handed it to his father. The old man began to tremble all over, for he realised that his son had been the victim of a misunderstanding. For the Mongolians used the same word for *strap* as for *secret*. The old man had meant to tell his son to kill the stranger because he had stolen his *secret*. But seeing that he had brought back his *strap*, he cried: 'The West has won! It is the will of heaven.' He then warned the herdsmen that they must all run fast to their flocks and herds, or they would be swallowed up by the waters. He himself remained in his tent, prostrating himself and awaiting death with resignation.

Dawn had hardly broken when a rumbling roar was heard underground, like the sound of a majestic mountain torrent falling over rocks. It came rapidly nearer and nearer and the waters of the little pond near the old man's tent began to boil. Soon the earth began to quake, the subterranean waters welled up and spread like a mighty sea over the great plains; it overwhelmed countless head of cattle and many families who had no time to escape. The old man was the first to perish.

The lama brought the secret of the great catastrophe back to the kingdom of Oué, and found his compatriots in great consternation: they had heard a terrifying noise in the valley, but no one could imagine the cause. He told the story of the blind old man, and then they all understood that the sound they had heard had been caused by the subterranean lake as it travelled to the East. They enthusiastically resumed their building, and completed a magnificent temple, that stands to this day. Many families settled round the temple, and little by little there grew up the city of Lhasa: *Lha-Ssa*, the Land of Spirits.

This strange story of the origin of the Blue Sea was told us for the first time in the Koukou Noor; we heard it again at Lhasa, almost unchanged. We have no idea to what historical circumstance, if any, it may correspond.

We stayed in the Koukou Noor nearly a month. Continual

rumours of brigands forced us to change camp five or six times, following the Tartar tribes who move on at the slightest pretext, without however ever going far from the marvellous grazing lands that surround the Blue Sea.

Towards the end of October, the Tibetan Embassy arrived. We joined this great company, swollen as it advanced by the addition of a number of Tartar caravans which, like us, took this excellent opportunity to travel to Lhasa. Previously, the Tibetan government sent an embassy to Peking every year. In 1840, it was attacked on the outward journey by a large force of Kolo; the battle lasted a whole day. The Tibetans succeeded in putting the brigands to flight and continued their march during the night. But next day they realised that the ambassador himself, the Tchanak Kampo or Grand Lama accredited to the court of Peking, was missing. For several days they sought him without avail; they concluded that in the confusion of the fighting he must have been carried off by the Kolo. The embassy continued its journey nevertheless, and arrived in Peking without its head. The emperor was of course much distressed by this occurrence.

In 1841 there was again a brigand attack, and again a disaster. This time the Tchanak Kampo was not carried off by the Kolo, but he suffered a great sabre wound in the stomach and died a few days later. When the emperor heard of this new disaster he was, so the story goes, inconsolable. He sent dispatches to the Dalai Lama, saying that in view of the difficulties and dangers of the journey, there was in future to be an embassy only every three years. As a result, the one we had just joined was the first since 1841. It had left Lhasa in 1844, had been fortunate in not meeting any brigands on the way and its Tchanak Kampo had therefore been neither captured nor killed.

The day after we left the Koukou Noor, we placed ourselves at the head of the caravan, then stopped by the wayside to watch this great company go by and get to know our fellow travellers. The number of men and animals in the caravan can be reckoned as follows: 15,000 yaks, 1,200 horses, as many camels, and 2,000 men, Tibetans and Tartars. Some were on foot, others riding yaks, the majority on horse or camelback. All the riders were armed with lances, sabres, arrows and matchlocks. Those on foot, called *lakto*, led the long files of camels or drove the unruly herds of yaks. The Tchanak Kampo travelled in a large litter carried by a pair of mules. Beside the great concourse of men and animals all bound for Lhasa, there was an escort of three hundred Chinese soldiers provided by the province of Kansou, and two hundred Tartar warriors detailed by the princes of Koukou Noor to protect the Holy Embassy of the Dalai Lama as far as the frontiers of Tibet.

The soldiers from Kansou carried out their task in a typically Chinese manner. For fear of some unpleasant encounter, they kept prudently at the tail of the caravan; they spent their time singing, smoking and playing the fool, quite at ease without a

thought of the brigands. They followed the unusual routine of waiting each day until the whole caravan had moved off; then they conducted a search of the various camps, appropriating everything that had been left behind. Since they took up the rear, they were also in an excellent position to pick up anything that the rest had dropped. The Tartar soldiers behaved quite differently. They could be seen constantly galloping out in front and on the flanks of the caravan, climbing to vantage points on the hills and riding into deep valleys, to spy out any brigand ambushes.

The caravan's order of march was quite well organised, especially at the beginning. Normally we set off two or three hours before sunrise, so as to be able to camp about noon and give the animals the rest of the day for grazing; reveille was sounded by a cannon shot; everyone then got up, fires were lit in all the tents and whilst some loaded the pack animals others boiled the water and made the buttered tea; we all drank a few bowlfuls in a hurry, ate a few handfuls of *tsamba* and then struck camp. A second cannon shot was the departure signal. Certain experienced horsemen acted as organisers and took the lead; they were followed by the long files of camels; then came the yaks, which were divided into separate herds of two or three hundred, each in charge of several *lakto*. The horsemen had no fixed place; they came and went in all directions exactly as they pleased. The plaintive cries of the camels, the grunts of the yaks, the neighing of the horses, the noisy shouts of the men, the shrill whistles made by the *lakto* to rally the pack animals and dominating it all the innumerable bells which the yaks and the camels wore round their necks, together produced a great, confused concert of sound which surprisingly did not tire one but seemed on the contrary to give everyone courage and energy.

In this way the caravan made its way across the desert by companies and platoons, stopping each day on the plains, in a valley or on a mountainside, creating makeshift townships of tents of many different shapes and colours, which could vanish each morning, then re-form in ever-changing patterns. How strange for these vast and silent wastes to be invaded by so great and noisy a multitude! When we looked at all these tents, these herds, these men who were both herdsmen and soldiers, we were again and again reminded of the children of Israel, marching in search of the Promised Land, across the wilderness of Midian.

On leaving the shores of the Blue Sea, we went westward, perhaps with a slight bias towards the south. The first days were a delight; the weather was perfect, the route beautiful and easy, the water pure, the pasture rich and plentiful. We never gave a thought to the brigands. It was a trifle cold at night, but we overcame this by wearing our fur coats. We began to wonder what was so terrible about this famous Tibetan passage; we could think of no more comfortable or agreeable way of travelling. Alas, the spell was not long in breaking.

Six days after we started came the crossing of the Pouhain Gol, a river which springs from the foot of the Nan Chan hills and flows into the Blue Sea. Its waters are not very deep, but as the river is divided into twelve channels running very close to each other, it occupies a total width of more than three miles. Unfortunately we arrived at the first channel long before dawn; it was frozen, but the ice was not thick enough to bear us. Arriving first, the horses were afraid and refused to go forward; they stopped on the brink, giving the yaks time to catch up. Soon the whole caravan was concentrated at one point: impossible to describe the chaos and confusion which reigned in this great crush, all wrapped in pitch darkness. At last, some of the horsemen urged their horses forward and broke the ice in several places. Then the caravan entered pell-mell into the river; the animals jostled one another and splashed the water all over the place, ice cracked, men shouted: the tumult was complete. When we had crossed the first channel, we had to go through it all again at the second, then the third and so on. When daylight came the Holy Embassy was still splashing about in water; finally, after much toil and trembling, both moral and physical, we were happy to leave behind us the twelve channels of the Pouhain Gol, and find ourselves on dry land; but all the charm had vanished, and we began to find this a vile way of travelling after all.

And yet everyone else seemed to be celebrating. The crossing of the Pouhain Gol had, it seemed, gone remarkably well. One man had broken his legs and two yaks had drowned: that was all. No one bothered to count the things that had been lost or pilfered during this long period of disorder.

When the caravan set off again in due order, it was a truly comic sight. Both men and animals were hung more or less all over with icicles. The horses were most dejected, evidently encumbered by their tails, which hung all of a piece, stiff as boards, as if made of lead rather than hair. Attached to the long hair on the camels' legs there were the most magnificent icicles, which clanged together with a musical sound. Yet the camels clearly disliked these charming ornaments, for from time to time they tried to dislodge them by stamping their feet. The yaks were real caricatures; nothing funnier can be imagined:

they walked with legs wide apart, bearing the weight of a forest of stalactites which hung from their bellies down to the ground. These poor beasts were so misshapen, so covered in icicles, that they looked as if they had been preserved in sugar candy.

For the first few days we were rather lonely and isolated amid this great throng. We knew no one. However, it was not long before we made friends, for there is nothing like travel for getting people together. The travelling companions that we found, and beside whom we pitched our tent each day, were neither merchants nor pilgrims, nor persons attached to the embassy, nor plain travellers like ourselves; they were four lamas who were of a class apart. Two of them were from Lhasa, one from the further side of Tibet and one from the kingdom of Torgot. As we journeyed they told us their long and picturesque story, a summary of which we give below.

The three Tibetan lamas had become the disciples of a Grand Lama with the title of Altere, who proposed to build, not far from Lhasa, a temple whose size and magnificence would surpass all those existing. One day he told his disciples that, all the plans having been completed, it was time to begin collecting alms on a large scale to provide the enormous sums required for the sacred building. All four set off, full of zeal and piety, in a northerly direction. They crossed the whole of Central Asia, as far as the kingdom of Torgot, quite close to the frontier. On the way they stopped at all the lamaseries and the dwellings of the Tibetan and Tartar princes. Everywhere they went they were given generous donations, for, besides the considerable appeal of the cause itself, the Altere Lama had letters of introduction from the Dalai Lama, from the Bandchan [Panchen] Remboutchi and from the superiors of all the most renowned lamaseries of Tibet. In Torgot, a rich Tartar lama, moved by the piety of these intrepid alms collectors, donated all his flocks and herds and pleaded with the Altere Lama to allow him to join the party and help in the work of gathering funds in the Tartar lands. The Altere Lama, equally moved by such pure enthusiasm and unselfishness, accepted his gift and received him as a disciple. So now they were five.

From Torgot they went eastwards from tribe to tribe, and everywhere they went they augmented their herds of horses, oxen, sheep and camels. They reached as far as the Khalkas, where they remained for a long time at the lamasery of Great Kouren, for the donations of the Tartar pilgrims were inexhaustible. From there they turned south as far as Peking, where they converted their great herds into gold and silver. After a long stay in the capital of the empire they set off again through the wildernesses of Tartary, collecting as they went, until they arrived at Kounboum. In this famous and holy establishment, where the qualities of good lamas were appreciated, the zeal and piety of the alms-collectors acquired great renown; they were venerated publicly, and masters anxious to lead their disciples to perfection pointed them out as models.

The Altere Lama, after three years travelling in the cause, was longing to return to Lhasa and devote the considerable funds he had collected to the building of his temple. He was delighted therefore when he learnt of the arrival of the Tibetan Embassy. It was decided that he would join it on its return from Peking, and that he would thus have protection when crossing the dangerous Kolo country. Meanwhile, he would prepare for the journey.

But alas, the best laid schemes of mice and men gang aft agley, at the very moment when they seem about to come to fruition. One fine day a special courier from the emperor arrived at Sining Fou, bearing dispatches in which the Grand Mandarin of the city was commanded, after consulting with the Grand Lama of Kounboum, to arrest the Altere Lama, accused of a whole series of frauds committed during the last three years, by means of certain forged letters of introduction attributed to the Dalai Lama. The orders of His Imperial Majesty were duly carried out. The amazement of the poor Altere Lama can easily be imagined, and above all that of his four disciples whose innocence was complete. The embassy, which they had been counting on for protection, had been instructed by the Tibetan government to find and seize the Altere Lama, whose amazing successes had come to light in Lhasa through the indiscretions of pilgrims.

After his arrest the defenceless Altere Lama was sent under escort to Lhasa. He was made to take the route of the emperor's courier through Ssetchouan. Once in Lhasa, he was to be judged by his peers. Meanwhile, his vast treasure was confiscated in the name of the Dalai Lama, for what could be more just than for that dignitary to come into possession of gold and silver which had been levied thanks to the all-powerful influence of his name? As for the four disciples, it was decided that they should wait for the Tibetan Embassy and return with it, bringing fifty-eight fine camels that the Altere Lama had acquired, and which would be at the disposal of the Tibetan government on arrival at Lhasa.

These four unfortunate disciples were the fellow travellers which our good fortune had provided. The memory of their fallen master haunted them ceaselessly, but the feelings which his memory evoked were not always the same. They sometimes thought of him as a saint and sometimes as a crook. One day they would pronounce his name with reverence, bowing over their joined hands, and the next they would curse him, spitting in the air as a sign of contempt. The lama from Torgot especially was baffled by the whole unfortunate affair. From time to time he expressed regret at having donated all his flocks and herds to a man who was beginning to show every sign of being a fraud, but he easily comforted himself, for after all, how otherwise would he have been able to travel and see all the great lamaseries? These four lamas were really good fellows and excellent company. Every day they had new tales to tell us of their long adventures, and more than once their stories helped us to forget for a time the hardships and miseries of the journey.

One constant cause of the sufferings we had to endure was undoubtedly our assistant cameleer, Charadchambeul. At first this young lama had seemed to be a little saint; but later we realised that we had brought with us a small devil in human form. The following incident opened our eyes to the truth about him, and gave us a taste of what we would have to suffer on his account.

The day after crossing the Pouhain Gol, after travelling for part of the night we noticed on one of our camels two large parcels, carefully wrapped, which we had not seen before. We supposed that some traveller, unable to find a convenient place for them on his pack animal, must have asked Charadchambeul to look after them for the day; we then dismissed the matter from our minds. When we arrived at the camping place, as soon as the baggage had been unloaded we saw with surprise that our young friend took the two parcels, wrapped them up surreptitiously in a felt rug and hid them at the far end of the tent.

Clearly such behaviour called for an explanation. We asked Charadchambeul what this new baggage was doing in the tent. He came close and in a confidential whisper informed us that during the night Buddha had granted him a boon, and had caused him to find something good on the path. Then he added, with a sly smile, that in Lhasa this 'good thing' would sell for some ten ounces of silver. These words were greeted with frowns on our part, and we asked to see the good thing in question. Charadchembeul first carefully shut the tent door, then he excitedly unwrapped his so-called 'find'. It consisted of two large leather bottles, containing a kind of spirit distilled in the province of Kansou, and sold at a fairly high price. On these two bottles there were Tibetan characters which gave the name of the owner, a well-known person. We were charitable enough not to allow ourselves to think that Charadchambeul had stolen these bottles during the night; we preferred to imagine that he had picked them up along the way. But our assistant cameleer had it all worked out: he claimed that these bottles belonged to him, that Buddha had given them to him and that all he had to do now was to hide them carefully so that the owner should not see them. Trying to argue from a moral standpoint with such a fellow was a waste of time. We told him firmly that these bottles being neither ours nor his had no place in the tent or on the camel's back during the journey, and that we had no desire to arrive in Lhasa with the reputation of being thieves. So that he should take our words seriously, we told him that if he did not remove the bottles from the tent we would go straightaway and warn the owner. He was somewhat shaken by these words. Finally, in order to encourage him to return them himself, we suggested that he should take them to the ambassador, with a request that the latter should return them to their owner. The Tchanak Kampo would certainly be impressed at his honesty; he might give him a reward or at least would remember him and might help him at Lhasa. After long noisy arguments, this solution was adopted. Charadchambeul went to see the Tchanak Kampo, who said to him: 'You are a good lama. A lama who has justice in his heart is pleasing to the spirits.' Charadchambeul came back extremely angry. He said that we had made him behave like a fool, and that all he had got from the Tchanak Kampo was empty words. From then on, he hated us implacably. He only carried out his work by fits and starts; he did his best to waste the food supply; he daily heaped impertinences and curses on our heads; and often, wreaking his wrath on the animals, he beat them mercilessly over the head, nearly knocking them out. It was impossible to sack the fellow there, in the middle of nowhere. We simply had to practise patience and resignation, and try not to provoke that untamed nature of his more than necessarily.

Five days after crossing the Pouhain Gol, we arrived at the Toulain Gol, a narrow shallow river which we crossed without trouble. The caravan stopped next near a lamasery that seemed to have been quite prosperous, but which was now entirely deserted. The temples and the lamas' cells were everywhere falling in ruins. Bats and enormous rats had made their home there. We were told that brigands had besieged the place for three days and had finally captured it; they had then massacred a large number of the inmates and sacked the buildings. Since then no lamas had dared settle there. Yet the country was not quite deserted, as we first thought it was. Walking over the rocky hills of the neighbourhood we came across a few flocks of goats and three poverty stricken tents tucked into the hollows of ravines. The unfortunate herdsmen came out to beg a few leaves of tea and a little *tsamba* from us. Their eyes were haggard and their faces pale and emaciated. They told us that they did not know where to go for a peaceful life: the fear of brigands so dominated their lives that they had even lost the courage to escape.

Next day the caravan moved on; but the Chinese escort remained camped on the river bank: their task was over. After a few days' rest they would turn round and make for home. The Tibetan merchants said that now the Chinese soldiers had gone they would be able to sleep in peace, without fear of thieves.

On 15 November we left the splendid plains of the Koukou Noor and entered the land of the Tsaidam Mongols. Immediately after we had crossed the Tsaidam river the appearance of the country changed abruptly. It became a sad and savage land; the barren stony earth supported nothing but a few dried-up bushes impregnated with saltpetre. This depressing area seemed to have had its effect on the inhabitants, who all looked as if they suffered from melancholia. They spoke very little, and their language was so rough and guttural that other Mongols often found it hard to understand them. Rock salt and borax abounded in this barren soil, whilst good pasture was almost nonexistent. Pits two or three feet deep were dug in which the salt collected, crystallised and purified itself without human intervention. Borax was collected in small reservoirs, which were full to the brim. The Tibetans imported it to sell to the goldsmiths and silversmiths who used it to induce the fusion of metals. We spent two days in the Tsaidam country. We had a feast on *tsamba* and goat's meat, which the herdsmen exchanged for bricks of tea. The yaks and the camels also feasted—on the nitre and salt that they found everywhere lying on the ground. The whole caravan tried to gather its strength for the crossing of the Bourhan Bota, a mountain famous for the poisonous vapours that were said to shroud it continually.

We set off at three in the morning, and after following a winding route through hilly country we arrived by nine o'clock at the foot of the Bourhan Bota. The caravan stopped briefly as if to gather its strength; we scanned the steep way upward and anxiously pointed out to each other a light mist which, we were told, was a poisonous vapour. Everyone seemed full of foreboding. After taking the hygienic precautions prescribed by tradition, that is, eating two or three cloves of garlic, we then began to climb. The horses soon refused to carry their riders, and everyone was on foot; little by little we all went pale and began to suffer from nausea; our legs refused to function, we lay flat on the ground, then got up for a few more steps forward, then lay down again, and in this pathetic manner made our ascent of the Bourhan Bota. What a miserable experience! Our strength drained away, we felt giddy, our limbs seemed disjointed, we suffered a sensation similar to seasickness; yet we realised that we simply had to summon up enough strength not only to drag our own bodies along but also to beat the animals again and again, since they insisted on lying down and staying where they were. One party, as a safety precaution, stopped halfway in a cleft in the mountain where the poisonous vapours were supposed to be less thick; the rest, for similar reasons, made a supreme effort to get to the top without dying of asphyxiation from that air laden with carbonic acid gas. Like these, we managed to get to the top in one go. Once there we could at last breathe with ease. The descent was child's play and we could put up our tent well away from the deadly air that we had left on the other side.

The curious thing about Bourhan Bota was that the poisonous gas was only on the north-east flank; on the other side the air was pure. Apparently the poisonous vapours were simply carbonic acid gas. People attached to the embassy told us that when it was windy the vapours were hardly noticeable; they were only dangerous when it was calm. Carbonic acid gas, being heavier than air, must have become concentrated at ground level and remained there until strong winds dispelled it and rendered it harmless. When we made the ascent the weather was fairly windless. We noticed that when we lay down we breathed with much greater difficulty; on horseback, we could hardly feel any ill effects. Because of the gas it was very difficult to get a fire going; the *argols* burnt without a flame and made a lot of smoke. But how the gas was formed or where it came from we have no idea. We will only add, for those who like to find significance in place names, that Bourhan Bota means Bourhan's kitchen, Bourhan being of course another name for Buddha.

During the night that we spent on the further side of the mountain, snow fell to a considerable depth. The party of those who had been afraid to finish the ascent caught up with us during the morning; they told us that they had been able to get to the top without too much trouble, because the snow had caused the vapours to disappear.

The climb over Bourhan Bota was a mere rehearsal for what was to come. A few days later Mount Chuga put our strength and courage to a sterner test. As the day's march was going to be long and hard, the cannon shot, our normal signal for departure, was sounded one hour after midnight. We made our tea with melted snow; we had a good meal of *tsamba* flavoured with chopped garlic and set off. When the great caravan began to move forward, the sky was cloudless and a brilliant moon lit up the carpet of snow which covered everything. Since Mount Chuga was not steep on the near side we were able to reach the top by first light. The sky soon became overcast and a gale got up which blew ever stronger and stronger. The far side of the mountain was so deep in snow that the animals sank up to their bellies; they could only progress by a series of leaps, and often fell into clefts and could not be extricated: a number died in this fashion. We rode against a wind so strong and so icy that it was at times impossible to breathe and in spite of our good furs we felt all the time that we would die of cold. To avoid the blizzard which the wind constantly hurled in our faces, we took the cue from some of our fellow-travellers and rode backwards on our horses, letting their instincts guide them. When we reached the bottom and could shelter our eyes from the wind, we could see more than one man whose face was frozen. Father Gabet was mourning the temporary death of his nose and ears. Everyone's skin was chapped and scorched by the cold.

The caravan stopped at the bottom of Mount Chuga, and each group went off to hunt for shelter in a great close-knit maze of gullies. Fainting with hunger and crippled with frost, what we really needed to restore us was a hostelry with a good fire, a well-stocked table and a well-warmed bed; but the Chuga is far behind the Alps in the question of comfort; the Buddhist monks have not yet had the idea of settling there in order to succour poor travellers. So we had to put up our tent in the snow, and then go searching for *argols*. It really was a pitiful sight to see a multitude of people wandering about, busily burrowing in the snow in the hope of turning up the odd cow pat. After a long and painful search we had found just sufficient to melt three large pieces of ice, which we had to hack out of a nearby pond. As our fire was not hot enough to make it boil, we had to be satisfied with dipping our *tsamba* in lukewarm water and swallowing it quickly, for fear of it freezing in our fingers. That was all the supper we had after that gruelling day. We then rolled up in our goatskins and our blankets and, huddled in a corner of the tent, waited for the cannon shot which would be the signal for us to resume our pleasure cruise.

Here, in this delightful spot, we parted from the Tartar soldiers who had been our escort since we left the Koukou Noor; they could not extend their generous protection any further, as that very day we would be leaving Tartary and entering Near Tibet. Now that the Chinese and Tartar soldiers had left us, the embassy would have to rely on its own resources. As already mentioned, this great body of two thousand men was fully armed; and everyone, with few exceptions, was prepared to act, if need be, like a good soldier; but it must be admitted that the original brave and warlike aspect of the caravan had considerably altered since the crossing of the

Bourhan Bota. There was no more singing or laughing, or prancing about on horses; all those moustaches which had bristled so bravely when we set off were now modestly concealed behind the lambskins in which we wrapped ourselves up to the eyes. All these brave soldiers had made parcels of their lances, rifles, sabres and quivers and fastened them on to their pack animals. Death from brigands no longer entered our minds: it was death from cold that we now feared.

It was from Mount Chuga onward that our long ordeal really began. Snow, wind and cold beset us with a fury which increased daily. The Tibetan wilderness is, without any shadow of doubt, the most terrible place imaginable. Since the ground rose steadily, vegetation decreased as we advanced and the cold reached a frightening intensity. From then on, death hovered over the poor caravan. Lack of water and pasture quickly exhausted the strength of the animals. Each day, pack animals which could no longer drag themselves along had to be abandoned. A little later, it was to be the turn of the men. The route we followed gave us a foretaste of doom; for several days we had seemed to be passing through a vast graveyard where exhumed human bones and animal carcasses lay strewn everywhere, telling us that in this land of death and the unleashed forces of nature the caravans that had preceded us had had no better fate than we.

As a final stroke of ill-fortune, Father Gabet fell ill. He began to lose his health at the very moment when tough travelling conditions called for an even greater expense of energy and courage. The extreme cold that he had endured on Mount Chuga had completely broken his strength. He needed, to regain his normal health, rest, tonic draughts and a good nourishing diet. But all we could give him were barley meal and tea made with snow-water; and still in spite of his great weakness he had to keep riding his horse and battling with extreme weather conditions. And there were two months more of it, to come, in the depths of winter. The outlook was indeed grim.

By early December we found ourselves under the Bayen Kharat, a great chain of mountains which stretches north-east and south-west between the Yellow and the Blue Rivers. These two great rivers, after running parallel on either side of the Bayen Kharat, turn one northward and the other southward.

They then take extremely winding courses through Tartary and Tibet before entering China which they cross from west to east whilst gradually approaching each other and finally flow into the Yellow sea, not far from one another. The point at which we crossed the Bayen Kharat was not far from the sources of the Yellow River; they were on our left, and it would have taken two days' journey to go and visit them. But it was hardly the season for pleasure trips. An excursion to the sources of the Yellow River was far from our thoughts; for the moment the crossing of the Bayen Kharat was enough to keep us busy.

From foot to summit the whole mountain was covered with snow. Before undertaking the ascent, the chief members of the embassy took counsel. The question was not whether or not to cross the mountain; since Lhasa was the destination, it had to be done. Nor was there any question of waiting for the snow to melt; the debate was as to whether to make the ascent on that day or whether to wait for the next. The fear of avalanches was uppermost in everyone's mind, and the question of wind was paramount. Like all parliaments in the world, that of the Tibetan Embassy was soon divided into two parties, one for going on and one for waiting. To find a solution they consulted those lamas who had a reputation for foretelling the future; but this expedient was unable to restore unity. Some of the soothsayers predicted that the day would be calm, but the morrow it would blow a gale; others held the opposite view. The caravan was henceforward divided into two camps, the go-party and the stay-party or, in other words, the progressives and the conservatives. Of course, being French citizens, we instinctively sided with the progressives, that is, those who wanted to set off straightaway and get this tiresome mountain behind us. Indeed, we thought that commonsense was on our side. The weather was calm at the moment, and we had no idea what the morrow would bring. So we began to scale these mountains of snow, sometimes on horseback but more often on foot. When on foot, we let our mounts go first and caught hold of their tails. This is a most satisfactory way of climbing a mountain. Father Gabet suffered horribly; but God, in His infinite goodness, gave us the strength and the courage to overcome. The weather remained calm, and we were not crushed by any avalanche.

Next day the 'stay-party' set off at dawn and successfully

made the crossing. As we were kind enough to wait for them, they caught us up and together we entered a valley where the temperature was reasonable. The good quality of the pasture caused the caravan to take a day's rest. A deep lake in which we dug a well gave us abundant water. Fuel was also available, for as embassies and pilgrims normally rested in this valley after crossing the Bayen Kharat, there were always plenty of *argols*. We lit great fires which burned continually. We burnt everything we could find, without fear of depriving those who came after us. Our fifteen thousand yaks saw to it that any deficit was made up.

We left the great Bayen Kharat valley and pitched our tents on the banks of the Mouroui Oussou River. Near its source it bears this name, which means 'Winding Water'; further down it is called Kin Cha Kiang (River of Golden Sands); when it reaches the province of Ssetchouan, it becomes the famous Yang Tze Kiang or Blue River. When crossing it over the ice, we saw a curious sight. From our camp site some way off we had already noticed indeterminate dark-coloured objects stretching in a line across the river. Even when we got much nearer, we could not make out what they were. Only when we were quite close did we realise that more than fifty wild oxen had been frozen into the ice. Presumably they were trying to swim across the river just when the water was on the point of freezing and got caught in it without having the strength to shake off the ice. Their fine heads, crowned with great horns, were above water; but the rest was in the ice, which was so transparent that we could easily make out their postures: they seemed to be swimming still. The eagles and the crows had picked out their eyes.

Wild oxen are common in the wilds of Near Tibet. They move in large herds and tend to keep to the summits. In the summer, they go down into the valleys to drink in the streams and ponds; but during the long winter season they stay on the heights, and eat snow and a species of very tough grass. They are extremely large, their coat is long and black, but they are remarkable above all for the size and splendid shape of their horns. It is unwise to hunt them, for they are said to be very fierce. When a small group is isolated from the herd, it is possible to use grape-shot against them; but a number of guns should fire simultaneously, for if the quarry is not killed there is a considerable risk that it will charge the hunters and tear them to pieces. One day we saw one of these beasts licking happily at some nitre in a little hollow surrounded by rocks. Eight men, armed with matchlocks, left the caravan and stalked it; eight shots fired at once; the ox raised its head, glared in the direction the shots had come from, then ran off at full gallop and crossed the plain leaping and bellowing horribly. It was thought that it had been wounded but that, seeing the caravan, it had been too scared to attack its hunters.

The 'wild mule' (Tibetan wild ass) is also quite common in this region. After crossing the Mouroui Oussou we came across them nearly every day. The naturalists have named it '*hemi-onus*', or horse-half-ass; it is the size of a mule, but the body is finer, the movements are more graceful and lighter; the coat is

reddish on the back but fades almost to white under the belly. The head is big and ugly, contrasting with the elegance of the body; when moving it holds its head high, with its long ears straight up. At the gallop it turns its head towards the wind and holds up its mule-like tail. The neigh of these beasts is clear and musical; they are so fast that the Tartar and Tibetan horsemen cannot catch up with them. They can only take them by means of an ambush laid at their watering places, where the hunters shoot them with arrow or rifle; the meat is excellent eating, and the hides are used for boot-leather. They are a true species, not cross-breeds, and are impossible to domesticate. We were told that even if they were caught very young and brought up with other foals, it was still impossible to break them in, either for riding or as pack animals. The moment they are untethered they escape and return to the wild state. But so far as we could see, their characters are not particularly fierce; from time to time we saw them frisking with the horses of the caravan when these were grazing near the camp; but at man's approach (and they can scent and recognise man from a long distance) they made off immediately. The lynx, the chamois, the reindeer and the ibex are also common in Near Tibet.

A few days after crossing the Mouroui Oussou, the caravan began to break up; those who rode camels wished to push ahead, to avoid being held back by the slow pace of the yaks. Moreover the type of country was such that so large a company could no longer camp in the same place. The pasture was so thin and poor that there was not enough to go round. We joined up with the camel riders, and left the yaks behind. Later our party split up again; once unity was broken, a number of petty caravan leaders arose, and there was frequent disagreement about camping sites and departure times.

We were gradually approaching the highest part of Upper Asia, when a terrible north wind, which blew for a fortnight, was an added and near fatal hazard. The sky remained cloudless, but the cold was so frightful that only at midday could we feel any warmth at all from the sun; and even then only when we got out of the wind. For the rest of the day and especially at night we were continually in fear of being frozen to death. Deeply chapped faces and hands were universal. Such cold is impossible to appreciate if one has never experienced it, but we perhaps can give some idea of what it was like by mentioning one small but significant detail. Each morning before setting off we had a meal, and then did not eat again until reaching camp in the evening. As our *tsamba* was not sufficiently appetising to consume enough in one go to keep us going till then, we used to prepare three or four balls of the stuff by kneading it in tea, and keep them in reserve for eating during the day. We would wrap the boiling hot paste in a hot cloth and place it next to the skin of our chests; over this we had our clothes, namely: a thick sheepskin vest, then a lambskin waistcoat, then a short fox-fur coat, then a loose woollen robe. Every day of that fortnight our *tsamba*-cakes froze; when we took them out they were like solid putty, yet they had to be eaten, at the risk of breaking one's teeth, to avoid perishing of hunger.

The animals, weakened by fatigue and privation, found it harder and harder to survive such cold. The mules and horses, being less resistant than the camels and the yaks, needed special care. We had to cover them with large felt rugs which we tied underneath, and we wrapped their heads in camelhair. In other circumstances all these bizarre accoutrements would have excited our hilarity; but we were too miserable to laugh. Despite all these precautions, the caravan's animals were decimated by death.

The many frozen rivers that we had to cross were an additional source of hardship and disaster. Camels are so clumsy, their gait is so unsure, that we were obliged to make a track for them by spreading sand or earth on the ice, or by breaking up the surface with our axes. Then we had to lead them carefully in single file to keep them on the right path: if they tripped or slipped, disaster followed; they would crash heavily to the ground, and getting them up again would be a major task. They would have to be unloaded, then dragged on their sides to the river bank; then carpets would have to be spread on the ice; sometimes even that was useless; you could hit them or tug at them and they made no effort at all to get up. Then they had to be left to their fate, for it was impossible to wait, in that terrible place, long enough for a camel to make up its silly mind to get on its feet again.

So many afflictions together eventually wore down the travellers into a state approaching despair. Now not only the animals were dying; men too succumbed to the cold, and were abandoned, still alive, by the wayside. One day when the exhausted state of our animals had forced us to slow down and we had fallen slightly behind the company, we saw a traveller sitting alone beside the way on a boulder; his head was bent, his arms were tight against his side and he was as motionless as a statue; we called him several times, but he made no reply; there was no indication that he had even heard us. 'What madness,' we said to each other, 'to stop in such weather. He will certainly die of cold.' We called again, but still no movement. We dismounted and went over to him. We then recognised him: a young Tartar lama who had often been to visit us in our tent. His face was waxen, and his half-open eyes were glazed. Icicles hung from his nose and the corners of his mouth. There was no response when we spoke and we thought for a moment that he was dead. But then he opened his eyes and fixed them on us with a horrible expression of stupidity. He was frozen stiff, and we realised that he had been abandoned by his companions. It seemed so dreadful to let a man die in this way without trying to save his life that without hesitation we took him with us. We dragged him off that awful stone on which he had been put and hoisted him on to Samdadchiemba's little mule. We wrapped him in a blanket and so led him to the camp. As soon as the tent was up, we went to visit the poor young man's companions. When they learned what we had done they prostrated themselves in gratitude; they praised our kindness, but said that all our trouble would be in vain, for there was no saving him. 'He is frozen,' they said, 'and the cold will soon reach his heart!' We could not share their hopelessness. We returned to our tent, accompanied by one of them, to see if the patient showed any sign of recovery, but when we arrived he was dead.

More than forty members of the caravan were left in the desert, still alive, and it was quite impossible to do anything for them. The sick were mounted on camel or horseback whilst there was still hope; but when they could no longer eat, speak, nor keep themselves in the saddle, they were left by the wayside. How could one stop and tend them in an uninhabited waste, with the menace of wild beasts, brigands and above all lack of food? It was heartrending to see these dying men abandoned by the way; as a final gesture, a wooden bowl and a little bag of flour were left beside each one; then the caravan went sadly on. When we had all passed by, the crows and the vultures which ceaselessly wheeled above us swooped down on these wretches, who no doubt had enough life left in them to feel the talons that tore them.

The north winds made Father Gabet's illness much worse. Each day his state became more alarming. He was too weak to walk and therefore unable to keep warm through exercise; his hands and his face were frozen; his lips were already blue, and his eyes dead; then he became too weak to stay in the saddle. All we could do was wrap him in blankets, tie him like a parcel on to a camel and put our trust in God.

One day when we were winding our way along a valley, our

hearts full of sad thoughts, we suddenly saw two horsemen appear on the ridge of one of the surrounding mountains. At this period we were in company with a small group of Tibetan merchants who, like us, had let the main body of the caravan go ahead, in order not to exhaust their camels by keeping up too quick a pace. 'Tsong Kaba!' cried the Tibetans. 'There are horsemen over there; but we are in deserted country where there are no herdsmen.' Hardly were these words out before we began to see other horsemen appearing at various points: and when we saw them bearing down on us at speed all together we could not suppress a tremor of fear. What could these horsemen be up to in this uninhabited region, and what did they want of us? We were soon convinced that we had fallen into the hands of brigands. Their appearance did nothing to reassure us: each had a slung rifle, and two sabres one on either side of his belt; they had long black hair down to their shoulders, their eyes flashed and each man wore a wolf's skin on his head. We were surrounded by twenty-seven of these alarming characters, and there were only eighteen of us, by no means all of whom were experienced warriors. Both sides dismounted, and a courageous Tibetan from our party went forward to parley with the brigand chief, distinguishable by two little red flags fluttering behind his saddle. After a long and animated conversation the Kolo* chieftain said, 'Who is that man?' pointing at Father Gabet, who, tied on his camel, was the only one who had not dismounted.

'He is a great Lama from the Western Heavens, and the power of his prayers is infinite,' replied the Tibetan merchant. The Kolo raised his two joined hands to his forehead and gazed at Father Gabet who, with his frozen face and his bizarre cocoon of motley-coloured blankets, looked not unlike one of those terrifying idols in a pagan temple. After a moment's contemplation of the famous Lama from the Western Heavens, the brigand spoke a few words in a low voice to the Tibetan merchant; then, with a sign to his companions, he and the rest mounted and galloped off over the mountains.

'We'll go no futher,' said the Tibetan merchant, 'let's camp here; the Kolo are brigands, but they are great-hearted and generous; when they see that we are not afraid to stay here,

---

*The *Kolo*: usually referred to as the Ngolog or Ngolo tribe: e.g. André Migot in *Tibetan Marches* (1946) and André Ghihaut, *Tibetan Adventure* (1940). (Trans.)

where we are in their hands, they will not attack us. And also, I think that they have considerable respect for the power of the Lamas of the Western Heavens.' So, following his advice, we all set about pitching camp.

The tents were hardly up when the Kolo reappeared on the skyline and galloped towards us at their usual speed. The chief alone came into our camp; the others waited a little outside. He addressed the Tibetan he had spoken to before.

'I have come,' he said, 'for an explanation of something that I do not understand. You are aware that our camp is over that mountain, and yet you dare to pitch your tents here, quite close. How many men have you in your party?'

'We are only eighteen; and you, I think, are twenty-seven. But men of courage never take flight.'

'So you want to fight?'

'If there were not a number of sick amongst us, I would answer "Yes", for I have met the Kolo face to face before.'

'You have already fought the Kolo? When? What is your name?'

'Five years ago, at the affray over the ambassador; I still have a reminder of that day,' and he bared his arm, marked with a long sabre scar. The brigand laughed and again asked him his name.

'I am Rala Tchembé,' said the merchant. 'Maybe you know that name?'

'Yes, all the Kolo know it, it is the name of a brave man,' said the Kolo and jumped off his horse; he drew a sabre from his belt and presented it to the Tibetan. 'Here,' he said, 'take this sabre, it is my best. We fought more than once; when next we meet, we shall meet as brothers.' The Tibetan accepted the gift and gave the brigand chief in exchange a magnificent bow and quiver which he had bought in Peking.

The Kolo who had remained outside the camp, seeing that their chief was fraternising with the headman of the caravan, dismounted, tied their horses in pairs by the bridles and came to drink a friendly bowl of tea with the poor travellers who were at last beginning to breathe again. All these brigands were extremely amiable; they asked for news of the Tartar-Khalkas, whom they were particularly anxious to meet, because during the previous year they had killed two of their men who had to be avenged. Politics were also discussed. The brigands claimed to be great supporters of the Dalai Lama, and bitter enemies of the emperor of China; this was why they seldom failed to plunder the embassy on its way to Peking, since they held that the emperor was unworthy to receive gifts from the Dalai Lama, but normally respected it on its return, because it was right and proper that the emperor should send gifts to the Dalai Lama. After graciously accepting the tea and *tsamba* of the caravan, the brigands wished us a good journey and set off back to their camp. Despite all these brotherly gestures we slept with one eye open. The night was untroubled, however, and next day we peacefully resumed our journey. Amongst the many pilgrims who have taken the road to Lhasa, there are few indeed who can boast of having seen the brigands so near at hand, and suffered no harm from them.

We had just escaped one danger, but, we were told, another even greater, though of a different nature, awaited us. We were beginning to climb the huge chain of the Tant La Mountains. According to our travelling companions all the sick would die on the plateau, and even the healthy would suffer greatly. Father Gabet was condemned to certain death by the experienced travellers. After six days' painful climb up a number of mountains, ranged as in an amphitheatre one above another, we finally arrived on this famous plateau, maybe the highest point of the world. The snow seemed to form a permanent crust, to be part of the soil. Although it crackled under our feet we hardly left the slightest footprint. The only vegetation was a grass, growing here and there in clumps, short, sharp, smooth, of a woody texture, hard as iron but not brittle; it would have made very good upholsterers' needles. The animals were so famished that, willy nilly, they had to graze on this terrible stuff. We could hear it crunch as they bit, and they could only get a few mouthfuls of it down after a fierce struggle which made their lips bleed.

Beyond the edge of this magnificent plateau we could see below us the summits and peaks of a number of great ranges of mountains, stretching far away to the horizon. We had never seen anything to compare with the splendour of this stupendous sight. For the twelve days that we travelled on the top of the Tant La we had good weather; the air was windless, and each day God sent a health-giving warm sunshine that tempered to some extent the cold of the atmosphere. Yet the air, much rarefied by the great altitude, was incredibly bracing. Enormous eagles followed our band of travellers, and every day several corpses were left behind for them. It was decreed that Death should also take toll of our small caravan; but it took only our little black mule. We were sad but resigned. The gloomy predictions made about Father Gabet proved quite wrong. Quite the contrary, this plateau did him a deal of good. His health and normal strength gradually returned. This almost unexpected gift of Providence made us forget all our past hardships. We regained our courage, and trusted that God would let us reach our destination.

The descent from the Tant La was long, rough and steep. For four whole days we went down a kind of giant staircase, of which each step was a mountain. At the bottom, we found hot springs of great magnificence. Amongst great rocks, many pools had been hollowed out by nature, in which the water boiled as if in a pot over a hot fire. In places it spouted from cracks in the rocks, innumerable little jets shooting in all directions in a most bizarre manner. There were some pools in which the water boiled at times so violently that great columns of water rose and fell intermittently, as if a great pump were at work. From these springs thick steam rose continuously, to condense into whitish clouds. The water was all sulphurous. After churning and leaping over and over again in the pools amongst the granite rocks it finally succeeded in escaping and flowed down into a little valley, forming a wide watercourse which ran over a bed of golden pebbles. These waters, though boiling, did not remain liquid for long. The extreme cold of the air cooled them so fast that at a little over a mile from the springs the stream was frozen almost solid. There are many thermal springs in the Tibetan mountains. The doctor-lamas realise that they have great medicinal properties; they frequently prescribe them for their patients, both for baths and for drinking.

From the Tant La mountains onwards, we noticed a gradual descent all the way to Lhasa. As we went, the cold became less intense and the soil produced stronger and more varied grasses. One day we camped in a great plain where the grazing was marvellously abundant. As our animals had long suffered from terrible starvation, it was decided to stop for two days and to let them enjoy this opportunity.

Next morning, as we were peacefully making tea inside our

tent, we saw in the distance a troop of horsemen bearing down on us at full speed. Our blood froze at the sight, and we stood a moment petrified. When we had recovered from the shock, we rushed to Rala Tchembé's tent. 'The Kolo! The Kolo!' we shouted. 'Here comes a great troop of Kolo!' The Tibetan merchants, who were sitting drinking their tea and dunking their tsamba, laughed and asked us to come and sit down.

'Take tea with us,' they said. 'There are no more Kolo to be afraid of here; these horsemen are friendly. We are beginning to reach inhabited country; behind that hill over there on the right there are a large number of black tents. The horsemen you took for Kolo are local herdsmen.' These words brought us comfort, and comfort bringing appetite, we were glad to sit down and share the Tibetan merchants' breakfast. But no sooner had they poured us a bowlful of buttered tea than the horsemen arrived at our tent door. Far from being brigands they were splendid fellows who had come to sell us butter and fresh meat. Their saddles looked like butchers' shops, with numerous joints of mutton and venison hanging along the horses' flanks. We bought eight legs of mutton, which being frozen were easy to carry. They cost us an old pair of Peking boots and the saddle from our little mule, which luckily was also from Peking. Everything that comes from Peking is greatly prized by the Tibetans, especially by those who are still herdsmen and nomads. Hence the merchants who accompanied the embassy had carefully marked all their bales of merchandise 'Goods from Peking'. Snuff is greatly in demand in Tibet. All the herdsmen asked us if we had any Peking snuff. I, the only snuff-taker of the party, had once had some, but for the past week I had been filling my snuff-box with a horrible mixture of earth and ashes. Inveterate snuff-takers will appreciate the grimness of my situation.

Condemned as we had been for the last two months to live exclusively on barley-meal dipped in tea, the mere sight of our joints of mutton seemed to act as a tonic on our stomachs and to strengthen our scraggy limbs. The rest of the day was devoted to culinary operations. For spice and seasoning we had only garlic, but it was so frozen and dried up that there was next to nothing inside the skin. We took all we had left and stuck it into two of the legs of mutton which we put into our biggest pot to boil. As there was an abundance of *argols* on this happy plain we were able to make a good enough fire to cook our priceless supper. The sun was on the point of setting and Samdadchiemba, who had just inspected one of the joints with his thumbnail, was triumphantly announcing that the meat was done to a turn, when we heard all around us cries of disaster: '*Mi yon! Mi yon!* Fire! Fire!' We bounded out of our tent. The fire had started indeed inside the camp, burning the dry grass, and threatening to destroy our tents; the flames spread everywhere with terrifying speed. All the travellers, armed with felt rugs, were trying to beat it out, or at least prevent it from reaching the tents. These, fortunately, escaped destruction. The fire, though pursued in all directions, found a way out and escaped into the wilds. Then, fanned by the wind, it spread over the wide prairie, consuming the pasture as it went. We thought that there was nothing more to fear, but shouts of 'Save the camels! Save the camels!' soon made us realise how little experience we had of the dangers of fire in the wilderness. We then saw how the camels stood stupidly waiting for the flames to envelop them, instead of running away from them, like the horses and the cattle. So we tore off to save ours, which were still some way from the fire. But the flames were there almost as soon as we were. Soon we were

surrounded by fire. We pushed and beat those silly camels to try and force them to run, but in vain: they stood still, turning their heads to look at us coolly, as if asking us what right we had to come and stop them from grazing. We could have killed them! The flames ate up the grass at such speed that it soon reached the camels. Their long thick coats caught fire, and we had to run at them with felt rugs to put out the flames as they ran over their bodies. We were able to save three whose coats were only singed. But the fourth was in a pitiful state; it hadn't a hair left on the whole of its body; nothing remained but skin, and this too was horribly burnt.

The area of grazing land that had been destroyed by the fire was about a mile and half long by three quarters of a mile wide. The Tibetans again and again blessed their lucky stars that they had succeeded in stopping the fire, and we heartily joined in when we realised the extent of the danger we had run. They told us that if the fire had gone on much longer it would have reached the black tents, and that then the herdsmen would have pursued and certainly slaughtered us. Hell knows no fury like that of these poor dwellers in the wilds when, by mistake or on purpose, someone reduces to ashes the pasturelands which are their only means of livelihood. It is tantamount to destroying their cattle.

When we resumed our journey, the burnt camel was not dead, but it was unusable; the three others had to fill the gap by sharing the load of their unfortunate fellow between them. In any case, the loads were much lighter than when we had left the Koukou Noor; our sacks of meal were almost empty; and since the crossing of the Tant La we had been reduced to a ration of two bowlfuls of *tsamba* a day. We had got our sums more or less right before we left, but we had not reckoned on the wastefulness of our two camel drivers: the one out of foolishness and carelessness, the other out of malice. Fortunately we were about to reach a large Tibetan supply base, at which we would be able to stock up.

For several days now our route took us along a succession of valleys, with here and there a few black tents and some large herds of yaks. Then at last we pitched our camp outside a large Tibetan village. It was on the Na Pichu River, marked on the Andriveau-Goujon map in its Mongol form of Khara Oussou; both mean 'Black Waters'. Na Pichu was the first Tibetan settlement of any size on the road to Lhasa. It consisted of some adobe houses, and a large number of black tents. There was no sign of any cultivation. Although the inhabitants were settled, they were herdsmen like the nomadic tribes, and cattle-raising was their only occupation. We were told that long ago a king of the Koukou Noor had made war on the Tibetans, had conquered a large part of the country and given the Na Pichu area to the soldiers he had brought with him. Although by now these Tartars had merged with the Tibetans, we did see a few Mongol yurts amongst the black tents. This historical event may perhaps also explain why a number of Mongol expressions were in use locally, and had become part of the Tibetan language.

All caravans bound for Lhasa had to stop at Na Pichu for some days, to change their means of transport, because the route from then on was so rocky that camels could go no further. Our first task therefore was to sell ours; they were in such poor shape and so exhausted that nobody wanted them. Finally a man claiming to be an animal doctor turned up: he probably knew a way of improving their condition, for we sold him three of them for fifteen ounces of silver, and threw in the 'burnt' one for nothing. These fifteen ounces of silver were just what we needed to hire six yaks to carry our baggage to Lhasa.

Our second task was to get rid of our assistant camel driver, the lama from the Ratchico mountains. After paying him off handsomely we told him that if he intended going on to Lhasa he must choose other companions, and that he could regard himself as freed from any obligations contracted with us. So at last we were parted from this fellow who, by his malice, had so increased the hardships we had had to bear on our journey.

We feel that we have a duty to warn anyone who for any reason might have to stop at Na Pichu that he would do well to be on his guard against thieves. The inhabitants of this Tibetan village are remarkable rogues; they exploit Mongol and other caravans to a shocking extent. At night they adroitly slip into the tents and take what they can lay their hands on; even by day they ply their profession with a cool skill which would be the envy of the cleverest crooks in Paris.

After stocking up with butter, *tsamba* and some joints of mutton, we went on towards Lhasa, which was now only about a fortnight's march away. We had as company some Mongols from the kingdom of Khartchin, who were on pilgrimage to

Lhasa, the 'Eternal Sanctuary'; they had taken their Grand Chaberon with them, that is, a Living Buddha who was the superior of their lamasery. He was a young man of eighteen; his manners were pleasant and refined, his expression was open and artless, contrasting strangely with the role he was made to play. At the age of five he had been declared a Buddha and Grand Lama of the Buddhists of Khartchin. He was going to Lhasa to spend some years in one of the great lamaseries, in the study of prayers and other knowledge required by his position. A brother of the king of Khartchin and several high-ranking lamas acted as his retinue. To be a Living Buddha was evidently a heavy burden for this young man. We could see that he would have enjoyed laughing and playing; he would have preferred to canter around on his horse, but was forced to proceed solemnly between a guard of honour of two horsemen who never left him. When we camped, instead of sitting all the time on cushions inside his tent, trying to look like an idol in a lamasery, he would much have preferred to be free in the wilds, busy with the tasks of nomadic life, but none of that was allowed. His life-task was to act the Buddha, and he must have no part in the everyday affairs of ordinary mortals. This young Chaberon enjoyed coming from time to time to chat with us in our tent; with us at least he could put off his official divinity and belong to the human race. He was most interested to hear us talk of Europe and the Europeans. He questioned us with artless candour about our religion, and greatly admired it; and when we asked him if it would not be better to be a worshipper of Jehovah than to be a Chaberon, he answered that he did not know. He disliked being asked about his previous lives and continual reincarnations; such questions made him blush, and in the end he told us that he found it painful when we spoke of such matters. This poor boy was clearly caught in a maze of religion of which he understood not a word.

The road from Na Pichu to Lhasa was mostly rocky and very hard going. When we reached the Koiran mountain chain it became extremely difficult indeed. Yet as we went along we were of good cheer, as we saw more and more signs of habitation. The sight of black tents in the distance, of many pilgrims on their way to Lhasa, of frequent inscriptions written on cairns by the wayside, and of many small caravans of yaks which we met from time to time all helped to lighten the fatigues of the journey. At a few days' march from Lhasa, the population ceased to be entirely nomadic. A few cultivated fields appeared in the wilderness, and gradually black tents gave way to houses. Then finally there were no more herdsmen and we were amongst an agricultural people. Fifteen days after we had left Na Pichu we arrived at Pampou, which, because of its closeness to Lhasa, was regarded by pilgrims as the gateway to the holy city. Pampou, erroneously marked on the map as Panctou, was a fine plain watered by a large river, which irrigated the land by means of a number of canals. There was no village as such, but large flat-roofed farmhouses were dotted everywhere, mostly well white-washed. They were all surrounded by large trees, and each one had a little turret like a dovecot from which floated many-coloured pennants covered with Tibetan characters. After more than three months spent in dreary deserts, with nothing to see but wild beasts and brigands, the plain of Pampou seemed to us the most beautiful place on earth. Our long hard journey had brought us so close to the savage state that we were lost in ecstasy at anything connected with civilisation. The houses, the ploughs, even a simple furrow seemed exciting. But what struck us most of all was the extraordinary mildness of the temperature. Although it was the end of January, the river and the canals had only a little thin ice along the edges; and hardly anyone was dressed in furs.

At Pampou we again had to reorganise the caravan. Yaks normally go no further than this; they are replaced by donkeys, very small but strong and trained as pack animals. As it was difficult to find enough donkeys for the baggage of the lamas from Khartchin and for our own, we were forced to stay two days. We used these days in an attempt to do something about our appearance. Our hair and our beards were so shaggy, our faces so sooty from the smoke of the tent, so cracked with the cold, so thin, so misshapen, that we felt sorry for ourselves when we looked at ourselves in a glass. As for our clothes, they were no better than we were.

The people of Pampou were most of them very well off; so they were continually gay and carefree. Each evening they gathered in front of their farms and we saw men, women and children jigging to a voice accompaniment. When the dances were over, the farmer plied everyone with a sourish drink made of fermented barley. It was like beer without the hops.

After two days' search in all the farms of the plain, enough donkeys had been collected to equip the caravan and we started off. One mountain stood between us and Lhasa, but it was undoubtedly the hardest and steepest of all that we had come across in our journey. The Tibetans and the Mongols climb it with great reverence; they believe that whoever has the good fortune to reach the top receives absolution for all his sins. Whether or not this is so, it is certain that climbing this mountain is a long, hard act of penance. We left at an hour after midnight, and it was not until nearly ten in the morning that we reached the summit. We were forced to do almost all the climb on foot, as riding was most difficult owing to the steepness and the rocky terrain.

The sun was just about to set when we had negotiated all the zig-zags of the descent. We came out into a wide valley, and on our right we saw Lhasa, capital of the Buddhist world. A multitude of ancient trees; large white houses, flat-roofed and turreted; countless temples with golden roofs; the Buddha La, with the palace of the Dalai Lama on it: all this we saw, an impressive and majestic city.

At the entrance to the city, the Mongols whom we had got to know on the journey and who had arrived a few days before us met us and invited us to put up at a lodging that they had arranged for us. It was 29 January 1846; eighteen months had elapsed since we had left the valley of Black Waters.

[6]

THE FIRST DAYS IN LHASA

After an eighteen months' battle against innumerable hardships and set-backs, we had reached our destination, but not the end of our troubles. We had no longer, it is true, to fear death in uninhabited territory from starvation and cold, but we would have to face up to trials and tribulations of another kind, if we were to speak to this pagan people of Christ crucified for the salvation of mankind. The physical struggle was over, but the moral struggle was about to begin. For this too we relied on the infinite goodness of God, confident that He who had protected us in the wilderness against the inclemency of the weather would be willing to aid us against the malice of men, here in the heart of the Buddhist world.

The day after our arrival in Lhasa, we hired a Tibetan guide and explored the various districts of the city in search of rented lodgings. Most of the houses in Lhasa were large; they were high, with several storeys and flat roofs which sloped slightly for drainage purposes; they were whitewashed all over, apart from some of the edges and the window and door frames which were painted red or yellow. Reformed Buddhists are particularly fond of these colours: they are called lamaic colours and are regarded as sacred. As the houses were whitewashed annually they were beautifully clean outside and looked newly built; but the interiors did not in any way live up to this fair promise. The rooms were dirty, smoky, smelly and cluttered with furniture and utensils in disgusting disorder. Tibetan houses were so to speak whited sepulchres, reminding one of Buddhism itself and of all other false religions, which are always careful to cover the corruption and falsehood within with a layer of fair-seeming dogma and moral rectitude.

After a long search, we chose quite a small lodging, part of a large house with about fifty tenants. Our modest apartment was on the top floor; twenty-six wooden steps led up to it, without a banister and so steep and narrow that it was wise to go on all fours to avoid breaking one's neck. We had a large square room and a small corridor which we called 'the closet'.

The room was lit by a window facing north-east with three thick wooden bars, and by a round skylight in the roof, which had many uses. It let in the light, the wind, the rain and the snow; but let out the smoke from our fire. The Tibetan form of heating consists of an earthenware bowl placed in the middle of the room, in which *argols* are burnt. As this is a fuel which often gives off more smoke than heat, there was a distinct advantage in having a hole above our heads: this invaluable

skylight enabled us to keep a fire going without risk of stifling from the smoke. There was of course from time to time the trifling inconvenience of a shower of rain or snow descending on one's shoulders; but this was nothing to us after our nomadic life. Our furniture consisted of two goatskin rugs, one on each side of the fireplace, two saddles, our tent, some pairs of old boots, two battered trunks, three ragged robes hanging on nails, our blankets done up in a roll and a heap of dried dung in a corner. In other words, we had straightaway adopted Tibetan ways. The 'closet', dominated by a fine brick cooking

stove, was both kitchen and larder; here we had installed
Samdadchiemba, who, after giving up his post as camel driver,
combined the functions of cook, butler and stable-boy. Our
two white horses were lodged in a recess of the courtyard,
resting on their hard-won laurels, waiting for an opportunity
to be given a new master; these poor beasts were so emaciated
that we could hardly put them up for sale until they had
acquired a little flesh between skin and bones.

As soon as we had settled in, we made a detailed exploration
of Lhasa and had a look at its inhabitants. It was not a large
city; the circumference was at most six miles. Unlike Chinese
cities, it was not walled. We were told that walls had once
existed, but were entirely destroyed in a war with the Indians
from Bhutan: not a trace now existed. Beyond the suburbs,
there were many gardens planted with great trees, making a
magnificent ring of verdure round the city. The main streets
were very wide, straight and clean, at least in dry weather; the
suburbs were utterly and revoltingly filthy. As already stated,
the houses were mostly large, tall and fine looking; some were
stone, others brick and a few adobe; but as they were always so
freshly whitewashed one house looked as good as another. In
one of the suburbs there was an area where all the houses were
built entirely of cow and sheep horns: these peculiar buildings
were extremely strong and most attractive to look at. As the
cowhorns were smooth and pale, and the sheephorns dark and
rough, they made a fascinating combination, forming patterns
of great variety. The spaces between the horns were filled with
mortar. These were the only houses not whitewashed; the
Tibetans had had the good taste to leave them as they were,
without any attempt to add to their strange barbaric beauty.
Needless to add that the inhabitants of Lhasa were great eaters
of beef and mutton; their horn houses were sufficient proof of
it.

The Buddhist temples were the most striking buildings in
Lhasa. We will give no description here, as they were all more
or less similar to those we have described elsewhere. We need
only add that they were larger, richer and more profusely
covered with gold.

The palace of the Dalai Lama thoroughly deserved the fame it
universally enjoyed. To the north of the city and no more than
a quarter of an hour's walk from it stood a low rocky eminence,

conical in form. It rose out of the middle of the wide valley like
an islet in a great lake. This was the Buddha La, or Mountain of
Buddha, Holy Mountain; it was on this majestic natural pedestal
that the worshippers of the Dalai Lama had built a magnificent
palace in which resided their Living God in flesh and blood. It
was a group of several temples, varying in size and splendour;
the central one was four storeys high, and dominated the rest;
it was topped by a dome which was entirely covered with gold
leaf, and surrounded by a gilded colonnade. Here the Dalai
Lama lived; from the top of this high sanctuary he could watch
on ceremonial days his myriad worshippers coming and going
in the plain below, to prostrate themselves at the foot of the
holy mountain. The smaller palaces, grouped round the great
temple, were the dwelling places of countless lamas of all sorts,
whose task it was to serve the Living Buddha at all times, and to
act as his court. A double avenue of tall trees led from Lhasa to
the Buddha La; it was always full of foreign pilgrims, telling
their beads, and of lamas from the court dressed in magnificent
vestments and riding richly caparisoned horses. Around the
Buddha La there was great activity at all times, but people were
mostly grave and silent and appeared to be wrapped in pious
thoughts.

In the town itself the population behaved quite differently;
there was much shouting and jostling, and eager buying and
selling. Trade and piety brought a great number of foreigners
to Lhasa, making the city the rendezvous of all Asiatic peoples;
the streets were always thronged with pilgrims and dealers,
with an astonishing variety of features, costumes and languages. This great multitude was to a large extent a floating
population, changing daily. The stable population of Lhasa
consisted of Tibetans, Pebouns, Katchi and Chinese.

The Tibetans belong to the great family of races collectively
known as Mongols; they have black hair, sparse beards, small
slanting eyes, high cheek-bones, short noses, wide mouths and
thin lips; their complexions are rather swarthy; however, in
the upper class, a number have faces as white as Europeans.
They are of medium height; they are as agile as the Chinese,
and as strong and vigorous as the Tartars. We noticed that they
were fond of gymnastic exercise and loved dancing; they had a
graceful springy walk. They continually hummed prayers or
popular songs as they went about the streets. There was much

generosity and openness in their natures; they were intrepid in battle and courageous in the face of death; they were as religious as the Tartars, but less credulous. Cleanliness was not one of their strong points; yet they loved luxury and gorgeous clothing.

The Tibetans did not shave their heads; they let their hair grow shoulder-length, and shortened it from time to time with scissors. A few years before our visit the Lhasa dandies had adopted the Chinese fashion of the pig-tail, which they adorned with gold ornaments set with precious stones and coral beads. The normal headgear was a blue brimless hat with a wide border in black velvet, and a red pompom on top; on feast days they wore a large red hat similar to a Basque beret but wider and decorated round the edge with a long thick fringe. A wide robe fastened on the right by four hooks and drawn in at the waist by a red belt, and red or purple cloth boots completed the simple yet quite elegant costume of the Tibetans. From their belts there usually hung a yellow taffeta bag containing the inevitable wooden bowl, and two richly embroidered little oval purses, with nothing inside: they were purely decorative.

The women's costume was very similar to the men's; but over the robe they wore a short motley tunic. Their hair was in two plaits and hung down over their shoulders. The lower class women wore a small yellow cap, rather like the liberty cap worn at the time of the French revolution. Great ladies wore simply an elegant crown, made of tiny beads. Tibetan women followed a custom, or rather obeyed a rule, which was almost incredible and surely unique: before going out of doors they daubed their faces with a kind of black sticky varnish, rather like a grape jelly. As the purpose of this was to make themselves look ugly, they applied this revolting form of make-up at random, with the result that they hardly looked human. We were given the following account of the origin of this monstrous practice: about two hundred years before our visit, the Nomekhan, or Royal Lama who then governed Tibet, was a man of strict puritanical morals. At this period Tibetan women did not set out to make themselves ugly; on the contrary, they had an exaggerated love of luxury and adornment, which had given rise to grave disorder and unbridled immorality. The contagion even spread to the holy family of lamas; the lamaseries relaxed their ancient strict discipline and were invaded by practices which were leading to their complete dissolution. In order to put a stop to a licentiousness that had become almost universal, the Nomekhan published a decree forbidding women to appear in public without daubing their faces in the manner we have described. This strange law was motivated by high moral and religious considerations; it threatened those who disobeyed it with the most severe punishments, especially with the anger of Buddha. It must have needed extraordinary courage to publish such a decree; but the most extraordinary thing about it was that the women should have been willing to put up with it. There is no hint, in the traditions handed down, of the slightest resistance, of the tiniest rebellion. They simply carried out the law, blacked their faces with gusto and made themselves into perfect frights; and so it continued up to the time of our visit. It seems to have become a point of dogma, an act of piety. The women who made themselves most hideous were considered to be the most pious. In the country districts, the decree was so scrupulously observed that no inspector could ever find fault; but at Lhasa it was not unusual to meet in the streets women who, disregarding the law and all the proprieties, were brazen enough to appear in public with unvarnished faces, just as nature made them. Those who behaved in this manner had a very bad reputation and always hid whenever they saw a policeman coming.*

It was claimed that the Nomekhan's decree caused a great improvement in public morals. We have no definite evidence to the contrary; however we can say that the Tibetans were far from being models of morality; a great deal of bad behaviour went on, and we are tempted to believe that the blackest, ugliest face-varnish is powerless to reform an immoral people. Christianity alone would be capable of curing the pagan nations of the shameful vices with which they are beset.

One thing that might indicate that there was less immorality in Tibet than in certain other pagan lands is the fact that

*Sir Joseph Dalton Hooker, in his *Himalayan Journals* (1854), refers to 'the Tibetan custom of daubing the face with black pigment to protect the skin from the excessive cold and dryness of those lofty regions', and says that 'a ludicrous imposition was passed on the credulity of MM. Huc and Gabet'. I have found no other reference to the custom however, and in his introduction John Keay appears to accept Huc and Gabet's view. (Trans.)

women enjoyed great freedom. Instead of languishing imprisoned in their houses, they led a busy active life. Apart from
household work, they ran all the small trades. They hawked
the merchandise round the streets, ran market stalls and almost
all the retail shops. In the countryside they took a large share in
the farm work.

The men, although less hard-working and active than the
women, were far from idle. They were mainly engaged in wool
spinning and weaving. The cloth they produced was called
pou-lou; it was very close-woven and extremely strong. It was
made in a very wide range of qualities, from the coarsest and
shaggiest to the finest, most beautiful merinos. A rule of the
reformed Buddhists laid it down that all lamas must wear red
pou-lou. Large quantities were consumed in Tibet itself, and the
caravans carried considerable loads to North China and Tartary. The lowest quality *pou-lou* was very cheap, but the top
qualities were excessively dear.

The joss-sticks well-known in China by the name of *tsan
hsiang* (perfumes of Tibet) were one of the main products of
Lhasa. They were made of the powdered wood of various
aromatic trees, to which musk and gold-dust were added.
These ingredients were worked into a purple paste which was
then moulded into thin rods some three or four feet long. They
were burnt in lamaseries or before the shrines of household
idols. Once lit, they never went out, and gave off odours of
exquisite sweetness. The Tibetan merchants who accompanied
the ambassadorial caravans to Peking took large quantities
with them and sold them at exorbitant prices. Imitations were
made in Northern China, and put on the market as the real
thing; but they were markedly inferior.

The Tibetans had no porcelain, but made all sorts of pottery
of an unusually high quality. However their table-service
consisted of course of only one wooden bowl each, carried
either in the bosom or in an elaborate pouch attached to the
belt. These bowls were fashioned from the roots of certain
special trees which grow in the Tibetan mountains. They were
gracefully shaped, but simple and without decoration. They
were given a light coat of varnish, which left the natural colour
and graining of the wood unaltered. Throughout Tibet, everyone from the poorest beggar to the Dalai Lama ate out of a
wooden bowl. However, all bowls did not look alike to the

Tibetans, as they might to us Europeans. There were bowls and bowls, some to be bought for a few small coins and others as dear as a hundred ounces of silver, about a thousand francs; and if you ask what difference there was between the various qualities, we should have to reply frankly that with the best will in the world we were unable to see any of importance. The Tibetans used to say that top quality bowls had the property of neutralising poisons.

A few days after our arrival in Lhasa, we went into a wooden bowl shop to renew our stock, which was already old and in bad condition. A Tibetan woman, her face well covered with black varnish, stood behind the counter. This lady, judging from our somewhat exotic and unusual appearance that we must be persons of distinction, opened a drawer and displayed two small boxes of artistic design, in each of which was a bowl wrapped in three layers of tissue paper. After examining them with some nervousness, we asked the price.

'*Tchik-la, gatsé-ré?*' ('How much each?')

'Fifty ounces of silver each, your excellencies.' This stagger-ing reply made us feel slightly faint, for with all our resources we could at most have bought four of such bowls! When we had somewhat recovered we put the two precious bowls carefully back into their boxes and went round the shop looking at the many sets of bowls that were openly on display on the shelves.

'And these, how much are they?'

'One ounce of silver the pair, your excellencies.' We put down an ounce of silver and carried off our two bowls in triumph, for they looked to us absolutely identical to the ones priced at the equivalent of five hundred francs each. When we got back home, our landlord, to whom we straightaway showed them, told us that for an ounce of silver one could buy at least four bowls of that type.

Pou-lou cloth, joss-sticks and wooden bowls were the three main products which the Tibetans made successfully. Everything else was poor or mediocre, and their simple arts and crafts are not worth mentioning. Nor was their agricultural production at all remarkable. Tibet, almost entirely mountainous, a land whose rivers are rushing torrents, had very little arable land. Only in the valleys could seeds be sown with some hope of success. There was little wheat, and less rice. The main crop was *tsing-kou* or black barley, which was made into *tsamba*, staple food of the entire population, rich or poor. Lhasa was well provided with mutton, horse and yak meat; there was also excellent fresh fish, and the most delicious pork. But all of these were usually so expensive that they were beyond the purse of the working classes. In fact, Tibetans subsisted on a poor diet. Their meals normally consisted of only buttered tea and *tsamba*, kneaded roughly with the fingers. The rich man's diet was identical, and it was pitiful to see such food caten out of a bowl that had cost a hundred ounces of silver. Meat, when there was any, was served between meals, a matter of whim or greed, rather as we eat fruit or pastries. Usually two dishes were served together, one of boiled meat and one of raw; the Tibetans ate both with equal appetite, without any seasoning whatsoever. They had however enough good taste not to eat without drinking. From time to time they filled their beloved bowls with a bitter malt beer, which was not unpleasant in flavour.

Tibet, so poor in agriculture and industry, was rich in metals to an incredible extent; gold and silver could be found so easily that even the simple shepherds knew how to refine them. We saw them sometimes at the bottom of a ravine or in a cranny in the mountainside, crouching over a fire of goat *argols*, amusing themselves by heating up in a crucible the gold dust that they had collected whilst grazing their flocks. Owing to this abundance of metals the currency was of little value, and in consequence goods were always very expensive. The Tibetan monetary system consisted only of silver coins, which were slightly larger but thinner than our franc pieces. On one side they bore inscriptions in Tibetan, Parsee or Indian characters; on the obverse there was a crown composed of eight little round flowers. To provide small change, these coins were cut up, and the number of florets remaining on a fragment determined its value. The complete coin was called a *tchan-ka*; a half was a *tché-ptché*, which therefore had only four florets. The *chokan* had five, and the *kagan* three. In big commercial deals, silver ingots were used; they were weighed on a balance with a scalebeam, graduated according to the decimal system. The Tibetans usually counted on their beads; a few, especially the merchants, used the Chinese abacus or *souan pan*; the learned worked with Arabic numerals, which seem to have reached Tibet very early. We saw several lamaic manuscript books containing astronomical tables in Arabic figures; the pages were numbered in the same way; some of these were slightly different from those in use in Europe, particularly the five, which was inverted.

From the few facts given above about Tibetan production, it can be concluded that Tibet was perhaps at this time both the richest and the poorest country in the world. Rich in gold and silver, poor in everything that makes for the prosperity of the masses. Gold and silver, collected by the people, were absorbed by the rich and powerful, especially by the lamaseries, which like great reservoirs drained off all the wealth of this large country. The lamas, to whom most of the currency passed via the gifts of the faithful, increased it hundredfold by means of usury, employing methods which shocked even the Chinese. The alms they received were used to lure more money from everyman's purse. The money having all accumulated in the coffers of the privileged classes and the necessities of life being extremely expensive, the inevitable result was that a large proportion of the population was continually plunged in abject poverty. There were a considerable number of beggars in Lhasa. They went from door to door begging a handful of *tsamba*. Their method was to hold out a closed fist, thumb upwards. We should add, in the Tibetans' favour, that they showed compassion and charity; the poor were rarely sent away empty-handed.

The most numerous of the foreign resident population were the Peboun, Indians from Bhutan, on the other side of the Himalayas. They were short, strong and vivacious; their faces were rounder than the Tibetans'; they had very dark complexions and small, black, cunning eyes; on their foreheads they wore a scarlet mark which they renewed each day. They all wore a robe of purple *pou-lou*, and small felt cap in a slightly darker shade of the same colour. Out of doors they wore in addition a long red scarf which was wound twice round the neck, with both ends hanging down over the shoulders.

The Peboun were the only metalworkers of Lhasa. In their quarter of the town were to be found all the smiths working in iron, brass, lead or tin, the foundrymen, goldsmiths, jewellers, mechanics and even the physicians and chemists. Their workshops and laboratories were partly underground. The entances were low and narrow, and three or four steps below street level. Over every housedoor was painted a red globe with a white crescent over it, evidently representing the sun and the moon. But why they did this, we forgot to enquire.

There were very fine craftsmen amongst the Peboun metalworkers. They made gold and silver vases for the lamaseries and all sorts of jewellery, which would certainly stand competition with that of European workmanship. They also made the beautiful goldleaf temple roofs, which are completely weathcrproof and always retain their freshness and their brilliance. They were such masters of this craft that they were in demand in the far corners of Tartary for the adornment of the great lamaseries there. They were moreover the dyers of Lhasa: their colours were so brilliant and their dyes so fast that although the cloth might wear out it never faded. They were only allowed to dye *pou-lou*. Imported cloth had to be used as it was: there was an absolute ban on dying it. This was no doubt with the intention of protecting the local product.

The Peboun were a jolly childlike people; in their leisure hours they always seemed to be laughing and romping about; at work, they always sang. They were Indian Buddhists. Although not adopting Tsong Kaba's reforms, they respected the lamaic ceremonies and practices. They would all go, on high feast days, to prostrate themselves at the foot of the Buddha La, and offer their devotions to the Dalai Lama.

The second most important group of foreigners living in Lhasa were the Katchi, Moslems from Kashmir. They stood out from the inferior races amongst whom they lived by their turbans, their long beards, their gravity, their noble intelligent faces and the cleanliness and richness of their attire. They had their own governor in Lhasa, whose authority was recognised by the Tibetan government. He was also their religious leader, acting both as Pasha and as Mufti. The Katchi had been in Lhasa for some centuries. They had left their country to escape from the despotism of a certain Pasha, which had become intolerable. Since then, their descendants had been so contented in Tibet that they had given up any idea of returning to their homeland. They had retained links with Kashmir, but the news that they had received was not such as to encourage them to leave their adopted country. The Katchi governor, with whom we became quite friendly, told us that the Pelings of Calcutta, that is, the British, were now masters of Kashmir. 'Pelings,' he told us, 'are the most cunning of men. They are getting control of all parts of India, but it is always by trickery rather than by open force. Instead of overturning the authorities, they cleverly try to win them over to their side and share the spoils with them. In Kashmir there is a saying: "The world is Allah's, the land is the Pasha's, but the East India Company rules."'

The Katchi were the richest traders of Lhasa. They owned all the drapers' shops and those selling luxury and toilet goods; they were also money-changers, trafficking in gold and silver. Hence the fact that there were almost always Pharsee characters on the Tibetan coins. Each year a few of them went to Calcutta for the purposes of trade; the Katchi alone were allowed to cross the frontier and enter British territory; they travelled on passports provided by the Dalai Lama, and a Tibetan escort accompanied them over the Himalayas. The goods they brought back from Calcutta were trumpery stuff: ribbons, laces, knives, scissors, a certain amount of ironmongery, and a small assortment of cotton goods. The silks and the cloth which they sold in their shops, and in which they did a brisk trade, all came from Peking by caravan; the cloth was of

Russian origin and therefore much cheaper than they could buy in Calcutta.

The Katchi had a mosque in Lhasa, and were strict observers of Mahomet's laws; they openly despised all the superstitious practices of the Buddhists. The first to arrive in Lhasa had taken Tibetan wives, whom they forced to give up their own religion and become Moslems. They later adopted the rule of marrying only amongst themselves; so that gradually, in the heart of Tibet, there grew up a little separate race, with its own costume, customs, language and religion. As they did not prostrate themselves before the Dalai Lama nor go into the lamaseries to pray, they were reputed to be godless. But since they were mostly rich and powerful, people would draw aside to let them pass, and put out their tongues as a sign of respect. In Tibet, the form of greeting is to take your hat off, put out your tongue and scratch your right ear: these three operations are performed simultaneously.

The Chinese we saw in Lhasa were mostly soldiers or law-court officials; very few had settled in the city. Throughout their history the Chinese and the Tibetans have been closely concerned with each other; they have often been at war, and have often violated each other's rights . The Tartar-Mandchou dynasty, as we have already had occasion to state, realised from the very beginning how important it was to win the friendship of the Dalai Lama, because of his paramount influence amongst all the Mongol peoples. So from then on, there have always been two senior mandarins stationed at Lhasa with the title of Kin Tchai (or, to use the Mandchou form, Amban), that is, ambassador. These persons have had the offical function of presenting the formal homage of the Chinese emperor to the Dalai Lama on certain specified occasions and of guaranteeing China's support in any difficulties he may have with his neighbours. At any rate these have been the declared objectives of this permanent representation; but its real function has been to flatter the religious scruples of the Mongolians and gain their support for the reigning dynasty, in the belief that the Peking government has the greatest respect for the divine person on the Buddha La. Another advantage for the Chinese has been that the two Kin Tchai can easily, from Lhasa, keep an eye on developments in the various countries round the edges of the empire, and advise their government accordingly.

In the thirty-fifth year of the reign of Kien Long, Peking had two Kin Tchai at Lhasa, one called Lo and the other Pou. It was customary to speak of them both together, combining their names, as the Kin Tchai Lo-Pou. The word *lo-pou* in Tibetan means turnip, and so this method of referring to them was hardly polite, but since the people of Lhasa had never approved of a Chinese presence in their country, they used it all the more. Moreover, the behaviour of these two mandarins had for some time given offence to the Tibetans: they increasingly meddled in government matters and openly flouted the Dalai Lama's authority. It was the last straw when they brought a large force of Chinese troops into Tibet, on the pretext of protecting the Dalai Lama against certain Nepalese tribes which were being troublesome. Everyone realised that China was trying to extend the empire and dominate Tibet. The Tibetan government, we were told, put up a valiant fight, and the Nomekhan used every power he had to contain the encroachments on the two Kin Tchai. One day when he was on his way to the palace of the Chinese ambassadors, a young lama threw into his litter a note on which the following words were written: '*Lo-pou, ma, sa,*' which means: 'Don't eat turnips, avoid turnips.' The Nomekhan understood perfectly that, by this play on words, he was being warned to beware of the Kin Tchai Lo-Pou; but, as the warning lacked clarity and precision, he continued his way. Whilst he was in private session with the two ambassadors, members of their bodyguard suddenly burst into the room, stabbed the Nomekhan and cut off his head. A Tibetan cook who was in a neighbouring room had come running in when he heard the victim's screams; he seized the bloody head, stuck it on the end of a pike and ran through the streets of Lhasa, crying: 'Vengeance on the Chinese! Death to the Chinese!' The whole city was soon alerted and up in arms; the mob advanced on the palace of the Kin Tchai and horribly tore them to pieces. The people's anger was so great that all the Chinese were attacked indiscriminately; they were tracked down like wild beasts, not only in Lhasa but wherever they had set up military posts. There was terrible slaughter. We were told that the Tibetans only laid down their arms when they had mercilessly pursued and massacred all the Chinese as far as the frontiers of Yunnan and Ssetchouan.

When the news of this hideous catastrophe reached the

court at Peking, Emperor Kien Long immediately made a great levy of troops throughout the empire, and ordered them to advance on Tibet. The Chinese, as in almost all the wars they have fought against their neighbours, were beaten, but they won the peace. Relations were reestablished on the old footing, and since then peace has never been seriously disturbed between the two governments.

The Chinese military presence in Tibet was small at the time of our visit. Between Ssetchouan and Lhasa they kept poorly manned guardposts at points along the route for the protection of the emperor's couriers. In Lhasa itself their garrison consisted of a few hundred soldiers, whose purpose was to uphold and protect the position of the ambassadors. From Lhasa southwards towards Bhutan they had another line of guardposts, not very well kept. On the frontiers, jointly with Tibetan troops, they guarded the high passes separating Tibet from the first British positions. In the rest of Tibet there were no Chinese; entry was strictly forbidden them.

The Chinese soldiers and mandarins living in Tibet were paid by the Peking government; they usually stayed for three years; they were then replaced and returned to their home provinces. A few, when their service was over, obtained permission to settle in Lhasa or in the towns along the Ssetchouan road. In Lhasa there were not many; it would be hard to say what they specialised in to make their fortunes. Most of them were jacks of all trades, with many wily ways of coaxing Tibetan *tchan-kas* into their pockets. Some took Tibetan wives; but marriage ties were insufficient to keep them in their adopted country for life. When, after some years they felt that they had put enough aside, they simply went back to China, leaving wives and children behind them, except for their sons, whom they preferred not to abandon. The Tibetans, we found, feared the Chinese, the Katchi looked down on them and the Peboun laughed at them.

Among the many types of foreigner living in or passing through Lhasa, there was not one that we at all resembled. We noticed at once how the strangeness of our appearance drew everyone's attention. When we walked abroad we were stared at, and various surmises were made *sotto voce* about our origins. We were taken for two muftis newly arrived from Kashmir, for Brahmins from India, for lamas from Northern

Tartary and for merchants from Peking who had disguised themselves in order to join the Tibetan embassy. But all these theories were soon exploded, when we assured the Katchi that we were neither muftis nor Kashmiri, the Peboun that we were neither Indians nor Brahmins, the Mongols that we were neither lamas nor Tartars and the Chinese that we were neither merchants nor from the Middle Kingdom. When we had convinced everyone that we were none of these things, the word spread around that we were 'white Azaras'. We liked the sound of this description, but could hardly adopt it without finding out more about it. So we made enquiries, and were told that the Azaras were the most fervent of all the worshippers of Buddha; that they were a large Indian tribe whose members often made the pilgrimage to Lhasa; and that since we were neither Tibetans nor Katchi nor Pebouns nor Tartars nor Chinese, we must be Azaras. There was only one small snag in this: all the Azaras who had so far been seen in Lhasa had black faces; so it had been decided to solve the problem by calling us white Azaras. Again we bowed at the shrine of truth, and declared that we were not Azaras, neither black ones nor white ones.

All these theories about our origins were at first quite amusing; but they soon took on a more serious aspect. Ill-intentioned persons suggested that we might be Russians or British; and it was finally decided that we must be the latter. It was freely suggested that we were Pelings from Calcutta, that we had come to spy on Tibet's military potential, to make maps and to prepare for an invasion. All national prejudice apart, it was undesirable to be taken for subjects of Her Britannic Majesty. Such a misunderstanding could only render us most unpopular, and could have led to our execution by quartering; for the Tibetans have got it into their heads, for some reason, that the British are an aggressive people of whom they had best beware.

To cut short all the gossip that was circulating about us, we decided to comply with a regulation in force in Lhasa, whereby all foreigners wishing to reside any length of time in the city must report to the authorities. So we called on the chief of police, and declared that we had come from the Western Heavens, from a great kingdom called France, and that we had come to Tibet to preach the Christian religion of which we were ministers. The person to whom we made this declaration was as dry and hard as any bureaucrat. He calmly took his bamboo writing stick from behind his ear and began to write down, without hesitation, what we had just told him. He did however mutter two or three times the words 'France' and 'Christian religion', like one who is puzzled at what he hears. When he had finished he wiped his well-inked writing stick on his hair and replaced it behind his right ear, saying:

'*Yakporé,*' ('That is good').

'*Témouchu,*' ('Remain in peace'), we answered; and after putting out our tongues we departed, pleased with ourselves at having regularised our situation. From then on we went about our business with a firmer step, with greater assurance, and caring nothing for the gossip which buzzed around us. The situation of legality which we had entered gave us confidence and a new courage. How pleased we were to find ourselves at last in a hospitable country, able to breathe freely, after living so long in China, always under constraint, always on the wrong side of the law, always having to think up ways of deceiving the government of His Imperial Majesty.

We were not at all surprised at the lack of interest shown by the Tibetan authorities at our declaration. Enquiries we had already made about the status of foreigners at Lhasa had convinced us that we should not have any difficulties. The Tibetans did not share the Chinese principle of excluding all other races; anyone was allowed entry into Lhasa; anyone could come and go freely, carry on a trade or a craft without check on his freedom. If Tibet was forbidden to the Chinese, this was due to the Chinese government, which, in accordance with its narrow, suspicious policy, prevented its own citizens from visiting neighbouring countries. It is probable that the British would have been as free to enter Tibet as anyone else, if the progress of their advance across India had not struck the Dalai Lama with justifiable alarm.

We have already spoken of the many striking parallels between the lamaic and the Catholic religions. Rome and Lhasa, the pope and the Dalai Lama, might also provide interesting comparisons. The Tibetan government, being purely lamaic, might seem to some extent modelled on the ecclesiastical government of the papal states. The Dalai Lama was the political and religious ruler of the whole of Tibet; in his hands resided all legislative, executive and administrative powers. A code of common law and certain rules laid down by Tsong Kaba were the instruments of his great authority. When the Dalai Lama died, or to use the Buddhist terminology, when his soul was transmigrated, a child was chosen who continued the indestructible incarnation of the Living Buddha: this choice was made by the great assembly of Houtouktou lamas (saints or Living Buddhas) whose priestly rank was second only to that of the Dalai Lama himself. Later, we shall give some details of the customs and rules of this strange election. As the Dalai Lama was not only the political and religious ruler of the Tibetans, but also their visible God, he could not of course without loss of dignity descend from his high sanctuary to deal with day to day human questions. He therefore dealt only with matters of the highest importance: he reigned, but did little governing. In any case his way of ruling depended entirely on his own choice and desires: there was no charter or constitution to control his methods.

After the Dalai Lama, whom the Tibetans sometimes also call Kian Ngan Remboutchi or Sovereign Treasure, came the Nomekhan or Spiritual Emperor. The Chinese called him the Tsan Wang or King of Tibet. He was appointed by the Dalai Lama from among the Chaberon Lamas. He retained the post for life, and could only be overthrown by a *coup d'état*. The entire government was in his hands and in those of four ministers known as Kalons. The latter were chosen by the Dalai Lama from a list of candidates drawn up by the Nomekhan: they did not belong to the priestly class, and might be married; their appointment was for an unlimited time. If they showed themselves unworthy, the Nomekhan reported to the Dalai Lama, who would dismiss them if he agreed. The lower officials were chosen by the Kalons, and were usually lamas.

The provinces were divided into principalities, all governed by Houtouktou lamas. These petty priest-potentates were appointed by the Dalai Lama and recognised his supreme authority. They were mostly of a warlike disposition, harassing their neighbours with battle, fire and pillage.

The most powerful of these lama princes was the Panchen Remboutchi; he resided at Djachi Loumbo, capital of Further Tibet. This city was only eight days' march to the south of Lhasa. The reputation of the Panchen Lama at the time of our stay was extraordinary; his supporters claimed that his spiritual authority was as great as the Dalai Lama's, and that the sanctuary of Djachi Loumbo was no less holy than the Buddha La. It was however generally agreed that the temporal power of the Dalai Lama was greater than that of the Panchen Lama. We could see that, sooner or later, a great power stuggle was bound to develop between Lhasa and Djachi Loumbo, causing tragic disunity amongst the Tibetans.

This Panchen Remboutchi was some sixty years of age; we were told that he was a fine impressive figure, astonishingly energetic for his years. He claimed to be of Indian origin: his first incarnation took place several thousand years before in the land of the Azaras, no less. Those clever people who mistook us for 'white Azaras' when we first arrived urged us to go on a pilgrimage to Djachi Loumbo, promising us that as compatriots of the Panchen Lama we would be made welcome. Lamaic scholars, learned in Buddhist genealogies, could explain how it was that the Panchen, after many marvellous reincarnations in Hindustan, finally appeared in Further Tibet and set up his residence at Djachi Loumbo. Whatever his biography, in which fortunately we do not have to believe, it was clear that this clever lama had achieved an astonishing popularity. The Tibetans, Tartars and other Buddhists all referred to him as the 'Great Saint', and never spoke his name without joining their hands and raising their eyes; they believed that his knowledge was universal; he could speak, they said, all the languages in the world without ever having studied any of them, and could converse with pilgrims from any country. The Tartars had such great faith in his powers that they continually invoked his name. In danger, in affliction, in all painful and difficult tasks, they always called on the magic name of the *Bokte*, the Saint.

The pilgrims who visited Tibet all went to Djachi Loumbo to prostrate themselves at the feet of this Saint of Saints, and present their offerings. The Tartar caravans brought him incalculable sums annually. In return for the gold and silver ingots that he packed away in his coffers, the Panchen distributed to his worshippers rags torn from his old clothes, bits of paper printed with mottoes in Mongol or Tibetan, terracotta statuettes and red pills guaranteed to cure all sorts of diseases. The pilgrims accepted all this rubbish reverently and put it religiously into a little bag which they wore round their necks.

Whoever made the pilgrimage to Djachi Loumbo, laymen or

lamas, men or women, enrolled in the brotherhood of the
Kelans, formed by the Panchen Remboutchi. Almost all Buddhists aspired to the honour of belonging to this association,
which might one day spark off some tragic event in Upper Asia.
Everybody seemed worried about the future; there was a
presentiment of a great catastrophe. These were the strange
prophecies which were rife when we were there:

When the Panchen Remboutchi died, he would not be re-
incarnated as before in Further Tibet. His new incarnation
would appear to the north of Lhasa, in the steppes where the
Ourianghai live, in the land called Tien Chan Pe Lou, between
the Celestial and the Altai mountains. While he lived there for
some years unknown, preparing himself by seclusion, prayer
and good works for the great events of the future, the Buddhist
religion would die within the hearts of all men, surviving only
in the brotherhood of the Kelans. In those unhappy days, the
influence of the Chinese in Tibet would increase; they would
spread over the hills and vales and would try to seize the
empire of the Dalai Lama. But that would last only a short time.
There would be a general insurrection; the Tibetans would
take to arms and would slaughter in one day all the Chinese
young and old, and not one would escape over the frontier.

A year after this bloody day, the Chinese emperor would
equip a great army which would march against Tibet. There
would be a tremendous resistance; the rivers would run with
blood, but the Chinese would end by seizing Tibet. However
this triumph would be short-lived, for it was then that the
Panchen Remboutchi would arise in power; he would call all
the Kelans of the holy association; those who were already
dead would come alive again and they would all gather in the
great plain of Tien Chan Pe Lou. There the Panchen would
distribute arrows and rifles to all, and would turn this multitude into a great army which he himself would command. The
Kelan brotherhood would march behind the Saint of Saints,
and would fling themselves on the Chinese who would be
hacked in pieces. Tibet would be conquered, then China, then
Tartary, then the great empire of the Oros (Russians). The
Panchen would be proclaimed world leader, and under his
holy influence lamaism would soon revive: splendid lamaseries would rise everywhere and the whole world would recognise the infinite power of Buddhist prayers.

These predictions, of which we have given but a short summary, were told us repeatedly and in the greatest detail. The strange thing was that no one seemed to have the slightest doubt about their truth: everyone spoke as if they were absolutely inevitable. The Chinese living at Lhasa also seemed to believe the prophecies, but they were sensible enough not to let them worry them unduly; they hoped that the disasters would be long delayed and that they would either be dead or at least see them coming in time. We were told that the Panchen Remboutchi himself was enthusiastically preparing for the revolution which he was destined to lead. Although somewhat advanced in years, he frequently took part in military exercises; all the time not spent in fulfilling his functions as Living Buddha was devoted to studying his future role as supreme commander of the Kelans. We were told that he shot a good arrow and was master of the lance and the matchlock. He kept great herds of horses for his future cavalry, and packs of huge dogs which, combining amazing strength with extraordinary intelligence, were due to play a major role in the great army of the Kelans.

These insane and extravagant ideas had got so great a hold over the masses, and especially over the minds of the members of the Kelan brotherhood, that we felt that they might well, one of these days, spark off a revolution in Tibet. When nations become obsessed with the future in this way, something is bound to happen. After the death of the Grand Lama of Djachi Loumbo, a bold adventurer would only have to go to Tien Chan Pe Lou, proclaim himself to be the Panchen Remboutchi, and call up the Kelans: this would probably be enough to cause an uprising of these fanatics.

One immediate result of the formation of the Kelan brotherhood was to endow the Panchen Remboutchi with an eminence which little by little undermined that of the Dalai Lama. This result was obtained the more easily since at the time of our stay the latter was a nine-year-old boy, and each of his three predecessors had died a violent death before attaining his majority, fixed by the law at twenty. The Panchen Remboutchi, clearly a clever and ambitious man, would hardly have failed to exploit this period of four minorities to transfer some of the Dalai Lama's spiritual authority to himself.

In 1844 the violent deaths of the three predecessors of the

current Dalai Lama gave rise to events which affected Tibet, Tartary and even China, and which were of such importance that some account of them must be given here. The unprecedented phenomenon of three Dalai Lamas in succession dying in the flower of their youth had plunged the population of Lhasa into deep consternation. Gradually rumours began to spread, first whispered, then aloud, that foul play had been involved. More than this, stories began to circulate in the streets and in the lamaseries, giving exact details of the crimes: it was said that the first Dalai Lama had been strangled, the second crushed by the roof of his bedroom, and the third poisoned with his numerous relatives, who had all come to settle in Lhasa. The superior of the great lamasery of Kaldan, who was a devoted supporter of the Dalai Lama, had suffered the same fate. Public opinion blamed the Nomekhan for all these murders. The four ministers knew perfectly well that this was in fact true, but they were impotent to avenge the deaths of their sovereigns: they were too weak to stand up to the Nomekhan, who was supported by many powerful friends.

This Nomekhan was a Si Fan, from the principality of Yang Tou Sse in the province of Kansou. The supreme title of 'Tou Sse' was hereditary in his family, and a large number of his relatives had lived in Lhasa for some generations and were extremely influential in the affairs of Tibet. The Nomekhan from Yang Tou Sse was still young when he was appointed to the post which commanded greater authority than any, apart from the Dalai Lama himself. We were told that a few years after his rise to power he began to show not only ambition but an unbridled desire for domination. He used his great wealth and the influence of his relatives to surround himself by subordinates who were entirely loyal to him. He particularly endeavoured to gain support amongst the lamas, and with this in mind he took under his immediate protection the famous lamasery of Sera, situated about a mile and a half from Lhasa and comprising more than fifteen thousand Buddhist monks. He heaped it with favours, granted it great privileges and endowments and appointed a number of its members to posts in his administration. The lamas of Sera responded by regarding the Nomekhan with due enthusiasm; they considered him a saint of the highest order, and listed his perfections in language as high-flown and exaggerated as the protocol of the perfections of Buddha. Supported by the party he had created around him, the Nomekhan threw all caution to the winds for the attainment of supreme power, and carried out the successive murders of the three young Dalai Lamas in order to retain the regency in his hands. Such was the Nomekhan from Yan Tou Sse, or so he was pictured to us during our stay in Lhasa.

To overthrow a man so well dug in as this was clearly extremely difficult. The Kalons, realising that open opposition would result in their ruin, decided to work in secret towards the downfall of this vile man. The council of Houtouktous elected a new Dalai Lama, or rather, designated the child into whose body the soul of the Living Buddha had transmigrated. He was enthroned on the summit of the Buddha La. The Nomekhan, in company with all other dignitaries, prostrated himself at his feet and worshipped him with due piety, no doubt at the same time making a private determination to cause his transmigration for the fourth time when he judged that the right moment had come.

The Kalons took secret precautions against another disaster of this sort. They came to an agreement with the Panchen Remboutchi of Djachi Loumbo, and it was decided that, to put an end to the wicked career of the Nomekhan, it was necessary to obtain the support of the irresistible power of the emperor of China. A petition was therefore drawn up and signed by the Panchen and the four Kalons; it was then despatched secretly to Peking with the 1844 embassy.

For three main reasons, the Peking government could not fail to give the Tibetans the protection which they had requested at this grave juncture. Firstly, the Tartar-Mandchou dynasty had solemnly declared itself protector of the Dalai Lama. Secondly, since the Nomekhan came from Yang Tou Sse in the province of Kansou, he was to some extent a legal responsibility of the Chinese emperor; thirdly, this was an excellent opportunity for the Chinese to establish their influence in Tibet and carry out their plans of domination. The petition was therefore most favourably received, and it was immediately decided to send to Lhasa an ambassador sufficiently energetic and adroit to destroy the power of the Nomekhan. The emperor picked out the mandarin Kichan and appointed him for this difficult task.

Before going any further, we must say something of Kichan, a man already well known in China who had played an important role in the British affair in Canton. He was a Tartar-Mandchou by origin; he began his career as scrivener in one of the six High Courts of Peking. His unusual capacities soon came to notice, and although still very young he quickly climbed to the top of the magistrature. At the age of twenty-two he was governor of the province of Honan, at twenty-five he was viceroy; but he was demoted from this position for failing to foresee and prevent an overflowing of the Yellow River which caused great damage to the province which had been entrusted to his care. His disgrace did not last long and he was reinstated in his previous position and sent as viceroy to the provinces of Chanton, Ssetchouan and Petchely, in that order. He was decorated with the Red Button, the Peacock's Feather and the Yellow Tunic, together with the title of Heou Ye or Prince Imperial. He was finally appointed Tchoung Tang, the highest dignity which a mandarin can attain. There are only eight Tchoung Tang in the empire; four Mandchous and four Chinese; they form the emperor's Privy Council and have the right to correspond directly with him.

Towards the end of 1839, Kichan was sent to Canton as viceroy of the province with the rank of Imperial Commissioner; he had full powers to negotiate with the British on behalf of his government, and re-establish the peace which had been disturbed by the injudicious and violent measures taken by Lin, his predecessor. The quality of Kichan's intelligence is revealed by the fact that as soon as he got to Canton he recognised the great superiority of the Europeans over the Chinese and realised that it was impossible to wage war against them. He therefore immediately opened negotiations with Mr Elliot, the British plenipotentiary, and peace was concluded by the transfer to the British of the small island of Hong Kong. To cement the good relations which had thus been established between Emperor Tackouang and Queen Victoria, Kichan gave the British authorities a magnificent banquet, to which M. de Rosamel, captain of the corvette *La Danaïde* which had anchored a few days before off Macao, had the honour to be invited. Everyone was delighted with the courtesy and friendliness of the Imperial Commissioner.

Only a few days passed before intrigues hatched in Peking by ex-Imperial Commissioner Lin succeeded in causing the emperor to declare null and void the treaty which had just been

signed in Canton. Kichan was accused of having been corrupt-
ed by British gold and of having sold territory of the Celestial
Empire to the 'sea-devils'. The emperor sent him a furious
letter, in which he said that he had committed a mortal crime,
and ordered him to return to Peking immediately. The poor
Imperial Commissioner was not executed as everyone expected; the emperor, in his fatherly mercy, pardoned his life and
only stripped him of all his titles and decorations, confiscated
his goods, razed his house to the ground, sold his wives by
auction and exiled him into far Tartary.

The many influential friends that Kichan had at court did not
abandon him in his misfortune; they worked with courage and
perseverance to restore him to the emperor's good graces. In
1844 he was finally recalled from exile and sent to Lhasa, as
ambassador extraordinary, to deal with the problem of the
Nomekhan. He set off decorated with the Blue Button instead
of the Red which he had worn before his fall; he was given
back the Peacock's Feather, but the privilege of wearing the
Yellow Tunic was still withheld. His friends in Peking clubbed
together and built a splendid house for him. The post of Kin
Tchai, up in the Tibetan mountains, was still considered to be
an exile, but it was a step towards a complete restitution of his
former glory.

Immediately after his arrival in Lhasa, Kichan deliberated
with the Panchen Remboutchi and the four Kalons, and arrested
the Nomekhan. Next, he submitted all persons in the service of
the accused to an interrogation and, to help them speak the
truth, arranged for long bamboo needles to be inserted in their
fingernails. By these means, as the Chinese say, 'truth was
separated from error', and the Nomekhan's crimes were
brought into the light of day. The Nomekhan himself confessed
everything, without any need for torture; he admitted having
deprived the Dalai Lama of three lives; he had caused him to
transmigrate with violence, first by strangulation, next by
suffocation and finally by poison. A confession was drawn up
in Chinese, Tartar and Tibetan. The Nomekhan and his accomplices signed it. The Panchen Remboutchi, the four Kalons
and the Chinese ambassador attached their seals, and it was
immediately forwarded to Peking by special courier. All this
took place behind closed doors and in complete secrecy.

Three months later the Tibetan capital was plunged into a

state of great agitation. Placarded on the great doorway of the Nomekhan's palace and in the main streets of the city was an imperial edict, in three languages, on yellow paper and bordered with pictures of winged dragons. After high-flown sentiments about the duties of kings and all rulers great and small; after exhorting potentates, monarchs, princes, magistrates and the nations of the four seas to walk in the paths of justice and virtue, under pain of incurring the wrath of Heaven and of the Great Khan, the emperor listed the crimes of the Nomekhan, and condemned him to perpetual exile on the banks of the Sakhalien-Oula in deepest Manchuria. At the end, came the conventional phrase, 'Tremble and Obey!'

The inhabitants of Lhasa hurried to gather round these placards, which they were unaccustomed to see on the walls of their city. The news of the Nomekhan's condemnation spread like wildfire through the crowd; many groups of men could be seen, in excited but low-voiced discussion. Faces were passionate, and on all sides a buzzing of lowered voices could be heard. The Tibetan people were less concerned with the well-deserved fall of the Nomekhan than the intervention of the Chinese authorities, by which everyone was angered and humiliated.

In the lamasery of Sera, the opposition was more energetic by far. As soon as the news of the imperial edict arrived, the insurrection was spontaneous and general. Those fifteen thousand lamas, all devotees of the Nomekhan, rushed to seize lances, rifles, sticks, anything they could find, and ran towards Lhasa, only a mile and a half away. The citizens could see and hear them coming from the clouds of dust and the frightful din that they raised in their riotous advance. 'The lamas from Sera! The lamas from Sera!' was the cry which arose from the whole city almost simultaneously, and which filled all hearts with fear. The lamas descended like an avalanche on the residence of the Chinese ambassador, and broke open the doors to repeated cries of 'Death to Kichan! Death to the Chinese!' But they found no one on whom to wreak their vengeance. The ambassador, warned in time of their approach, had run to shelter in the house of one of the Kalons, and the members of his staff had scattered through the town. The crowd of lamas then divided into several groups; some went to the Nomekhan's palace, the others attacked the houses of the Kalons, vociferously demanding that the Chinese ambassador should be handed over to them. There were long and bitter struggles over this, during which one of the four Tibetan ministers was torn to death; the others were injured to greater or lesser extent.

Whilst the attack was going on at the houses of the Kalons with the objective of capturing Kichan, the largest group of lamas had broken down the doors of the prison in which the Nomekhan had been shut, and were proposing to carry him in triumph to the lamasery of Sera. The Nomekhan was strongly

opposed to this plan and used all his influence to quieten the lamas' excitement. He told them that their thoughtless revolt had worsened his situation instead of improving it. 'I am,' he said, 'the victim of a plot; I shall go to Peking, I shall enlighten the emperor and I shall return in triumph amongst you all. For the present we must all obey the imperial edict. I shall depart as I have been commanded. You must all return peacefully to your lamasery.' These words did not alter the lamas' resolution; but, as night had fallen, they returned in a confused mob to Sera, with the intention of planning their action better on the morrow.

When morning came, the lamas began to bustle about in their great monastery, with the intention of again invading the city of Lhasa; but to their great surprise they saw in the plain quite close to the lamasery a number of tents and a multitude of Tibetan and Chinese soldiers fully armed and blocking their way. At this sight, everyone's courage vanished away; the conch sounded and these temporary soldiers, throwing down their arms, returned to their cells, tucked their books under their arms and went quietly to the temple to recite, as they did every day, the morning prayers.

A few days later the Nomekhan, with a strong escort, took the road to Ssetchouan, going obediently into the exile to which he had been condemned. The people of Lhasa never understood why this man, who had not recoiled before the murder of three Dalai Lamas, failed to take advantage of the insurrection of the lamas of Sera. It is certain that, had he given the word, all the Chinese in Lhasa would have been killed and possibly all Tibet engulfed in war; but he was not a man of such a stamp: he had the cowardly energy of a murderer, but not the audacity of a revolutionary leader.

Kichan, drunk with success, wanted to exercise his power also against the Tibetans who had been the Nomekhan's accomplices. This idea did not appeal to the Kalons, who told him that only they had the right to judge those who were in no way dependants of China, and against whom the emperor's protection had not been invoked. The Kin Tchai did not insist; but in order not to appear to be giving in to the Tibetan authorities, he made the official reply that he would leave them to deal with these minor murderers, because it was beneath the dignity of a representative of the great emperor to become involved.

A new Nomekhan was then appointed in the place of the banished man: the choice fell on the Chaberon of the lamasery of Ran Tchan, a boy of eighteen. The Dalai Lama and the new Nomekhan both being minors at the time that we arrived in Lhasa, the post of regent was filled by the senior Kalon. His major preoccupation was to find ways of resisting the encroachments and the arrogance of the Chinese ambassador, who tried by every means to take advantage of the current weakness of the Tibetan government.

7

THE GOSPEL IN LHASA

As soon as we had reported to the Tibetan authorities, telling them who we were and why we had come to Lhasa, we felt able—now that our activities were above-board—to get in touch with Tibetan and Tartar lamas and begin, at last, our missionary activities. One day when we were sitting at our modest fireside talking about religion with a lama who was a considerable Buddhist scholar, there burst in suddenly upon us a rather elaborately dressed Chinaman: he claimed to be a trader, and was most anxious, he said, to buy our merchandise. We told him that we had nothing to sell.

'What, nothing?'

'Nothing at all—except those old riding saddles that we no longer need.'

'Good, good! That's just what I want; I need saddles,' and whilst he examined our poor wares he put countless questions about where we came from and the places we had visited before arriving in Lhasa. Meanwhile in came a second Chinaman, then a third, then two lamas wrapped in beautiful silk scarves. All these visitors wanted to buy something from us; they badgered us with questions and seemed meanwhile to be casting anxious searching glances into all the nooks and corners of our room. We kept on telling them that we were not merchants, but it was useless. Though we had neither silks nor drapery nor iron-mongery for them, they were quite happy to make do with our saddles; they turned them over and over; sometimes they pronounced them to be very good, sometimes very bad; finally, after beating about the bush for a long time, they departed promising to return.

The visit of these five characters gave us furiously to think; their behaviour and their speech were most unnatural. Although arriving separately they were obviously all in league and bent on the same objectives. Their wish to buy was clearly only a pretext hiding other intentions: they were crooks or informers rather than real traders. 'Let's wait calmly,' we said to each other, 'maybe it will all come clear in time.'

Since it was dinnertime we sat down—or rather remained squatting round the fire—and took the lid off the pot in which for the last few hours a good-sized lump of yak-meat had been boiling. Samdadchiemba, in his role as head waiter, hooked it up to the surface of the liquid by means of a wide wooden spatula, then caught it in his fingernails and flung it on to a piece of board, where he proceeded to cut it into three equal portions. We took one each, put it into a bowl and, with the assistance of some rolls which had been baking in the ashes, we

calmly began to eat, without much worrying about crooks and informers. We had reached the dessert, that is, we were rinsing out our bowls with buttered tea, when the two lamas, self-styled traders, reappeared.

'The regent,' they said, 'awaits you at his palace: he wants to speak to you.'

'Are we to suppose that the regent is also interested in buying our old saddles?'

'It's nothing to do with saddles or any other merchandise. Come quickly and follow us to the regent's palace.' So now we knew: the government was interested in us; but for what purpose? For good or for ill? Would it be freedom or chains? Would it be life or death? That we did not know, nor could we guess.

'Let's go and see the regent,' we said to each other, 'and put our trust in the Lord.' We put on our best robes and our magnificent fox-fur hats, and then told the henchmen that we were ready.

'And that young man?' said one of them, pointing at Samdadchiemba, who was looking at him in a far from friendly manner.

'That young man is our servant. He will look after the house until we return.'

'No, no, he must come too: the regent wants to see all three of you.' Samdadchiemba, to smarten himself up, shook his big sheepskin robe and put on a little black cap cheekily over one ear, and we all left together after padlocking the door of our apartment.

After walking at top speed for five or six minutes we arrived at the palace of the First Kalon, prime minister and regent of Tibet. We crossed a large courtyard, in which a crowd of lamas and Chinese were standing: they began to whisper as we appeared. We were then made to stop at a half-open gilt double door: our guide disappeared down a little corridor to the left, and a moment later the door opened wide. At the far end of a simply decorated room a man sat cross-legged on a thick cushion covered in tigerskin: it was the regent. With his right hand he beckoned to us. We came forward to where he sat, and saluted him by putting our hats under our arms. A bench covered with a red rug stood on our right hand. We were invited to sit on it, which we immediately did. Meanwhile the gilt door had been closed, leaving in the room only the regent and seven persons who stood behind him: namely, four lamas who looked modest and composed; two Chinese who struck us as subtle and sly; and a man whose long beard, turban and bold expression proclaimed him to be a Muslim. The regent was aged about fifty; his broad, smiling face was extraordinarily white-complexioned, and had a dignity that was truly regal; his black eyes, under long lashes, were intelligent and full of kindness. He wore a yellow robe lined with sable; a diamond earring hung from his right ear, and his long, ebony-black hair was done up in a topknot, held in place by three small gold combs. His broad red cap, edged with pearls and surmounted by a coral ball, lay beside him on a green cushion.

As soon as we had sat down the regent silently began to

examine us with a long careful gaze. He cocked his head now to the right, now to the left, with a half-mocking, half-kindly smile. This pantomime finally became so comic that we couldn't help laughing. 'Well!' we said in a low voice and in French, 'this gentleman seems good-natured enough; we shall be all right.'

'What language are you speaking?' asked the regent in a most friendly tone, 'I did not understand what you said.'

'We spoke the language of our country.'

'Come now, repeat aloud what you said so quietly.'

We then repeated: *'Ce monsieur paraît assez bon enfant.'*

'Now, can *you* understand that?' he said, turning to those who stood behind him. They all bowed together and replied that they did not understand. 'You see, no one here understands the language of your country; translate your words into Tibetan.'

'We were saying that in the face of the First Kalon there was great kindness.'

'Ah so, you think I am very kind? But I am very cruel. Am I not very cruel?' he asked, turning to his entourage, who smiled but made no reply. 'You are right,' he continued, 'I am kind, for kindness is the duty of a Kalon. I must be kind to my people, and also kind to foreigners.' He then made a long speech very little of which we understood. When he had finished we told him that, not being sufficiently versed in the Tibetan language, we had been unable to follow his meaning completely. The regent gave a sign to one of the Chinamen, who took a step forward and translated the speech, of which the following is a summary: we had been summoned, but there was no intention of disturbing us. The contradictory rumours that had been current since our arrival in Lhasa had decided the regent to interrogate us himself to find out where we came from.

'We are from the Western Heavens,' we told him.

'From Calcutta?'

'No, our country is called France.'

'But you are Pelings?'

'No, we are French.'

'Can you write?'

'Better than speak.' The regent turned, said a few words to a lama, who disappeared and returned a moment later with paper, ink and a bamboo stylus.

'Here is paper,' said the regent. 'Write something.'

'In what language? In Tibetan?'

'No, in the language of your country.' One of us took the paper on his knees and wrote: 'For what shall it profit a man if he shall gain the whole world, and lose his own soul?'

'Ah, so that is the writing of your country? I have never seen the like. And what does it mean?' We wrote the translation in Tibetan, in Tartar and in Chinese, and it was passed to him.

'I was not deceived,' he said, 'you are men of great learning. I see that you can write in all languages, and you express thoughts as profound as in the prayer-books.' Then he repeated, with a shake of his head, 'For what shall it profit a man if he shall gain the whole world, and lose his own soul?'

Whilst the regent and his entourage were praising our great scholarship, we heard some shouts from the crowd in the courtyard, and the resounding tones of a Chinese tom-tom.

'Here comes the Peking ambassador,' said the regent. 'He wishes to interrogate you himself. Be quite frank with him about yourselves, and count on my protection. I rule this country.' So saying he went out attended by his suite, leaving us alone in the audience chamber.

The idea of falling into the hands of the Chinese filled us momentarily with alarm, and the thought of those terrible persecutions which have at various times ravaged the Christian communities of China came forcibly to our minds; but we were soon comforted by the thought that, alone and isolated as we were in the middle of Tibet, we could hardly compromise anybody. This thought gave us courage.

'Samdadchiemba,' we said to our young disciple, 'the time has now come to show that we are brave, that we are Christians. Anything may happen to us; but let us keep eternity always in mind. If we are treated well, we will thank God; if we are treated ill, we will still thank Him, for we shall have the good fortune to suffer for our faith. If they kill us, the martyr's crown will be the reward of our labours. To go to Heaven after only eighteen months, is that not a successful journey? Is it not the greatest of good fortune? What is your opinion, Samdadchiemba?'

'I have never been afraid of death. If they ask me if I am a Christian, you'll see if I tremble or not.'

Samdadchiemba's admirable frame of mind filled our hearts with joy and completely allayed the apprehension we had felt at the disagreeable turn of events. We were on the point of thinking about the questions that we might be asked and the replies we should make; but we decided against such worldly prudence. We felt that the moment had come for strict observance of the words that Our Lord addressed to his disciples: 'Ye shall be brought before rulers and kings for my sake . . . Take no thought beforehand what ye shall speak.' We decided only that we would salute the mandarin in the French manner, and would not kneel in his presence. We felt that, when one has the honour to be a Christian, a missionary and a Frenchman, one can without arrogance remain standing in the presence of any Chinaman, whoever he may be.

After a few minutes' wait, a young Chinaman, elegantly dressed and with exquisite manners, came to announce that Kichan, Great Ambassador of the Great Emperor of China, was waiting to question us. We followed this pleasant attendant, and were ushered into a hall decorated in the Chinese manner, in which Kichan was sitting on a three foot high platform covered in red cloth. He sat behind a small black lacquer table, on which were an escritoire, brushes, a few sheets of paper and a silver box containing snuff. Below the platform there were four scribes, two on each side. The rest of the room was filled by a crowd of Chinese and Tibetans, who seemed to have put on their best clothes for the show.

Kichan, though some sixty years old, looked strong and vigorous. His face was by far the noblest, the most affable and the wittiest that we had ever seen on a Chinaman. As soon as we had taken off our hats, with the best little bow that we could muster, he said:

'It is well, follow your own customs. I hear that you speak correctly the language of Peking, and I want a few words with you.'

'We make many mistakes, but your great intelligence will be able to fill the gaps when our meaning is obscure.'

'Now that is indeed the pure language of Peking! You Frenchmen are very talented in all sciences: you are French, are you not?'

'Yes, we are Frenchmen.'

'Oh, I know the French! There used to be a number in Peking, and I knew some of them.'

'You must also have known some at Canton, when you were Imperial Commissioner.' This memory caused His Lordship to knit his brows; he took a large pinch of snuff from the box and sniffed it with some ill-humour.

'Yes, true: I met many Europeans at Canton. You are of the religion of the Lord of Heaven, are you not?'

'Indeed, yes. We are even preachers of that religion.'

'I know, I know. And you no doubt came here to preach that religion?'

'That was our only object.'

'Have you already passed through many countries?'

'We have crossed China and Tartary, and here we are in the capital of Tibet.'

'With whom did you stay when you were in China?'

'We do not answer such questions.'

'And if I order you to do so?'

'Then we cannot obey.' At this point our judge, vexed, banged the table with his fist. 'You know,' we told him, 'that Christians are not afraid. Why then try to intimidate us?'

'Where did you learn Chinese?'

'In China.'

'Where exactly?'

'In a number of places.'

'And can you speak Tartar? Where did you learn that?'

'In Mongolia, in the Grasslands.'

After a few more unimportant questions, Kichan said that we must be tired, and invited us to sit down. Suddenly changing tone and manner, he turned to Samdadchiemba, who with hand on hip had remained standing slightly behind us.

'And you,' he said in a hard angry voice, 'where do you come from?'

'I come from Ki Tou Sse.'

'Wherever is Ki Tou Sse? Who has ever heard of it?'

'Ki Tou Sse is in the San Tchouan.'

'Ah, you come from San Tchouan, in the province of Kansou! Child of the Middle Kingdom, on your knees!' Samdadchiemba turned pale, his hand left his hip, and he stood modestly at attention.

'On your knees!' thundered the mandarin.

Samdadchiemba knelt, and said: 'Kneeling, standing or sitting, it's all more or less the same to me: a working chap like me isn't used to comfort.'

'Ah, so you're from Kansou,' said His Lordship, taking great pinches of snuff, 'so you're from Kansou, you're a child of the Middle Kingdom! Good, good. In that case, I'll deal with you, you are my business. Child of the Middle Kingdom, answer your Father and your Mother, and take care to speak no lies. Where did you meet these two foreigners? How did you enter their service?' Samdadchiemba calmly gave a long account of his life, which appeared to be of some interest to his hearers; then he described how he met us in Tartary and why he had decided to accompany us. Our young disciple spoke with dignity, but above all with a discretion that we had not expected.

'Why did you join the religion of the Lord of Heaven? Do you not know that the Great Emperor forbids it?'

'Your humble servant joined that religion, because it is the only true one. How could I believe that the Great Emperor would ban a religion which commands one to do good and to shun evil?'

'It is true, the religion of the Lord of Heaven is holy, that I know. Why do you serve foreigners? Do you not know that it is forbidden by law?'

'How can an ignorant man like me know who is a foreigner and who is not? These men have done me nothing but good; they have always urged me to practise virtue; why should I not follow them?'

'How much do they give you in wages?'

'I go with them to save my soul, not for money. My masters have never let me want either for rice or for clothes; that is enough for me.'

'Are you married?'

'As I was a lama before I joined the religion of the Lord of Heaven, I never married.' Laughing, the judge then put an improper question to Samdadchiemba, who hung his head and remained silent. One of us then rose and said to Kichan:

'Our religion not only forbids impure actions, but also thoughts and words: we are not even allowed to listen to lewdness.' These words, calmly and gravely spoken, caused a slight blush to rise in the cheeks of His Excellency the Chinese ambassador.

'I know, I know,' he said. 'The religion of the Lord of Heaven is holy; I know something about it, I have read the books of its doctrine; anyone who would follow its teachings faithfully would be irreproachable.' He signed to Samdadchiemba to rise; then turning to us, he said:

'Night has come; you must be tired, it is time for supper. Go: if I need you tomorrow, I will call you.'

Ambassador Kichan was quite right; it was very late, and the various emotions we had undergone during the evening had been no sort of substitute for supper. As we left the Sino-Tibetan audience room we were accosted by a venerable lama, who informed us that the First Kalon was expecting us. We crossed the courtyard, which was lit by red lanterns; we then turned right into a hazardous staircase up which we climbed, prudently hanging on to the robe of our guide. After traversing a long terrace lit by the dim light of the stars, we were ushered into the regent's apartments. The great high chamber in which we found ourselves was brilliantly lit by butter lamps. Walls, ceiling and even floor were completely covered with gilt and brilliant colours. The regent was alone. He invited us to sit beside him on a rich carpet, and tried to convey, by words and even more by gestures, his concern for us. It was immediately clear that preparations were being made to allay our hunger.

This pantomime was interrupted by the arrival of someone who left his shoes at the door; it was the governor of the Katchi or Kashmiri Muslims. He greeted the company with a salute and the word '*Salamalek*', then leant against a column which rose from the middle of the room and apparently supported the wooden roof. The Muslim governor spoke Chinese very well, and had been summoned by the regent to act as interpreter. Then a servant brought a small table and set it down in front of us, and we were served supper at Tibetan government expense. We will say nothing for the present of the regent's cuisine, first because our ravenous appetites prevented us from savouring the quality of the dishes, and secondly because on that occasion our minds were more taken up with politics than with gastronomy. However we did notice that Samdadchiemba was not present, and asked what had become of him. 'He is with my servants,' the regent told us, 'you need not worry about him, he shall lack for nothing.'

During and after the meal, there was much talk of France and of the countries we had visited. The regent then drew our attention to the pictures that adorned his room, and asked us if we could paint as well as that.

'We cannot paint at all,' we answered. 'Scholarship and the preaching of the doctrine of Jehovah are our only occupations.'

'Now don't tell me that you can't paint; I know that your countrymen are very clever at that.'

'Yes, those whose profession it is, but the ministers of religion do not normally go in for it.'

'Although you are not particularly gifted in that direction, you are not completely ignorant of it? You doubtless know how to draw maps?'

'No, we do not.'

'What? In all your journeys you have never drawn, have never made, a single map?'

'Never.'

'Oh, it's impossible.' We could not help wondering at the regent's persistence in his questions on such a subject, and told him how surprised we were. 'As I see that you are honourable men,' he said, 'I will deal frankly with you. You know how suspicious the Chinese are; since you have lived long in China you must know them as well as I. They are convinced that you are travelling abroad in order to explore all countries and make maps of them. If you do draw, if you do make maps, you can tell me about it without danger: you can count on my protection.' Evidently the regent feared an invasion; he may have imagined that we were on a mission preparing the way for some great army poised to descend on Tibet. We tried to allay his fears, assuring him of the extremely peaceful nature of the French government. We admitted however that amongst our effects there were a quantity of plans and maps, and that we even had one of Tibet. At these words the regent's jaw set suddenly, but we hastily added that all these plans and maps were printed, and that we were not the authors. We took the opportunity to tell the regent and the Kashmiri governor about the extent of the geographical knowledge of the Europeans. They were most astonished when we told them that ten- or twelve-year-old children in our country had a correct and comprehensive knowledge of all the countries in the world.

The conversation went on far into the night. The regent at last got up and asked us if we were not ready for a little rest.

'We were only waiting for the Kalon's permission to return to our lodgings.'

'Your lodgings? But I have ordered a room to be prepared for you in my palace; you will stay here tonight, tomorrow you will return home.' We tried to make excuses, whilst thanking the regent for his kindness, but soon realised that we were not free to refuse what in our innocence we had taken for an act of courtesy. We were prisoners, that was all there was to it. We bid the regent a rather chilly goodnight and followed a person who, after leading us through many rooms and passages, brought us into a kind of closet, which could quite truthfully be described as a prison, since we were not permitted to leave it and go elsewhere.

Two cots had been made up for us, which were in fact much better than our own. However, we missed our wretched bunks, on which we had for so long enjoyed the sleep of freedom during our long wanderings in the desert. Lamas and attendants of the regent crowded in to visit us. Some had been to bed and got up again, and we began to hear in that vast silent palace the sound of doors opening and shutting and the hurried footsteps echoing along the corridors. They crowded round us and examined us with an avidity which we found unbearable. In the eyes which stared at us from all sides there was neither sympathy nor malice; there was mere curiosity. For these people we were nothing more than exhibits in a zoo; and how unpleasant it is to be on show before an indifferent crowd.

When we judged that these intruders had gazed and whispered their fill, we informed them that we were going to bed and that we should be extremely obliged if they would be kind enough to withdraw. They all bowed; some even put out their tongues; but no one moved. It was clear that they wanted to watch us going to bed. We thought this rather indiscreet of them but felt that we should have to humour them up to a point. So we knelt down, made the sign of the cross and said our prayers aloud. No sooner had we begun than the whispering ceased, and a religious silence descended. When prayers were over we again invited our visitors to leave us alone and, so as to make our words more effective we blew out the lamp. The crowd, suddenly plunged in darkness, decided to burst out laughing and grope their way out. We closed our prison door and went to bed.

As we lay on Premier Kalon's beds we were ready for a chat, but rather unwilling to go over the day's adventures one by one. Those sham traders who wanted to buy our saddles, our appearance before the regent, Ambassador Kichan's interrogation, our supper at public expense, our long talk with the regent: all seemed like the baseless fabric of a vision. Our whole day had been a long nightmare. Our journey itself, our arrival in Lhasa, began to seem incredible. We wondered if it were really true that we, missionaries and Frenchmen, could be here in the states of the Dalai Lama, in the capital of Tibet, in bed in the palace of the regent himself! All our adventures, past and present, became jumbled in our heads. But above all the future seemed fraught with thick black clouds. How would it all end? Would they say: 'You are free, go where you wish'? Would we be left to languish in this prison? Or would we be strangled? Such thoughts were enough to quicken the heartbeat and bring on a headache. But how good it is to be able to trust in the Lord in the midst of tribulation! How happy is he who has faith in Providence when alone, abandoned and helpless! So we told each other that we must accept what came, and count on God's help. Not a hair of our heads would fall without His leave.

With all these thoughts we slept a light, troubled sleep. As soon as the first light of dawn began to appear the door of our cell opened softly and the Katchi governor came in. He sat down beside us, between our two cots, and asked us in a kind and friendly voice if we had passed a reasonable night. He then handed us a little basket of cakes made in his household, and some dried fruits from Ladakh. These attentions touched us deeply : it was like suddenly coming across an old and devoted friend.

The Katchi governor was thirty-two years old; his fine and noble countenance was full of a kindness and a frankness that gave us great confidence. His eyes, his words, his behaviour, everything about him seemed to express a liking for us. He had come to let us know what would be happening to us during the day.

'In the morning,' he said, 'the Tibetan authorities will go with you to your lodgings. Seals will be put on all your possessions, which will then be taken to the lawcourts where they will be examined, in your presence, by the regent and the Chinese ambassador. If you have no hand-drawn maps in your luggage, you can set your minds at rest: you will be left in peace. On the other hand, if you do have some, you had better warn me now, because some way out will have to be found. I am on excellent terms with the regent'—this had been clear enough the previous evening during supper—'who sent me himself to tell you all this in confidence.' He then added, lowering his voice, that all this fuss had been made by the Chinese, against the wishes of the Tibetan government. We told the Katchi governor that we had no hand-drawn maps. Then we gave him a detailed account of everything that was locked up in our two trunks.

'Since they are to be examined today,' we said, 'you will judge for yourself if we are people whose word can be trusted.' The Muslim's face burst into a smile.

'Your words have completely reassured me,' he said. 'There is nothing compromising about any of the things you have mentioned. Maps are regarded as very dangerous here, especially since the affair of a certain Englishman named Moorcroft, who infiltrated Lhasa disguised as a Kashmiri. After living here twelve years he left, but was murdered on the road to Ladakh. In his luggage a great collection of maps and sketches was found, drawn by him during his stay in Lhasa. This incident has made the Chinese authorities very suspicious of such matters. Since you have drawn no maps, all is well. I shall now tell the regent what you have said.' We took advantage of the Katchi governor's departure to get up, for we had unceremoniously remained lying in bed during his long visit. We said our morning prayers, composing our minds as best we could, and then tackled the breakfast that the regent had just sent in. It consisted of bread rolls stuffed with brown sugar and minced meat, and a richly buttered pot of tea. We tackled with greater appetite the cakes and dried fruits that the Katchi governor had brought. It was not long before three lama-ushers appeared to announce our orders for the day, namely the fact that our effects were to be examined. We respectfully obeyed the command of the Tibetan government and proceeded in the direction of our lodgings. Between the regent's palace and our house we noticed that a great to-do was in progress. The streets were being swept, the garbage was being rapidly removed and long strips of red and yellow *pou-lou* were being hung on the fronts of the houses. We were wondering what it all meant, who all these demonstrations of loyalty and respect were intended for, when we heard loud cheers behind us. Turning our heads we recognised the regent. He was riding on a fine white horse and was surrounded by a large troop of horsemen. We arrived at our lodgings almost at the same moment as he. We opened the padlock that fastened the door, and invited him to do us the honour of entering our apartment.

Samdadchiemba, whom we had not seen since our audience with the Chinese ambassador, was also present. He was quite stunned: he could make neither head nor tail of what was going on. The regent's servants, with whom he had spent the night, had not been able to enlighten him. We gave him a word of reassurance, to the effect that we were not all going to be made into martyrs straightaway.

The regent sat down in the middle of our room, on a gilt chair that had been brought for the purpose from the palace; then he asked us if what he saw in our room was all we possessed.

'Yes, that is all we have, neither more nor less. All we have, to conquer Tibet with.'

'These are sly words,' said the regent, 'I never thought that you were dangerous to that extent. Now, what is that?' he added, pointing to a crucifix that we had hung on the wall.

'Ah, if you knew all about that, you would not say that we were not dangerous. With that, we hope to conquer China, Tartary and Tibet.' The regent laughed, for he thought that we were joking, deadly serious though we were.

A scribe squatted at the regent's feet and made an inventory of our trunks, our ragged garments and our kitchen utensils. A lighted lamp was brought; the regent took from a small purse hanging round his neck a golden seal with which all our belongings were marked. Nothing was spared, our old boots, even our tent-pegs, everything was daubed with reddish-brown wax, and solemnly marked with the Dalai Lama's seal.

When this long ceremony was over, the regent informed us that we now had to proceed to the lawcourts. Porters were straightaway fetched; this was quickly done: a police-lama had only to appear in the street and summon the passers-by in the name of the law, men, women and children, to enter the house immediately to carry out a task for the government. In Lhasa the forced labour system worked extremely well. The Tibetans accepted it cheerfully, without any resentment.

When the fatigue party had arrived in sufficient numbers, our possessions were shared out amongst them; our apartment remained completely empty, and we set out with some ceremony for the lawcourts. A Tibetan horseman, sabre in hand and a rifle slung over his shoulder, led the procession. Then came the porters, between two files of police-lamas; the regent on his white horse with a mounted guard of honour followed our baggage; and last of all, behind the regent, we two poor French missionaries followed on foot, accompanied by a large mob of inquisitive onlookers whose presence was an unwelcome addition to the procession. Our bearing was far from proud. Led like criminals, or at least suspects, we had perforce to walk humbly with downcast eyes through the large crowd which milled about us. Our situation was, of course, painful and humiliating, but the thought of our Saviour dragged to the council chamber through the streets of Jerusalem was enough to sweeten the bitter draught we had to swallow. We prayed that He would sanctify our humiliations through His own, and accept them in memory of the sufferings of His passion.

When we reached the lawcourt, the Chinese ambassador and his staff were already installed. The regent said to him:

'You wished to examine the possessions of these foreigners. Here they are, examine them. These men are neither as rich nor as powerful as you think.' There was resentment in his voice, and indeed he could hardly have enjoyed playing the policeman in this way. Kichan asked us if we had only two trunks.

'Two only,' we told him. 'Everything we have is here. In our house there is not a rag, not a bit of paper left.'

'What have you got in those two trunks?'

'Here are the keys: open them, empty them, examine them at your leisure.' Kichan reddened and took a step back. His Chinese delicacy had been wounded.

'Are these trunks mine?' he said hotly. 'What right have I to open them? If something were missing afterwards, what would you say?'

'Never fear: our religion forbids us to judge our neighbour rashly.'

'Open your trunks yourselves. I wish to know what they contain, for that is my duty. But you alone have the right to touch what is yours.'

We broke the Dalai lama's seal and removed the padlocks;

then these two trunks at which everyone had been gazing for some time were at last opened for public inspection. We removed the objects one by one and displayed them on a large table. First came some books in French and Latin, then others in Chinese and Tartar, then some church linen, ornaments, sacred vessels, chaplets, crosses, medals and a splendid collection of lithographs. Everyone was lost in wonder at the sight of this little European museum: wide-eyed they nudged each other and clicked their tongues in admiration. Nothing so beautiful, so rich, so marvellous had ever been seen before. They took everything that shone yellow for pure gold. Everyone beamed with delight and the fact that we might be suspect or dangerous seemed to be quite forgotten. The Tibetans put out their tongues and scratched their ears at us, and the Chinese made gushing little bows. Our bag of medals especially was the cynosure of all eyes. There was an air of expectancy, as if they hoped that before leaving the court room we would be sharing out those shining gold pieces.

The regent and Kichan, who were men of superior stamp and who certainly did not covet our treasure, had nonetheless forgotten their judges' roles. The sight of our beautiful coloured pictures enthralled them. The regent sat with joined hands

staring openmouthed whilst Kichan held forth, displaying his knowledge and explaining how the French were the world's most distinguished artists. In Peking once, he said, he had known a French missionary who could sketch portraits with such a likeness that it was uncanny. He would keep the paper hidden in his sleeve, and draw the features stealthily, but before you could smoke a pipe of tobacco it was finished. Kichan asked us if we had any watches, telescopes, magic lanterns and so forth. We then opened a little box that no one had noticed before and which contained a microscope. We

fitted up its various parts and all eyes were now turned to this strange machine, made of pure gold, of course, which was certainly about to work wonders. Kichan alone realised what it was. He explained its uses to the public, in a pretentious and conceited manner. Then he asked us to put some small insect under the lens. We gave His Excellency a sidelong glance, then dismantled the microscope piece by piece and put it back into its box.

'We thought,' we said to Kichan, 'that we were here for a judgment, and not to give a show.'

'Judgment? What judgment?' he said. 'We wanted to examine your possessions, find out who you were, that is all.'

'And the maps? Aren't you interested in them?'

'Yes, yes, that's the important point. Where are your maps?'

'Here they are,' and we unfolded the three maps that we had, namely: a map of the world in two hemispheres, a Mercator's projection and a map of the Chinese empire. The sudden appearance of these maps was a bad shock to the regent; the poor man changed colour several times in the course of a minute, as if we had produced our death warrants.

'We are so glad', we said to Kichan, 'that you are here. If you had not been, we should never have been able to convince the Tibetan authorities that we did not draw these maps ourselves. But an educated man like yourself, a man so familiar with European matters, will know at once that we could not possibly have done so.' Kichan looked very pleased at the compliment.

'There's no doubt about it,' he said. 'One can see at a glance that these maps are printed. Here, look,' he said to the regent, 'those maps were not drawn by these men; they were printed in the kingdom of France. You wouldn't know the difference, but I have long been familiar with Western things.' These words had a magical effect on the regent; he beamed all over; he looked at us with eyes full of joy and nodded graciously to us, as if to say: 'Everything's all right; you are good men.'

It was impossible to proceed further without giving a geography lesson. We kindly bowed to the wishes of the regent and the ambassador, and pointed out on the Mercator's projection, China, Tartary, Tibet and all the other countries of the globe. The regent was dumbfounded to find how far we were from our homeland, and how long was the route we had had to follow by sea and by land to pay him a visit in the capital of Tibet. He looked at us amazed, then he gave the thumbs-up gesture with his right hand and said: 'You are men like that,' which means in the gesture-language of Tibet: 'You are splendid fellows.' After we had shown him the main features of Tibet, the regent asked us where Calcutta was.

'There,' we said, pointing to a tiny circle by the sea.

'And Lhasa? Where is Lhasa?'

'Here it is.' For a little while the eyes and the finger of the regent travelled the route from Lhasa to Calcutta and back again.

'The Pelings of Calcutta are very close to our frontiers,' he said, grimacing and shaking his head. 'No matter,' he added, 'here are the Himalayas!'

The geography lesson being over, the maps were folded up and put back into their cases, and we then turned to the religious objects. Kichan knew quite a lot about these. When he had been viceroy of the province of Petchely he had persecuted enough Christians to have had numerous occasions to become familiar with everything connected with the Catholic ritual; so of course he gave a display of his knowledge. He explained the pictures, the sacred vessels, the ornaments; he was even able to state that in the box of sacred oils there was an excellent remedy for the dying. Whilst Kichan was explaining all this, the regent became absent-minded; his eye was continually caught by a long pair of sacramental tongs, which, with their two wide lips, seemed to work strongly on his imagination; he questioned us with his eyes, and seemed to be asking whether this horrible instrument were not some infernal machine. He was reassured only when we had shown him some wafers which we kept in a box. Only then did he realise the use of that strange object.

That kindly man was all smiles and bubbling with triumph when it was clear that amongst all our possessions there was nothing at all compromising.

'Well,' he said to the Chinese ambassador, in a sly voice, 'what do you think of these men? What shall we do with them?'

'These men are French, they are ministers of the religion of the Lord of Heaven and they are honest men; we must leave them in peace.' These favourable words were received by those in the room with a low murmur of approval, and we two missionaries answered from the bottom of our hearts: *Deo gratias!*

The fatigue party loaded up with our luggage and we returned home looking no doubt more cheerful and relaxed than when we had left. The news of our acquittal had quickly spread through the town, and the Tibetan crowd came running from all directions to congratulate us. We were greeted eagerly, and the word 'French' was being said all round us. From now on, the 'white Azaras' were quite forgotten.

When we reached our apartment we handed round a few *tchan-kas* to the porters, so that they could drink our health in a pot of Tibetan small-beer, and appreciate the generosity of the French, who do not make people work for nothing.

When everyone had left we were alone at last, with time to think; at which point we became conscious of two very important things: the first, that we had not dined, and the second, that our two steeds were no longer in their stalls. Whilst we were wondering how we could rustle up a meal in a hurry, and how we could find out what had happened to our horses, who should appear at the door and solve both our problems but the Katchi governor himself! That excellent fellow, realising that our session at the lawcourts had prevented us from putting our pot on to boil, had come with two servants bearing a basket full of provisions. It was a celebration banquet that he had prepared for us.

'And our horses? Have you any news of them? They have disappeared from the courtyard.'

'I was going to tell you. They have been in the regent's stables since yesterday evening. Whilst you were away, they were neither hungry nor thirsty. I have heard that you intend to sell them. Is it true?'

'Yes, it's true, they cost so much to keep. But they are so thin, who would buy them in that state?'

'The regent wants to buy them.'

'The regent?'

'Yes, the regent. Don't laugh, it's not a joke. How much do you want for them?'

'Oh, whatever he wishes.'

'Then your horses are bought.' Saying this the Kashmiri undid a small package he was carrying under his arm and placed on the floor two silver ingots each weighing ten ounces. 'There,' he said, 'is the price of your two horses.' We thought that our animals, thin and worn out as they were, were not worth that much, and conscientiously said so to the Katchi governor: but it was impossible to make any change in the transaction, which had all been settled in advance. The regent thought that the horses, though thin, must be of good stock because they had not succumbed to the hardships of our long journey. In addition they had extra value for him, in that they had travelled in many lands and especially had grazed the pastures of Kounboum, birthplace of Tsong Kaba.

Twenty ounces of silver added to our meagre purse was a

small fortune, and we could afford to be generous. So on the spot we took one of the ingots and laid it on Samdadchiemba's lap.

'That's for you,' we said, 'there's enough there to buy a fine new outfit from head to foot.' Samdadchiemba thanked us, in a loud, surly voice; then the muscles of his face relaxed, his nostrils distended and his big mouth burst into a smile. Next, he could no longer contain his joy; he threw his ingot into the air and caught it several times, crying: 'What a wonderful day!' He was quite right; that day, so badly begun, had turned out better than we could have hoped. We now enjoyed an honourable position at Lhasa, and we could henceforth work freely for the propagation of the gospel.

The following day was even better, and in a way marked the high point of our success. In the morning we went with the Katchi governor to see the regent, in order to thank him for his support. We were received with great cordiality. The regent told us in confidence that the Chinese were suspicious of our presence in Lhasa, but that we could count on his protection and remain freely in the country where no one would have the right to meddle with us.

'You are very ill-lodged,' he added, 'I thought your room was dirty, small and inconvenient; I want foreigners such as you, men who have come so far, to be comfortable in Lhasa. Are not foreigners well-treated in your land of France?'

'They are given first-class treatment. If only you could go there one day, you would see how our emperor would treat you!'

'Foreigners are guests; you must therefore leave the lodging that you found for yourselves; I have given the order for a proper lodging to be prepared for you in one of my houses.' We accepted this generous offer with alacrity and gratitude. Free, comfortable accommodation was not to be sneezed at in our position; but above all we realised the value of residing in a house belonging to the regent himself. Such a notable favour, such a demonstration of protection from the Tibetan authorities, was bound to give us great moral prestige with the inhabitants of Lhasa and facilitate our task as missionaries.

When we left the palace we went straight to the house we had been assigned; it was superb, it was perfect! That same evening we moved into our home.

Our first task was to create a small chapel in our house. We chose the largest and finest room, we carpeted it as best we could and then adorned it with sacred pictures. How our hearts rejoiced now that at last it was possible to pray publicly at the foot of the cross in the very heart of the capital of Buddhism, where perhaps the symbol of our Redeemer had never before been seen to shine! What a comfort it was to us to be able at last to speak loud and clear the word of life to these poor peoples, who had lived for so many centuries in the shadow of death! This little chapel was in fact a poor thing, but for us it was the hundredfold that God has promised to those who give up all for His sake. Our hearts were so full, that we felt that two years of hardship and suffering in the desert were a small price to pay for such joy.

Everyone in Lhasa wanted to visit the chapel of the French lamas; some merely asked us for an explanation of the pictures round the wall and left again, putting off until some future time any instruction in the holy doctrine of Jehovah: but many did feel moved, and showed great interest in the study of the truths that we had come to reveal to them. They came to us diligently every day, worked hard reading the summary of the Christian faith which we had written at the lamasery of Kounboum, and begged us to teach them some 'true prayers'.

It was not only Tibetans who showed enthusiasm for the study of our holy religion. There were Chinese, including the secretaries of ambassador Kichan, who came often to see us to discuss the great doctrine of the West; one of these, to whom we had lent several books written in Tartar-Mandchou, became convinced of the truth of Christianity and of the need to embrace it, but he lacked the courage to declare his faith openly whilst he was still a member of the embassy staff; he preferred to wait until he was able to return to his country. God grant that his resolution has not weakened!

A doctor from the province of Yunnan showed more nobility of soul. This young man had lived in so strange a way since he had arrived in Lhasa that he was generally known as 'the Chinese hermit'. He never went out except to visit his patients and seldom went to see any but the poor. The rich applied to him in vain; he never even answered them, except when driven to it by the need for some cash; for he took nothing from the poor, to serve whom he devoted his life. When not visiting the sick he spent his time in study; he even passed the greater part of the night over his books. He slept little, and ate only one meal a day, consisting of barley meal; he never touched meat. One only had to look at him to see that he led a life of hardship: his face was extremely pale and thin, and although he was not more than thirty years of age, his hair was completely white.

One day he came to see us whilst we were reciting the breviary in our little chapel; he stopped a few paces inside the door, and stood waiting gravely and in silence. A large coloured picture representing the crucifixion had evidently caught his attention; for as soon as we had finished our prayers he asked us bluntly, without any of the usual preliminaries, to explain its meaning. When we had answered his question he crossed his arms over his chest and without uttering a single word he stood motionless, his eyes on the image of the crucifixion; he stood thus for nearly half an hour; then his eyes filled with tears; he held his arms out towards the figure of Christ, fell on his knees, struck the ground three times with his forehead and then stood up crying: '*There* is the only Buddha that men should worship!' Then he turned to us and, after bowing deeply, said: 'You are my masters; take me for your disciple.'

This man's behaviour was strangely impressive; we could not help feeling that God's grace had descended on his heart. We briefly outlined the main points of the Christian doctrine to him, and at everything we said he answered only, 'I believe', with a truly astonishing conviction of faith in his voice. We showed him a little crucifix in copper gilt, and asked him if he would accept it as a gift. His only reply was a deep, eager bow; once the crucifix was in his hands, he asked us to give him a cord, and immediately hung it round his neck. He also wanted to know what prayer he could recite before the cross.

'We can lend you various books in Chinese, in which you will find the doctrine explained and many forms of prayer.'

'My masters, it is well; but I should like a short, easy prayer that I can learn immediately and repeat often and everywhere I go.' We taught him to say, 'Jesus, Saviour of the world, have pity on me.' For fear of forgetting the words, he wrote them on a piece of paper which he put in a small purse which he hung on his belt; then he left us, saying that the memory of that day would for ever remain with him.

This young doctor worked with great zeal to master the truths of the Christian religion; but what was most remarkable about him was that he made no attempt to hide the faith with which he was filled. When he came to see us, or when we met him in the street, the crucifix was always shining on his breast, and he would always greet us by using the words of his prayer: 'Jesus, Saviour of the world, have pity on me.'

While endeavouring to sow the seed amongst the people of Lhasa, we tried at the same time to introduce it into the regent's palace, hoping that one day we should reap a precious harvest there. Since the day of our 'trial' we had seen a great deal of the regent, and were now on terms of some intimacy. Almost every evening, when he had finished his important administrative duties he sent a message inviting us to come and share his Tibetan meal, to which he thoughtfully caused several Chinese dishes to be added for our benefit. Our conversations generally continued far into the night.

The regent was a man of great brilliance; of humble origins, he had risen step by step and through his own merit to the premiership. He had reached this high eminence only three years previously; until then he had always held posts involving much labour and hardship; he had frequently had to go vast distances from one end of Tibet to the other, to fight or to negotiate with neighbouring states or to supervise the activities of the Houtouktous who were governors of the different provinces. This active, troubled existence, hardly compatible with a life of study, had not prevented him from mastering the lamaic texts. Everyone agreed that the regent knew more about them than the most learned lamas. What was truly remarkable was the ease with which he handled business. One day whilst we were with him a number of paper scrolls were brought; they were despatches from the provinces; a secretary unrolled them one by one and held them up for him to read, kneeling on one knee. The regent ran his eye rapidly over them, but without interrupting the conversation that he was holding with us. As soon as he had absorbed the contents of a despatch he took his bamboo stylus and wrote out his orders at the end of the scroll; he thus dealt with all his affairs speedily and as if they were child's play. He was reputed to be a writer of merit, and of this we could not judge, but we can say that we never saw the Tibetan script so beautifully written as by him.

The regent was fond of talking about religion, and more often than not this was the subject of our conversations. At the beginning of our relationship, he spoke these remarkable words: 'All your long journeys were made for a religious purpose. You are right, for man's business in life is religion; I see that the French and the Tibetans are at one in this. We are not like the Chinese, who care nothing for questions of the soul. But your religion is not the same as ours; it is important to decide which is the truth. We shall therefore examine them both carefully and sincerely; if yours is the true one, we shall adopt it; how could we refuse to? But if it is ours, I hope you will be reasonable enough to adopt it yourselves.' This attitude seemed right—we could not have hoped for a better.

We began with Christianity. The regent, always courteous, insisted that as we were his guests, our beliefs should have priority. We went systematically through all the dogma and moral teachings. To our great astonishment, the regent showed no surprise at anything. 'Your religion,' he told us again and again, 'is identical with ours; the principles are the same, we only differ in the explanations. In everything that you have seen and heard in Tartary and Tibet you must have found much to criticise; but you must not forget that the many errors and superstitions that you have noticed have been introduced by ignorant lamas, and they are rejected by educated Buddhists.' He would only admit two points of difference between his religion and ours: the creation of the world and the transmigration of souls. The regent's beliefs, although at some points apparently close to the Christian doctrine, led in the end to vague pantheistic conceptions; but he claimed that our ideas would lead to the same conclusions, and undertook to convince us of the fact.

The Tibetan language, strongly religious and mystical in character, expresses with great clarity and precision all ideas connected with the human soul and the godhead. Unfortunately, we were insufficiently experienced in the language and were forced in our conversations with the regent to have recourse to the Katchi governor as interpreter; but as he was not very good at expressing metaphysical ideas in Chinese, it was often difficult for us to understand one another. One day the regent said to us: 'Truth is manifest; but when clothed in obscure words it cannot be perceived. So long as we have to use

Chinese as a vehicle, we shall never be able to understand each other. We shall only have profitable discussions when you are able to speak Tibetan with clarity.''No one agreed with this more wholeheartedly than we. We replied that we were much concerned with the study of the Tibetan language, and that we worked at it daily. 'If you wish,' he said, 'I will find you the means of learning it.' Saying this, he called a servant and spoke some words that we did not understand. A very young man, elegantly dressed, soon appeared and greeted us with great courtesy. 'This is my nephew,' said the regent, 'I give him to you as pupil and teacher; he will spend the days with you, and so you will be able to practise your Tibetan; in return, you will give him some lessons in Chinese and Mandchu.' We gratefully accepted this proposal, and were in fact able by these means to make rapid progress in the language of the country.

The regent much enjoyed hearing us talk about France. During our long visits, he continually questioned us on the manners, the customs and the products of our country. Everything we told him about steamboats, railways, balloons, gaslight, the telegraph, daguerreotypes and all our industrial products filled him with excitement and admiration for the greatness and power of France.

One day when we were speaking of astronomical observations and instruments, he asked us if he could be allowed to look closely at that curious instrument that we kept in a box: he meant the microscope. As we were in the best of humours and much better disposed than on the day all our effects had been examined, we hastened to satisfy the regent's curiosity. One of us ran home and returned immediately with the marvellous instrument. As we adjusted it, we tried to explain some of the basic principles of optics to our audience; but, perceiving that the theory excited little enthusiasm, we quickly passed on to an experiment. We asked if any gentleman present would be good enough to provide a louse. This was easier to find than any butterfly. A noble lama, secretary to his excellency the prime minister, had only to slip his hand into his armpit under his silk robe, to produce a fine specimen of a louse. We caught hold of it on each side of its body with our tweezers; but the lama immediately began to object; he wanted to stop the experiment, on the grounds that we would cause the death of a living creature.

'Have no fear,' we told him, 'your louse is only caught by the epidermis; in any case, it seems vigorous enough to survive this unpleasant experience.'

The regent, who as already explained was not as literal-minded as the common folk, told the lama to keep quiet and let us carry on. We therefore continued the experiment and placed the poor little struggling creature under the lens, held by the tip of the tweezers. We then invited the regent to apply his right eye to the lens at the top, whilst simply closing his left. 'Tsong Kaba!' exclaimed the regent. 'That louse is a big as a rat!' After watching it for a moment, he raised his head and hid his face in his hands, saying that it was a horrible sight. He tried to dissuade the others from looking, but completely without success. Each in turn bent over the microscope and recoiled uttering exclamations of horror. The secretary-lama, noticing that his little creature had more or less stopped moving, begged a reprieve. We removed the tweezers, dropping the louse into the hands of its owner. But oh dear! the victim was motionless. The regent said with a laugh to his secretary 'I think your louse is sick. See that it takes some medicine, or it may not recover.'

By now no one wanted to see any more living creatures, so we continued the performance by showing our small collection of slides. They were enthusiastically received, and on all sides we heard praise for the amazing cleverness of the French. The regent said to us 'Your railways and your airships no longer surprise me so much; men who can invent an instrument like this can do anything.'

The First Kalon became so infatuated with everything about our country that he took a notion to study the French language. One evening we brought him, at his request, a French alphabet, with the corresponding Tibetan character under each letter. He glanced at it, and when we offered to explain it told us that it was unnecessary; it was quite clear.

The following day, as soon as we arrived, he asked us for the name of our emperor.

'Our emperor is called Louis Philippe.'

'Louis Philippe, Louis Philippe. Right.' He took his stylus and began to write; after an instant he gave us a piece of paper on which he had written, in well-shaped letters: LOUY FILIPE.

During the short period of our prosperity in Lhasa we also

enjoyed a fairly close relationship with Kichan. He summoned us several times to talk politics or, to use the Chinese expression, to talk of idle things. We were most surprised at how much he knew about European affairs. He had much to say of the British and Queen Victoria.

'It appears,' he said, 'that that woman is extremely clever, but in my opinion her husband is in an absurd position: she won't allow him to play a part in anything. She has made a beautiful garden for him, full of fruit trees and flowers of every kind, and there he remains imprisoned, spending his whole life walking in the garden. I am told that there are other countries in Europe where the women rule. Is it true? Are their husbands also shut up in gardens? Does this also happen in France?'

'No, in France the women are in gardens and the men conduct the business.'

'Now that is right and proper: the other way would lead to disorder.'

Kichan asked us for news of Palmerston, whether he was still Foreign Secretary.

'And Ilu (Elliot): what has become of him? Do you know?'

'He was recalled; your dismissal caused his.'

'A pity; Ilu was a good-hearted man, but he was unable to make decisions. Was he executed or exiled?'

'Neither. In Europe we do not go as far as you do in Peking.'

'Yes, true, your mandarins are luckier than we are. Your government is better than ours. Our emperor can't know everything, yet he has to decide everything, and no one ever dares to criticise what he does. Our emperor says: "That is white." We kowtow and say: "Yes, that is white." Then he points to the same thing and says: "That is black." We kowtow again and answer, "Yes, that is black."'

'But supposing you were to say that nothing can be both black and white?'

'The emperor might perhaps say to the bold man who said that: "You are right." But he would then have him strangled or beheaded. Unlike you, we have no "Council of all the Chiefs" (Tchoung Teou Y) by which Kichan meant the Chamber of Deputies. 'If your emperor intended to carry out an injustice, the Tchoung Teou Y would be there to prevent him.'

Kichan told us the strange story of how the British affair of 1839 had been handled in Peking. The emperor summoned the eight Tchoung Tang or Grand Counsellors who made up his privy council and spoke to them about the events that had taken place in the South. He told them that adventurers from the Western Seas had committed rebellious acts and that they must be captured and punished, in order to set an example to any others who might be tempted to follow their example. After expressing this opinion, he asked his counsellors for theirs. The four Mandchou counsellors kowtowed and said:

'*Tcha, tcha, tcha, tchou-dze-ti fen-fou*: Yes, yes, yes, those are the Master's orders.'

The four Chinese counsellors kowtowed in their turn and said:

'*Che, che, che, hoang chang-ti tien-ngen*: Yes, yes, yes, it is the heavenly gift of the emperor.' After that there was nothing to say and the council was dismissed.

This story is perfectly authentic, as Kichan was one of the counsellors in question. He added that he himself was convinced that the Chinese could only stand up militarily to the Europeans if they changed their weapons and their old habits, but that he would take care never to tell the emperor what he thought, because not only would it be useless but it might well cost him his life.

Our close relations with the Chinese ambassador, the regent and the Katchi governor were a great help in attracting the confidence and approval of the population of Lhasa. As we saw how the number of those who came to visit us and take instruction in our holy religion increased daily, our hopes grew and our courage strengthened. But in spite of these comforting feelings, there was one thought which constantly nagged at us: we deeply regretted that we were unable to show the Tibetans the beautiful and moving spectacle of the rituals of Catholicism. We always felt that with their love of the external shows of religion they would have been deeply affected by them.

The Tibetans, as we have already said, are extremely religious; but, apart from a few contemplative lamas who retire to the mountain tops and spend their lives in rocky caverns, they are little given to mysticism. Their piety does not turn inwards; they prefer to express it by actions. Hence their enjoyment of pilgrimages, noisy ceremonials in lamaseries, and prostrations on roof-tops. They take their beads with them everywhere, and tell them noisily; prayers are always on their lips, even when they are conducting business.

In Lhasa there was a most moving custom, which we were quite jealous of finding amongst infidels. Around evening, just as daylight was fading, all the Tibetans put down what they were doing and gathered together—men, women and children, according to sex and age—in different parts of the town and in the public squares. They formed into groups, and squatted on the ground; then began the slow murmur of chanted prayers. The sound rising from so many of these choirs together filled the city with a vast solemn harmony which moved the soul most deeply. The first time we witnessed this spectacle we could not help drawing a painful contrast between this pagan town and the cities of Europe, where people are ashamed to make the sign of the cross in public.

The prayers which the Tibetans chanted in their evening gatherings varied according to the seasons of the year; but the one they said when telling their beads was always the same, and consisted only of six syllables: *Om, mani padme houm*. This phrase, which the Buddhists called in short the *mani* was not only continually recited but was written up everywhere, in the streets, in the squares and indoors. On all the banners to be seen flying over doors or from the tops of buildings there was always a *mani* printed in Landza, Tartar and Tibetan characters. Some rich and pious Buddhists supported bands of sculptor-lamas whose function was to spread the use of the *mani*; these strange missionaries went off, hammer and chisel in hand, through the countryside, the mountains and wildernesses, engraving the sacred formula on the boulders and rocks in their way.

According to the celebrated orientalist Klaproth, *Om, mani padme houm* is the Tibetan transcription of a Sanscrit phrase brought to Tibet from India. About the middle of the seventh century AD the Hindoo Tonmi Sambhodha introduced writing into Tibet; but the king, Srong Bdzan Gombo, considered the Landza alphabet which he adopted at first to be too complicated and too difficult to learn, and he commissioned the Hindoo to design a new one, both simpler and better adapted to the Tibetan language. So Tonmi Sambhodha shut himself up for some time and composed the Tibetan characters in use today, which are thus only a modification of the Sanscrit. He also introduced the king to the secrets of Buddhism, and taught him the sacred formula *Om, mani padme houm,* which spread rapidly thoughout Tibet and Mongolia.

The phrase has a meaning in Sanscrit which is complete and unambiguous, but none in Tibetan. *Om* is, for the Hindoos, the mystical name of God, with which all prayers begin. It is composed of A—the name of Vishnu; O—that of Siva; and M—that of Brahma. At the same time *Om* is the interjection oh!, the expression of a religious emotion, and is therefore in a sense a declaration of faith. *Mani* means jewel, precious object; *padma* is the lotus and *padme* the locative case of the same word. Finally, *houm* is a word expressing a wish and is equivalent to Amen. The literal sense is therefore: 'Oh! the jewel in the lotus. Amen!'

To Buddhists of Tibet and Mongolia this simple, clear meaning was not enough. They have racked their brains to find a mystical interpretation of each one of the six syllables of which the phrase is composed. They have written one heavy tome after another in which the wildest theories are produced to explain the meaning of their *mani.* Lamas often say that the doctrine contained in these words is boundless, and that the life of a man is too short to plumb its depths.

We were curious to know what the regent would have to say about it. He told us as follows: 'The forms of life (in Tibetan, *semdchan;* in Mongol, *amitan*) are divided into six classes: angels, devils, men, quadrupeds, birds and reptiles. Each of the syllables of *Om, mani padme houm* corresponds to one of these classes. The forms of life move to and fro within the six classes by continual transformations according to their merit or lack of it, until they reach perfection; they are then absorbed and lost in the great essence of Buddha, that is, in the eternal soul, into which all souls, after their temporary reincarnations, will unite and merge. The forms of life have means of attaining sainthood which vary according to the class they belong to and which enable them to rise into a higher class, attain perfection and finally merge in the eternal soul. Men who recite *Om, mani padme houm* very frequently and piously will not fall back when they die into the six classes corresponding to the six syllables of the *mani,* but will reach the fullness of their being by absorption into the eternal and universal soul of Buddha.'

We do not know if the explanation given to us by the regent is the one generally adopted by educated Buddhists in Tibet and Mongolia. It strikes us, however, that there is an analogy between it and the literal sense of: 'Oh! the jewel in the lotus. Amen!' Since the jewel is the symbol of perfection and the lotus the emblem of Buddha, these words could be said to express the desire to attain perfection, to be united with the Buddha, absorbed in the universal soul. The formula of the

mani might then be paraphrased: 'Oh! may I reach perfection and be absorbed in Buddha. Amen!'

According to the regent's explanation, the *mani* is a sort of abstract of the all-embracing pantheism which is at the root of all Buddhist beliefs. The educated lamas say that Buddha is the essential, independent Being, beginning and end of all. The earth, the stars, men, everything that exists is a partial and temporary manifestation of Buddha. Everything was created by Buddha, in the sense that everything comes from him, as light comes from the sun. All beings which emanate from Buddha have had a beginning and will have an end; but as they have come out of the universal essence, they must also return thither. Like the waters which form the rivers and which came originally from the sea, they will after a long or a short time eventually flow back again into its immensity. Thus Buddha is eternal; his manifestations are also eternal, in the sense that they always have been and always will be, although taken separately, each one must have a beginning and an end.

Without much caring whether it is consistent or not with the foregoing, the Buddhists believe in addition in an unlimited number of divine incarnations. They say that Buddha takes a human body and comes to live amongst men, in order to help them attain perfection and union with the universal soul. These Living Buddhas form the numerous class of Chaberons, of which we have already spoken. The most famous at the time of our visit were: at Lhasa, the Dalai Lama; at Djachi Loumbo, the Panchen Remboutchi; at Grand Kouren, the Guison Tamba; at Peking, the Tchang Kia Fuo, a kind of Grand Almoner of the imperial court; and in the land of the Ssamba, at the foot of the Himalayas, the Sa Dcha Fo. The latter, we were told, had a particularly strange function. He prayed continually night and day, that snow might fall continually on the summits of the Himalayas. For, according to a Tibetan tradition, there was on the other side of the mountains a wild and cruel people who were only waiting for the snows to melt to come and cut the Tibetan tribes to pieces and seize their country.

Although all Chaberons are Living Buddhas, they nevertheless form a hierarchy, with the Dalai Lama at the top. All the others recognise or should recognise his supremacy. The Dalai Lama at the time of our stay, as already stated, was a nine year old child. He had already been in the palace on the Buddha La for six years. He was Si Fan by origin, and came from a poor and obscure family of the principality of Ming Tchen Tou Sse.

When the Dalai Lama dies, or to speak Buddhistically, when he sheds his human envelope, his successor is chosen in the following manner. Prayers and fasts are ordered in all lamaseries. In Lhasa, the inhabitants—being those most affected by the outcome—redouble their zeal and piety. There is a constant pilgrimage round the Buddha La and through Lhasa, City of Spirits; everyone holds a whirling prayer-wheel, the sacred formula of the *mani* is heard incessantly night and day in all parts of the city, and incense burns profusely. Those who believe that they have the Dalai Lama in their family inform the authorities in Lhasa, who then proceed to establish whether or not these children qualify as Chaberons. Before the choice of a Dalai Lama can proceed, three confirmed Chaberons have to be found. They are sent for and brought to Lhasa. The

Houtouktous of the lamaic states then assemble. They spend six days in retreat, in fasting and in prayer shut up in a temple of the Buddha La. On the seventh day, three golden dockets engraved with the candidates' names are placed in a golden urn. The urn is shaken, the senior Houtouktou takes out one of the dockets and the infant whose name is on the docket is immediately proclaimed Dalai Lama. He is paraded in great pomp round the streets of the City of Spirits; as he passes the crowd falls prostrate, and finally he is placed in his sanctuary.

The two Chaberons in swaddling-clothes who also competed are taken back to their families by their nurses; but as compensation for failure to win the prize the government makes them a small gift of five hundred ounces of silver.

The Dalai Lama is worshipped by the Tibetans and the Mongols as a god. His prestige in the Buddhist lands is really astonishing. But stories that his excrement is respectfully collected and used to make amulets which the faithful enclose in little bags which they hang round their necks are complete exaggerations. It is also untrue to say that the Dalai Lama appears to the admiring faithful with snakes twined round his head and his arms. Such statements as these, which are to be found in certain geography textbooks, are completely lacking in foundation. During our stay in Lhasa we questioned many people on these points, and every one of them laughed in our faces. Unless it is assumed that everybody, from the regent to the *argol*-merchant, was in a conspiracy to deceive us, it will have to be admitted that the tales that gave rise to these myths were without foundation.

We did not succeed in seeing the Dalai Lama; this was not because it was made particularly difficult for the pious or the curious to do so, but we were prevented by a rather odd circumstance. The regent had promised to take us to the Buddha La, and we were about to make this eagerly awaited expedition when it was decided that we might give the Dalai Lama smallpox. An epidemic of this had just started at Lhasa and it was thought that it had been brought from Peking in the great caravan which had recently arrived. As we had been members of this caravan we were asked to postpone our visit rather than risk exposing the Dalai Lama to infection. The suggestion was so reasonable that we could hardly object.

The Tibetan fear of smallpox was extraordinary. They spoke

of it with horror as the greatest scourge that could attack the human race. Nearly every year there were disastrous epidemics at Lhasa; the only preventive measure that the government knew was to banish the unfortunate families that were affected. As soon as there was an outbreak of smallpox in a house, all the residents were forcibly evacuated out of the town, and became refugees in the mountains or deserts. No one was allowed to communicate with these unfortunates, who quickly died of hunger and hardship or were eaten by wild beasts. We of course told the regent about the invaluable method in use in Europe against smallpox. One of the reasons for the regent's friendship and protection was his hope that we might one day introduce vaccination into Tibet. The missionary fortunate enough to do the Tibetans so valuable a service would acquire an influence over their minds which would be able to compete with that of the Dalai Lama himself. The introduction of vaccine into Tibet by missionaries might herald the fall of lamaism and make possible the establishment of Christianity in that pagan land.

Leprosy and scabies were quite common in Lhasa. These skin diseases were caused by the dirt which was universal especially amongst the poor. Cases of rabies were not uncommon. We were only surprised that this dreadful illness was not even more widespread, in view of the hordes of starving dogs which prowled day and night though the streets of Lhasa; these beasts were so numerous that the Chinese would say ironically that the three main products of the capital of Tibet were lamas, women and dogs: *lama, ya-teou, keou.*

This plague of dogs came from the great respect that the Tibetans had for the animal, and for their use in the disposal of the dead. There were four methods of disposal in use in Tibet: burning, immersion in rivers and lakes, exposure on mountain tops and—the most honourable and most popular of the four— the cutting up of the body into pieces and feeding it to dogs. The poor man's grave was simply the neighbourhood dogs; but for persons of distinction it was done more ceremoniously; in certain lamaseries sacred dogs were bred for the purpose, and that is how rich Tibetans were disposed of.

8

EXPULSION FROM LHASA

We already made a brief mention of Moorcroft's journey to Tibet when speaking of the Tibetan government's exaggerated fear of draughtsmen and map-makers. One day the Katchi governor brought with him one of his compatriots, named Nisan, who for a long time had been Moorcroft's servant at Lhasa. This man gave us a long account of his old master, and the details he gave us confirmed what we had already heard. Since the story of this British traveller was too strange to be ignored, we feel that a short digression would not come amiss.

The story as we heard it in Lhasa was that Moorcroft arrived there from Ladakh in 1826; he was wearing Muslim costume and spoke the Parsee language so fluently that the Kashmiri of Lhasa accepted him as one of themselves. He rented a house in the city and lived there for twelve years with his servant Nisan whom he had brought from Ladakh and who fully believed that his master was a Kashmiri. Moorcroft had bought some herds of goats and yaks and put them out to grass with Tibetan herdsmen in mountain valleys not far from Lhasa. Under cover of visiting his herds, he made frequent sorties into the country, during which he made sketches and drew maps. Knowing no Tibetan he apparently avoided contact with the local inhabitants. Twelve years later he set off to return to Ladakh, but when passing through the province of Ngari he was attacked and murdered by a troop of brigands. The latter were tracked down and arrested by the Tibetan government and were found to have on them some of the Englishman's effects, including his collection of sketches and maps. This was the first intimation that the Lhasa authorities had had that Moorcroft was British.

Before parting company from his servant, Moorcroft had given him a letter and told him that if he ever went to Calcutta and showed it to anyone there he would make his fortune. This was presumably a letter of introduction. But the capture of Moorcroft's effects caused so great a stir that Nisan, for fear of becoming implicated, destroyed the letter. He told us that the writing in it was similar to our own.

The details of this story were given us by the regent, the Katchi governor, Nisan and other inhabitants of Lhasa. We had never heard of Moorcroft before we arrived there, but with all these independent sources it would seem beyond doubt that he really did arrive there in 1826, lived there twelve years and was murdered on the road from Lhasa to Ladakh. However, Charles Ritter in his *Géographie Universelle* tells a different story, hardly compatible with the one we were told in the capital of Tibet. According to Ritter, Moorcroft, in 1812, went on a journey which lasted two months, after which he was commissioned by the East India Company to go to Turkestan to procure horses for the improvement of the Indian stud. He set off with this objective in November 1819 and reached Ladakh where he stayed two years. In October 1822 he set off in the direction of Kashmir, and on 25 August 1825 he died at Andkou, on the road between Herat and Balkh. The news of his death was contained in a letter from his travelling companion, Mr Tribeck, dated from Balkh on 6 September 1825, and addressed to a Captain Wade at Loudiana.

It is clearly impossible to reconcile these two accounts. But if Moorcroft never went to Lhasa, how is it that the Tibetans knew so much about him? Why should they want to invent such a tale? On the other hand, how can we explain Tribeck's letter giving news of his friend's death in 1825, just when—according to the Tibetan account—he would be setting off for Lhasa?

We will make no attempt to resolve these contradictions, but it may be relevant here to mention our own case, which presents certain parallels with the Moorcroft affair. Some time after our return to Macao from Tibet, we read the following article in the Bengal Catholic Herald, of Calcutta:

'Canton, 12 September: The French missionaries of our city have recently received the tragic news of the death of two fathers of their mission in Mongolian Tartary . . .' After a brief description of Chinese Mongolia, the article continues: 'A French Lazarist called Huc arrived about three years ago to reside with a group of Chinese families who had settled in the Valley of Black Waters, about six hundred miles from the Great Wall. Another Lazarist, whose name is unknown to me, joined him with the intention of founding a mission amongst the Buddhists of Mongolia. They studied the Mongolian language amongst the lamas of neighbouring monasteries. It seems that they were accepted as foreign lamas and treated in a friendly manner, especially by the Buddhists who are very ignorant and who mistook the Latin of their breviaries for Sanscrit—which they cannot read but for which they have a secret veneration, because the rites in their prayer-books, which are in Mongol translated from Sanscrit, are printed in red letters.

'When the missionaries felt that they were sufficiently fluent in the language they set off for the interior to begin their missionary activities. Since then nothing was heard of them apart from rumours; but last May the news came through from farthest Mongolia that they had been tied to horses' tails and dragged to their death. The reasons for this are not yet known.'

Whilst our death was being announced in these positive terms, we were on the last stages of our long journey and about to arrive at Canton, healthy enough to contradict the stories current about us. But if by chance we had perished amongst the mountains of Tibet, or been murdered, everyone would have remained convinced that we had been tied to horses' tails and died in Mongolia. It would have been considered most unlikely that we had ever been as far as the capital of Tibet, and later, if some European traveller had heard about us in Lhasa, it would have been as difficult to square these two accounts as the two stories about Moorcroft. This is why we felt we ought to mention our evidence about the latter, although without any wish to invalidate documents accepted by scientific journals in London.

We had been in Lhasa no more than a month, and already the holy doctrine of Jehovah and the great kingdom of France were respected and admired in that populous city. The peace we enjoyed, the notable protection afforded us by the Tibetan government, our warm reception from the public all filled us with hope that with God's help we could, in the very capital of Buddhism, lay the foundations of a mission whose influence would soon spread as far as the nomad tribes of Mongolia. It seemed that the moment had come when pilgrims from Tartary would at last be able to take instruction, in Lhasa itself, in the only doctrine which can save souls and civilise the nations.

Once our position in Lhasa seemed secure, we began to think of ways of regaining contact as soon as possible with Europe. The desert route was impracticable. We had it is true succeeded on that one occasion, miraculously as it seemed, in crossing those wastes infested with brigands and wild beasts, but the thought of organising a courier service on such terrain was out of the question. Even had it been safe enough, it would have been far too long. The Indian route seemed the only practicable one. From Lhasa to the British frontier post there was scarcely a month's march. If we could establish a correspondent on the far side of the Himalayas and another at Calcutta, we could open up communications with France which, if not quick or easy, would at least be workable. As such a plan could only be carried out with the consent of the Tibetan government, we put it to the regent, who immediately agreed. It was therefore decided that during the summer season Father Gabet would embark on a journey to Calcutta, with a Tibetan escort which would accompany him as far as Bhutan.

But at the very moment when these plans were maturing to set up a mission at Lhasa, the author of all evil was working to ruin them by removing us from the country which he seems to have chosen as the centre of his empire. Hints had been dropped of sinister moves in the wind, from which we gathered that the Chinese ambassador was secretly plotting to have us expelled from Tibet. We were not at all surprised at these rumours of persecution, for from the very beginning we had realised that if any difficulties were to arise they would come from Chinese mandarins. It was clear that Kichan could not bear to see the Tibetans open their doors so readily to the very religion and the very foreigners to which the Chinese, with their absurd prejudices, had closed their frontiers for so long. Christianity and the reputation of France had become too popular with the population of Lhasa for the Chinese not to be jealous. Any agent of the court of Peking was bound to resent such popularity in view of the possibility of eventual foreign influence in a country which China regarded as within its vital sphere of influence. A decision had therefore been made that the two ministers of the religion of the Lord of Heaven must be made to leave Lhasa.

One day Kichan summoned us, and after many honeyed words he let drop the remark that Tibet was too cold and too poor a country for us and that we ought to be thinking of returning home to France. He said this as if it had been the most natural and unobjectionable thing in the world. We asked him if he meant the remark as a piece of advice or an order.

'Both,' he answered coldly.

'If that is the case,' we told him, 'we must first thank you for your sympathetic interest in pointing out that this is a cold and a poor country. But you must realise that men like us are not in search of comfort and wealth; had we been so we would have stayed in France, for it is the best of all countries. But in so far as you mean your remark to be taken for an order, here is our reply: we were allowed in Tibet by the Tibetan authorities, and do not recognise your authority, or anyone else's, to revoke this.'

'What, you are foreigners, and yet you mean to stay?'

'Yes, we are foreigners, but we know that the laws of Tibet are not the same as those of China. The Peboun, the Katchi and the Mongols are all foreigners like us; yet they are left in peace, no one troubles them. Why should the French be arbitrarily excluded when this country is open to all? If foreigners are all to leave Lhasa, how about yourself? Is not your title of ambassador clear evidence that you too are only a foreigner?' At these words Kichan bounced on his crimson cushion.

'I a foreigner?' he exclaimed, 'I who represent the power of a great emperor? Who was it who only a few months ago condemned the Nomekhan and sent him to exile?'

'Yes, we know that story; but there is one difference between us and the Nomekhan, and that is that the Nomekhan came from Kansou, a province of the empire, and we come from France, where your great emperor has no dominion; moreover the Nomekhan had murdered three Dalai Lamas, whereas we have done no harm to anyone. Have we any other aim than to make known the true God to men, and teach them how to save their souls?'

'Yes, as I've told you before, I believe you to be honest men; but after all the religion that you preach has been declared harmful, and forbidden by our great emperor.'

'To the words that you have just spoken, we have only this to answer: the religion of the Lord of Heaven has never needed your emperor's permission in order to be a holy religion, any more than we, its missionaries, have needed it to come and preach it in Tibet.' The ambassador decided at this point to close the discussion; he dismissed us coldly with the assurance that he would see to it that we left Tibet.

We went straight to the regent to tell him of the regrettable interview we had had with Kichan. He already knew what the

Chinese mandarins were plotting against us. He tried to re-assure us, and said that as protector of thousands of foreigners in the country, he would be strong enough to protect us. 'In any case,' he added, 'even if our laws forbade the entry of for-eigners, you would be outside them. As men of religion, men of prayers, you are at home everywhere and foreigners nowhere: such is the doctrine taught in our holy books. It is written: "The yellow goat has no homeland, and the lama no family."

Since Lhasa is the meeting-place and special resort of men of prayers, as such you will always find freedom and protection here.'

This Buddhist view of the cosmopolitan nature of the man of religion is not just a mystical concept confined to their books; it has become, as we ourselves had seen, adopted as a normal attitude in the lamaseries. When a man shaves his head and dons the religious costume, he gives up his old name and takes a new one. If a lama is asked where he comes from, he replies: 'I have no homeland, but I live in such-and-such a lamasery.'

This way of thinking and acting is even admissible in China, amongst the bonzes and other men of religion, who are often referred to by the generic name of *Tchou-Kia Jen*, men outside the family.

For the next few days a struggle raged about us between the Tibetan government and the Chinese ambassador. Kichan used the tactic of posing as the defender of the Dalai Lama. His argument went as follows: He had been sent to Lhasa by his emperor to protect the Living Buddha, and it was therefore his duty to remove anything which might endanger him. Any ministers of the religion of the Lord of Heaven, however well-intentioned, would be preaching a doctrine which in the long run would tend to undermine the Dalai Lama's authority. Their avowed object was to substitute their religion for Buddhism, converting all the inhabitants of Tibet whatever their age, class or sex. What would become of the Dalai Lama when he had no worshippers? Would not the introduction of the religion of the Lord of Heaven into the country lead directly to the fall of the sanctuary of the Buddha La, and consequently to the ruin of the lamaic hierarchy and the Tibetan government? Can I, he would say, who am here to defend the Dalai Lama, allow men who spread so dangerous a doctrine to remain in Lhasa? If this doctrine were to take root, and proved impossible to eradicate, who would be responsible for such a disaster? What should I answer my emperor when he reproached me for negligence and cowardice? You Tibetans, he told the regent, do not understand how serious this is. Because these men are virtuous and well-behaved, you think they are not dangerous; that is an illusion. If they stay long in Lhasa they will bewitch you all. There is not one of you who can stand up to them when it comes to religion. Nothing can stop you from becoming converted to their creed, and in that case the Dalai Lama is finished.

The regent was unaffected by the ambassador's attempts to persuade him that we were dangerous. He maintained that our presence in Lhasa could do no possible harm to the Tibetan government. 'If the doctrine brought by these men is false,' he would say, 'the Tibetans will reject it. If on the other hand it is true, what have we to fear? How can truth be harmful to men? These two French lamas', he would add, 'have done no harm; their intentions towards us are excellent. How can we, without cause, deprive them of the freedom and the protection that all foreigners enjoy here, especially men of prayers? Have we the right to commit what is clearly an act of injustice here and now, for fear of a possible misfortune in the future?'

Whilst Kichan reproached the regent for neglecting the interests of the Dalai Lama, the regent accused Kichan of taking advantage of the minority of the sovereign to lord it over the Tibetan government. We ourselves, the bone of contention in this unfortunate conflict, refused to recognise the authority of the Chinese mandarin and declared that we would not leave the country without receiving formal orders to do so from the regent, who constantly assured us no one would ever extract such orders from him.

The quarrel became daily more bitter until Kichan decided to expel us on his own responsibility. Things reached such a point that we felt it only prudent to yield to circumstances and cease to put up any further opposition for fear of compromising the regent and possibly provoking a dangerous conflict between China and Tibet. If we had continued to react against the injustice of persecution, there was a danger that the Chinese would overreact by using us as a pretext in their plans to take over the government of Tibet. If on our account a rupture occurred between Lhasa and Peking, we were bound to be held responsible; the Tibetans would turn against us and the cause of Christianity in their country might suffer great damage in consequence. We therefore thought that it was better to bow our heads and patiently accept the role of the persecuted. Our behaviour would at least prove to the Tibetans that we had come among them with peaceful intentions, and that there was no question of our using violence to try and stay among them.

There was another reason which strengthened our decision. It occurred to us that this tyrannical behaviour of the Chinese towards us might set off a train of events whereby missionaries could one day safely establish themselves in Tibet. In our innocence we imagined that the French government would take exception to this provocative act on the part of China, whereby their persecution of Christians and Frenchmen was extended to foreign countries more than a thousand leagues from Peking. We were convinced that the representative of France at Canton would be bound to make a strong protest to the Chinese authorities, and obtain proper compensation for the act of force we had suffered. In holding this opinion, we—as humble and obscure missionaries—were far from claiming any personal importance for ourselves; but, we admit, we were proud enough to believe that as Frenchmen we would be entitled to the protection of our own government.

After a good deal of careful thought on these lines we called on the regent. When he heard that we had decided to leave Lhasa he was upset and embarrassed. He told us that he deeply regretted not being able to ensure a peaceful and secure life for us in Tibet, but that alone and without his sovereign's support he had not been strong enough to contain Chinese aggression which for some years past, taking advantage of the Dalai Lama's minority, had taken unheard-of liberties in the country. We thanked the regent for his goodwill and left him. Our next call was on the Chinese ambassador. We told Kichan that yielding to force and in the absence of any protection we had decided to leave Lhasa, but that we protested against this violation of our rights.

'Yes, of course,' said Kichan, 'that's the right thing to do, you must be off; it's best for you, best for me, best for the Tibetans, best for everybody.' He then told us that he had issued orders for the preparations necessary for our speedy departure; the mandarin and the escort who would accompany us had already been appointed. It had even been decided that we should leave in a week and that we should follow the route which leads to the Chinese frontier. We were both surprised and indignant at this; how could anyone be cruel enough to condemn us to an eight month journey, whereas if we went in the direction of India we could be at the first European frontier-post in twenty-five days, from which we would be sure of finding secure and easy means of reaching Calcutta. We protested strongly but in vain; nor were we any more successful when we asked to be allowed to stay a few days longer to rest from our recent long journey and allow the great wounds caused by the desert frosts time to heal. There was nothing we could say that would mollify the Chinese ambassador.

Realising this we stopped asking for favours and changed our tone. We were yielding to force, we said, but we wished the representative of the Peking government to know that we should report to our government as follows: firstly, we should say that the Chinese ambassador at Lhasa had arbitrarily and forcibly ejected us, on the empty pretext that we were foreigners and ministers of the Christian religion, which he pronounced to be harmful and condemned by his emperor; and secondly that contrary to all principles of justice he had prevented us from leaving by an easy direct route of only twenty-five days and instead forced us to take another lasting eight hard months and leading across the interior of China; and lastly we would denounce to our government the cruelty with which he made us take to the road without allowing us a longer rest; for, in view of our state of health we regarded this as tantamount to attempted murder. Kichan replied that he cared nothing for what the French government might think or do, and that his conduct was solely governed by the will of his emperor. 'If my master knew', he said, 'that I had allowed two Europeans freedom to preach the religion of the Lord of Heaven in Tibet, I should be finished. This time I should have no chance of escaping execution!'

On the following day Kichan summoned us to read us a report that he had written about us and that he was sending to the emperor. 'I don't want it to go before reading it to you,' he said, 'in case I have made any errors of fact or said anything that you dislike.' Having succeeded in his main aim, Kichan was now disposed to be friendly. His report was harmless enough; he spoke neither ill nor well of us and simply listed without comment the places we had visited since we had left Macao. 'Is the report to your liking,' asked Kichan, 'or have you some criticism?' I then told him that I had a most important criticism to make. 'Go ahead, I'm listening.'

'What I have to say does not affect us, but it affects you very closely.'

'Well, what is it?'

'It is confidential; send all these people away.'

'These people are all servants of my household: fear nothing.'

'We have nothing to fear; the danger is yours.'

'Mine? No matter, members of my suite may hear everything.'

'You can repeat to them what I have to say to you if you wish, but I cannot speak in their presence.'

'Mandarins may not have secret conversations with foreigners: that is forbidden by law.'

'In that case, I have nothing to say; send your report as it stands, and if anything happens to you, you have only yourself to blame.' The ambassador grew thoughtful; he took pinch after pinch of snuff and after long cogitation he told his suite to retire and leave us alone with him.

When they had gone, I took the floor, saying to Kichan:

'Now you will understand why I wanted to speak in secret, and how important it is for you that no one hears what I have to say; and if you think that we are dangerous men, remember that we even avoid hurting those who persecute us.' Kichan was pale and abashed.

'Come now,' he said, 'out with it; no beating about the bush: what have you to say?'

'In your report there is one error: you say that I left Macao with my Brother Joseph Gabet, but in fact I entered China four years after him.'

'Oh, if that's all it is, it's easy to correct.'

'Yes, quite easy. This report, you say, is for the emperor?'

'Of course.'

'Then you must tell the emperor the whole truth, and nothing but the truth.'

'Yes, yes, the whole truth; let us correct the report: now when did you enter China?'

'In the twentieth year of Taokouang (1840).' Kichan took his brush and wrote this in the margin. 'What moon?'

'In the second moon.' When Kichan heard this he put down his brush and gazed fixedly at me. 'Yes,' I repeated, 'I entered the Chinese empire in the twentieth year of Taokouang, in the second moon; I crossed the province of Canton, of which at that moment you were viceroy. But why do you not write this down? Does not the emperor have to know the whole truth?' Kichan winced. 'Now do you understand why I wanted to speak to you alone?'

'Yes, I know that Christians are not ill-natured. Does anyone here know about this?'

'No, no one.' Kichan tore up the report and wrote a new, entirely different, one: the dates of our entry into China were left vague, and there was a pompous eulogy of our learning and our saintliness. He really thought, poor man, that we wanted the Emperor of China to have a good opinion of us.

Kichan's orders were that we should set off as soon as the

Tibetan New Year festival was over. We had not yet been in Lhasa two months, and we had had two New Years, one European and one Chinese; now was the Tibetans' turn. Although the latter have a lunar calendar like the Chinese, the two do not tally: Lhasa is always one moon behind Peking.

The Chinese, the Mongols and most peoples of Eastern Asia use a chronological system of sixty-year cycles, made up of ten signs called trunks and twelve called branches. In the Tartar and Tibetan systems, the signs of the ten-year cycle are named after the five elements, repeated twice, or by the names of the five colours with their feminine shades. The years of the twelve-year cycle are named after twelve animals.

As this cycle is repeated every sixty years, it is essential to have a method of distinguishing one cycle from another, or great chronological confusion could result. For this purpose the emperors give a special name to the years of their reign, and thus all ambiguity is avoided. Thus a Mongol would say: the twenty-eighth year of Taokouang, which is the year of the Ram of Fire (1848). The current sixty-year cycle in China began in 1805, and the Taokouang years date from 1820, when the present emperor came to the throne. The names of the sixty-year cycles (Choundje, Kanghsi, Young-Tcheng, Kienlong, Kiaking, Taokouang) are not the names of the Mandchou dynasty emperors themselves, but names given by them to the years of their reign.

The Tibetans also use the ten- and twelve-year cycles, but by making more combinations of them arrive at a 252-year cycle. The first twelve years are named simply after twelve animals; then these same names are combined with those of the five elements, repeated twice until the seventy-second year of the cycle. Then these combinations are repeated followed by the word *pô* (male), which takes us to year 132; then the word *mô* (female) which takes us to year 192; finally the words *pô* and *mô* alternate until the end of the cycle.

This chronological system, being too complicated for general use, is only used in the lamaseries, and then only by the most educated lamas. The ordinary people live from day to day, without an inkling of the existence of such a system of combined cycles. Apart from the regent we met no one in Lhasa who could tell us what year it was; the importance of naming the dates and the years did not seem to be understood at all. A high official in Lhasa, a lama with a considerable reputation, told us that the Chinese system of counting the years was a great nuisance, and not nearly as good as the simple Tibetan system: namely to say this year, last year, a hundred years ago and so forth. When we objected that history would become thoroughly confused by this method, he said: 'All we need to know about the old days is what happened. What is the point of knowing exactly *when* it happened?'

This contempt for, or at least indifference to, chronology is evident in most of the lamaic texts; they are often orderless and dateless, merely a collection of anecdotes piled one on top of another, with no definite facts either on people or events. Fortunately, since Tibetan history frequently mingles with Tartar and Chinese, the latter can be used to disentangle the former.

We were not only struck during our stay at Lhasa by Tibetan vagueness about the years, but noticed that they were equally confused about the days of the month. Their calendar is a hopeless muddle simply because of superstitious notions of lucky and unlucky days; all days reputed to be unlucky in any one moon are simply ignored: they don't count. So, for example, if the fifteenth of the moon is an unlucky day, they count the fourteenth twice and then jump to the sixteenth. Sometimes there are several unlucky days one after another; no matter: they are all cut out, until the next lucky day. The Tibetans do not appear to find this at all inconvenient.

New Year for the Tibetans, as for all peoples, is a time of festival and rejoicing. The last days of the twelfth moon are spent in making preparations; they stock up with tea, butter, *tsamba*, barley wine and joints of beef or mutton. Best clothes are taken out of the cupboards; the furniture, for once, is dusted; there is polishing, scrubbing, sweeping: a little order and cleanliness appear indoors. Since this only happens once a year each home takes on a new look; the household altars come in for special attention; the old idols are repainted, and pyramids, flowers and ornaments to decorate the family Buddhas are fashioned out of fresh butter.

The first *Louk-So*, or festival rite, begins at midnight; everyone stays up, waiting impatiently for that mystic solemn hour which ends the old year and begins the new. As we had little interest in witnessing this point of intersection between two

Tibetan years, we had gone to bed at our usual time. We were fast asleep when we were suddenly wakened by a general shout of joy. Then there was an outburst of bells, cymbals, conches, tambourines and all the Tibetan musical instruments, making the most terrible din imaginable, a kind of tin-kettle music to welcome the New Year. We thought for a moment it would be a good idea to get up and have a look at the Tibetans enjoying themselves, but the cold was so intense that we were loath to abandon our warm blankets and decided to attend the public festivities only in spirit. Loud bangs, which eventually thundered on our door and threatened to break it down, made us abandon this excellent plan. Reluctantly, we dragged ourselves from our warm beds, slipped on our robes, opened the door and let in some of our Tibetan friends who bid us to the New Year feast. Each one was carrying a little earthenware pot full of hot water, in which floated little dumplings made of wheat flour and honey. One of these visitors produced a long silver needle, ending in a hook, and invited us to fish in his pot. We made excuses at first, saying that we never ate during the night, but he insisted so charmingly and put out his tongue so politely, that we had to give in and join in the *Louk-So*. We each fished a dumpling, and chewed it a moment to get the flavour. It was difficult not to make a face, but *toujours la politesse*, we had to swallow them. If only this had been all! But the *Louk-So* was merciless; the many friends we had at Lhasa arrived one after another almost without interruption and we had to eat honey dumplings until dawn.

The second *Louk-So* was another round of visits, but with a different ceremonial. No sooner had dawn appeared than the Tibetans came out on to the streets, each one carrying a pot of buttered tea in one hand and a shiny gilt dish in the other, containing *tsamba* meal piled up into a pyramid and topped with three ears of barley; on that day no one pays a visit without bringing *tsamba* and buttered tea with him. On entering, the New Year visitor kowtows three times before the household altar which is decorated and lit up for the occasion; he burns some leaves of cedar or some other aromatic tree in a large copper incense-pot and then offers tea to all those present, after which he hands round the dish, from which everyone takes a pinch of *tsamba*. The householder then makes a similar offer to the visitor. There is a saying at Lhasa that the

Tibetans celebrate New Year with *tsamba* and buttered tea, the Chinese with red paper and fire crackers, the Katchi with delicacies and tobacco and the Peboun with singing and frolics.

This is true enough, but the Peboun have not quite got the monopoly of gaiety. The Tibetans also go in for jollity, including much singing and dancing. Groups of children, the hems of their robes hung with numerous little bells, go from house to house giving little concerts which are not without charm. The

verses of their songs are sweet and sad, but after each verse comes a rollicking chorus. During the singing of the verse the children sway slowly to and fro with the rhythm, rather like the pendulum of a clock but when the chorus comes they prance around, stamping rhythmically. The sound of their little bells and of their hobnailed shoes makes a kind of wild accompaniment which is very pleasing to the ear, especially from a little distance. When these young enthusiasts have finished their concert, it is customary for the hosts to hand round cakes fried in walnut oil and little butter-balls.

In the main squares and in front of public buildings we saw troupes of actors and acrobats amusing the public from morning till night. Unlike the Chinese, the Tibetans did not seem to have a repertoire of plays: their performers were on the stage the whole time, sometimes singing and dancing, sometimes performing acrobatics. Above all they excelled at ballet. Their skill at dancing, leaping and pirouetting was really astonishing. They wore long pheasant feathers in their caps, black masks adorned with fantastically long white beards, wide white trousers and green tunics down to their knees, drawn in at the waist with yellow belts. Attached to their tunics at intervals were long cords ending in pompoms of white wool. When the dancers swayed in rhythm, the pompoms made a graceful accompaniment to the movements of their bodies; when they spun round the pompoms rose up and made a wheel round them, making their pirouettes seem even faster than they were.

We also witnessed a form of gymnastic display known as 'the Dance of the Spirits'. A long rope made of leather thongs plaited strongly together was tied to the top of the Buddha La and reached to the foot of the mountain. The Spirit Dancers walked up and down this rope with the agility of cats or monkeys. Sometimes on arriving at the top they held out their arms like divers and slid down the rope with the speed of an arrow. The inhabitants of the province of Ssang are reputed to be the great experts at this.

The strangest thing that we saw at Lhasa during the New Year festivities was what the Tibetans called the Lha-Ssa-Morou, a total invasion of the city by innumerable bands of lamas. It began on the third day of the first moon. All the lamaseries of the province of Oué opened their doors and tumultuously along every road leading to Lhasa came crowds of lamas, on foot, on horseback, riding donkeys and yaks, carrying with them their prayer-books and their cooking paraphernalia. The city was soon swamped in this avalanche of lamas, which descended from all the surrounding mountains. Those who could not find room in private houses and in the public buildings camped in the squares and in the streets or put up their little travelling tents in the surrounding countryside. The Lha-Ssa-Morou lasted six whole days. All this time the lawcourts were shut, the normal course of justice was in abeyance, the ministers and civil servants more or less lost their authority, which they abandoned to that great army of

Buddhist monks. Disorder and total confusion reigned. Mobs of lamas prowled round the streets, shouting, chanting prayers, clashing, quarrelling and sometimes fighting bloody battles with fisticuffs.

Although they behaved in this rowdy manner, it was not for frivolous amusements that they had come to Lhasa: it was piety that had brought them. They had come to get the Dalai Lama's blessing and to make a pilgrimage to the monastery called the Morou, in the centre of the city: hence the name of this festival. This monastery was notable for the rich ornaments in its temples and for the order and cleanliness which made it a model for all the lamaseries of the province. On the western side of the main temple was a large garden surrounded by a cloister full of printing shops. Here plates were engraved and Buddhist texts were printed by workers from the lamasery. Since the processes used were similar to the Chinese, which are sufficiently well-known, we will not describe them. The lamas who came here each year for the Lha-Ssa-Morou took the opportunity to buy books.

In the Lhasa area alone there were more than thirty large monasteries. Of these, Khaldan, Preboung and Sera were the most important. There were more than fifteen thousand lamas in each. Khaldan, which means Heavenly Bliss in Tibetan, was the name of a mountain some twelve miles to the east of Lhasa on top of which the lamasery was built. According to the lamaic texts it was founded in A D 1409 by Tsong Kaba himself, the Buddhist reformer and founder of the sect of Yellow Hatted lamas. Tsong Kaba resided there and it is there that his soul left his body when it was absorbed into the universal essence. The Tibetans told us that his miraculous body was still to be seen, fresh, incorruptible, sometimes speaking, and, by a continuous miracle, floating in the air without any support. We are unable to comment on this belief, as our stay at Lhasa was too brief to allow a visit to Khaldan.

The lamasery of Preboung, or Ten Thousand Fruits, lay six miles to the west of Lhasa on the side of a high mountain. In the middle of it stood a magnificently ornate pavilion, sparkling with gold and colour. It was reserved for the Dalai Lama who went there once a year to explain the sacred books. Mongolian lamas who had come to Tibet to study prayers and obtain degrees in the lamaic hierarchy mostly resided at Preboung, which was therefore sometimes known as the Monastery of the Mongols.

Sera was situated to the north of Lhasa, and no more than a mile and a half from the city. The temples and the lamas' quarters were all built up the side of a mountain wooded with holly and cypress. Alongside passes the pilgrim route from Tartary. The view of the buildings ranged one above the other against the green background of the mountainside was extremely beautiful and picturesque. In the clefts of the mountain well above the monastic buildings we saw a number of cells inhabited by contemplative lamas, which looked very difficult of access. Sera was famous for its three great temples on several storeys, of which the interiors were almost entirely covered in gold : hence the name, which comes from the Tibetan

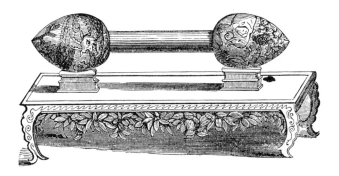

word *ser*, meaning gold. In the main temple, lay, religiously preserved, the famous *tortché* or sanctifying instrument which, the Buddhists believed, had come flying through the air from India and placed itself in the Sera monastery. It was made of bronze and roughly like a pestle in shape. It was meant to be held by the middle, which was smooth and cylindrical; both ends were thicker and oval in shape : they were carved with symbolic figures. Every lama had to have a little *tortché* made on the model of this one : when they said their prayers, and during religious services, this object was essential : sometimes they had to hold it in their hands, sometimes place it on their knees, then hold it again and turn it in their fingers, according to instructions marked in their service books. The *tortché* at Sera was the object of a considerable cult. All pilgrims went to prostrate themselves before it in the niche where it rested. In the New Year festival it was carried in procession with great pomp through the streets of Lhasa, so that the people could pay homage to it.

Whilst the throngs of lamas were enjoying their noisy festival, we, with heavy hearts, were silently preparing for departure. We had to dismantle our little chapel where we had enjoyed such consolation, so many hopes, but alas for so short a time. After trying to plough and sow a small corner of this great desert, we had to leave it, realising that the thistles and thorns would soon grow again, no doubt, and stifle the precious shoots of salvation that were beginning to sprout. Bitter and grievous were our thoughts; our hearts were near to breaking and all we could do was to pray that the Lord would send to these children of darkness missionaries more worthy than we to bring them the torch of faith.

The day before we were due to leave, one of the regent's secretaries came to see us with two large silver ingots as a present from him. We were deeply touched by his kindness, but felt that we should not accept them. That evening, when we went to his palace to say goodbye, we took back the two ingots. We placed them on a little table in front of him, explaining that this was not because we had any complaint to make: on the contrary, we should always remember with gratitude the good treatment we had received from the Tibetan government during our short stay in Lhasa. We said that we were convinced that, had it depended on the regent, we should always have enjoyed a peaceful and honourable life in Tibet. However, as regards this silver, we could not accept it without compromising our conscience as missionaries and the honour of our country. The regent was not at all put out by our decision. He told us that he understood and respected our unwillingness, and would not insist, but that he would like to make us a gift before we parted. Then, pointing to a dictionary in four languages that he had often seen us examine with interest, he asked us if this would be acceptable. We felt we could say yes to this without compromising our dignity in any way. We then told the regent how happy we should be if he would accept, as a reminder of France, the microscope that had so aroused his curiosity: our offer was readily accepted.

As we were about to leave, the regent stood up and addressed us in these terms: 'You are leaving; but who can tell what the future has in store? You are men of great courage to have come this far. I know that in your hearts you have a great and holy resolve: I think that you will never forget it; I too will remember it always. I think I have made myself clear: circumstances do not allow me to say more.'

'We understand your words,' we told him, 'and their implication. We shall pray our God to grant you the wish you have expressed.' Then with heavy hearts we left this man who had been so full of kindness to us and on whom we had built our hope of spreading the Christian word, with God's help, amongst the unfortunate peoples of Tibet.

When we got home we found the Katchi governor waiting for us; he had brought some food supplies for our journey, excellent dried fruits from Ladakh and cakes made with wheat flour, butter and eggs. He insisted on spending the whole evening with us and helping us pack. As he intended to go shortly to Calcutta, we asked him to tell the first Frenchman he met in British India about us. We also gave him a letter addressed to the representative of the French government in Calcutta, in which we gave a short account of our stay in Lhasa and the reasons for our departure. We thought this a sensible thing to do, now that we were setting off on a journey of some two thousand miles on very bad roads often along the edge of precipices. We thought that if it were God's will that we should find a grave in the midst of the Tibetan mountains, our friends would at least know what had become of us.

That evening Samdadchiemba came to say goodbye. Since the day when the Chinese ambassador had decided to have us expelled from Tibet, our dear convert and disciple had been removed from us. Needless to say we had found this hard to bear, but neither the regent nor we ourselves were in a position to protest. Since Samdadchiemba was born in the province of Kansou he was subject to Chinese authority. Although our influence with Kichan was not great, we did get a promise from him that Samdadchiemba would not be ill-treated and that he would be allowed to return to his family in peace. We have since learned that he kept his word. The regent was extremely good to Samdadchiemba. As soon as he was separated from us, the regent ensured that he lacked for nothing; he even sent him a fairly large sum of money to set him up on his journey. With what we could afford to add to this Samdadchiemba had a tidy sum of money, enough for the journey and a decent home-coming. We advised him to do his duty by his old mother, teach her the Faith, see that she was baptised before she died, and when this occurred, return to live amongst Christians.*

To tell the truth, Samdadchiemba had not an attractive character: he was rough, wild and sometimes insolent, and this did not make him a good travelling companion; but he was fundamentally straight and loyal, and this made up for all his faults. When we said goodbye we were deeply moved, and found, rather to our surprise, that we had developed a great affection for this young man. But we had travelled so long and so hard a road together, had shared so much hardship and misfortune, that without our realising it our lives had become, so to speak, welded together. The law of affinity, which binds men together, works much more strongly in suffering than in prosperity.

Early next morning two Chinese soldiers came to inform us that we were expected to breakfast with His Excellency Ly Kouo Ngan (a name which means Ly, Pacifier of Kingdoms). This was the mandarin whom Kichan had appointed to accompany us as far as China. We accepted his invitation, and as the convoy was going to assemble at his house we brought our luggage also.

Ly, Pacifier of Kingdoms, came from Tcheng Tou Fou, capital of the province of Ssetchouan. He was an army mandarin. For twelve years he had served in Gorkha, a province of Bhutan, where he had had quick promotion, reached the rank of Tou Sse and been appointed officer commanding the troops guard-ing the frontiers of the British possessions. He was decorated with the Blue Button and enjoyed the privilege of wearing seven sable-tails on his hat. Ly was only forty-five, but he was so broken down and decayed that he looked seventy. He had hardly any teeth, his hair was thin and grey and his dim, glassy eyes shunned any bright light; his flabby wrinkled face, his emaciated hands, his thick legs on which he could hardly stand—all this pointed to some form of over-indulgence. We thought at first that this premature ageing was due to the opium

---

*We recently had news of Samdadchiemba. After staying over a year in his own village, he returned to our Mongolian missions, and settled in the Christian village of Siwan, outside the Great Wall. R-E. Huc, 1852.

habit, but he told us himself, the very first time that we met him, that it was due to the drinking of spirits. He had asked for, and been granted, his retirement, and was going back to his family to repair his broken health by following a strict healthy diet. Kichan's only reason for hastening our departure was so that we could accompany this mandarin, who, owing to his rank as a Tou-Sse, had the right to an escort of fifteen soldiers.

Ly Kouo Ngan was very well educated for an army mandarin; his knowledge of Chinese literature and, especially, his highly observant character, gave his conversation wit and interest. He spoke slowly, with something of a drawl, and knew how to put suspense and vividness into a story. He liked talking philosophy and religion; he even had splendid plans for attaining perfection when, at home in the bosom of his family, he could spend the days playing chess with his friends and going to the theatre. He believed neither in bonzes nor in lamas; as for the religion of the Lord of Heaven, he knew little about it: he would have to study it before making up his mind to adopt it. Meanwhile his whole religion consisted in a fervent cult of the Great Bear. He put on aristocratic airs and graces; unfortunately he sometimes forgot, and then his plebeian origin showed through. Needless to add that His Excellency the Pacifier of Kingdoms was a great lover of silver ingots; otherwise he would have been no Chinaman, and certainly no mandarin.

Ly Kouo Ngan's breakfast was an elegant feast, all the more so to us after two years of eating more or less like savages. From eating with our fingers we had almost forgotten how to use chopsticks. When we had finished, our host told us that everything was ready but before setting off it was his duty to go, with his soldiers, to the ambassador's residence to take his leave. He asked us if we would like to go with him. 'Certainly,' we replied, 'let's go there together, you out of duty and we out of politeness.'

Together we all entered the room where Kichan was sitting. The fifteen soldiers stopped just inside the door and kowtowed three times, striking the floor with their foreheads; they then stood in line. The Pacifier of Kingdoms also kowtowed, but the poor fellow could not get up again without our help. We as usual put our caps under our arms. Kichan then made a separate little speech to all three parties.

Speaking to us first, he used a smooth, affected tone: 'Now,' he said, 'you're on your way back home; you won't have any complaints about my behaviour towards you, which has been perfectly correct. I am not letting you stay here, but it is the emperor's will and not mine; I am not letting you take the road to India, because it is against the laws of the empire; if it were not so, old as I am, I would escort you myself to the frontier. The route you will be following is not as terrible as has been made out; true, there will be snow; true, there will be high mountains and cold weather. You see that I hide nothing from you: why should I? But at least you will have men to protect you, and every night you will have a lodging; there will be no need to put up your tent. Is this not better than the route you took to come here? You will have to travel on horseback; I cannot let you have a palanquin, they are unobtainable here. My report to the emperor will leave in a few days' time; as my couriers travel night and day, it will reach its destination before you. When you are safely arrived at the capital of Ssetchouan, the viceroy, Pao, will take care of you, and my responsibility ceases. You can leave with confidence and in good heart. I have already sent orders that you are to be well treated all along the route. May the lucky star be your guide until the journey's end!'

'Although we feel ill-used,' we said in reply, 'we nevertheless wish you well. Since it is to high rank that you aspire, we hope that you will regain all the honours you have lost, and acquire even greater ones!'

'Ah, my star is an unlucky one, an unlucky one!' said Kichan, taking a large pinch of snuff from the silver bowl beside him.

Turning to the Pacifier of Kingdoms, Kichan suddenly adopted a tone of great solemnity. 'Ly Kouo Ngan,' he said, 'since the emperor permits you to return home, you must now leave: you will have these two travelling-companions, and this should be a great consolation, for the road as you know is long and tiresome. These men are full of justice and mercy; you will therefore live in peace with them. Take care never to grieve them, either by word or by deed. And here is another important thing I have to tell you: as you have served the empire for twelve years on the Gorkha frontiers, I have instructed the accountant to send you five hundred ounces of silver; it is a gift from the emperor.' At these words, Ly Kouo Ngan, finding his legs all of a sudden unusually supple, dropped recklessly on to his knees.

'The celestial boons of the Great Emperor', he said, 'have always been mine to receive; but, unworthy servant that I am, how could I, without a blush of shame, accept such a gift as this? I humbly beg Your Excellency to permit me to hide my face, and deny myself this undeserved favour.'

To which Kichan replied: 'Do you imagine that your self-denial would mean anything to the emperor? What are a few ounces of silver? Come on, take this small amount of money, since you're offered it; there'll be enough for a cup of tea with your friends. But when you reach home, mind you don't start drinking spirits again. If you want to live a few more years, no spirits. I tell you this, because a father and mother should give their children good advice.' Ly Kouo Ngan struck the ground three times with his forehead and then came and stood beside us.

Lastly, Kichan harangued the soldiers, changing his voice yet again. He was now blunt and abrupt, with a touch of anger: 'Now you soldiers. . .' At these words the fifteen fell on their knees as one man, and remained in that posture until the end of his speech. 'Now, how many are you? Fifteen, I think.' He counted them with his finger. 'Yes, fifteen. You fifteen men are on your way home, your service is finished. You will escort your captain as far as Ssetchouan, and also these two foreigners; on the way you will serve them faithfully and will always be respectful and obedient. Do you understand me clearly?'

'Yes, we understand.'

'When you pass through the villages of the Poba (Tibetans), you are not to exploit the people, or you will be sorry for it. In the posting-houses, you are not to pilfer the goods of others. Do you understand me clearly?'

'Yes, we understand.'

'Do not harm the flocks, respect the crops, do not set the forests alight. Do you understand me clearly?'

'Yes, we understand.'

'You must always agree amongst yourselves. Are you not all soldiers of the empire? Then do not curse and quarrel. Do you understand me clearly?'

'Yes, we understand.'

'Anyone who misbehaves will have no hope of escaping punishment. His fault will be carefully examined and severely punished. Do you understand me clearly?'

'Yes, we understand.'

'Since you understand, obey and tremble!' When this short but impressive last word had been spoken, the fifteen soldiers struck the ground three times with their foreheads and stood up.

As we were about to leave his residence, Kichan took us aside for a private word. 'Shortly', he said, 'I am leaving Tibet and returning to China. So as not to have to take too much luggage with me, I am sending off two large boxes with your party; they are covered in yakhide.' He then told us the characters they were marked with. 'I am putting these two boxes in your care. Every evening, when you arrive at the posting-house, have them put in the room where you are spending the night. At Tcheng Tou Fou, capital of Ssetchouan, deliver them to Pao Tchoung Tang, the viceroy. Also keep a good eye on your own belongings; for on the route you are taking there are many petty thieves.' After promising Kichan that we would do as he asked, we rejoined Ly Kouo Ngan, who was waiting for us at the main gate.

It was curious that the Chinese ambassador should have entrusted his treasure to us, when he had at his disposal a senior mandarin whose normal function it would have been. But Kichan's dislike of foreigners stopped short of the point where his own interests were concerned. He no doubt felt that his boxes would be safer with missionaries than with any Chinaman, even a mandarin. We appreciated this token of confidence; it was a tribute to Christian honesty and a bitter reflexion on the Chinese character.

We proceeded to Ly Kouo Ngan's house, where eighteen horses were saddled and waiting in the courtyard. The three best had been set aside for the captain and for ourselves. The fifteen others were for the soldiers, and were shared out by lot.

Before we mounted, a Tibetan woman, strong-limbed and quite cleanly dressed, appeared: it was Ly Kouo Ngan's wife. He had married her six years before and was about to leave her for ever; they had had only one child which had died as an infant. Since this couple would never meet again, a few words of goodbye at such a heart-rending moment would have been normal. It all took place in public, and went like this:

'Well, we're off,' said the husband. 'You must stay here, in peace in your room.'

'Now take care of yourself,' said the wife, 'take care of yourself and look after your swollen legs.' She then put her hand in front of her eyes to give the impression that she was crying.

'Now look at that,' said the Pacifier of Kingdoms, turning to us, 'these Tibetan women are funny; I've left her a good well-built house and a lot of new furniture, but she cries just the same! What more does she want?' After these affecting and tender farewells we all mounted and the squadron advanced through the streets of Lhasa, carefully choosing those least encumbered with lamas.

When we were out of town, we saw a large group of people who seemed to be waiting for us; they were the inhabitants of Lhasa we had got to know well whilst we were there. Most of them had begun the study of Christianity and had seemed to be on the road to conversion. They were waiting to say goodbye, each with the gift of a *khata*. Amongst them was the young doctor, still wearing round his neck the cross we had given him. We dismounted to speak words of consolation to these

Christian hearts; we urged them to abandon the superstitious cult of Buddha, to worship the Christian God and to trust in his infinite mercy. It was a bitter moment when we had to leave behind all these dearly beloved candidates for baptism, to whom we had only pointed out the way to eternal salvation, and whose first steps on the road we had been unable to guide. Alas, we could do nothing more to help them, except pray the Almighty to have mercy on their souls, redeemed by the blood of Jesus Christ.

When we were on the point of remounting we saw a horseman galloping towards us: it was the Katchi governor who had had the idea of coming with us as far as the Bo Tchou river. We were deeply touched by this token of friendship, though not surprised, for throughout our stay in Lhasa he had shown again and again how sincerely attached he was to us. We had so much to say to each other that we rode very slowly, and it took us an hour to reach the Bo Tchou. There we found a Tibetan escort provided by the regent to accompany us as far as the Chinese frontier; it consisted of seven men and a senior lama with the rank of Dheba or district governor; altogether our caravan now had twenty-six horsemen, and a number of drovers for the yaks which carried our baggage.

Two large ferries were waiting to take the horses and their riders over. The horses jumped on board, then quietly stood in line side by side: they had obviously done this before. Then the riders embarked, except for the Dheba, Ly Kouo Ngan and ourselves. We realised that we were meant to cross in some more upper-class manner, but no boat was visible anywhere.

'But how are we going to cross?' we asked.

'Look, there comes the boat.' Then we saw a boat, and a man, approaching across fields, but the normal positions were reversed: the man was carrying the boat, instead of the boat the man. It was such a large boat for one man to carry that it was an extraordinary sight. When he reached the bank he put it down and pushed it into the water without apparent effort. Either the man was very strong or the boat was very light; he looked quite ordinary, and when we examined the boat the problem was solved. Although quite large it was made of a number of cowhides strongly sewn together and attached to a bamboo framework.

After bidding an affectionate goodbye to the Katchi governor, we stepped into the boat: but we nearly went through the bottom at the first step: they had forgotten to warn us to step only on the canes of the framework. When we were all on board, the boatman began to punt with a long pole and in no time we were across. We jumped ashore and the boatman, with the boat on his back, disappeared across the fields. These boats have the disadvantage that they cannot stay long in the water without rotting. After use, they must be left bottom up on the beach to dry. Maybe a good coat of varnish would preserve them and allow them to take the water for longer.

When we had remounted we took a last look at the city of Lhasa, still visible in the distance, and said in our hearts: 'Thy will be done!' Then we followed the caravan in silence. It was 15 March 1846.

9

FROM LHASA TO TSIAMDO

On leaving Lhasa we travelled for some days along a wide valley which was all cultivated land. We saw numerous farm-houses, mostly surrounded by trees. Work had not yet started, for the winters in Tibet are long and hard. Herds of goats and yaks wandered sadly about the dusty fields, occasionally tug-ging at the hard stubble of the *tsingkou*, a kind of barley which is the main crop of these ungiving acres. The valley was entirely covered with little fields divided by low thick walls made of large boulders. The work of clearing this rocky land must have cost the first farmers much toil and patience: these great stones had had to be dug out one by one and rolled—no easy task—to the edges of the fields. It was a depressing-looking countryside when we saw it, enlivened only by occa-sional caravans of lamas on their way, singing and fooling about, to the festival of the Lha-Ssa-Morou. We could also hear shouts and laughter coming from farmhouses along the road-side, which showed that the New Year festivities were not yet over.

Our first day's march was a short one. Well before sunset we stopped at Detsin Dzoûg a large village about eighteen miles from Lhasa. A big house had been made ready to receive the caravan for the night. We dismounted and were immediately led by the headman of the village into a room with a fine fire of *argols* burning in a large earthenware bowl in the middle. There were thick cushions covered in green *pou-lou* on which we were invited to sit, and buttered tea was produced. We were plied with so many kind attentions that we were soon purring with content. This way of travelling seemed the height of luxury: what a contrast with the hard life we had led in the desert, when a halt for the night meant an increase in hardship. To travel without having to pitch a tent or feed the animals, without having to light a fire or cook a meal, was like a dream-world come true. Merely to find on dismounting a warm room and a jug of buttered tea seemed to us the height of indulgence.

Soon after our arrival the senior lama, whom the regent had appointed to escort us as far as the Chinese frontier and with whom so far we had only exchanged a few civilities during the river-crossing, came to pay a formal call. He was a stocky little man of about fifty years of age. He had been a civil administrator in various parts of Tibet; before being posted to Lhasa he had been Dheba of a district near Ladakh. His broad, rather wrinkled, face beamed good nature; he was as simple and open as a child. He told us that the regent had appointed him to make this journey expressly on our behalf, so as to make sure that we had everything that we needed whilst we were in territory ruled by the Dalai Lama. He then introduced two young Tibetans, and sang their praises in a long pompous speech. 'These two men,' he said, 'have been specially appointed to serve you during the journey. Whatever you order, they will promptly carry out. As regards your meals, since you are not used to Tibetan food, it has been agreed that you will take them with the Chinese mandarin.'

So, after a few more minutes' conversation with lama Dsiamdchang, we had the honour to sup with Ly the Pacifier of Kingdoms, whose room was next to our own. Ly Kouo Ngan was most affable, and spoke in detail about the route we were to follow and which he was travelling for the eighth time. So that we might follow the details of the route from day to day, he lent us a Chinese book describing the itinerary from Tcheng Tou, capital of Ssetchouan, to Lhasa. It was called: *Oué Tsang Thou Tche*, that is, *A Description of Tibet*, with illustrations. This volume, which included several other Chinese monographs on Tibet, had been compiled by a mandarin named Lou Hoa Tchou who, in the fifty-first year of Kien Long (1786) had been quartermaster of the Chinese army. Father Hyacinth, Russian archimandrite of Peking, has published a translation of this work, a kind of geography of Tibet. M. Klaproth, after revising, correcting and annotating this translation, published it in the *Journal Asiatique* of Paris. The part of this work which deals with the route between Lhasa and Ssetchouan and which we consulted daily during our journey is remarkably accurate, but so dry and factual that it is only of interest to specialists or to travellers on the route. It is simply a list, stage by stage, of the places that occur on the route. As a sample, we transcribe the section dealing with our first day's march:

From Detsin Dzoûg to the halt at Tsaï Li	
From Tsaï Li to shelter at Lhasa	
At Detsin Doûg there are a number of hostelries, in which travellers usually stay some time. Near the road is a posting-house; from there it is 40 *li* to the convent of Tsaï Li.	40 *li*
At Tsaï Li there is a *Dheba* who provides wood and hay. This canton is separated only by a river from Lhasa territory. That city is reached after 20 *li*. There is a military commander.	20 *li*
Total	60 *li*

We set off from Detsin Dzoûg before dawn, as we had a long stretch in front of us. We continued along the same valley we had entered when we left Lhasa; but, as we advanced, the mountains surrounding the valley floor grew taller and closer, the valley narrowed and became rockier, the farms were fewer and the inhabitants lost that well-clad civilised look that always betokens the proximity of large towns. After twenty-seven miles of fast unbroken riding, we stopped to take a little rest and food at a large half-ruined monastery in which a few dirtily dressed old lamas were living. They were too poor to provide anything to the commissariat apart from some tea with milk, a jug of beer and a small ball of butter. But by adding to these some girdle-cakes and a saddle of mutton that Ly Kouo Ngan's cook had had the foresight to prepare the previous night, we had a fairly substantial meal.

As soon as we had satisfied our hunger and stretched our limbs, we thanked these poor monks by giving them a *khata* and remounted. It was already late and we still had some fourteen miles to go before reaching the post-house. It was dark when we arrived at Midchoukoung. We immediately called our Tibetan valets and told them to prepare our beds as soon as possible; we felt that after a long day spent on bad horses we could be excused from any social activities. So after eating a light supper and saying our prayers, we said goodnight to the Pacifier of Kingdoms and the musician-lama and crept in under our blankets.

When we woke next morning the sun was already shining in all its splendour; yet everything was quiet in the courtyard of the inn: no yaks grunted, no horses neighed and the usual din made by a departing caravan was lacking. We got up, wiped the sleep out of our eyes and opened the door to see what was happening. Ly Kouo Ngan and Dsiamdchang were sitting in the sun in a corner of the yard. As soon as they saw us they came over and, with much beating about the bush, explained that we should have to stop there for the day because there were difficulties in finding post-horses and yaks.

'Such a nuisance,' they said, 'such an unwelcome hitch, but we can do nothing about it; the delay is all due to the New Year festivities.'

'On the contrary,' we answered, 'it's excellent news: we're in no hurry. Let's take our time, and have frequent rests, and all will go well.' Our two escort commanders were most relieved to hear this. These two good fellows had really thought that we were going to complain because of a day of enforced rest. They were utterly wrong. On our previous journeys, it is true, we had often been extremely impatient of delay, but this was because we had an objective and were in a hurry to reach it. But now it was different, and we were happy to regard ourselves, as far as possible, as tourists. We also felt that it was unreasonable to be in a hurry when leaving a place under duress.

Midchoukoung was a staging-post for changing the *oulah*, that is, the horses, the pack-animals and their drovers. This forced-labour service had been organised by the Tibetan government all along the road which led from Lhasa to the Chinese frontier. Chinese and Tibetan official travellers alone had the right to avail themselves of it. The Lhasa government issued passports on which was clearly marked the number of men and animals which those villages forced to contribute to the *oulah* had to provide. The Chinese handbook on Tibet had the following to say about this system of forced labour:

As regards the local service called the *oulah*, anyone with any property, man or woman, is forced to contribute; people from distant parts, if they occupy an entire house, have no exemption. The number of men who have to be provided for this service is fixed according to the means of each man. The elders and the Dheba choose who is to contribute and decide, by the size of each man's house, how many men he must give to the *oulah*. In a small village three, four and up to ten men are taken. Small families hire the poor to act as proxies, or pay, daily, a half ounce of silver for the whole family. Those over sixty are exempt. When required, oxen and horses, donkeys and mules are requisitioned in the richer houses; the poor club together, and three or four families give a single animal.

The Chinese mandarins, who always try to turn everything into money, have found a way of exploiting the *oulah* provided for them by the Tibetan government. Before leaving Lhasa, they contrive by devious means to get a large number of animals entered on their passports; they insist only on having the number that they need and draw a compensation for the remainder which rich Tibetans prefer to pay them rather than expose their animals to the dangers of the road. Others take all the animals to which their papers entitle them and use them to carry Tibetan merchandise to China. Ly Kouo Ngan, who proclaimed so vehemently his lack of interest in money when Kichan offered him a gift from the emperor, had different ideas when it came to the *oulah*. During the day we spent at Midchoukoung, we happened to see the relevant charge sheet and were most surprised to read that we had been allotted two horses and *twelve* yaks. Yet our baggage consisted only of two trunks and some bedding.

'Why all these yaks?' we asked the Pacifier of Kingdoms. 'How are two trunks shared out amongst twelve?'

'Oh, it's a mistake,' he answered. 'The scribe made an error.' Out of politeness we had to pretend to believe this explanation.

However it quite frequently happens that the Chinese incur losses over the *oulah*; there are certain areas where the inhabitants find this form of tax unacceptable. It is no use showing these rough proud mountain folk a piece of paper marked with the seals of the Dalai Lama and the Chinese ambassador; they remain unmoved. Speeches urging them to obey the law get only one answer: 'Per man, so much; per house, so much; per yak, so much.' Chinese diplomacy here breaks down, and the *oulah* have to be paid for.

The people of Midchoukoung treated us with great courtesy. The village elders provided a performance by a troupe of players who had got together locally for the New Year celebrations. The theatre was the large courtyard of the inn where we were staying and before the performance the players, masked and wearing bizarre costumes, played loud savage music for a long time to summon the audience. When everyone had arrived and was seated in a circle, the Dheba of Midchoukoung came solemnly to present our two leaders and ourselves with a 'Scarf of Felicity' and to invite us to sit on four thick cushions which had been placed under a tree in a corner of the yard. When we were seated the whole troupe began to move in a circle, performing a sort of devil's dance to the music, faster and faster until we were giddy. Then came a series of capers, pirouettes, feats of strength and battles with wooden sabres, all accompanied either by singing, dialogue, music or imitations of the cries of wild beasts. There was one member of the troupe more grotesquely masked than the others who was the comedian and had a monopoly of jokes and repartee. Our knowledge of Tibetan was insufficient to allow us to appreciate how good these were, but judging from the excitement and laughter he aroused in the crowd he must have been a witty enough fellow. We found the show well worth watching and the Tibetans enjoyed themselves hugely. When they had danced, capered and sung for more than two hours the performers ranged themselves in a semi-circle in front of us, took off their masks, put out their tongues and bowed deeply. We each presented the leader of the troupe with a 'Scarf of Felicity', and the performance was over.

That afternoon we invited Ly Kuou Ngan to come for a little walk; in spite of his weak legs he accepted our proposal readily and we set off to explore the neighbourhood. Midchoukoung was a populous place, but evidently a poor one. The houses were mostly built of pebbles roughly cemented with clay. Many were tumbling down, and large rats were living in the ruins. Here and there there were Buddhist altars, carefully white-washed, their cleanliness contrasting with the grey smoky colour of the village. There was a Chinese guard post at Midchoukoung, of a lance-corporal and four men. They kept a few horses, and their post was used as a relay by couriers carrying dispatches for the Chinese administration.

When we got back to the inn, we found a noisy gathering of men and animals in the courtyard which only that morning had been a theatre. The recruitment of our *oulah* was going on: it was to consist of twenty-eight horses, seventy yaks and twelve drovers. At nightfall the Dheba came to tell us that all had been organised according to the holy orders of the Dalai Lama, and that we could set off on the morrow, either early or late, as we wished.

At dawn we mounted and said goodbye to Midchoukoung. After a few hours we left—rather as if emerging from the end of a great funnel—the long valley we had followed all the way from Lhasa, and entered a wild rough country. For five days we travelled in a maze of valleys, twisting to right and to left, sometimes almost retracing our steps to avoid chasms or skirt impassable mountains. We rode all this time along the bottom of ravines, on the steep, stony banks of rushing rivers: our horses jumped rather than walked. However strong, a horse unused to such country would not last long. Only on one half day were we able to travel fairly safely and agreeably; this was when we found ourselves once again by the river we had crossed near Lhasa; it ran placidly down a gentle slope, and its broad, smooth banks made an excellent road. The nights we spent in cold, damp, draughty hovels; but we were so tired out when we reached them that we slept like logs.

Before reaching the town of Ghiamba, we had to cross the Loumma Ri mountain. To quote from the Chinese handbook:

This mountain is high but not steep. It extends to a width of about forty *li*. The snow, ice, and frowning peaks which the traveller has encountered before reaching this mountain, terrifying to the heart and dazzling to the eyes, make it seem, by comparison, a flat plain easy to cross.

The top of Loumma Ri was indeed easily reached; we went up a gentle slope without once having to dismount, which is most unusual on a Tibetan mountain. But the other side was very hard going because of the snow which was falling fast; the horses often slipped; sometimes their back feet slid to join their front ones; but they never fell. The rider felt a slight swinging motion, but gradually got used to it.

The Pacifier of Kingdoms wanted to go down the mountain on foot in order to warm up a little, but after a few uncertain steps he tottered weak-kneed and fell headlong, making a deep, wide trench in the snow. He rose up in a fury, ran to the nearest soldier and showered him with curses and belaboured him with his whip, because he had not dismounted to support him. All the Chinese soldiers immediately jumped off their

horses and came to kowtow before their colonel and apologise.
In fact they had all failed in their duty, for according to Chinese
etiquette, when a chief dismounts all subordinates must
straightway do likewise.

When we reached the bottom of Loumma Ri we followed a
little river which wound its way through a fir forest so thick
that the daylight hardly came through. Thick snow had lodged
on the wide branches of the trees, from where the wind blew it
on to the caravan. These small avalanches, falling unexpectedly
as they did, made us jump and cry out with surprise; but the
animals, who no doubt had been through this forest before in
similar weather, took no notice. They kept their normal pace,
without shying, and simply shook their ears when the snow
became a nuisance.

No sooner out of the forest than we had to dismount and
clamber upwards for an hour over very nasty piles of rocks.
When we reached the top we all looped the bridles round the
horses' necks and let them find their own way down the steep
slope with precipices everywhere that we now had to negotiate. The men either went backwards as on a ladder, or when
they could, slid down over the snow; we all succeeded in
reaching the bottom, and there were no arms or legs broken.

We followed a narrow valley for another couple of miles,
and then at last saw, under a high mountain, a vast number of
houses, and in their midst two enormous temples. It was the
posting station of Ghiamba. Shortly before we entered the
town we came upon a squad of eighteen soldiers drawn up in
line, commanded by two junior mandarins decorated with the
White Button. Both soldiers and mandarins stood with bare
sabres and slung bows. It was the Ghiamba garrison, fully
armed and in their best uniforms, waiting to greet the Pacifier
of Kingdoms with military honours. At the caravan's approach,
the eighteen soldiers and the two mandarins knelt down,
turned their sabres point downwards on the ground and
shouted all together: 'To Tou Sse Ly Kouo Ngan, from the
unworthy garrison of Ghiamba, health and prosperity!' Ly
Kouo Ngan and his escort then immediately stopped, dismounted and ran to the soldiers of the garrison to insist on their
rising from their knees. This was followed by much bowing
and scraping by both parties, so we left them to it and went on
our way. When we reached the town we had our own little

official reception. Two Tibetans, dressed up for the occasion, ceremoniously took hold of our horses' bridles and led us to the house which had been prepared for us. The Dheba, or First Magistrate, of the district, was waiting there for us; he presented us with Scarves of Felicity and ushered us into a room where there was a table on which tea, butter, girdle-cakes and dried fruits stood ready.

Whilst we were doing justice to this modest collation, we were told that we should have to stay two days at Ghiamba because the Dheba, having received news of our approach only that morning, had not had time to send for the animals, whose grazing grounds were quite distant from the town. We were quite pleased about this, but Ly Kouo Ngan and Dsiamdchang were most upset. We tried to comfort them by pointing out that when things get out of control, the only thing is to possess one's soul in patience. They agreed with this in theory, but found it difficult to put into practice. However, they later had to agree that this delay had been a blessing in disguise, for during the two days we were in Ghiamba the sky was so dark, the north wind blew with such force and so much snow fell that according to local opinion it would have been folly to set off. To judge from weather conditions in the valley, a hurricane must have been raging in the hills.

Next day we were visited by two resident Chinese officers. One bore the rank of Pa-Tsoung, the other of Waé-Wei. The former was a handsome fellow, strong-limbed, with a resonant voice and quick movement. A broad scar across his face and a long black moustache gave the finishing touches to the fine figure of a soldier. For four years he had been on active service in Kashkhan as a private, and then had been awarded his new rank and the Peacock's feather. The Waé-Wei, a young man of twenty-six, was also of a good height, but his languid, effeminate appearance was in notable contrast with the manly looks of his colleague. His face was white, soft and very frail-looking; his eyes were humid and listless. We asked him if he were ill: 'No,' he said in an almost inaudible voice, 'my health is excellent.' He blushed slightly as he spoke, and we realised that our question had been indiscreet, so changed the subject. This poor young man was a confirmed opium smoker. When they had gone, Ly Kouo Ngan said: 'The Pa-Tsoung is a man born under a lucky star; he will quickly climb the ladder of the military mandarin service; but the Waé-Wei was born under a bad fog: ever since he took to the "European smoke", Heaven has forsaken him. Before a year is over, he will have said goodbye to this earth.'

The torrential rain which fell almost all the time we were in Ghiamba prevented us from seeing very much of this populous trade-centre. There were a large number of Peboun, Indians from Bhutan, who—as at Lhasa—were engaged in arts and crafts. There was almost no agriculture. Some black barley grew in the valley, but hardly enough for local consumption. The wealth of the neighbourhood came from wool and goat-hair, of which cloth was made. Apparently amongst these grisly mountains there were excellent pastures which fed large flocks. Lapis lazuli, antlers and rhubarb were three commodities in which there was a brisk trade with Lhasa, Ssetchouan and Yunnan. The mountain slopes round Ghiamba were reputed to grow the best quality rhubarb. This district also abounded in all sorts of game. The forest we traversed after leaving mount Loumma Ri was known for partridges, pheasants and several types of wild fowl. The Tibetans have no idea how to serve these dishes which in Europe are so sought after by gourmets: they eat them boiled without any sort of seasoning. The Chinese, as in everything else, are well ahead of their neighbours in this matter. Ly Kouo Ngan's cook could prepare venison to perfection.

On the day fixed for our departure, the *oulah* were ready at dawn. The wind had stopped completely and it was no longer raining. But it was by no means a fine day: a thick chilly mist filled the valley and hid the surrounding peaks. However we had to leave, for all the locals agreed that, considering the season, it was the best possible weather. 'So long as you are in the valley,' they told us, 'you won't see much, but once you are on the heights visibility will be good. Usually, when there's a mist in the valley it's snowing in the hills.' These words were not exactly reassuring, but snow was something we would have to put up with, for everyone told us that from Ghiamba to the Chinese frontier not a single day would pass without our having snow along our route.

We were about to mount our horses when the Dheba of Ghiamba presented us with two pairs of spectacles, to protect our eyes from snow dazzle. We could not help laughing at the sight of these peculiar optical appliances. Instead of glass there was gauze made of horsehair, so convex that the shape resembled a walnut shell. To keep the eyepieces on, there were strings which looped behind the ears and fastened together under the chin. We thanked the kind Dheba most warmly, for in the circumstances his present was invaluable. We had already suffered considerably from the glare when crossing the Loumma Ri.

On the outskirts of the town, there was the garrison on parade once again, waiting to present arms to Ly Kouo Ngan. These men standing in line in the thick fog, their bare sabres glinting in the gloom, were so ghostly that nearly all the horses shied. These greeting ceremonies were repeated all along our route wherever there were Chinese soldiers. They exasperated Ly Kouo Ngan; with his bad legs, he could get on and off his horse only with great difficulty, so they were a real torture to him. He would send one of his men on ahead with orders that no reception party should be sent out, but in vain; they only sent a bigger and better one, under the impression that he was simply being modest in trying to deny himself the honours due to his rank.

At just over a mile from Ghiamba we crossed a wide rushing stream by a bridge made of six great fir trunks which were unplaned and so badly fastened together that they rolled under one's feet. No one tried to ride over, which was lucky for one of the soldiers; his horse slipped on the damp unsteady footway and one of its front legs went through right up to the breast, between two of the tree-trunks, and was caught there as in a vice. If the man had been riding he would undoubtedly have been flung down into the torrent and dashed on to the rocks. The unfortunate animal was finally, and with great difficulty, hoisted out of its agonizing position. To everyone's surprise, its leg was not broken and it was completely unhurt.

Once over this wretched bridge we continued our rugged advance over steep mountains and in deep snow. For four days there was no village in this wild terrain. Each night we slept in the Chinese guard post, round which there were a few shepherds' cabins, built of bark. Yet in these four days we changed *oulah* three times without the slightest delay. The advance orders had been so well given that when we arrived at the guard post everything was ready waiting for our departure

next morning. Had we not known that in this apparently deserted region there were gorges well populated with shepherds living in tents, this quick change of *oulah* would have been impossible to explain. In general, it was only in towns that the caravan suffered delays and difficulties.

On the fourth day after leaving Ghiamba, after crossing a big lake over the ice, we stopped at the stage-post of Atdza, a small village whose inhabitants cultivated a few tiny fields and which lay in a little valley surrounded by mountains wooded to the top with holly and pine. About the lake, the Chinese handbook says, 'The unicorn, a very strange beast, is found in the neighbourhood of this lake, which is forty *li* long.'

The unicorn, long regarded as a fabulous beast, really exists in Tibet. It often appears in the paintings and sculptures of Buddhist temples. Even in China it frequently occurs in the landscape paintings which decorate inns in the northern provinces. The inhabitants of Atdza spoke about this animal, but without attaching any greater importance to it than to any other species of antelope which abound in the mountains in their area. We were not lucky enough to see a unicorn during our travels in Upper Asia, but everything we were told about the animal seemed to confirm the curious details that M. Klaproth has published on this subject in the recent number of the *Journal Asiatique*. We think it may be relevant to quote here an interesting note which this erudite orientalist appended to the translation of Lou Hoa Tchou's handbook published in that journal:

The Tibetan unicorn is called in their language, *serou*; in Mongol, *kere*; and in Chinese, *tou-kiao-chô*, meaning 'the animal with one horn', or, *kiao-touan*, 'straight-horn'. The Mongols sometimes confuse the unicorn with the rhinoceros, called in Mandchou, *bodi gourgou* and in Sanscrit, *khadga*, by calling the latter animal also *kere*.

The unicorn is mentioned for the first time by the Chinese in a work dealing with the history of the first two centuries A D. It is there stated that the wild horse, the *argali* (wild sheep) and the *kiao-touan* are animals foreign to China, that they are to be found in Tartary, and that the horns of the latter are used as bows, known as 'unicorn bows'.

Chinese, Muslim and Mongol historians all describe the following traditional event, said to have occurred in 1224, when Genghis Khan was preparing to invade Hindustan. The Mongolian version states:

The conqueror, having subdued Tibet, marched against Enedkek (India). As he was climbing Mount Djadanaring, he saw coming to meet him a wild beast, of the kind called *serou*, which has only one horn on the top of its head; this beast knelt down three times before the monarch as if to show its respect. When all showed their amazement, the conqueror exclaimed:

'The empire of Hindustan is, we are told, the birthplace of the majestic Buddhas and Bodhisatvas, and of the powerful Bogdas, or Princes of Antiquity. What therefore can it mean when a dumb beast greets me like a man?' After these words, he returned to his homeland.

Although this is a fable, it nevertheless points to the existence of a one-horned beast in the Tibetan mountains. There are also places which take their name from the presence of a large number of them, living in herds, such as the canton of Serou Dziong, that is, Village of the Riverbank of the Unicorns, in the eastern part of the province of Kham, near the Chinese frontier.

A Tibetan manuscript examined by the late Major Lattre called the unicorn 'the one-horned *tsopo'*. One horn of this animal was sent to Calcutta; it was fifty centimetres long and eleven centimetres round; it diminished in size from the root to the point. It was nearly straight, black, and slightly flattened on the sides; it had fifteen rings, but these protruded only on one side. Mr Hodgson, British Resident in Nepal, succeeded in obtaining a unicorn, thus finally solving the problem of the existence of this type of antelope, known as *tchirou* in Southern Tibet near the borders with Nepal. It is the same word as *serou*, the pronunciations varying according to the different dialects in north and south.

The skin and the horn, sent to Calcutta by Mr Hodgson, belonged to a dead unicorn from the menagerie of the Raja of

Nepal. It had been presented to that prince by his friend the lama of Digourtchi. The people who had brought the unicorn to Nepal told Mr Hodgson that the *tchirou*'s favourite habitat was the beautiful valley or plain of Tingri, which is watered by the Arroun. To get to this valley from Nepal, one has to go through the gorge of Kouti or Nialam. The Nepalese call the valley of the Arroun, Tingri-Meïdam, from the town of Tingri, which is on the left bank of that river; it is full of salt deposits, around which the *tchirous* gather in herds. These animals are described as being very shy when in the wild state; they allow no one to approach, and make off at the slightest sound. If they are attacked, they resist courageously. The male and the female are similar in appearance.

The *tchirou* is graceful, like all antelopes, and has the beautiful eyes common to the species. It is reddish in colour, like the fawn, on the upper part of the body, and white below. Its distinctive characteristics are: first, one black horn, long and pointed, with three slight curves and rings towards the base; these rings are more protuberant on the front than on the rear of the horn; next, two tufts of hair sprouting from the outside of each nostril; there are long bristles round nose and mouth, giving the animal a heavy appearance. The coat of the *tchirou* is hard and gives the impression of being hollow, like that of all animals living to the north of the Himalayas which Mr Hodgson had been able to examine. The hair of the coat is about five centimetres long; it is so thick that it feels like a solid mass to the touch. Under the coat, the *tchirou*'s body is covered with a fine soft down, like almost all the quadrupeds living in the high regions of the Himalayas, especially the Kashmir goats.

Dr Abel has suggested that the *tchirou* be given the scientific name of antelope Hodgsonii, after the scholar who proved its existence.[*]

At Atdza we changed the *oulah*, although we only had some twenty-six miles to go before reaching the Lha-Ri posting station. We needed animals which were fresh and familiar with the very bad stretch that lay before us. Only one mountain lay

---

*Sir Joseph Dalton Hooker (*Himalayan Journals*, 1854) gives an illustration of the *Chiru* antelope (antilope Hodsoni) and says: 'It is the so-called "unicorn of Tibet" of Huc and Gabet's narrative—a name which the profile no doubt suggested.' i.e. It has straight horns so close together that from the profile they look as one. (Trans.)

between us and Lha-Ri, and to cross it, we were told, we would have to leave at first light if we wished to arrive before dark. We consulted our Chinese handbook, and found the following jolly description:

Next, one crosses a great mountain whose summits rise up sheer. The ice and the snow do not melt at any season. Its chasms are as steep as cliffs by the sea, often the wind fills them with snow. The paths are almost impassable, so steep and slippery is the descent.

Clearly, this short but forcible description promised no pleasure trip for the morrow. We would gladly have changed places with any of the intrepid tourists who, for love of snow and ice, go annually—by carriage—into the Alps, which are mere miniatures of the Tibetan mountains.

One discouraging sign was that the men of the caravan and the local inhabitants themselves seemed worried. The question was whether the snow, which had fallen heavily for five days and had not had time to settle down, would make the mountain impassable, whether we should fall into crevasses or be crushed by avalanches; and whether in consequence it would not be wiser to wait a few days, in the hope that the snow would be scattered by the wind, partly melted by the sun or frozen hard by the cold. The answers to none of these questions seemed very reassuring. To avoid the alternatives of cowardice on the one hand and rashness on the other, a council was held before bedtime to which we summoned some old local hillfolk. After much discussion it was decided, first, that if next morning dawned calm and still, we could set off without undue risk; and second, that if we did go, the pack animals should precede the horsemen, in order to trample a path for them. When this solution had been reached, we tried to get a little rest, though with little confidence in the plan and trusting rather in Divine Providence.

When we awoke, some stars were still shining, growing pale in the first light of dawn; the weather was quite perfect. Preparations for departure were therefore made, and as soon as the last shades of night had fled we began to climb the fearsome Mountain of Spirits, Lha-Ri. It rose up before us like a huge block of snow, without a single tree, or blade of grass, or black patch of any sort to mar the uniformity of that dazzling whiteness. As agreed, the yaks, followed by their drovers, went first, in single file; then the horsemen, also in file, followed in their track, and the long caravan, like an enormous snake, wound its way slowly in great spirals up the side of the mountain. It was not steep at first; but the snow was so horribly deep that there was continual danger of being buried in it. The yaks in the leading positions had to advance by a series of jumps; we could see them searching anxiously from side to side for the least dangerous places, sometimes disappearing entirely in drifts, leaping about in the masses of shifting snow like porpoises in the sea. The horsemen who followed in their wake were on more solid terrain. We advanced step by step in a deep, narrow trench between two walls of snow chest-high. The yaks grunted, the horses gasped and panted, and the men, to urge on the caravan, sang out in unison and in rhythm like watermen on a windlass. Gradually the way became so steep that the caravan seemed to be clinging to the mountainside. It was no longer possible to stay on horseback, so we all dismounted, caught hold of our horses' tails and set off again with renewed vigour. The sun in splendour shone on these mighty mountains of snow, making a myriad sparkles which dazzled the sight. Fortunately, our eyes were protected by those invaluable spectacles, the gift of the Dheba of Ghiamba.

After a long and unspeakably wearisome climb, we arrived, or rather were hoisted, on to the top of the mountain. The sun was already past the zenith. We stopped a moment, to tighten saddle-girths, brace the baggage and knock from the soles of our boots the maddening lumps of packed snow that had stuck there in the shape of inverted cones. Everybody was in high spirits; we all felt a thrill of pride at having got so high, at standing on the top of this colossal column. It was marvellous to look back at the deep winding rut we had made in the snow, a brown line across the immaculate whiteness of the mountain.

The descent was even steeper but it was shorter and required less effort. In fact its very steepness made it easier, for we simply let ourselves go. The only danger was that if one went too fast one might leave the path and land up—permanently—at the bottom of a ravine. In such country this can well happen. So our descent was brisk, sometimes standing, sometimes sitting, without other mishap than a few spills and long slides, funny rather than frightening.

Just before we reached the bottom of the mountain, the entire caravan stopped on a small plateau on which stood an *obo*, or Buddhist monument, a heap of stones topped with streamers and with bones covered in Tibetan inscriptions. A group of tall majestic fir trees surrounded the *obo*, and covered it with a magnificent dome of verdure.

'Here we are at the glacier of Spirit Mountain,' said Ly Kouo Ngan. 'Now for some fun.' We looked in astonishment at the Pacifier of Kingdoms. 'Yes, that is the glacier. Look over there.' We walked in the direction he was pointing and, leaning over the edge of the plateau we saw an immense glacier, steeply convex in shape, and edged on either side by frightening precipices. We could just see, through a light covering of snow, the greenish colour of the ice. We took a stone from the Buddhist monument and threw it on to the glacier. There was a ringing sound, and the stone, sliding rapidly, left a wide green ribbon behind it. No doubt about it, this was certainly a glacier, and we understood so far the words of Ly Kouo Ngan; but we could not see where the fun lay in having to travel on such a route. Ly Kouo Ngan was however right on both counts, as we were soon to discover.

The animals were made to go first; the yaks, and then the horses. A magnificent yak was the first to go. He stepped forward sedately to the edge of the plateau, stretched out his neck, sniffed the ice for a second, and blew steam in thick puffs through his wide nostrils. Then he bravely placed both forefeet on the glacier, and shot off immediately as if propelled by a spring. He held his legs wide apart as he went down, but kept them as still as if they had been made of marble. When he got to the bottom, he somersaulted, but ran off grunting and leaping across the snowfields. All the animals, one by one, went through the same performance, which was really fascinating to watch. The horses by and large made rather more fuss about launching themselves than the yaks; but one could easily see that both had been long accustomed to this exercise.

It was then the turn of the men, who were as intrepid and as successful as the animals, although the method used was quite different. We sat cautiously down on the edge of the glacier, holding our heels together and pressing them down hard on the ice. Then, using a whip as a rudder, we sailed off over the frozen waters with the speed of a train. A sailor would have said that we were making at least twelve knots. In our long and numerous journeys, we have never encountered a method of transport which was so comfortable, so speedy and above all so refreshing. At the bottom of the glacier, each man retrieved his own horse as best he could, and we continued our way in the common fashion. After descending a gentle slope we left the Mountain of Spirits behind us and entered a valley in which scattered patches of snow remained in spite of the sunshine. For a short while we followed the banks of a little frozen river, and then at last we reached the posting stage of Lha-Ri. As at Ghiamba, there was a military reception at the entrance to the town. The local Dheba came with an offer of service, and we entered the lodging that had been prepared for us in a Chinese pagoda called Kouan Ti Miao, that is, Temple of the God of War. From Lhasa to Lha-Ri it is reckoned to be a thousand and ten *li* (about three hundred and fifty miles); we had been on the road for a fortnight.

As soon as we had settled in our lodging it was agreed, by Ly Kouo Ngan, Dsiamdchang and ourselves, that we would stop a day at Lha-Ri. Although the *oulah* were ready and waiting, we thought it wise to make a short halt and recuperate our strength sufficiently to face another difficult mountain that stood in our path.

The large village of Lha-Ri was built in a gorge amidst sterile desolate mountains; there was not a sign of cultivation anywhere, and the *tsing-kou* had to be brought from elsewhere. The inhabitants were almost all herdsmen; they had sheep, yaks and especially goats whose fine soft hair was used to make top quality *pou-lou* and especially that beautiful material used for the Kashmir shawl. The people here were much less civilised than at Lhasa: there was something hard and savage about their faces; their clothes were dirty and their houses were no more than large shapeless hovels, built of uncut stone and roughly daubed with clay. Yet on the mountainside, a little above the village, was a very large lamasery with a rather fine temple: the Kampo who was Superior at the lamasery was also civil administrator of the canton. There were a large number of lamas to be seen, doing absolutely nothing; at all hours of the day they lay or stood about the streets of the town trying to warm their limbs in the sunshine clad in tattered red and yellow rags. It was disgusting to see them.

At Lha-Ri the Chinese government maintained a supply base for food, in charge of a civil mandarin with the title of Leang Tai, or Quartermaster, decorated with the White Crystal Button. The Leang Tai was paymaster to the guard posts along the route. Between Lhasa and the Chinese frontier there were six of these supply bases. The one at Lhasa was the most important, and its Leang Tai had control over the five others and received an annual salary of seventy ounces of silver, whereas his colleagues only got sixty. The upkeep of the base at Lhasa cost the Chinese government forty thousand ounces of silver a year; the base at Lha-Ri only cost eight thousand. The garrison at the latter town consisted of a hundred and thirty soldiers, commanded by a Tsien Toung, a Pa-Toung and a Waé-Wei.

The day after our arrival at Lha-Ri, the Leang Tai, instead of making a personal call on the leaders of the caravan, simply sent us by way of visiting card a sheet of red paper with his name written on it; the messenger explained that the Leang Tai was confined to his room seriously ill. Ly Kouo Ngan whispered to us, smiling mischievously, 'The Leang Tai will be better the moment we have left.' When we were alone, he said: 'I thought this would happen; every time a caravan arrives, Leang Tai Sue [the mandarin's name] is dying; everyone knows that. According to custom, he should have prepared a first-class banquet in our honour today, and he is pretending to be ill in order to get out of it. Sue is the complete miser. He dresses no better than a palanquin bearer, he eats *tsamba* like a Tibetan barbarian; he plays no games, he drinks no wine. At night his house is unlit; he gropes his way to bed in the dark and always gets up late for fear of being hungry too early. Such a being is no man, he is a tortoise egg. Ambassador Kichan wants to have him sacked, and quite right too. Have you got purveyors like that in your country?'

'Heavens no! The Leang Tai of the Kingdom of France never go candle-less to bed, and when the *oulah* come through their town, they never fail to prepare a good dinner.'

'Quite right, that's the proper thing to do. But this Sue Mou Tchou—' At these words we couldn't help laughing, for they mean, Sue the Sow. 'By the way, do you know', he continued, 'how he came to have this nickname?'

'It's a shameful one to have.'

'Shameful indeed, but its origin is interesting. Sue, before he was sent to Lha-Ri, was mandarin in charge of a small district in the province of Kiang Si. One day two peasants turned up at his court and asked him to pronounce judgment on a sow the ownership of which was in dispute between them. Sue gave judgment as follows: "Having separated truth from falsehood, I can see clearly that this sow is neither yours, nor yours. I therefore declare that it is mine. Let this judgement be respected." The court officials took possession of the sow, and Sue sold it at the local market. Ever since, Mandarin Sue is known as Sue the Sow.' This story made us regret that we would have to set off without ever setting eyes on this interesting individual.

The weather was unsettled when we left Lha-Ri; our first day's march was only twenty miles and was unremarkable except for a large lake some two and a half miles wide by three and a half long. It was frozen, and we were able to cross it very easily as it was covered by a light fall of snow. We spent the night in a wretched hamlet called Tsa-Tchou-Ka, near which there are some hot springs. The Tibetans bathe in them and claim that they have miraculous properties.

The next day was fraught with fatigue and hardship: we went over the Chor-Kou-La Mountain, which in height and steepness is even worse than Lha-Ri. We began the climb full of apprehension, for the heavy grey sky seemed to promise wind or snow: God's mercy preserved us from both. Towards midday a light wind got up from the north, cold enough to chap the skin of our cheeks very quickly, but not strong enough to blow the snow which lay thick on the mountain.

When we reached the top, we rested a while in the shelter of a big stone *obo*, and had our lunch and smoked a pipe of tobacco. During this frugal meal Ly Kouo Ngan told us that during the wars of Kien Long against Tibet the Chinese troops, embittered by the fatigues and privations of the long journey, had mutinied when crossing the Chor-Kou-La. 'It was here on this plateau,' he told us, 'that the soldiers seized their officers, and after tying them up threatened to throw them into that gully, if they did not promise them an increase in pay. The generals gave their word that their demands would be satisfied, the mutiny was called off, the mandarins were untied and the march continued as before to Lha-Ri. On arrival, the generals kept their promise, pay was increased; but the unit was ruthlessly decimated for insubordination.'

'And what did the soldiers say to that?' we asked.

'The ones not chosen by lot to be executed thought it very funny, and considered that their chiefs had been very clever.'

On leaving the summit of Chor-Kou-La we followed a fairly level route, and kept for the next few days on the heights of a great mountain system with many branches whose peaks and cliffs we could see stretching away into the distance. From Lhasa to Ssetchouan, along the whole of that great distance, there are continuous vast chains of mountains, divided by cataracts, deep ravines and narrow defiles. Sometimes these mountains are piled and jumbled together in the most monstrous shapes; at others they follow one another in a regular progression, like the teeth of an immense saw; the view changes constantly before the traveller's eyes with infinite variety. Yet in the midst of all this diversity, the continual sight of mountains has a uniformity which eventually becomes monotonous. Since a detailed account of the journey would inevitably share this monotony, we shall, to avoid boring repetitions, skip the ordinary mountains, mentioning only the most important, those which—to use the Chinese expression—'claim travellers' lives'. This is indeed the custom of the mountain people themselves: anything that does not actually go soaring up into the clouds is to them a 'plain', and anything which is not a precipice or a labyrinth is a 'smooth road'.

The heights on which we travelled after climbing the Chor-Kou-La were locally considered to be flat. From here to Alan-To, the men of the Tibetan escort told us, there are no mountains: the road is like *that* all the way, they said, showing us the palms of their hands. However, they added, you have to be very careful, for the paths are sometimes slippery and narrow. Now this is what that flat-as-your-hand road was really like. Immediately after leaving the summits of Chor-Kou-La we entered a long series of grim defiles with perpendicular walls of rock on both sides. We had to follow these defiles at a great height along a ledge so narrow that the horses had only just room to put down their hooves. As soon as we saw the yaks start off on this appalling path and heard the muffled roar of the waters far below, we lost our nerve and dismounted. But everyone immediately shouted at us to remount: the horses

were used to it, they said, and would be more sure-footed than we; we must let them find their own way and simply keep firm in our stirrups and avoid looking over the edge. We offered up a prayer and set off after the others. We soon realised that we could not have kept our footing for long on that evil slippery ground. We had the sensation that an invincible force was dragging us down into the fathomless depths below. For fear of becoming giddy we kept our eyes towards the cliff, which was sometimes so sheer that there was no ledge at all for the horses' feet: when that happened there were tree-trunks for the horses to pass over, laid on to stakes driven horizontally into the mountain. The very sight of these terrifying bridges made us come out into a cold sweat all over. Yet there was nothing to do but go ahead; to go back or to dismount were both out of the question.

After two whole days of being permanently suspended between life and death, we at last left this path, the most horrible and most dangerous imaginable, and arrived at Alan-To. Everyone was in great spirits, full of mutual congratulations at not having rolled down into the abyss. With a kind of feverish exaltation we told each other of the terror we had felt in the most difficult stretches. The Dheba of Alan-To, on hearing that no man had been lost, said that we had had extraordinary luck. Three yaks, with the baggage they were carrying, had gone over the edge, it was true, but such accidents didn't count, they were not worth mentioning. Ly Kouo Ngan told us that he had never passed through the Alan-To defile without witnessing the most horrible accidents. On his last journey, four soldiers had been flung over the edge with the horses that carried them. Everyone had stories to tell that made one's hair stand on end. They had avoided telling us beforehand for fear that we might have refused to go on. In fact, if we had had an inkling, when we were still at Lhasa, of the terrors of Alan-To, Ambassador Kichan might have found it much more difficult to persuade us to undertake this journey.

From Alan-To, where we changed *oulah*, we descended through a thick fir forest, into a valley where we stopped after a march of thirty miles in a village called Lang-Ki-Tsoung. This staging-post was one of the pleasantest of the whole journey. It stood in the middle of a plain surrounded by low hills covered in tall timber-trees. The ground was quite fertile, and the inhabitants seemed to cultivate it with much care. The fields were watered by a copious stream, which carried a large quantity of gold dust. For this reason the Chinese call this valley Kin Kow, Golden Gorge.

The houses of Lang-Ki-Tsoung were built in a remarkable manner; they were made entirely of tree-trunks stripped of their bark and cut off at each end so that they should be more or less the same width for the whole of their length. Big stakes are first driven into the earth, to a great depth, with only about two foot above ground. On these stakes prepared fir-trunks are then placed horizontally: these form the floor and the base of the house. Remarkably thick solid walls are then made with similar trunks placed one above the other. The roof is then made out of trunks covered with wide strips of bark, laid like slates. The effect is of a great cage with bars closely set

together. Any gaps between the trunks are filled with cowdung.
Some of the houses made in this manner were very large, of
several storeys; they were very warm, and completely dry.
The only disadvantage was that the floors were very uneven
and disagreeable to walk on. If it ever occurred to the inhabitants of Lan-Ki-Tsoung to give ballroom dances in their
houses, they would have to change their building methods.

Whilst we were sitting in silence patiently waiting for
supper to be served, the Dheba of Lang-Ki-Tsoung and the
corporal of the Chinese guard-post came to tell us that there
was a small matter to be discussed. 'What matter?' said Ly
Kouo Ngan, rather hotly. 'What matter? Oh, I know, the *oulah*
are not ready.'

'It's not that,' replied the Dheba. 'No one has ever had to
wait for the *oulah* at Lang-Ki-Tsoung. You can have them
tonight if you want. But I have to warn you that Mount Tanda
is impassable; for eight consecutive days so much snow has
fallen that the route is not yet open.'

'We managed to cross the Chor-Kou-La, so why not the
Tanda?'

'What is the Chor-Kou-La to the Tanda? These mountains
cannot be compared. Yesterday three men from the Tanda
district wanted to try the mountain and two of them disappeared in the snow; the third arrived here this morning,
alone and on foot, for his horse was also buried. Of course,'
added the Dheba, rather grimly, 'you can leave when you
want; the *oulah* are at your disposal; but you will have to pay
for any yaks or horses which die on the journey.' After deliver-
ing his ultimatum, this Tibetan diplomat put out his tongue,
scratched his ear and left.

Whilst the Pacifier of Kingdoms, lama Dsiamdchang and
other experienced members of the caravan held an animated
discussion on the question, we took our Chinese handbook in
which we found the following passage:

Tanda Mountain is extremely steep and difficult to climb; a
stream runs down it winding through a narrow ravine; in
summer its bed is muddy and slippery; in winter it is covered
with ice and snow. Travellers armed with sticks travel along it
in single file like a line of fish. It is the most difficult stretch on
the road to Lhasa.

Reading this last sentence we almost dropped the book. We read it again; yes, there it was, as plain as a pikestaff: 'It is the most difficult stretch on the road to Lhasa.' The prospect of having to face something even worse than Alan-To was a considerable shock. At that moment Ambassador Kichan seemed to us no better than a murderer, and a cowardly one at that: not daring to kill us in Lhasa, he had sent us to perish in the snow. But our depression soon passed; God in His bounty gradually renewed our courage, and we joined the group still engaged in discussion. It was decided that, on the morrow, a group of our men would leave before dawn to measure the depth of the snow, and see for themselves what the situation was.

They were back by midday, with the news that Mount Tanda was impassable. This news disappointed everybody: even we, usually in no hurry, were quite put out. The weather was fine, and it seemed likely that if we did not take advantage of it new snow would come and our departure would be postponed indefinitely. Whilst we were anxiously debating what to do, the Dheba arrived with a solution: he was prepared to send a herd of yaks on two consecutive days to trample down the snow on the mountain track. 'If we do this, and if the weather keeps fine,' he said, 'I think you will be able to make it.' The Dheba's proposal was eagerly and gratefully accepted by all.

Whilst waiting for the yaks to beat out a road for us, we enjoyed a few days' pleasant and health-giving rest at Lang-Ki-Tsoung. The Tibetans in this valley were more civilised than any we had come across since Lhasa. Morning and evening they contributed in abundance to our table: they brought pheasants, venison, fresh butter and a small, sweet tuber that they found in the mountains. Our prayers, walks and a few games of chess helped to make these days of waiting truly delightful. The chessboard we used had been given us by the regent; the pieces were in ivory, and were in the form of delicately sculptured animals. The Chinese, of course, love chess, but their game is very different from ours. The Tartars and Tibetans also have it, and the strange thing is that their board is exactly the same as ours; the pieces, though shaped differently, have the same value and make the same moves, and the rules of the game are identical. What is even more surprising is that they say 'Chik' for Check, and 'Mat' for mate. These expressions, which are neither Tibetan nor Mongolian, are used by everyone, yet no one can explain their origin or their true meaning. The Tibetans and Tartars were amazed when we told them that we also said 'check' and 'mate'. It would be interesting to make an archaeological study of chess, its origin, its transmission from country to country, its introduction into Upper Asia with the same rules and the same terminology as in Europe. Such a study belongs by right to *Palamède, Revue française des échecs.* We have come across Tartars who were first-class chess-players: they play fast, with less concentration than the Europeans, but their game is no less good.

After three days' rest, the Dheba told us that the yaks had sufficiently beaten down the track, and we set off. The sky was overcast, and there was a fairly strong wind. When we reached the foot of Tanda, we could see a long dark trail, like a huge caterpillar, winding its way up the steep slopes of the mountain. The drovers from Lang-Ki-Tsoung said that it was a party of lamas returning from the pilgrimage of Lha-Ssa-Morou, who had camped for the night at the end of the valley. It was encouraging to see all these travellers, and we started our climb with some enthusiasm. Before we reached the summit the wind began to blow with fury and take the snow with it: the whole mountain seemed to be disintegrating. The climb was so steep that it was too much for man or beast. The horses fell repeatedly and had they not been stopped by great piles of snow, would have rolled down as far as the valley we had just left. Father Gabet, who had never completely recovered from the illness caused by our first journey, nearly failed to reach the top of Tanda; when his strength failed and he was no longer able to hang on to the tail of his horse, he fell exhausted and was almost buried in the snow. The men of the Tibetan escort went to his assistance, and after long and painful efforts managed to hoist him as far as the summit. He was more dead than alive; he was ghastly pale, and panted with a noise like a death-rattle.

On the plateau we found the lama pilgrims who had preceded us; they were all lying in the snow, each with his long spiked stick beside him. A few donkeys, laden with baggage, were huddled together, shivering in the wind with their ears down. When we had got our breath back, we started the descent. As it was almost perpendicular, all we could do was to lie down and let ourselves go, and in this way we made rapid progress. The snow was now an advantage: it was thick enough to cover the unevenness of the ground and we could slide without danger. Only one donkey was lost: through straying too far from the track it crashed down into a gully.

When we reached Tanda village, Ly Kouo Ngan shook the snow off his clothes, put on his dress-cap and went with his soldiers to a little Chinese pagoda which we had passed on entering the place. The story goes that during the Kien Long wars against the Tibetans, a Leang Tai in charge of victualling the Chinese army was crossing Mount Tanda in winter on his way to Lha-Ri. Whilst he was riding along the edge of a chasm filled with snow, a chest full of silver fell off the back of a yak; seeing this, the Leang Tai leapt from his horse on to the chest, which he held fast in his arms, and rolled to the bottom of the chasm without letting it go. When spring came and the snow had melted, so the story goes, the Leang Tai was found, standing on his silver chest. Emperor Kien Long, to honour the devotion of his supplies officer, had him sanctified as the Spirit of Tanda Mountain and built a pagoda for him. Mandarins travelling to or from Lhasa never failed to visit it and kowtow before the image of the Leang Tai. Chinese emperors often deify in this way those civil or military officers who have distinguished themselves in some conspicuous manner. To worship at such shrines is the official religion of mandarins.

After leaving Tanda village we travelled twenty miles across a plain called Piam-Pa which, according to the Chinese handbook, 'is the largest in Tibet'. If this is true, Tibet is indeed a terrible place; for not only is this so-called plain everywhere broken up by hills and ravines, it is also narrow enough for one to be able, from the middle, to spot a man standing at the foot of the mountains on either side. After crossing the plain, for some seventeen miles we followed a small stream which wound its way through the mountains to Lha-Dze, where we changed *oulah*.

From Lha-Dze to Barilang was thirty-three miles; two-thirds of the way were taken up by the well-known Kchak-La Mountain; it is classified as a 'killer' mountain, *Yao Ming Ti Chan* in Chinese: a mountain which claims the lives of travellers. We made the ascent and descent without accident. We were not even very tired, for we were by now in training for the hard life of daily climbing mountains.

After Barilang the route was quite easy; from it we could see, here and there, smoke rising from wretched Tibetan dwellings in isolated mountain gorges. We passed a number of black tents and many herds of yaks. After thirty-three miles we reached Chobando, a small town which seen from a distance was unusual and attractive, because all the buildings—houses and lamaseries—were painted with a solution of red ochre. The town was built with its back to a mountain, and on the other side was enclosed by a river which was not wide but deep. We crossed it by a wooden bridge which swayed and groaned under our feet and seemed about to come to pieces at any moment. Chobando was the most important military post that we had come to since leaving Lha-Ri: it consisted of twenty-five soldiers under an officer with the rank of Tsien Tsoung. He was an intimate friend of Ly the Pacifier of Kingdoms: they had served together for a number of years on the Gorkha frontier. The Tsien Tsoung invited us to supper, and somehow was able to serve, in the midst of this wild mountainous country, a superb meal of all sorts of Chinese delicacies. During the meal the two comrades in arms had a splendid time recalling their old adventures.

Just as we were going to bed, two horsemen wearing belts hung with little bells arrived in the inn yard; they stopped for a few moments and then went off at the gallop. We were told that it was the special courier, carrying Ambassador Kichan's dispatches to Peking. It had left Lhasa only six days before and had already travelled two thousand *li*—some seven hundred and twenty miles. Normally dispatches took only thirty days from Lhasa to Peking: such a speed will not perhaps seem very impressive, especially compared with that of European couriers; but when the incredible hazards of the route are taken into account it will appear astonishingly rapid. The express couriers who carry the dispatches across Tibet travel day and night; they always travel in pairs, a Chinese soldier and a Tibetan guide. At every thirty to forty miles there is a change of post-horses, but the men are changed less frequently. They travel attached to their saddles by broad straps. They habitually observe a day's total fast before riding; and whilst they are travelling simply swallow two boiled eggs whenever they arrive at a relay station. The men who follow this hard calling seldom live to an old age; many perish falling into chasms or buried in snow; other fall victims to illness easily contracted in such murderous regions. We have never understood how these couriers could travel by night through the Tibetan mountains, where there are perilous precipices at every turn.

Chobando was remarkable for two monasteries, residences of a large number of Yellow Hatted lamas. In one of them there was a big printing-works, providing sacred texts for the lamaseries of the province of Kham.

Leaving Chobando, after two long and difficult days winding through mountains and immense forests of pine and holly, we arrived at Kan-Yu-Kiao. This village was built on the steep banks of the Souk-Tchou river, where it flowed between two mountains: a wide, deep and rapidly flowing river. We found the inhabitants in deep distress: it was only very recently that a wooden bridge over the river had given way. Two men and three yaks, who had been on it at the time, had perished. The remains of the bridge, made of large tree-trunks, were still visible: the fact that the wood was clearly rotten indicated that it had collapsed from old age. The sight of these tragic ruins made us thank God for having delayed us three days before climbing Mount Tanda. Had we arrived at Kia-Yu-Kiao before

the bridge fell, it would probably have collapsed under the
weight of the caravan. Unexpectedly, this accident caused us
no delay. The local Dheba quickly had a raft built, and next
day we were able to get going by dawn. Men, baggage and
saddles crossed the river by raft, and the animals swam.

Some twelve miles after leaving Kia-Yu-Kiao, we came to a
wooden bridge spanning a deep ravine. Since our minds were
still full of the disaster at Kia-Yu-Kiao, we approached this
perilous construction with some apprehension. As a precaution, the animals were first sent over one at a time: the bridge
creaked and swayed but held good, the men followed. We
walked slowly, on tip-toe, trying to make ourselves as light as
possible. We got over safely, and the caravan re-formed and set
off again. After climbing a mountain which though small was
rocky and steep, with a torrential river running at its foot, we
spent the night at Wa-Ho-Tchai, a staging post consisting of a
guard-post, a little Chinese temple and three or four Tibetan
houses.

We had no sooner arrived than the snow began to fall in
large flakes. Elsewhere such weather would have been merely
disagreeable, but at Wa-Ho-Tchai it was disastrous. We were
due to cover a distance of some fifty-three miles next day, on a
plateau famous throughout Tibet. The hand-book gave the
following details of the route:

On Wa-Ho mountain there is a lake. So that travellers shall not
lose their way in the thick fogs which are common here,
wooden signal-posts have been planted. When the mountain is
covered with deep snow, one can find one's way by these
posts, but it is important to make no noise and travellers must
keep absolutely silent; otherwise ice and hail will descend on
them in abundance and with amazing speed. On the whole
mountain there are neither animals nor birds, for it is frozen
throughout the year: on its sides, and for a hundred *li* (thirty-
five miles) around, there is no habitation. Many Chinese
soldiers and Tibetans die of cold on this mountain.

The soldiers of the guard-post at Wa-Ho-Tchai, seeing that the
snow had set in seriously, opened the doors of the little pagoda
and lit a quantity of little red candles in front of a sinister-
looking idol with a sword in his right hand and in the other a
bow and a quiverful of arrows. They then played a roll on a

small drum and on a tambourine. Ly Kouo Ngan put on his best uniform and went off to kowtow in front of the idol. When he returned we asked him in whose honour the pagoda had been built. 'But it's the pagoda of Kiang Kiun (General) Mao Ling.'

'And what did this general do, to be so honoured?'

'Ah, I see you do not know this story from times past. I will tell it to you. During the reign of Kang Hsi, the empire was at war with Tibet. Mao Ling was sent against the rebels as commander-in-chief. When he was about to cross over Wa-Ho mountain, with a force of four thousand men, local guides warned him that during the crossing silence must be observed by all or they would be buried in snow. The general immediately sent an order to this effect, and the army set off without a sound and in complete silence. As the distance was too great for the soldiers, encumbered with baggage, to cover it in one day, they camped on the plateau. In accordance with the rule established for the cities of the empire and for camps in time of war, a cannon-shot was fired as soon as it was dark. Mao Ling had not dared to break a rule fixed by military discipline. No sooner had the shot been fired than enormous masses of snow descended from the sky on to the camp. The general and all his soldiers were buried in the snow, and their bodies have never been found: only Mao Ling's cook and three servants were saved: they had gone ahead and had already arrived at the village where we are now. Emperor Kang Hsi created General Mao Ling tutelary genius of Mount Wa-Ho and built this pagoda to him, so that he could protect travellers against the snow.'

When Ly Kouo Ngan had finished his story, we asked him what powerful being it was who sent this terrible quantity of hail, ice and snow whenever one made a noise crossing Mount Wa-Ho. 'That's easy,' he answered. 'It can only be the Spirit of the Mountain, the *Hsia Ma Tcheng Chen*, the Toad-which-has-become-a-god.'

'A deified toad?'

'Why, yes. You know that on the top of Wa-Ho there is a lake?'

'Yes, we've been reading about it in the handbook.'

'Well, on the edge of that lake, there is a great toad. He is hard to see, but he can be heard grunting and croaking for a hundred *li* around. This toad has lived on the shores of this lake since heaven and earth existed. As he has never left that lonely place, he has become an immortal, the Spirit of the Mountain. When men make a noise and trouble the silence of his lair, he becomes angry and punishes them by heaping them with hail and snow.'

'Why, you're really quite serious. Do you really believe that a toad can become immortal and turn into a spirit?'

'Why not, if he prayed every night to the Great Bear?' When Ly Kouo Ngan got on to his hobby-horse about the Great Bear, it was impossible to reason with him, so we simply smiled and made no reply. 'I see you're laughing because I spoke of the "seven stars",' he resumed. 'I was wrong to mention them; I should have just said that the toad of Wa-Ho became immortal because he had always lived in solitude on a wild mountain inaccessible to men. Is it not the passions of men which pervert all created beings and prevent them from achieving perfection? Would not animals eventually become spirits, if they did not breathe an air poisoned by man's presence?' This idea struck us as more philosophical than the first, and so we gave it the benefit of a serious reply. Ly Kouo Ngan, who was a reasonable man when he kept off the Great Bear, finally began to doubt the power of the immortal toad and the effectiveness of General Mao Ling's protection. When we were about to say our evening prayers, he said: 'Whatever may be the truth about the toad and the general, it is certain that tomorrow's march will be hard and dangerous; since you are lamas of the Lord of Heaven, pray Him to protect the caravan.'

'We do that every day,' we told him, 'but because of tomorrow's danger we shall do so tonight in a special way.'

We had been in bed at most two hours when one of the soldiers from the guard-post came noisily into our room, hung a large red lantern on a peg fixed in the wall and told us that the cock had already crowed once. We had to get up and get ready smartly, for some fifty-three miles lay between us and the next relay-post. There was a starry sky, but so much snow had fallen in a short time during the evening that it had added a layer a foot thick on top of the old snow. This turned out to be ideal, for it made a carpet which lay on top of the frozen snow—almost as slippery as a glacier—with which Wa-Ho is perpetually covered.

The caravan started off long before dawn; it advanced

slowly and silently over the winding trails of the mountain, lit by starlight on snow. The sun was beginning to redden the horizon when we arrived on the plateau. Fear of the Great Toad vanished with the darkness and the silence we had all observed was broken. First the drovers began to curse aloud any yaks which wandered or gambolled off the path. Gradually the travellers began to make a few remarks about the mildness of the weather and the unexpectedly easy going; eventually the toad's anger was entirely defied; everyone began to chat, shout and sing, without a thought apparently of a deluge of snow and hail. The caravan had never been noisier.

The plateau of Wa-Ho was indeed a dreary place. There was nothing to be seen anywhere but snow in all directions; not a tree, not even the track of a wild beast, broke the monotony of this vast plain. The only things to be seen were the long poles, blackened by age, which had been put there to guide the caravans. On the whole long mountain, there was not even a place where travellers could prepare their tea and eat a little food. Those who were not strong enough to spend twenty hours without eating and drinking, ate as they went along a few handfuls of snow and some *tsamba* dough prepared in advance.

All day the sky was clear and serene; not a single little cloud hid the sun's rays. This over-good weather caused us considerable suffering; the glare from the snow was so dazzling and strong that the horsehair spectacles were insufficient to protect our eyes from being seriously inflamed.

Just as darkness began to fall on the mountain we reached the edge of the plateau. The descent was by a steep narrow path, and after countless twists and turns along a deep gorge we finally arrived at the relay-post of Nenda-Tchaï, where everyone spent the night in considerable pain. We all groaned and cried out: it felt as if our eyes were being torn out. Next day it was impossible to travel. Lama Dsiamdchang, who was something of an apothecary, distributed remedies to all. Eye-lotions of all sorts were concocted, and we all spent the day with our eyes bandaged.

Thanks to the lama's remedies, next morning we were able to open our eyes and resume our journey. We were three stages from Tsiamdo; they were difficult and tiresome, for we were obliged to cross a large number of those vile wooden bridges suspended between precipices and over rushing rivers. We could never forget the recent disaster at Kia-Yu-Kiao. After following for seven miles a narrow path on the steep banks of the large river called Kiang-Tang-Tchou, we finally arrived at Tsiamdo. It was thirty-six days since we had left Lhasa. According to the Chinese handbook we had covered about two thousand five hundred *li* (eight hundred and seventy-five miles).

[10]

THE RETURN TO
CHINA

The Chinese government had established a supply base at Tsiamdo administered by a Leang Tai. The garrison consisted of about three hundred soldiers, with four officers, a Yeou Ki, a Tsien Tsoung and two Pa Tsoung. The upkeep of this military post and the guard-posts dependant on it cost ten thousand ounces of silver a year.

Tsiamdo, capital of the province of Kham, stood in a valley surrounded by high mountains. Once it had been enclosed by earth ramparts which at the time of our visit were completely in ruins; the remains were being used to repair the flat roofs of the houses. In any case Tsiamdo hardly needed artificial fortifications; it was sufficiently protected by two rivers, the Dza Tchou and the Om Tchou, which flow past the town, the former on the east side and the latter on the west, and then join south of the town to form the Lantsangkiang or Mekong River, which crosses the province of Yunnan and then Cochinchina from north to south, and runs into the sea in the Gulf of Tongking. Two big wooden bridges, one over the Dza Tchou and the other over the Om Tchou on either side of the town, led to two parallel roads: the Ssetchouan road and the Yunnan road. The postal couriers from Lhasa to Peking and all Chinese government employees, civil or military, used the Ssetchouan road; the other was hardly used, except occasionally by Chinese merchants who had purchased from their local mandarins the right to trade in Tibet.

The military posts established by Peking in the territory of the Dalai Lama were previously maintained and administered jointly by Ssetchouan and Yunnan. This arrangement was long a source of division and friction between the mandarins of the two provinces, and it was finally decided that the Viceroy of Ssetchouan should take over complete charge of all Chinese stationed in Tibet.

Tsiamdo gave the impression of being an old town fallen into a decline; large, very irregularly built houses were scattered in disorder over a great area, leaving wide open spaces often covered with rubble. Apart from a few modern buildings, the rest were obviously ancient. The large population was generally dirty, unkempt and profoundly idle.

We tried without much success to find out what they lived on. There were no crafts, no industry and practically no agriculture. The country round the town mostly consisted of sandy areas near the rivers, hardly suitable for growing grain crops. But some grey barley was grown there, though probably not enough for the needs of the area. There was some trade in musk, wild yak hides, rhubarb, turquoises and gold dust, possibly enough to purchase the necessities of life.

The was little enough to be seen, then, of luxury or elegance, but in contrast a large and magnificent lamasery stood on a flat-topped hill that dominated the town from the west. About two thousand lamas lived there; instead of each one having his own little house as in other lamaseries, they lived all together in great buildings grouped round the main temple. The latter, richly decorated, was regarded as one of the most beautiful and best endowed in Tibet. The superior of the lamasery was a Houtouktou Lama, who was also temporal ruler of the province of Kham.

At about one hundred and seventy-five miles from Tsiamdo in the direction of the Chinese frontier there is a town called Djaya which, with its dependant cantons, was ruled by a grand lama with the title of Tchaktchouba. This lamaic rank is slightly inferior to that of Houtouktou. At the period we were in Tibet a great struggle had developed between the Houtouktou of Tsiamdo and the Tchaktchouba of Djaya. The latter, a bold and enterprising young lama, had declared himself to be a Houtouktou on the basis of an old diploma granted him in one of his previous lives by the Dalai Lama. He therefore claimed rights of seniority and the governorship of Tsiamdo and its province, Kham. The Houtouktou of Tsiamdo, a very old lama, refused to step down, and claimed to hold documentary authority from the court at Peking ratified by the Dalai Lama. All the tribes and lamaseries of the province were involved on one side or the other. After long and useless disputes, written and verbal, they had resorted to arms; and for a whole year these wild fanatic peoples had fought a bloody civil war. Whole villages were destroyed and their inhabitants slaughtered. The fury of destruction brought ravage in its train: they chased the herds of goat and yak in the wilderness with arrows and with guns and burned the forests they met on their path.

When we arrived at Tsiamdo, the fighting had stopped a few days before and a truce had been called in the hope of reconciling both sides. Tibetan and Chinese negotiators had been sent jointly by the Dalai Lama and Ambassador Kichan. The young Houtouktou of Djaya had been summoned to this meeting, and for fear of treachery had turned up with a strong escort of his fiercest supporters. Several conferences had been held, without any satisfactory result. Neither side would give an inch, no reconciliation was possible and it seemed inevitable that fighting would be resumed with new fury. We got the impression that the young Houtouktou was the likely winner, as his supporters were more nationalistic and therefore more popular and stronger. Not that his title-document was any more authentic than that of his rival, but it was easy to see that the old Houtouktou of Tsiamdo had offended the pride of the tribes by calling on the Chinese for arbitration and seeking the protection of the Peking government. All foreign intervention is loathed and detested. Not only is this true in Europe, but also amongst the mountain peoples of Tibet and wherever men care for their independence and dignity.

Our stay at Tsiamdo was quite unaffected by the nervous tensions and passions which dominated the town. We were treated with the kindness and the courtesy we had encountered everywhere since leaving Lhasa. Each of the rival Houtouktous sent us a Scarf of Felicity, with a good provision of butter and joints of mutton. We stayed for three days, since our leader, the Pacifier of Kingdoms, was urgently in need of rest. The hardships of the journey had caused his health to deteriorate ; his legs were now so swollen that he could no longer mount or dismount without being helped by several people. The doctors and soothsayers of Tsiamdo were consulted, and gave their opinions which boiled down to nothing more than that if his condition improved it was not serious, but that if it got worse it might become dangerous. The best advice he got was to continue his journey by palanquin. A local Chinese mandarin was willing to sell him his, and find porters ; this would have been the sensible thing to do, but avarice raised its ugly head and the patient protested that he would find it more tiring in a palanquin than on a horse.

In addition to Ly Kouo Ngan's illness there was another reason for delay. A Chinese caravan that had left Lhasa a few days after us had arrived at Tsiamdo the same evening as ourselves. It consisted of a Leang Tai, or quartermaster, his son, a boy of eighteen, and a large escort of soldiers and servants. We wanted to let them go ahead, for if we had joined forces there would have been a risk of finding insufficient lodging and *oulah* for such a large party. The Leang Tai and his son travelled by palanquin, but despite the advantages of this form

of transport these distinguished gentlemen were so exhausted and despondent that there were serious doubts that they would survive as far as China. Civil mandarins, who lead a life of ease and comfort, are usually hardly capable of facing the extreme conditions encountered on the Tibet road. Few of those sent to fill the post of quartermaster ever see their beloved homeland again.

When we left, the old Houtouktou of Tsiamdo sent us an escort of four Tibetan horsemen to protect us until we reached the territory of the Tchaktchouba of Djaya. On leaving the town, we crossed a fine bridge made of great fir trunks, and joined the Ssetchouan road, which wound along the flank of a high mountain at the foot of which ran the rapid Dza Tchou river. After about seven miles we met at a bend in the mountain, in a deep narrow gorge, a small group of travellers which made a truly charming picture. In front came a Tibetan woman, astride a large donkey, and carrying a baby on her back firmly fastened with leather straps. She was leading, on a long halter, a packhorse laden with two oblong boxes, one on each flank. These two boxes each contained a child; their happy laughing faces could be seen framed by small windows. There did not seem to be much difference in their ages, but they must have had a different weight, for, to keep the balance, a large stone had been tied on the side of one of the boxes. Behind the horse so laden, came with slow walk a horseman who from his dress could easily be recognised as a retired Chinese soldier; behind him on the crupper rode a boy of about twelve years old. Finally, an enormous, shifty-eyed, sandy-haired dog of ill-tempered mien ended this curious caravan, which joined us and profited from our company as far as the province of Ssetchouan.

This Chinaman was an ex-soldier of the Tsiamdo garrison. Having fulfilled the three years of service fixed by law, he had obtained permission to remain in Tibet in order to engage in commerce. He had married there, and after making a sufficient sum of money he was returning to his native land with his whole family. We could not help admiring the courage, the energy and the devotion of this good Chinaman, so different from his selfish compatriots, who without the slightest scruple abandoned wives and children in foreign countries. He had to face, not only the dangers and hardships of a long journey, but also the mockery of those who had not the courage to follow his good example. Indeed, the soldiers of our escort soon began to scoff at him. 'That man', they said, 'clearly has an addled brain. To bring back from abroad money and goods, that's reasonable; but to take to the homeland a woman with feet that have not been bound and all those little barbarians is against all the rules. Maybe the idea is to make more money, showing off those Tibetan animals?' More than once this sort of talk excited our indignation, and we always made a point of defending this fine family man, praising his good behaviour and sternly reproving the barbarity and immorality of Chinese customs.

Shortly after we had accepted into our caravan the interesting little family from Tsiamdo, we left the Dza Tchou river on our right and crossed over a mountain with great trees and enormous rocks covered with large patches of lichen. Then we rejoined the river, followed it on a very rough track for a mile or two and arrived at Meng Phou. We had hardly done more than twenty-four miles but were worn out; during the three days we had spent at Tsiamdo we had lost the habit of riding, and it was quite an effort to regain our form. Meng Phou was a huddle of seven or eight little houses built of uncut stone in a wide, deep ravine.

Next day we travelled along the ridge of a high mountain on a track which continually dipped and rose from one rounded hilltop to the next. We were frequently having to cross over chasms by wooden bridges which, to quote the Chinese handbook, 'hang in the region of the clouds'. After twenty-one miles we reached Pao Tun, where we changed *oulah* and where we began to find the Tibetans less tractable and docile than on the other side of Tsiamdo. Their expressions were prouder and their manners blunter; in consequence the Chinese of the caravan became humbler, less demanding and prudently avoided using words of command.

From Pao Tun to Bagoung, for some thirty miles, we passed through limestone mountains which were bald and bare. There were no trees, no grass and not even moss; but in low places here and there in clefts in the rock there were saxifrages, vigorous enough and protesting, as it were, against this depressing sterility. One of these mountains, which the Chinese called Kou Loung Chan, that is, Hole Mountain, was most remarkable. There were a considerable number of holes and cavities in it, varying greatly in size and shape. Some looked like great doorways; the smallest were like bells or like round or oval windows. As the mountain face was a sheer cliff we were unable to visit these caves, but were close enough to see that they were of considerable depth. Their origin is no doubt volcanic, but the Chinese attribute them to the *Kouei* or evil genies. The Tibetans, on the other hand, believe that they were hollowed out by the guardian spirits of the neighbourhood and that, in ancient times, lamas of great sanctity made their retreat in them; they were transformed into Buddhas, and at certain times of the year the sound of lamaic prayers can still be heard inside the mountain.

Up to this point in our travels in Tibet the mountains had almost always been of granitic origin, great masses of stone piled one on the other and usually quadrangular, though rounded at the corners by the continuous action of wind and rain. The calcareous massif which we passed on our way to

Bagoung was therefore all the more remarkable. In fact the landscape as a whole was beginning to change completely. For more than a fortnight we saw nothing but limestone, including a marble as white as snow, fine grained and very dense. The herdsmen quarry great slabs of it, on which they carve the image of Buddha or the phrase: *Om, mani padme houm!* and which they then set up by the wayside. These carvings remain undefaced for many years, because there is a large proportion of silex combined with the carbonate of lime in this marble, and it is therefore extremely hard. Before arriving at Bagoung we passed along a track for two or three miles lined continuously on both sides with these pious inscriptions. We indeed came across a few lamas carving the *mani* on marble slabs.

We arrived at the little village of Bagoung shortly before nightfall. We made our way for our night's lodging to the Chinese guard-post, which consisted of several small houses built of magnificent slabs of white marble stuck together with mud or cowdung. On arrival we were told of the death of the Leang Tai, named Pei, who had caught us up at Tsiamdo. His caravan had arrived at Bagoung two days before. When the mandarin's porters had reached the guard-post, they had put down the palanquin and opened the curtains, as is the custom, to invite His Excellency to be good enough to enter the apartment prepared for him. But in the palanquin there was only a corpse. According to Chinese custom, the deceased's son must not leave his father's body on foreign soil; he must bring it home for burial in the ancestral tomb. Now, we were still deep in Tibet, and the family of Mandarin Pei was in the province of Tche Kiang, right at the far end of China. The road was long and hard, yet there was no alternative, filial piety would have to overcome all obstacles. A coffin, by chance, happened to be ready and waiting at the guard post. The mandarin's son bought it, very dearly, from the soldiers; the poles from the palanquin were fixed on to the coffin and the porters agreed, in return for an increase in wages, to carry a dead man instead of a live one as far as the frontier of China. The caravan had left Bagoung the day before we arrived.

The news of this man's death astonished and upset everyone. Ly Kouo Ngan especially, owing to his own state of health, was so scared that he lost his appetite for supper; but later that evening a new worry took his mind off these sad thoughts of death. The headman of the village called at the guard-post to announce that it had been decreed locally that the *oulah* would no longer be provided gratis: a horse would cost an ounce of silver and a yak half an ounce. 'The caravan which left yesterday', he added, 'had to pay these prices.' To prove that there was no arguing about this ruling, he quickly put out his tongue and departed.

This ultimatum struck the Pacifier of Kingdoms like a thunderbolt. He completely forgot the melancholy demise of the poor Leang Tai and concentrated on the disaster which now threatened his purse. We sympathised with him in his distress and did our best to make soothing noises, but really we couldn't care either way. If means of continuing our journey were not provided, we could always stay in Tibet, and we would have nothing against such an outcome. Meanwhile we went to bed, leaving it to our escort to worry about politics and economics.

Next morning when we got up there were no yaks or horses in the courtyard of the guard-post. Ly Kouo Ngan was utterly despondent.

'Are the *oulah* coming?' we asked. 'Shall we be leaving today?'

'These savages', he said, 'will not listen to reason. They don't know the meaning of obedience. I have decided to appeal to Proul Tamba. I have sent him a deputation. I have known him for a long time, and hope he will see that we have some *oulah*.' We had already heard a good deal about Proul Tamba; he was leader of the faction of the young Tchacktchouba of Djaya, and therefore an open opponent of Chinese influence. We were told that he was as educated as the most learned lamas of Lhasa; no one was his equal in bravery, and he had never been defeated in battle. Among all the tribes of the province of Kham his name was therefore something to be conjured with, acting as a kind of magic charm on the hearts of the people. Proul Tamba was, in some sort, the Abd el-Kader* of these rough mountain folk.

Proul Tamba's dwelling was only a couple of miles from Bagoung. The deputation that had been sent there was soon

Abd el-Kader (1807–1883): Algerian emir who fought against France and tried to organise an Arab empire. He was captured in 1847 and later became a faithful friend of France. (Larousse)

back, and announced that the Great Chief was on his way in person. This unexpected news put everyone, both Tibetan villagers and Chinese guard, into a state of commotion. 'The Great Chief is coming! We're going to see the Great Chief!' they called out excitedly. Ly Kouo Ngan quickly put on his best clothes, his silk boots and his ceremonial hat. The Chinese soldiers also did their best to smarten themselves up. Whilst the Tibetans ran out to meet their chief, Ly Kouo Ngan chose a magnificent *khata* from one of his trunks and stood in the doorway to welcome the great man. Our own part in this event was to remain on the sidelines, and observe the faces of the participants. Undoubtedly the most interesting of these was Ly Kouo Ngan's; here was a Chinese mandarin, usually so arrogant and insolent in front of Tibetans, suddenly become humble and modest, waiting nervously for a man he knew to be strong and powerful.

Then the Great Chief arrived. He was on horseback, with an escort of four horsemen. As soon as they had all dismounted, the Pacifier of Kingdoms went up to them, bowed deeply and offered the scarf to Proul Tamba. The latter signed to one of his men to accept the gift, and without a word crossed the yard and went straight into the room that had been prepared for the reception, in which we and Lama Dchiamdchang were waiting. Proul Tamba gave us a little nod and sat down without further ado in the place of honour on a large grey felt rug. Ly Kouo Ngan sat down on his left, Dchiamdchang on his right and we in front of him. There was a respectful distance between all five, and we formed a sort of large circle. Chinese soldiers and a crowd of Tibetans stood behind.

For a moment there was a deep hush. Great Chief Proul Tamba was at most forty years old, of medium height; his only garment was a long green silk robe, beautifully lined in wolf-skin and drawn in at the waist by a red belt. In addition he wore high purple leather boots, a formidable fox-skin hat and long broad sabre passed through his belt horizontally. Long ebony-black hair down to his shoulders gave his pale thin face an expression of great energy. His most remarkable feature was his eyes, large and blazing with indomitable pride and courage. Everything about him proclaimed a man above the rest of mankind, born to command. He looked at us closely one by one, with his hands resting on either end of his sabre, then drew from his bosom a packet of little *khatas* and got one of his men to give us one each. Next, he turned to Ly Kouo Ngan.

'Well, here you are back again,' he said in a voice that boomed like a bell. 'If they hadn't told me this morning that it was you, I shouldn't have recognised you. How old you've grown since you last came through Bagoung!'

'Yes, you're right,' said the Pacifier of Kingdoms in sancti-monious honeyed tones, dragging himself over the felt rug to get closer to the speaker, 'you're absolutely right, I'm very frail; but you're stronger than ever.'

'We live in times when one has to be strong. There is no peace in our mountains any more.'

'Yes, I heard that you had had a little dispute amongst yourselves.'

'The tribes of Kham have fought a bitter war for a year, and you call that a little dispute! You will only have to keep your eyes open as you travel, and you will see everywhere ruined villages and burnt forests. In a few days we shall have to get going again, because no one will listen to words of peace. This war could have been over after a few fights; but since you Chinese decided to meddle in our affairs the two sides have become irreconcilable. Oh, you Chinese mandarins, all you can do is bring disorder and confusion into our land. Things can't go on like this. You've been given a free hand for too long, and now there's nothing you don't meddle in! I can't think of the affair of the Nomekhan of Lhasa without trembling with anger in every limb. They say that the Nomekhan committed great crimes; it's not true. Those great crimes were invented by you. The Nomekhan is a saint. He's a living Buddha. Who ever heard of a living Buddha being condemned and sent into exile by such a man as Kichan, a Chinaman and a layman?'

'The order came from the Great Emperor,' said Ly Kouo Ngan in a low trembling voice.

'Your Great Emperor,' cried Proul Tamba turning angrily on the interruptor, 'your Great Emperor is only a layman himself. What is your Emperor compared to a Grand Lama, a Living Buddha?'

The Great Chief of the province of Kham then launched into a tirade against Chinese domination in Tibet. In turn he attacked the emperor, the viceroy of Ssetchouan and the ambassadors in Lhasa. Throughout, he kept on coming back to the case of the Nomekhan. We could see that he was much concerned with the fate of this man, whom he regarded as a victim of the government of Peking. The Pacifier of Kingdoms was careful to put up no opposition; he pretended to agree with everything Proul Tamba said by giving little nods of the head. Finally he hazarded a remark about our departure and the *oulah*.

'The *oulah*,' said Proul Tamba; 'from now on there will be no *oulah* for the Chinese, unless they pay a proper price. It's enough that we let the Chinese into our country at all, without being silly enough to supply them with free *oulah*. However, since I have known you for a long time, today we'll make an exception for your caravan. In any case, you are escorting two lamas from the Western Heavens, who have been recommended to me by the First Kalon of Lhasa, and to whom I owe this service. Where is the Dheba of Bagoung? Let him come forward!' The man who had come the night before to say 'No money, no *oulah*' stepped forward, knelt before the Great Chief and respectfully put out his tongue. 'Bring the *oulah* immediately,' said Proul Tamba, 'and let each man do his duty!' The Tibetans who were in the guard house all gave a great shout of acclaim and ran off to the next village. Proul Tamba got up, and after inviting us to take tea with him at his house, which lay on our route, he leapt on his horse and galloped off. The *oulah* soon arrived and the caravan was ready in no time, as if by magic.

After half an hour's march we arrived at the home of the Great Chief. It was a great tall building, not unlike a medieval castle. It was surrounded by a wide moat bordered with trees. A drawbridge was lowered for us; we dismounted to cross it and, passing through a large gateway, came out into a square courtyard in which his lordship Proul Tamba was waiting. The horses were tied to stakes in the middle of the yard and we were ushered into a vast hall which seemed to do duty as a temple. The enormous beams which supported the roof were entirely covered in gilt. The walls were hung with coloured banners covered in Tibetan inscriptions. At the far end there were three colossal statues of Buddha with tall butter lamps and perfume pans in front of them.

In one corner of the temple a low table and four double cushions in red *pou-lou* had been placed in readiness. Proul Tamba graciously invited us to sit down, and as soon as we had done so the lady of the house appeared in full dress, that is, with her face horribly daubed with black and her abundant hair adorned with gold spangles, red coral beads and little disks of mother-of-pearl. In her right hand she held the handle of a majestic teapot, the base of which rested on her left arm. We each produced our bowl, which was instantly filled to the brim with tea on top of which floated a thick layer of butter: it was a top quality tea. Whilst we were sipping this scalding liquid the lady of the house reappeared carrying two dishes in gilded wood, one containing raisins and the other walnuts.

'These are fruits of our country,' said Proul Tamba. 'They come from a beautiful valley which is quite near here. Have you such fruits under the Western Heavens?'

'Yes, many. You wouldn't believe how happy you make us in offering us these fruits, for they remind us of our homeland,' and so saying we took a pinch of raisins from the gilt dish. But, alas, their skin was hard and leathery and they were full of pips which ground in the teeth like gravel. We turned our attention to the walnuts, which were of magnificent size; but, another disappointment, the kernel was so solidly enclosed in hard compartments that it was only with the greatest difficulty that we could extract a few bits with our nails. We returned to the raisins, then back to the walnuts, then turn by turn, seeking but not finding a little nourishment to calm our protesting stomachs. We were beginning to wonder if Madame Proul

Tamba had been playing a bad joke on us, when two strong Tibetans appeared bearing a two-tiered table, on which were a whole kid and a magnificent haunch of venison. This unexpected sight made us jump, and the involuntary grins that came on our faces must have betrayed to our host how much we welcomed his second course. The raisin skins and the nutshells were removed, Tibetan beer came instead of buttered tea, and we set to work with great enthusiasm.

When we had emerged triumphant from this Homeric meal, we presented the Great Chief with a Scarf of Felicity and rode on our way. Not far from the castle we passed a limestone mountain with large holes near the top, and all over the steep sides Buddhist texts carved in giant characters. All the Tibetans in the caravan stopped and prostrated themselves three times. In this mountain lived a contemplative lama whom all the tribes of the province of Kham venerated profoundly. The local people told us that twenty-two years before, this holy man had retired into one of the caves. Since then he had stayed there without once emerging, spending his days and nights in prayer and in the contemplation of the thousand virtues of Buddha. No one was allowed to visit him. However every three years he gave a grand audience lasting eight days, and during this period his devotees could visit him freely in his cell, and consult him on things past, present and future. Plentiful offerings then arrived from everywhere, but the holy man kept nothing for himself. He distributed everything to the poor of the area. For what need had he of riches or the goods of this world? His cell, a hole in the rock, never needed repairs; his yellow robe lined with sheepskin was suitable for all seasons; once every six days only he had a meal consisting of a little tea and barley meal, which charitable people in the neighbourhood sent him on the end of a long rope which reached from his cave to the foot of the mountain.

A few lamas had become the disciples of this hermit and had decided to copy his way of life. They lived in cells hollowed out near that of their master. His best known disciple was Proul Tamba's father. He too had been a distinguished warrior, always at the head of his people. When he was advanced in age and his son capable of succeeding him, he had passed him the title of Great Chief. With his head shaven and clad in the sacred habit of the lamas, he had retired to solitude, leaving to younger and stronger arms the task of waging the struggle which had broken out between the two Houtouktous of the province of Kham.

The sun had not set when we arrived at the stage-post of Wang Tsa, some seventeen miles from Bagoung. It was a small village running along the foot of a hill of black earth, on which clumps of holly and cypress were growing. The houses were built of this black earth, giving the village a sombre funereal appearance. Here we began to notice traces of the civil war that had been raging. The Chinese guardhouse, built of big deal planks, had been burnt down. The many half-burnt fragments lying here and there made us a splendid bonfire which lasted the whole evening.

Next day when we set off we noticed an odd change in the caravan. The horses and yaks were the same ones we had been given at Bagoung: but all the Tibetan drovers had disappeared, every one of them; they had been replaced by women from Wang Tsa. When we asked why this was, Lama Dchiamdchang told us as follows: 'Today we are due to arrive at Gaya; it's an enemy village. If the men were to go there, there would inevitably be fighting and the men of Gaya would seize the animals of the caravan. But since the *oulah* are driven by women, there is no danger. Any men cowardly enough to fight with women and seize the cattle they have been put in charge of would be universally despised. Such are the customs in these parts.' We were amazed to meet, in these wild Tibetan mountains, customs and attitudes so similar to our own. It was pure French chivalry! We were therefore looking forward to seeing with what forms of courtesy and gallantry the ladies of Wang Tsa would be welcomed by the gentlemen of Gaya.

After crossing a high pass covered in great boulders half buried in old snow, we entered a valley which was entirely cultivated and where the temperature was fairly mild. We could see Gaya some way off, in a dip. The houses were tall and, with their observation towers, resembled forts. When we were within a few hundred yards of the place, an impressive squadron of cavalry suddenly emerged from it and galloped at full speed towards our caravan. These warriors, armed with slung rifles and long lances, seemed ready for the fray. However all their martial ardour vanished when they saw that our beasts were being driven by women. All they did was roar with laughter and mock the cowardice of their enemies.

When we entered the village, there was great excitement: men, women and children all made hostile noises, but there was no incident. We went to our lodging at a large three storey house, and dismounted in the courtyard. As soon as the horses had been unsaddled and the yaks unloaded, the ladies of Wang Tsa hastily drank a good bowlful of buttered tea that someone had had the courtesy to prepare and serve round to them, and immediately afterwards began the journey home with their *oulah*.

Our lodgings were quite comfortable, but what would be the outcome? Everyone had the important question of the *oulah* in mind, but no one had the courage to mention it outright, and we all went to bed leaving serious matters for the morrow. It was scarcely light when our courtyard was crowded with Tibetans who had come to take counsel on the question of how much to charge our caravan. From a second storey balcony we were able to get an excellent view of the unusual parliamentary meeting that was being held below. In this large crowd there was not one single individual who was not an orator—but they all spoke at once, and to judge from the ringing tones of the voices and the violence and expressiveness of the gestures the speeches must have been eloquent indeed. Some of the speakers climbed on top of the piles of baggage to be in a position to dominate the rest. But it seemed that from time to time the power of the word was insufficient to carry conviction, for they resorted to fisticuffs, caught each other by the hair and fought like dogs, until one parliamentarian more influential than the rest called his honourable colleagues to order. The peace was soon broken however and tumult returned, eventually reaching a great crescendo. It was so bad that we were sure that they would never agree and would end by unsheathing their sabres and cutting each other to pieces. But we were utterly wrong: when the company had shouted, roared, gesticulated and fought for more than an hour, they all suddenly burst out laughing, the meeting was over and everyone left in perfect order. Two men immediately came up to the second floor where the staff of our caravan had its headquarters and informed Ly Kouo Ngan that the heads of family of Gaya, after debating the question of *oulah*, had decided that the animals would be provided free to the Lamas of the Western Heavens and to the Tibetans from Lhasa; but that the Chinese would have to pay half an ounce of silver per horse and a quarter per yak. At this news Ly Kouo Ngan gathered all his strength together and poured invective on 'this tyranny', as he called it, 'this injustice'. The Chinese soldiers of the caravan, who were also present, shouted threats with the idea of intimidating the delegates from Gaya's parliamentary assembly. However the latter remained admirably proud and disdainful: one of them stepped forward and put his hand with a certain rough dignity on Ly's shoulder; he looked at him for a moment with large black eyes under bushy eyebrows and then said: 'Man of China, listen to me. Do you think that for us of the valley of Gaya there is any difference between beheading a Chinaman and beheading a kid? So tell your soldiers to stop snarling and using big words. Whoever saw a fox that could scare a wild yak? The *oulah* are on their way here; if you do not take them, if you do not leave today, tomorrow the price will be double.' The Chinese, realising dimly that violence might be fatal, tried guile and persuasion, but it was no use. Ly was finally compelled to open his safe-box and weigh out the required sum. The *oulah* soon turned up and the caravan was got ready hastily, in order to get as soon as possible out of Gaya, a village which the Chinese found barbarian and uninhabitable, but which had seemed to us extremely picturesque.

From Gaya to Angti, where we were to change *oulah* again, was only twelve miles. The Chinese were exasperated at having had to spend so much money for such a short journey; but they were only at the beginning of their troubles, for we were to meet even more intractable tribes than at Gaya. The snow, which had given us a few days' respite since we left Tsiamdo, now returned to the attack on the evening we reached Angti. During the night and the following day it fell so heavily that we could not go out of doors without sinking up to our knees in it. By an unfortunate coincidence we would have to cross, immediately after Angti, one of the steepest and most dangerous passes on the whole road. The Chinese handbook said as follows:

At Angti you cross a great snowy pass; the way is very steep; the accumulated snow is like a silver mist. The fog that the mountain exhales penetrates into the body and makes the Chinese sick.

According to a folk tradition, in ancient times a chief of the Angti tribe, a famous warrior feared for miles around, was buried in an avalanche one day when crossing the mountain. All attempts to find his body failed. A holy lama then declared that he had become the genie of the mountain, and a temple was built in his honour, which still stands and which all travellers visit to burn a few joss-sticks before setting off. When the storm wind rages, the genie of Mount Angti never fails to appear: not a man in the neighbourhood but has seen him a number of times. He always rides a red horse; he is dressed in long white clothes and rides calmly along the ridge of the mountain. If he meets a traveller, he takes him up behind him and then immediately disappears at the gallop; the red horse is so light that it leaves no trace, even on the snow, and no one has ever, to this day, discovered the White Horseman's lair.

We for our part were not so much worried about meeting the red horse and the White Horseman, as about the mountain itself; we were very apprehensive about the heavy snowfall which would make the track very dangerous. We had to wait for better weather and then send, as we had done before in similar circumstances, a succession of herds of yak to trample the snow and make a trail on the mountain. We stayed five days at Angti. Ly Kouo Ngan took advantage of this long halt to nurse his bad legs, the condition of which was daily more alarming. The problem of the *oulah* was debated at length at a number of meetings, and finally resolved in the same way as at Gaya, which of course annoyed the Chinese and caused them to protest loudly.

By far the most remarkable thing about Angti was its Dheba, or tribal chief. His name was Bomba and he was at most three foot high; the sabre that he wore in his belt was at least twice as long as he was. Despite this, the upper half of his body was magnificent, and his face was broad, strong and handsome. His shortness was due to a complete failure of his legs to develop, yet there was no sign of deformity in the feet. This almost complete leglessness did not prevent him from being surprisingly active. He went ceaselessly to and fro, as nimbly as anyone; of course he could not take long strides, but made up for this by rapid movements. He came bounding along, rolling from side to side, and always got there as soon as anyone else. They told us he was the best horseman and boldest fighter of the tribe. Once he had been hoisted on to his horse, on which he both sat and stood at the same time, he was invincible. In open air tribal gatherings which the mountain folk hold frequently to decide public and private matters, Chief Bomba was always the dominant figure, for his eloquence and his personality. When the *oulah* rate was being discussed at Angti, all eyes were turned, all ears listened, to the amazing Bomba. Perched on the shoulders of a big heavy countryman, he came and went like a giant in the rowdy crowd, dominating it even more by his words and gestures than by his stature.

The Chieftain of Angti took every opportunity to show us his particular sympathy and goodwill. One day he invited us to dinner at his house: this invitation was intended not only as a gesture of hospitality but also as a snub to the Chinese, whom he heartily detested and despised. After the dinner, which was unremarkable except for an abundance of raw and boiled meats and tea richly laced with butter, he conducted us round a hall hung with pictures and filled with armour and weapons.

The pictures filling the walls were crudely painted portraits of the most illustrious ancestors of the Bomba family; many were lamas, varying in age and rank, and a few were warriors in full rig-out. There was a large and varied collection of weapons: lances, arrows, and broadswords, some double-edged, some spiral and some saw-toothed; tridents, long staves ending in iron loops and breechlocks of the most curious design. For defence there were round shields in wild yakhide with copper studs; arm-pieces and thigh pieces in copper plate and suits of chainmail armour which were thick and closely woven and yet retained considerable elasticity. Bomba told us that these were from the old days: chainmail had not been worn since the rifle had come into general use in his country. As we have said, the Tibetans are too vague about time to be able to date their first use of firearms. Presumably they only became aware of gunpowder around the thirteenth century, at the time of Genghis Khan who is known to have used artillery. It is notable that, in the Tibetan mountains no less than in the Chinese Empire and on the steppes of Tartary, everyone can make gunpowder: each family makes its own supply. As we passed through the province of Kham we frequently saw women and children busily pounding carbon, sulphur and saltpetre. This home-made gunpowder is certainly not up to European standards, but when put in a rifle with a bullet on top of it there is a strong enough explosion to propel the bullet and kill a stag or a man.

After resting five days we set off, and immediately the climb to the Angti pass began. We met no red horse or White Horseman; no genie took us up behind him and rode away with us. There was nothing but snow to be seen anywhere, but snow so deep that even on the most notorious mountains we had never seen anything like it. Often the guides completely disappeared with the yaks they were riding in drifts from which they could only extricate themselves with the greatest difficulty. More than once we nearly turned back, giving up all hope of reaching the top.

The little Chinese and Tibetan family caravan which had joined us at Tsiamdo and had kept with us ever since was a sight that filled us with compassion. We almost forgot our own troubles whilst watching how these poor little creatures got covered in snow almost at every step, and had hardly the strength to cry out or weep. How we admired the courage and energy of that Tibetan mother as she ran to help one child and then another of her numerous family, finding a superhuman strength in her mother-love.

The Angti pass is so high and so steep that it took us the whole day to cross it. The sun had already set when we reached the bottom. We stopped a short while in some black tents belonging to nomad herdsmen; we swallowed a few handfuls of *tsamba* dipped in salty tea and set off again along a rocky valley where the snow had melted completely. For two hours, in total darkness, we followed the steep banks of a river which we could hear but not see. We were frightened of falling into it, but as the horses were familiar with the road we let them have their heads and they got us safely to Djaya. Our arrival in the middle of the night caused a commotion in the village. The dogs first raised the alarm with furious barking. Then all the doors opened and the people poured out into the streets carrying horn lanterns, torches and weapons of all sorts. They were all convinced that it was an enemy attack, but seeing the peaceful and even rather timorous appearance of the caravan they calmed down and everyone went home. It was after midnight before we could unroll our bedding and get a little sleep. It was first decided that we would stop for a day at Djaya: one day's rest is not excessive after crossing the notorious Angti pass.

Djaya was, as we have stated, the residence of the young Houtouktou who was at war with the Houtouktou of Tsiamdo. The town was in a beautiful valley, and was of considerable size; but at the time of our visit it was half in ruins. Some twenty days before at most it had been attacked by the supporters of the old Houtouktou. The fighting had been bitter and there had been many casualties on both sides. Whole sections of the town had been burnt to the ground; only great heaps of charred rubble and blackened woodwork remained. All the trees in the valley had been cut down and the horses had thoroughly churned up the earth of the cultivated fields. Djaya's famous lamasery was deserted. The cells of the lamas and the wall of more than six-hundred feet circumference which had surrounded them had all been demolished; nothing but a horrid mass of ruins remained. Only the main temples had been spared.

The Chinese government kept a small garrison of about twenty soldiers at Djaya, commanded by a Tsien Tsoung and a

Pa Tsoung. They were a dissatisfied lot, obviously hating their posting in this land torn by civil war; the warlike character of the local population allowed them no peace, day or night: they did their best to appear neutral—or rather to give the impression of siding both ways—but nonetheless found themselves between two cross-fires. Apparently Djaya has never made it easy for the Chinese: these proud peoples have always put up a strong resistance to Chinese domination. The Chinese handbook, which was written in the reign of Emperor Kien Long, had this to say:

The Tibetans who live in the canton of Djaya are haughty and wild; all attempts to tame them have been fruitless. They are reputed to be fierce, and that is their nature.

Their so-called wildness is nothing but an ardent patriotism and a justifiable hatred of the foreign yoke.

One day's rest was enough and we left Djaya. The Chinese were of course made to pay cash for hiring the *oulah*. These Tibetans were too 'wild' to let them have yaks and horses for nothing. We travelled for two days through a very low country, passing frequently through small villages and groups of black tents in the valley bottoms. There were many wooden bridges to cross, sometimes over calm streams and sometimes over rushing torrents. Shortly before arriving at the stage-post of Adzou Thang, we caught up with the group accompanying the coffin of the Leang Tai who had died at Bagoung. His son had also just died in a black tent, after some hours of terrible agony. The caravan, without a leader, was completely disorganised; most of the soldiers of the escort had made off, after ransacking their mandarin's luggage; only three had remained at their post and were trying to find ways of taking the two corpses to China. They had little hope of being able to continue their journey, being so few, and so the arrival of our caravan got them out of a great difficulty. A hearse had been organised for the father's body at Bagoung; now the same had to be done for the son. The porters of his palanquin had refused to carry him, because they feared that there would not be enough money to pay them. To load the corpse on to a yak was not practicable: the Tibetan drovers could never have been persuaded to accept a dead body, especially a dead Chinaman; so a trick had to be resorted to. The body of the young man was secretly cut up into four parts, then stowed in a chest that was put with the rest of the luggage. The Tibetans were told that, for the sake of filial piety, the son's body had been placed beside his father's, in the same coffin.

These two corpses we had acquired as travelling companions cast a gloom over the caravan and greatly depressed the Chinese. Ly the Pacifier of Kingdoms, who was getting weaker every day, was specially scared; he would gladly have got rid of these grisly reminders, but to do so would have exposed him to the very serious accusation of having prevented the proper burial of two mandarins who had died abroad.

From Adzou Thang we went on to spend the night and change *oulah* at a little village in the valley of Che Pan Keou, the Valley of Slates. The Chinese handbook said that the people of this valley were 'very gross, wicked and turbulent', which simply meant that they were not afraid of the Chinese and always made them pay dearly for the yaks and horses they provided.

The valley of Che Pan Keou, as its name implies, has a number of slate quarries. The Tibetans extract fine roof slates and also thick slabs on which they carve the likeness of Buddha and the phrase *Om, mani padme houm!* The slate is extremely fine grain, and contains a quantity of mica which gives it a brilliant silky lustre.

The stream which runs down the middle of the valley contains gold dust in large quantities, which is panned and smelted on the spot. Walking along the bank we picked up several fragments of melting-pots with numerous flecks of gold still stuck to them. We showed them to the Pacifier of Kingdoms, and the sight seemed to revive him and give him a new lease of life. His face suddenly flushed and his dim eyes sparkled with unaccustomed fire: the sight of a few scraps of gold seemed to have made him forget for a moment both his illness and the two corpses he was escorting.

Musk-deer abound in this valley of shale and slate. These cold-loving animals are to be found on almost all Tibetan mountains, but probably nowhere in such numbers as at Che Pan Keou. They are attracted no doubt by the pines, cedars, holly and cypress with which the area is covered, as they particularly like the strongly aromatic roots of these trees. The musk-deer has a small head, sharp muzzle with long off-white moustaches; its legs are slim and its rump broad and thick; it has two long curved tusks protruding from its upper jaw which it uses to tear out of the ground the aromatic roots on which it feeds; the hair on its coat is usually two or three inches thick; it is hollow like the hair of almost all animals living to the north of the Himalayas, very coarse and always bristled up on end; in colour the animal is black below, white along the middle and greyish on the back. A pouch, attached to the belly near the navel, contains the precious substance known as musk.

The people of Slate Valley shot so many of these animals that everywhere in their houses there were skins hanging on pegs stuck in the walls. They used the hair to stuff the thick cushions they sat on during the day and the mattresses they slept on at night. The musk itself was sold to the Chinese at great profit.

We stayed one night at Che Pan Keou. At the next three stage-posts the Tibetans were equally demanding on the question of the *oulah*; our Chinese escort were quite exasperated at the behaviour of these wild hill-folk who, they said, knew nothing of proper behaviour, or the difference between right and wrong. We however felt some sympathy with these rough, hardened fellows: their manners were not polished, it is true, but there was a true generosity and openness about them: under the rough exterior there was something of real value which was of greater importance.

When at last we arrived at Kiang Tsa, the Chinese began to breathe again, for we were coming to a less hostile area. The valley of Kiang Tsa is very fertile and the inhabitants seemed to be prosperous. Apart from the soldiers of the guard-post there were many Chinese from Ssetchouan and Yunnan who lived here as shopkeepers and craftsmen of the basic skills. We were told that after a few years they could put aside a tidy sum. The two military mandarins of the post, who were old comrades-in-arms of Ly Kouo Ngan, were shocked at his deplorable physical state and strongly advised him to continue his journey in a palanquin. We too tried to persuade him, and were glad when we finally overcame his miserly instincts. It had dawned on him at last that a dead man needs no money and that the first priority was to try and save his own life. The death of Pei's son had conveniently made available both his palanquin and his four porters, and these were all at Kiang Tsa. We stopped there for a day so that the palanquin could be repaired and the porters could prepare their sandals for the journey.

The country we entered south of Kiang Tsa looked less cold and arid than any we had yet seen. There was a noticeable downhill slope; we were still surrounded by mountains but they gradually grew less gloomy and wild; the frowning masses of granite cliffs had disappeared. Tall grasses and forests were everywhere; there was more wildlife to be seen. It was clear that we were entering a more temperate zone; only the summits of the mountains were still crowned with snow and ice.

Four days after we had left Kiang Tsa we reached the banks of the Kin Cha Kiang, the River of Golden Sands, which we had already crossed on the ice with the Tibetan Embassy two months before our arrival in Lhasa. When this magnificent river flows across China's fair plains, its waters are calm and blue, but in the Tibetan mountains it rushes and roars, ceaselessly hurling its great masses of water down the valley bottoms with terrifying and thunderous force. At the point where we met the river, it was enclosed between two cliffs which rose perpendicularly from its banks, leaving it only a narrow but extremely deep channel. The stream ran rapidly with a dull mournful sound. Here and there great blocks of ice floated along, spinning in the whirlpools and finally breaking up against the rocky sides.

For half a day we followed the right bank of the river. About midday we reached a small village where we found in readiness all that we needed for the crossing. The caravan split up and embarked in four large flat-bottomed boats; in no time we were over on the far bank. Not much further on at the mouth of a small valley lay the stage-post of Tchou Pa Loung. The Dheba provided excellent fresh fish for supper and for the night a room well protected against the wind with thick mattresses filled with musk-deer's hair.

Next day we followed a small river, a tributary of the River of Golden Sands. We were more cheerful because we had been told that before evening we should reach a land of great charm and beauty. So we kept peering anxiously ahead as we rode along; sometimes we stood up in our stirrups to get a longer view; but the landscape was in no hurry to change from prose to poetry. The same little river still ran on our left, babbling prosaically over its boulders; and on our right there was only a big reddish mountain, grim and bare, criss-crossed with deep ravines. Masses of white clouds driven by a sharp wind sped along the mountainside and merged ahead of us on the dark, foggy horizon.

About midday the caravan stopped at a hovel where we drank a bowlful of tea and ate a handful of *tsamba*. Then we climbed the red mountain to the top and from that high vantage point we were able to admire the magnificent, the delightful plain of Bathang. We had suddenly been wafted as if by magic above a land where the eye could feast on all the marvels of the richest and most varied vegetation. It was above all the contrast that was striking; on one side, a barren, dark land of mountains, almost uninhabited; on the other, a smiling plain in which a large population were working a fertile soil. The Chinese handbook said:

The canton of Bathang is a fine plain a thousand *li* [350 miles] in length, well watered by streams and springs; the sky is clear, the climate pleasant, and there is everything to delight the heart and eyes of man.

We rode quickly down the mountain and then began to travel through a veritable garden, with trees in blossom and green paddy fields. A gentle warmth gradually thawed our limbs and we were soon feeling the weight of our fur-lined coats. It was more than two years since we had actually sweated, and it seemed quite strange to be warm without standing in front of a fire.

On the outskirts of the town of Bathang the soldiers of the garrison were standing in line to present arms to the Pacifier of Kingdoms who, bundled up in his palanquin, carried out his inspection in a far from soldierly manner. The Tibetan population, who had all turned out, escorted the caravan to a fine Chinese pagoda which was to be our lodging. That evening the mandarins of the Chinese garrison and the senior lamas of the town came to visit us, bringing gifts of beef, mutton, butter, flour, candles, bacon, rice, walnuts, raisins, apricots and other local produce.

There was a supply base at Bathang, the fourth since Lhasa: like the others, it was managed by a civil mandarin with the title of Leang Tai. Thé Chinese garrison of three hundred soldiers was commanded by a Chopei, two Tsien Tsoung and one Pa Tsoung. The annual cost of the upkeep of the troops dependant on the post amounted to 9,000 ounces of silver, without counting the rice and *tsamba* meal rations. There were a large number of Chinese residents engaged in arts and crafts; some were even in agriculture, running Tibetan farms to advantage. This plain which lies like an enchantment in the midst of the Tibetan mountains is extremely fertile, and gives two crops a year. Its main products are: rice, maize, grey barley, wheat, peas, cabbages, turnips, onions, and other vegetables. The fruits include grapes, pomegranates, peaches, apricots and watermelons. Honey is also to be had in quantity. In addition there are cinnabar (sulphurate of mercury) mines from which mercury is extracted in large quantities. The Tibetans obtain pure mercury, eliminating the sulphur by a heat process, or by combining it with slaked lime.

Bathang is a big town with a large and prosperous population. As in all Tibetan towns, there are quantities of lamas. The main lamasery, known as the Great Convent of Ba, is ruled by a Khampo deriving his spiritual authority from the Dalai Lama. The temporal authority of the latter ends at Bathang. The frontiers of Tibet proper were fixed in 1726 at the end of a major war with the Chinese. Two days' journey before Bathang on the summit of Mount Mang Ling there is a stone monument marking the border as fixed at that date by the two governments. At the time of our visit, the area to the east of Bathang was politically independent of Lhasa. It was governed by Tou Sse — feudal princes — originally created by the Chinese Emperor and still recognising his authority as suzerain. These princelings must visit Peking every three years to present tribute to the emperor.

We stopped for three days at Bathang, the delay being caused by the illness of our leader, Ly Kouo Ngan. The daily hardships of our long journey had so exhausted the poor mandarin that his condition was more or less hopeless. His best course was to take advantage of the good climate of Bathang and let the caravan go ahead. His friends advised him to do this, but in vain. He was determined to continue the journey and tried hard to persuade himself that his illness was not serious. We however considered that he was so dangerously ill that it was our duty to use this period of rest and peace at Bathang by talking to him seriously about his soul and things eternal. Conversations we had had during the journey had given him the basic facts of the Christian faith. All that had to be done now was to bring home to him where he stood and convince him of how urgent it was to enter the way of salvation, openly and finally. Ly entirely agreed with us; everything we said was utterly true. He spoke eloquently to us of the shortness and fragility of life, of the vanity of the world, of the mysteriousness of God's ways, of the importance of salvation, of the truth of the Christian religion and of the need for all men to embrace it. On all these subjects he spoke sensibly and movingly. But when it came to the point, to the logical conclusion, namely that he should declare himself to be a Christian, everything went off the rails. He was quite determined to wait until he reached home and had retired from his profession of mandarin. We pointed out the danger he was running by putting off this all-important decision, but it was useless. 'So long as I am a mandarin in the service of the emperor I cannot enter the service of the Lord of Heaven,' he would say. This absurd idea was so firmly stuck in his head that there was no dislodging it.

On leaving Bathang we were forced to turn due northwards for some time, before again turning east; for since our departure from Tsiamdo twenty days before we had continually moved southwards. Caravans are forced to make this large detour in order to find a place where they can cross the great Kin Cha Kiang river in some safety.

The first day's march out of Bathang was delightful, for we rode in warm weather through a delightfully varied landscape. The narrow path we followed was edged with willows, pomegranate trees and apricot trees in blossom. But the next day we were back again in all the horrors and dangers of our earlier route. We had to cross a very high pass, with snow and a cruel north wind beating against us: what a contrast to the life of luxury we had been leading! After the pass, the snow turned to heavy icy rain, which penetrated to the marrow of our bones. As a last straw, we had to spend the night in a house with a roof so full of holes that wind and rain could enter freely. Yet we were so tired out that we slept after all. Next morning we woke up surrounded by mud; our bedding was soaked through and our limbs stiff with cold. We had to rub ourselves hard with lumps of ice to get the circulation going again. The wretched hamlet that provided this miserable lodging was called Ta So.

On leaving the Ta So valley we climbed by a narrow gorge on to a plateau deep in snow. Next we entered a magnificent forest, the finest we had seen in the Tibetan mountains. Great pines, cedars and hollies grew closely together, forming a roof of greenery which shut out the daylight and was a much better shelter from the rain and the snow than the houses of Ta So. The branches and trunks of these trees were covered with a thick moss which hung down in long thin threads. When new, the threads were an attractive green, but turned black when old, looking exactly like tufts of long, dirty, unkempt hair. The effect of all these old pine trees hung with what appeared to be heads of hair from every branch was extremely eerie. The prickly holly tree grows to a great height in the Tibetan mountains. In Europe it seldom grows bigger than a bush, here it is a tall tree; though not as tall as a pine, it has as thick a trunk and its foliage is even more abundant.

That day's march was long and tiring, and night had fallen when we reached Samba, where we were to change *oulah*. We were about to go to bed when it was noticed that one member of the Tibetan escort was missing. It was the one who had been appointed to be our servant. The small village was searched carefully but in vain. It was realised that he must have got lost in the forest, and the first thought was to send a search party: but how to find a man in the pitch dark in the middle of a great thick forest? So we all trooped up on to a hilltop nearby, shouted and lit a beacon. Round midnight the straggler appeared half-dead with fatigue. On his head he was carrying the saddle of his horse which, finding no doubt the road too long, had simply lain down in the middle of the forest and had refused to get on its feet again. Everyone was enormously cheered by the arrival of this young man, and so to bed.

We rose late next morning. Whilst the people of Samba were bringing the horses and pack animals for the caravan, we went for a short walk to see something of the place, since we had arrived there after nightfall. The village was a group of some thirty cottages built with large pebbles and roughly cemented, some with cowdung and others with mud. It was dismal enough, but the country round had its charm. Two streams, one from the west, the other from the south, met near to the village to become a river whose clear waters flowed across a vast area of meadowland. Completing the picture and giving it colour and life were a little bridge painted red, herds of goats and yaks happily grazing, storks and wild ducks fishing for their breakfast by the water's edge, a few huge cypresses dotted about, and the smoke rising from the houses and driven by the breeze along the hillsides. The sky was cloudless and calm and the sun, already well clear of the horizon, promised us a fine, warm day.

We walked slowly back to our lodging. As we approached we could see that the caravan was ready and on the point of departure. The pack animals were loaded; the horsemen, with robes tucked up and whip in hand, were waiting to mount. 'We're late,' we said, 'we must hurry,' and sprinted the last lap.

'No need to hurry,' said a Chinese soldier, 'Ly Kouo Ngan is not ready; he hasn't come out of his room yet.'

'Today', we answered, 'there's no big mountain to climb, the weather is good, if we start a little late it won't matter. However, go and tell the mandarin that the caravan is ready.' The soldier pushed open the door and went into Ly's room; he came out quickly, pale and wide-eyed.

'Ly Kouo Ngan is dead!' he said without raising his voice. We ran into the room: the poor mandarin was lying on his camp-bed, his lips curled back, his teeth clenched, his eyes contorted by death. When we felt his heart—his chest was still heaving slightly, there was some life left, but no hope. He was unconscious already, and after a few gasps he died. The fluid in his legs must have spread into his lungs and choked him.

Our leader's death was not unexpected, there was no reason for us to feel any shock, but there was something so sad and so pitiable about the way it had happened that everyone was bowled over by it. We in particular found it quite heart-rending. We bitterly regretted not having been beside this unfortunate man in his last hours, since he was one whom we so wished to lead from the darkness of paganism into the light of faith. God's ways are mysterious indeed! There is but one hope: since this poor soul knew and understood the truths of religion, it may be that God, in His infinite mercy, at the last moment granted him His grace.

The caravan did not travel that day. The animals were unsaddled and put to pasture; then the soldiers did what had to be done, according to Chinese ritual, so that their mandarin's body could be taken home to his family. We will not describe it in detail, because we propose to deal elsewhere with the whole question of Chinese customs.* Suffice it to say that the deceased was wrapped in a large shroud which had been given him by the Living Buddha of Djachi Loumbo. It was white, but covered all over with Tibetan texts and pictures of Buddha in black print. The Tibetans and other Buddhists have complete faith in these shrouds which are provided by the Dalai Lama and the Panchen Remboutchi. They believe that whoever is fortunate enough to be wrapped in one after death is bound to have a favourable transmigration.

The death of Ly Kouo Ngan left the caravan without a leader. There was of course Lama Dsiamdchang, to whom the leadership should have passed, by right and legitimate succession; but the Chinese soldiers were reluctant to accept his authority, and so we moved from a monarchy to a democratic republic. This lasted at most half a day. We, however, realising that the members of the caravan, both Tibetans and Chinese, were unready for so perfect a form of government; seeing that anarchy and confusion abounded, with public interest at heart and in an attempt to ensure the safety of the caravan, we declared a dictatorship. We then issued a large number of decrees, so that everything should be ready for our departure at dawn. The need for discipline was so strongly felt that there was no opposition and we were strictly obeyed.

We left Samba punctually. The caravan was a gloomy spectacle; with its three corpses it looked exactly like a funeral. After three days' march through mountainous country in mostly windy, snowy, cold weather we arrived at the stage-post of Lithang, where there was a Chinese supply-base and a garrison of some hundred soldiers. The mandarins of Lithang were: a Leang Tai, a Chopei and two Pa Tsoung. A few minutes after our arrival these gentlemen called on us. First and foremost, there was much talk about the illness and death of our leader. Then we had to explain who we were and why we were in the caravan. Our only answer was to produce a large document, signed and sealed by Ambassador Kichan and containing the instructions which had been given to Ly Kouo Ngan about us.

*Father Huc interlarded the third volume of his travels, *L'Empire Chinois* (not translated here), with detailed descriptions of Chinese customs. (Trans.)

'That is all in order,' said our visitors. 'Ly Kouo Ngan's death need make no change in your position; you will be well treated wherever you go. You have until now always lived in peace with the men of the caravan, and this will surely continue so to the end.' We certainly hoped so. But as, owing to human frailty, difficulties could easily arise during the journey especially with the Chinese soldiers, we were very anxious to have a responsible mandarin along with us. We said so, and were told that we could perfectly well go on as we were with our Tibetan and Chinese escorts as far as the frontier; and that from then on a mandarin could easily be found to take us to the capital of Ssetchouan.

'Right!' we said. 'Since you cannot give us a mandarin, we propose to travel in our own way, and go where we like. We do not guarantee even that on leaving here we shall not take the road back to Lhasa. You see that we are frank with you. Think about it.' Our four officials got up, saying that they were going to talk this important matter over, and that we should have a reply later that evening.

Whilst we were having supper, a Pa Tsoung, one of the four mandarins, arrived, dressed in his best uniform. After the usual polite preliminaries, he announced that he had been appointed to command our escort as far as the frontier. He added that never, in his most ambitious dreams had he imagined that he would have the honour of conducting people such as ourselves, and that he was embarrassed at having from the very first day to ask us a favour, namely that we would be good enough to rest at Lithang for two days, to regain our strength which must surely be exhausted by so long and so hard a journey. We realised that he needed a couple of days to finish some business or other and prepare for an unexpected journey. 'How thoughtful you are on our behalf!' we said. 'We will rest for two days, since you think that it should be so.' Legitimate authority having been reconstituted, our dictatorship ended. There were signs, however, that this was unwelcome to the men, who preferred having us to a mandarin.

The town of Lithang was built on the flanks of a hill that stood in the middle of a fairly extensive but almost entirely barren plain. Nothing grew but a little grey barley and some scanty grass on which some poor herds of goat and yak were grazing. The town was impressive from a distance; two large

lamaseries, richly painted and gilded, had been built on the top
of the hill and made an imposing sight. But inside the town
itself there were nothing but ugly, dirty, narrow streets, so
steep that one had to be a mountaineer not to lose one's
balance.

On this side of the River of Golden Sands, we noticed in the
tribes we encountered many changes in customs, costume and
language. It was clear that we were no longer properly in Tibet.
As we approached the Chinese frontier, the natives were less
proud and less rough; they were just a little greedy, over-polite
and cunning; their religious faith was neither so strong nor so
open. They did not speak pure Tibetan as spoken at Lhasa and
in the province of Kham: it was a dialect that was close to the
language of the Si Fan, and contained certain Chinese expressions. The Lhasa Tibetans of our party had the greatest difficulty in understanding and in being understood. In the
costume, only the headdresses had changed. The men wore a
grey or brown felt hat, not unlike our own felt hats when they
are straight from the press and not yet shaped on the block. The
women wear their hair in innumerable little plaits which hang
down over their shoulders; they then fix a large silver disk on
their heads, rather like a dinner-plate. The best dressed wear
two of them, one on each side, arranged so that the rims meet
above the head. The ordinance whereby women daub their
faces with black is not observed at Lithang: it is in force only in
the territories under the temporal rule of the Dalai Lama.

The largest of the Lithang lamaseries has a big printing
works for Buddhist texts. On feast days the lamas from the
surrounding area come to buy their books. Lithang does a brisk
trade in gold-dust, chaplets of black beads and bowls made of
vine-roots and box-wood.

As we left Lithang, the Chinese garrison paraded to present
arms to Ly Kouo Ngan. They followed the ceremonial exactly as
if he were still alive. When the coffin passed by, all the soldiers
went down on one knee and shouted: 'To Tou Sse Ly Kouo
Ngan, from the unworthy garrison of Lithang, health and
prosperity!' The little mandarin, decorated with the White
Button, who was now our leader returned the salute on behalf
of the deceased. This new head of our caravan was a Chinese of
Muslim origin. There was nothing whatever about him to recall
the fine physical type of his ancestors: his thin stunted body,

his sharp face with its jeering expression reminded one of a young shop-assistant rather than a military mandarin. He could talk the hindleg off a donkey. For the first day we found him quite amusing, but after that it became tiresome. As a Muslim, he felt that he must keep telling us about Arabia and its horses worth their weight in gold, about Mahomet and his famous sword that could cut metals, about Mecca and its walls of bronze.

From Lithang to Ta Tsien Lou, the Chinese frontier town, there are only some two hundred and ten miles, divided into eight stages. We found the last part of this terrible Tibet road no better than the rest. We crossed mountains, only to find still more mountains in front of us : always grim-looking mountains, always covered in snow and full of precipices. Nor had the temperature changed appreciably. We felt that since we had left Lhasa we had simply been going round in a circle. However, the villages were becoming more frequent, but without losing anything of their Tibetan character. The most important was Makian Dsoung, where there were shops kept by Chinese merchants for stocking caravans. At one day's march from here we crossed by ferry boat the Ya Loung Kiang, a wide fast-running river. Its source is at the foot of the Boyen Kharat mountains, near that of the Yellow River. It joins the Kin Cha Kiang or Blue River in the province of Ssetchouan. According to local tradition, the cradle of the Tibetan people was by the banks of the Ya Loung Kiang.

Whilst we were crossing the Ya Loung Kiang by boat, a herdsman was crossing by a bridge consisting only of a thick cable made of yak-hide, stretched tightly from one bank to the other. A kind of wooden stirrup hung by a strong strap from a pulley attached to the cable. The herdsman had only to stand facing backwards on the stirrup underneath the bridge, grasp the cable with both hands and jerk himself forward ; the weight of his body helped him along, and he was quickly over on the other side. Such bridges are quite common in Tibet. They are quite a practical means of crossing torrents and chasms, but they need some practice. We never ventured on one. Chain bridges are also often used, especially in the provinces of Ouei and Dzang. To build them, they first fix on the bank as many iron clamps as there are to be chains; over the chains they put planks which they sometimes cover with a layer of earth. As these bridges are extremely elastic, they are always provided with hand-rails.

At last we arrived safe and sound at the Chinese frontier, where the Tibetan climate gave us a cold farewell. Crossing the pass immediately before the town of Ta Tsien Lou the snow fell so thick and fast that we were almost buried in it. It followed us right into the valley, and we reached the Chinese town in

torrential rain. It was early in June 1846. We had left Lhasa nearly three months before. According to the Chinese handbook we had covered five thousand and fifty *li* (1760 miles).

Ta Tsien Lou means Arrow Forge. The town got this name because in A D 234 General Wou Heou, leading his army against the people of the south, sent one of his lieutenants to establish an arrow factory in the town. This area has passed to and fro between the Tibetans and the Chinese; for the last century it has been integrated into the empire. The Chinese handbook says:

The walls and the fortifications of Ta Lsien Lou are in dressed stone. Chinese and Tibetans live there side by side. It is here that the troops and their officers who are to be stationed in Tibet leave China. A large quantity of tea passes through here from China to Tibet, and the main tea fair takes place here.

Although the inhabitants of this canton are devoted to the Buddhist faith, they do try to make small profits; yet they are sincere and honest, and behave in a submissive and obedient manner, so that nothing, even death, can change their natural good nature. As they have been accustomed to Chinese government for a long time, they are the more devoted to it.

We rested three days at Ta Tsien Lou. During this period we had hot arguments, several times a day, with the chief mandarin of the town, who was unwilling to consent to our continuing our journey by palanquin. However he had to agree in the end, for we really could not face the thought of riding on horseback any more. Our legs had been astride so many horses of every age, size, colour and quality that they had had enough; they had an irresistible desire to lie peacefully in a palanquin. Their wish was finally granted, due to our determination and persistence.

The Tibetan escort, who had so faithfully accompanied us on this long hard journey, was now preparing to return to Lhasa. We gave Lama Dsiamdchang a letter for the regent, in which we thanked him for having given us so loyal an escort which had been a reminder every day of our journey of the good treatment we had received in Lhasa. When we said goodbye to these good Tibetans we could not help shedding tears, for gradually and without our realising it a bond had grown between us that it was very painful to break. Lama Dsiamdchang told us in confidence that he had been instructed to remind us when he left us of the promise we had given the regent. Could he count on seeing us again at Lhasa? We told him that he could; for at the time we were far from foreseeing what sort of obstacle would stand in the way of our returning to Tibet.

The following day at dawn we got into our palanquins and were carried, at public expense, to the capital of the province of Ssetchouan where, by order of the emperor, we were to receive solemn judgment from the grand mandarins of the Celestial Empire.

POSTSCRIPT
The End of the Story

Twelve days and three hundred and fifty miles later, the two missionaries arrived at Tcheng Tou Fou, capital of Ssetchouan province, where they were to receive 'solemn judgment'. Readers of the preceding chapters will not be surprised to learn that they emerged triumphant from this ordeal, developed a close friendly relationship with the viceroy and continued their journey with all the privileges accorded only to Chinese high officials. This status did not entirely protect them from varied fortunes on the road, but they finally reached Canton in October 1846, six months after leaving Lhasa, and thence crossed to the Portuguese island of Macao, the base from which they had originally entered China.

On arrival they received news that effectively destroyed their dream of one day being able to fulfil their promise to the regent and return to Lhasa to open a mission there. During their absence, indeed at the very time they had been in Lhasa, another Catholic missionary body, the *Société des Missions étrangères*, had been granted a charter by the Church authorities whereby they alone had the right to send missionaries to Tibet. Father Gabet then sailed for Europe and visited Rome in the hope of persuading the authorities to alter their decision, but in this he failed. In 1849 he was posted to Brazil, and died of yellow fever in Rio de Janeiro in 1853.

Father Huc remained in Macao for two years, writing up the notes he had made on the journey. The result was the two-volume *Souvenirs d'un voyage dans la Tartarie et le Thibet*, which, as the reader will have seen, takes the story only as far as the Chinese frontier. He was then again dispatched on a mission to Peking, but whilst in the north, his health, damaged on the Tibetan journey, gave acute cause for concern. He returned to Macao and then in January 1852 to France, where his book had already appeared with some success. A second edition quickly followed. He now had leisure to take up the story where he had left it, and completed the narrative in a two-volume work which he called *L'Empire Chinois* and which was published in 1854. But his health never recovered and he died in 1860, aged forty-seven.

Samdadchiemba, as we have seen, returned to his village and thence to a Christian mission in Mongolia. He lived into the 1880s at least, enjoyed some fame from his association with Gabet and Huc and was visited and questioned by later travellers. On at least one occasion he acted as guide across Mongolia to another Lazarist, the naturalist Armand David. A Belgian missionary who spoke to him in 1881 summed him up with the words: '*C'est un brave chrétien*'; a good Christian soul.

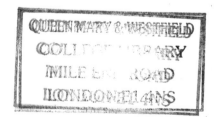

GOBI DESERT

K A N S

Chuga Mtn.

Tsaidam River

Pouhain Gol

Koukou
Noor L.

Ta Toung

Ping

Bayen Kharat Range

Sining Fou

Nien

Paehsie

Tant La Mountains

Mouroui Oussou

T   I   B   E   T

Na Pichu

Chobando

Tsiamdo

Lhasa

Alan-To

Ghiamba

Lha Dze

Bagoung

Midchoukoung

Diaya

C

Bathang

Lithang

Tchingto

Ta Tsien Lou

Blue   R

0 ———————————————— 300 miles

0 ———————————————— 500 kms